W9-AVE-672

Social History of Africa
MARRIAGE IN MARADI

Social History of Africa Series

Series Editors: Allen Isaacman and Jean Hay

African Workers and Colonial Racism
JEANNE PENVENNE
Agriculture and Apartheid
JONATHAN CRUSH AND ALLAN JEEVES (EDITORS)
Are We Not Also Men?
TERENCE RANGER
Burying SM
DAVID COHEN AND ATIENO ODHIAMBO
Colonial Conscripts
MYRON ECHENBERG
Cotton is the Mother of Poverty
ALLEN ISAACMAN
Cotton, Colonialism, and Social History in Africa
ALLEN ISAACMAN AND RICHARD ROBERTS (EDITORS)
Cutting Down Trees
HENRIETTA MOORE AND MEGAN VAUGHAN
Drink, Power, and Cultural Change
EMMANUEL AKYEAMPONG
Feasts and Riot
JONATHAN GLASSMAN
Gender, Ethnicity, and Social Change on the Upper Slave Coast
SANDRA GREENE
In Pursuit of History
CAROLYN KEYES ADENAIKE AND JAN VANSINA (EDITORS)
Insiders and Outsiders
BILL FREUND
Law in Colonial Africa
KRISTIN MANN AND RICHARD ROBERTS (EDITORS)
Marriage in Maradi
BARBARA M. COOPER
Money Matters
JANE GUYER (EDITOR)
The Moon is Dead—Give Us Our Money!
KELETSO ATKINS
Peasants, Traders, and Wives
ELIZABETH SCHMIDT
The Realm of the Word
PAUL LANDAU
"We Spend Our Years as a Tale That is Told"
ISABEL HOFMEYR
Women of Phokeng
BELINDA BOZZOLI
Work, Culture, and Identity
PATRICK HARRIES

MARRIAGE IN MARADI

GENDER AND CULTURE
IN A HAUSA SOCIETY
IN NIGER, 1900–1989

Barbara M. Cooper

HEINEMANN
Portsmouth, NH

JAMES CURREY
Oxford

Heinemann
A division of Reed Publishing (USA) Inc.
361 Hanover Street
Portsmouth, NH 03801-3912
Offices and agents throughout the world

James Currey Ltd.
73 Botley Road
Oxford 0X2 OBS
United Kingdom

ISBN 0-435-07414-8 (Heinemann cloth)
ISBN 0-435-07413-X (Heinemann paper)

ISBN 0-85255-677-2 (James Currey cloth)
ISBN 0-85255-627-6 (James Currey paper)

British Library Cataloguing in Publication Data
  Cooper, Barbara M.
    Marriage in Maradi : gender and culture in a Hausa society
    in Niger, 1900–1989. – (Social history of Africa)
    1. Hausa (African people) – Marriage customs and rites
    2. Niger – Social conditions
    I. Title
    306.8'089937

Library of Congress Cataloging-in-Publication Data
  On file at the Library of Congress

Cover design by Jenny Jensen Greenleaf
Cover photo: "Woman spinning" ("Niger–Fileuse"). Early colonial–no date, no
contributor. Elderly women to whom I showed this photograph liked it the
best of all the ones I am including in the book. They seemed to enjoy recalling
spinning and they expressed admiration for the woman's dignity and the modesty of her dress. French National Archives, Centre des Archives d'Outre-mer.
All rights reserved. 30F1 AOF 3280.

Printed in the United States of America on acid-free paper.
99 98 97 DA 1 2 3 4 5 6

CONTENTS

List of Maps and Figures vi

List of Photographs vii

Acknowledgments ix

Glossary of Acronyms and Foreign Terms xiii

Introduction xvii

1   Unpredictable Interventions: Emancipating Slaves and
    Regulating Marriage 1

2   Mediating Marriage: State Intrusion and Local Dispute Settlement 20

3   Ambiguities of Dependency: Negotiating Land and
    Labor in a Shifting Agricultural Economy 40

4   From Migrant to *Mai Gida* 62

5   Women's Worth and Wedding Gift Exchange 90

6   Wealth and Learning: Discourses on Prosperity and Domesticity 110

7   Coping with Conflicting Models: Nurturing Ties,
    Maintaining Ambiguity, and Opting Out 143

8   Of "Prostitutes," the Public, and Politics 168

Conclusion 193

Bibliography 201

Index 219

LIST OF MAPS AND FIGURES

Map 1
Contemporary Niger xvi

Map 2
Maradi Department xlix

Map 3
The City of Maradi Today l

Chart I
Marriages and Divorces Registered at the Tribunal, Oct. 1985- Sept. 1989 32

Figure 1
Actes de mariage 1956 160

Figure 2
Actes de mariage 1965 160

Figure 3
Actes de mariage 1970 161

Figure 4
Actes de mariage 1988 161

LIST OF PHOTOGRAPHS

Cover photo
Woman spinning (Niger–Fileuse) .... cover

Photo 1
Girl sifting pounded millet xxvi

Photo 2
A young Hausa woman bringing her husband his meal 42

Photo 3
Typical young women, from left to right: Zerma, Hausa, Bella 72

Photo 4
The merchant of cloth and enamelware 104

Photo 5
The school in Doutchi–a class 118

Photo 6
Hausa women–Gouchy (near Magaria) 150

All photographs reproduced courtesy of the French National Archives; please see captions below individual photographs for full details.

ACKNOWLEDGMENTS

This study could not have been completed without help from many individuals and institutions. My research was made possible through the generous funding of a U.S. Department of Education Fulbright–Hays Doctoral Dissertation Research Abroad Grant and a University of Florida Faculty Improvement Grant. My coursework in preparation for research was accomplished through a U.S. Department of Education Javitz Fellowship. I thank the government of Niger and the Ministry of Higher Education for granting me permission to do research in Niger. Boubé Gado of the Institut de Recherche en Sciences Humaines (IRSH) and Diouldé Laya and Traore Boubacar Mahamane of the Centre de l'Enseignement Historique et Linguistique par la Tradition Orale (CEHLTO) offered the resources of their institutions during my stay in Niamey.

In Maradi the Préfet Commandant Torda Heinikoye saw that my work was supported by all the relevant services. Sarki Buzu 'dan Zambadi generously allowed me to observe his court and to interview women in his home and throughout the city. Mallam Habou Magaji of the IRSH station in Maradi helped me get started on my work and provided invaluable advice on how to proceed at various moments; he also introduced me to Madame Hadiza Salifou Hassoumi who helped me transcribe my interviews and whose friendship was as valuable as her research assistance.

Diallo Abdoulaye and Ali Dogo of the Service Départemental de Plan in Maradi shared the *calendriers historiques* used in the 1988 census to help me establish local chronology. M. Harouna Issa gave me access to the documents of the Projet de Développement Rural de Maradi and shared his own study of women in the CPRs with me. Al Hajj Iro Magaji permitted me to explore the colonial documents of the Archives de la Préfecture de Maradi. The Mairie allowed me to study the marriage registers of the commune of Maradi, while the Tribunal de Première Instance shared more recent registers of marriage and divorce. Members of the Sudan Interior Mission extended their hospitality and shared their knowledge of the region both in Maradi and in Sebring, Florida. I would like in particular to thank Elizabeth Chisholm and Rita Salls, who shared their homes and recollections of Maradi with me in the Fall of 1990.

Much of my work in Maradi would never have come about without the wise guidance of the *chef de quartie*r of Sabon Gari, Soly Kané, who helped me find a home, introduced me to many of the women I worked with, and acted as my liaison with both the Mairie and the sarki's court. I would also like to thank Chef de Quartier Bagalam for his assistance in his neighborhood and in the Mairie. The women of the Association des Femmes du Niger (AFN) permitted me to observe their meetings, share in their celebrations, and interview many of their members; I must particularly thank Mme. Marie Lebihan, Hajjiya Cimma Mai Nono, and Hajjiya Habi Ta Bago for their energetic and warm assistance; I would like to thank all of the other members of the 'kunjiyar mata for their hospitality and for sharing their stories, humor, and homes with me.

I am deeply grateful to Iya Aisha Wandara, who introduced me to the diverse and overlapping worlds of the women of the aristocratic class, the Association des Femmes du Niger, the bori cult, and the village of Fura Girki. Our conversations not only helped me make sense of the Maradi community, but also provided me with many hours of gracious and enjoyable company. Many of the women of her family also shared their homes, friendship, and experiences with me, and as they are too numerous to mention here let me simply thank them as a whole. I would in particular like to thank her "granddaughter," Hajjiya Amina Mallam Sule, who assisted me in the collection of some of my material on wedding gifts and was more of a friend than an "informant."

Academic writing takes critique of previous scholarship as its stock in trade, and I hope that in engaging with the many scholars upon whose shoulders I stand I have not seemed to neglect their own invaluable efforts. My gratitude and admiration to Guy Nicolas, Claude Raynaut, Emmanuel Grégoire, and countless other scholars of Maradi and Hausaland more broadly upon whose works I have relied. My debt to them will be obvious in what follows. Students and colleagues at the University of Florida and at Bryn Mawr and Haverford Colleges have provided me with stimulating and challenging environments in which to think about my work. I must thank my editors, Allen Isaacman and Jean Hay for their sensible and supportive suggestions. Donald Moore, Roberta Ann Dunbar, Michael Watts, Achille Mbembe, Steven Feierman, and Neil Smith offered comments on portions of the book or the book prospectus that probably influenced my thinking more than they realized. Roberta Ann Dunbar, Alice Burmeister and Donald Moore offered frequent encouragement and shared useful materials with me. Numerous journal editors and anonymous readers have left their imprint on this work and have much improved it, whatever its remaining flaws.

I would like to thank Jennifer Yanco and family, Lisa and Marc Manganaro and the "Mango" kids, John Mason, Helen Ogilve and Irving Gershwin, Tina and Pascal da Campo, and Adeline Masquellier Fisher for helping me keep my humor and my perspective during this research and the many years of its incubation. The sense of community provided by the African Studies Center and Department of History at Boston University has also sustained me throughout this process; special thanks to Jim McCann, who got me into this business of African History in the first place, and to Barbara Diefendorf, who helped me keep track of the history part. Jean Hay has probably seen more incarnations of this work than anyone other than me, and I thank her for her unfailing generosity.

Sara Berry saw this study from its unlikely inception to its harried completion, never seeming to doubt that some order would eventually emerge from
the chaos: I thank her for being a wonderful teacher and an even more wonderful friend. Jane Guyer, like Sara, has gone well beyond influencing my thinking and reading my manuscripts to helping me stitch together a humane family life, and I thank her for her intellectual and emotional support. Above all I
would like to thank my husband, Richard Miller, whose contributions to this
work are immeasurable. This book is dedicated to Richard, Cara, and Rachel,
my best buddies in the world.

GLOSSARY OF ACRONYMS AND FOREIGN TERMS

AFN	Association des Femmes du Niger, national women's association initiated under Seyni Kountché
al hajj	man who has performed the pilgrimage to Mecca
al'kali	Muslim judge, *qadi*
albarka	blessings, prosperity
alhazai	(plural of *al hajj*) the merchant class, many of whom have performed the pilgrimage to Mecca
almajirai	Koranic students
amarya	new bride
arme	marriage
armen kulle	secluded marriage
armen sadaka	marriage of alms in which no *sadaki* is offered
armen soji	marriage to a soldier
armen tsari	strict seclusion in marriage, "guarded seclusion"
armen zummunci	"kinship" marriage, generally a cross-cousin marriage
arna	non-Muslim Hausa population of the Maradi valley practicing local religions
arziki	fortune, wealth, luck
arzikin mutane	wealth in people
aure	see *arme*
bajawara/bazawara	previously married woman who is not presently married
baraka/barka	see *albarka*
biki	ceremony or celebration surrounding marriage [*bikin arme*] or the naming of a child after birth [*bikin suna*]
bori	a spirit possession cult
budurwa	previously unmarried virgin (often translated as "maiden")
CFA	currency of French West Africa
'darme	to tie
'darmen arme	the public ceremony in which bridewealth is transferred from groom's kin to the bride's kin
dowo	dough used to make *fura*, a staple drink
fadama	heavy clay land in the river valley used to grow dry-season crops

xiii

fura	millet porridge, a staple food
gado	inheritance, heritage, inherited skill
gamana	land used in usufruct by a dependent (often a wife) of the household head
gandu	land managed by the household head
gargajiya	traditional, customary, passed from generation to generation
gara	"increase"; counter gifts offered by bride's family to groom and his family
gida	household, compound, house, home, lineage
gidan mata	"house of women," home of courtesans
gudummawa	"reinforcements" or help offered in the form of gifts at the time of a ceremony or celebration
hajjiya	woman who has performed the pilgrimage to Mecca
hé!	celebration at moment of transfer of the *gara* to the groom and his family, *kan kwarya*
igiya	rope or thread
igiyar arme	the ties binding a man and woman in marriage
ilimi	knowledge, education, learning
indigénat	code governing indigenous French subjects in the colonies
Izala	reformist Islamic movement founded in Jos, Nigeria
jigawa	light, sandy plateau land used to grow millet, sorghum, peanuts, and beans
kan kaya	the ceremonial "bearing of things" for the bride to take into her marriage
kan kwarya	"overflowing calabashes"; ceremony with drumming when the *gara* is offered to a groom and his kin by the bride's female supporters
karuwa	"courtesan," an unmarried woman who lives on her own or with other unmarried women and who supports herself through sexual favors
karuwanci	the practice of courtesanship or prostitution
kayan 'daki	the "things for the room," or decorative gifts to the bride for her to arrange in her room
kulle	the state of being in seclusion, a relatively relaxed seclusion. See also *tsare*.
'kunjiyar mata	women's association
kunya	shame, embarrassment, self-consciousness, respect
mai gida	the "owner of the house," the head of household, the male head of the family, a woman's husband
makaranta	Koranic school
mallam (male)	
mallama (female)	Koranic scholar
mata	woman, wife
matan arme	married woman

miya	sauce used to flavor the staple porridge, *tuwo*
MNSD	National Movement of the Society for Development, party initiated by Ali Saibou
PDRM	the Projet de Développement Rural de Maradi (the Maradi Rural Development Project)
PPN	Parti Progressiste Nigérien, local branch of the Rassemblement Démocratique Africaine (RDA) founded prior to independence; later served as base of Diori Regime
rimji	large-scale agricultural slavery; slave village, plantation
SIM	Sudan Interior Mission
sadaki	the bridewealth payment from the groom to the bride's family upon marriage
Samariya	traditional youth cooperative work group, later adapted as the state-sponsored national youth association
sana'a	a trade, often for men an inherited vocation; for women, any income-generating activity
sarauta	a titled position available to aristocrats and the courtly class
sarki	the chief or traditional leader
Sawaba	political party founded by Djibo Bakary, outlawed under the Diori Regime
sharia/shari'a	Islamic law, which in this region follows the Maliki school of law
takarda	paper, divorce papers, marriage registration, any certificate or diploma
tallakawa	commoners, peasantry, the poor
tarihi	formally a written history; more colloquially, tradition
tsare	strict seclusion
tuwo	staple food of millet grits or porridge
UFN	Union des Femmes du Niger, national women's association initiated under Diori Hamani
USTN	Union Syndicale des Travailleurs du Niger, the national labor union
zarafi	leisure, opportunity, wealth
zare	spinning cotton into thread
ziyara	visiting, local pilgrimage, visiting a shrine, tomb, or holy place
zummunci	friendship, kinship

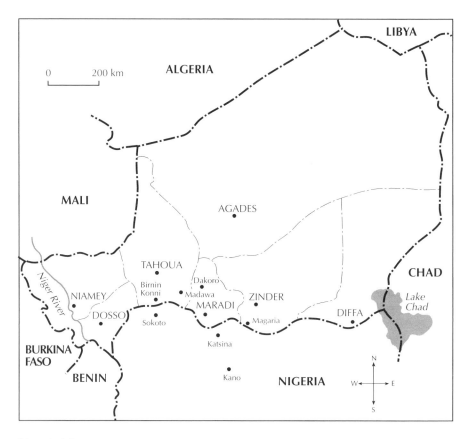

Map 1. Niger

INTRODUCTION

Marriage, History, and Tradition

Twentieth-century Maradi has undergone sociopolitical upheaval of enormous dimensions as a consequence of the abolition and decline of domestic slavery, the colonial imposition of taxation and cash cropping, the emergence of secular education and state employment, and the rise and redefinition of Islam. This book explores how both women and men have responded to these regional, national, and global processes by adapting, negotiating, and contesting their rights and duties in marriage, struggling to capitalize upon an environment that presents constantly shifting opportunities even as it imposes new risks and constraints. These contestations are played out in a number of complex and often contradictory processes: first, in the increasing elaboration of wedding rituals to establish the worth and standing of the bride and her mother, as marriage becomes a means of replacing involuntary female labor lost with the decline of slavery; second, in the reinterpretation of married women's rights to land, labor, and produce as men have been drawn into the production of crops for the global market; third, in the rise of urban seclusion and the parallel development of married women's house trades in response to Maradi's increased regional trade with Islamic northern Nigeria; and finally in verbal and visual debates about what constitutes a "married woman" in light of the growth of state education and employment.

It is not possible to make sense of the most important economic and political developments of the region in this century without also taking into consideration the social and cultural forms through which those developments have been understood and mediated. Focusing upon marriage has made it possible for me to bring together political economy and cultural analysis, for marriage is both a fundamental principle organizing productive and reproductive arrangements and a key element of Hausa cultural and social life. Because marriage also figures centrally in relations between men and women, it serves well as a point of entry into a consideration of how gender shapes and is shaped by broader processes.

My interest here is in gendered history broadly understood rather than women's history in the recuperative sense. Most histories of the Hausa-speaking regions have, until recently, been written without any serious consideration

xvii

of women and gender, and my initial impulse was, indeed, to redress this era-
sure of female agency and experience.[1] A number of useful studies of women
in the history of northern Nigeria have taken up this, often celebratory, project
(Boyd 1989; Sule and Starratt 1991; Mack 1991). Sociological and anthropological work on the Hausa region has often given greater attention to gender
(Schildkrout 1982, Hill 1969, 1972, 1977; M. F. Smith 1981; J. Nicolas 1967), occasionally casting women as victims of oppressive practices (Callaway 1987). My
approach differs from both celebratory histories of women and sociological
analyses of women's oppression because I do not see the women of the region
as either heroines or victims. Women have contributed powerfully to the systems and processes that define gender in the region, and therefore must be
understood to be complicit in the competing discourses that shape and are
shaped by their actions. In fact to speak of "Maradi women" in the first place is
deceptive, for this is hardly a homogeneous category. Women's culture and
women's interests in the region are fragmented in myriad ways. While I have
taken pains to attend to the means by which women actively resist the constraints placed upon them, I am also alert to the contradictions inherent in female agency, and to the ways in which women have themselves contributed to
the very structures that confine them. By addressing the role of gender in
Maradi's history through the subject of marriage rather than through women
as a category I hope to have avoided the essentializing tendencies of the latter
approach. This study, then, explores one of the central institutions through which
women and men differently situated within the social field have navigated the
rough waters of social, economic, and political change.

  I should confess that I did not at first intend to write a study of marriage
in Maradi at all. My original aim was to recast the tale of this Sahelian region
so that it would include the lives and experiences of the women who lived
there as farmers and traders, mothers and wives.[2] While I knew that marriage
would inevitably be part of the story, I had not anticipated that it would emerge
as the thematic core of my research. However, my interviews soon revealed
marriage and discourses about marriage to be sites of tremendously complex
negotiations, competing interests, confusions, and compromises. In order to
explain how the interview situation and the interviews themselves prompted
me to shift the focus of my study–not always fully consciously–towards marriage, I must first explain how I approached my fieldwork.

  When I arrived in Maradi in 1988, the male bureaucrats whose permission
and assistance I needed to launch my work determined, quite reasonably, that

---

[1] Many of these works broke important ground for later scholars and are still extremely useful.
For classic texts on Hausa history and culture see Hamani (1975), Hiskett (1973), Last (1967), Raynaut
(1972). For a recent work which gives evidence of the continued under attention to gender see
Miles (1994). Important exceptions to the neglect of gender would include Lovejoy (1988), Lovejoy
and Hogendorn (1993), Boyd and Last (1985), M.F. Smith (1981).

[2] Niger as a whole has a population of over 7 million, of whom some 120,000 live in the city of
Maradi. This study concerns the region of Maradi, comprising the southernmost arrondissements
of the Département de Maradi: Madarumfa, Guidan-Roumji, Aguié, and Tessawa. This region, with
a population of over 900,000, has the highest population density in Niger.

the best way for me to go about interviewing women was to work through the state-sponsored women's association (the Association des Femmes du Niger, or AFN). The male *chef de quartier* in each of five different neighborhoods in the city accordingly introduced me to the woman heading the neighborhood chapter of the association in his neighborhood, and I would ask her to help me set up an informal meeting with ten women of her own choice. These women were usually (but not always) also members of the AFN. The purpose of the gathering was for me to introduce myself, to break the ice, and to ask the women collectively in a relatively unthreatening setting a few questions that might give them some notion of what "talking about history" with this young white woman might entail. I would then conduct and tape record a series of unstructured private interviews on my own in Hausa with those women who seemed comfortable with me and who were willing, for whatever reason, to share some of their lives and experiences with me. I gradually worked from this central group of women to meet and interview other women in their lives (friends, neighbors, kin, co-wives, patrons, clients). These interviews were then contextualized, interpreted, and problematized in a dialectic with the quite different perspectives available in colonial and postcolonial era documents in the French Archives d'Outre-Mer in Aix-en-Provence, in the Archives Nationales du Niger in Niamey, and in the scattered collections in Maradi of the Tribunal, the Mairie, the Préfecture, and the Projet de Développement Rural de Maradi.[3] While documentary evidence was indispensable to my research (I devoted two months to work in the archives in France, a month in the archives in Niamey, and untold hours gathering the fugitive bits of evidence available in Maradi), it was the women's life histories themselves that came to occupy pride of place in my thinking. This is partly because the collection and interpretation of these tremendously rich "texts" was deeply engaging for me. However, the focus on interviews with women was also partially a strategic research decision. A tremendous expenditure of time and energy was necessary to earn me, a young woman and stranger with little authority, access to the uncatalogued collections of documents in Maradi controlled by a predominantly male bureaucracy.

---

[3] The location of documents cited in this work has been indicated with a prefix:

APM\Archives de la Préfecture de Maradi.

ANN\Archives Nationales du Niger (Niamey).

AOM\Archives d'Outre Mer (Aix-en-Provence, France); FOM refers to the documents in the Agence de la France d'Outre Mer collection, AP to documents in the Affaires Politiques of the Afrique Occidental Français collection, otherwise the reel number of the microfilm of the AOF collection is indicated.

PM\Projet de Développement Rural de Maradi; where the author of the document in this collection is not clear I have indicated PDRM after the prefix.

IP\Inspection Primaire, Commune de Maradi.

Interviews are indicated by the name of the woman in question and the date of the interview. I have assigned a pseudonym to most informants in order to protect their confidentiality, although I have attempted to use an equivalent nickname wherever the meaning of a woman's name seems important. Copies of the tapes are deposited with the Archives of Traditional Music at Indiana University in Bloomington.

I eventually determined that my energies would be most fruitfully employed by focusing upon oral research among women which a male scholar would have had more difficulty carrying out.[4]

Over the course of the eleven months of my research in Maradi proper, I came to work with many women who were not members of the Association de Femmes du Niger, women both younger and older than the generally middle-aged women of the AFN, and women who as servants, clients, sponsors, and patrons of the initial core might be, as we shall see, from quite different socio-economic backgrounds than my original contacts. By working in five neighborhoods of different character in the city of Maradi, as well as in the village of Fura Girki nearby, I was able to broaden my range of informants. I worked in the oldest core neighborhood where the Katsinawa aristocracy live, 'Yan Daka; the aristocratic spillover neighborhood of Bagalam, where the ties between the Katsinawa and Gobirawa ruling families of the cities of Maradi and Tibiri are most evident; the neighborhood in which many clients and commoners related to the Sarki's court (the court of the local ruler of Maradi) have settled, Mokoyo; a neighborhood in which many of the rural immigrants to the city (from the nineteenth century and more recently) and state functionaries (since 1960) have settled, Maradawa ("people of the Maradi valley"); and a newer neighborhood which has become popular among the merchant class and among "stranger" immigrants to the Maradi region, Sabon Gari ("New Town").[5]

I chose the neighborhoods in consultation with Mallam Habou Magaji of the Institut de Recherches en Sciences Humaines, a researcher and scholar whose assistance has contributed to many a study of the region. By tracing out women's networks linking different neighborhoods and attending to the different character (political, social, and economic) of different neighborhoods, I attempted to obtain as broad a cross-section of Maradi as was possible given constraints of time and funding. In retrospect it seems to me that my sampling was also powerfully shaped by some of the social implications of the rising *tsare* seclusion of the city. Since, as a historian, I needed to devote considerable attention to the memories and experiences of older women, I was not troubled that I spent less time in households with very young women. Younger women were often more closely secluded than older women, and had fewer experiences to relate. Conversations with them could run dry quite quickly, particularly if they had not succeeded in setting up a house trade or their children were not of school age. Such younger secluded women were also less tightly bound into the active female networks of women who attend *biki* celebrations as their own

---

[4]   I am heartily grateful to the administrators, secretaries, and clerks at a variety of offices in Maradi who graciously shared the documents I draw upon here with me. We in the United States often take our access to information rather for granted; in sharing their resources with me many Nigériens were exhibiting a generosity that was by no means a foregone conclusion. Please see my acknowledgements.

[5]   The city of Maradi was originally located in the valley of the Gulbin Maradi, but was forcibly moved to the plateau in 1945–46 after serious flooding. All of the pre-existing neighborhoods were reconstituted in the new location. Of the neighborhoods I chose to work in, only Sabon Gari post-dates the move to the plateau.

daughters come of age to marry. The more closely secluded a young woman was, the less likely it was that I would come to meet her through my strategy of networking. Consequently while I worked with a substantial number of women who would characterize themselves as being in seclusion, I encountered fewer young secluded women in the neighborhoods I selected than older women. Furthermore, and this is extremely important, in tracing out active women's networks I was not drawn into the very neighborhoods in which the most restrictive forms of seclusion predominate: Limanci for the wives of Mallamai, and Zaria for the wives of the new younger generation of *alhazai* merchants. While I did know several women in both of these neighborhoods, I am now struck by the social dynamics at work that contributed to the likelihood that I would spend less time with such women. In other words, the withdrawal of women in more restrictive forms of seclusion has important implications for a strategy of sampling through active social networks in a region such as Maradi. And conversely, the difficulty of gaining access to such women is, in a sense, a gauge of their social isolation. Not only are such women less likely to be integrated into female social networks, they are less likely to have permission to speak to individuals (even to other women) outside their households, and they are likely to be more reticent than women whose movements and behavior are less constrained. I did succeed in working with some closely secluded women, and many of my informants had been in such a marriage in the past and were willing to talk quite openly about those marriages once they were outside the constraints of that household. However, more work on the emerging forms of seclusion among wives of younger merchants needs to be done, and that work would entail attention to the rapidly developing differentiation among male Muslims who claim allegiance to different brotherhoods and movements, and to how different understandings of seclusion impinge upon the social networks upon which women rely so heavily.

Local gender dynamics had other important implications for my research. I had originally intended to work with both men and women; it very quickly became clear to me, however, that I was mining riches in my interviews with women that would instantly dry up were the women to perceive me as a conduit of information for men (in particular their husbands) about their activities and experiences.[6] I determined, with some reluctance, that I could not afford to lose the women's trust, and worked instead to get as broad an array of women's accounts as possible. This was only one of many compromises I found I had to make, compromises that have led me to be profoundly skeptical about the degree to which any researcher determines alone the shape or content of the research conducted.

All told, then, I worked with 111 women in the Maradi region, most of whom lived in the city of Maradi, but almost half of whom had either lived and worked in a rural setting at an earlier moment in their lives, or lived in

---

[6] This constraint may be heightened in populations which are acutely segregated by sex; Lila Abu-Lughod found herself having to make a similar commitment to women in working with Bedouins (1986:16, 26).

rural villages at the time of my research. I did not use a set interview schedule and I conducted the interviews without an interpreter in Hausa. I probably learned as much from simply visiting and observing these women over the course of the year as I did from the interviews themselves. My approach was to learn all I could about a limited number of women whose lives were interconnected in various ways rather than to collect larger quantities of survey data. While my sample was broad, it was obviously in no sense a "random" sample: because I am a historian I intentionally skewed my sample to overrepresent middle-aged and elderly women, whose memories of changes in the city over time were of particular interest to me.[7] Furthermore I deliberately chose to work with a diffuse network of women because I was convinced that the only way to make sense of women's lives was to trace them out in relation to one another. How did women of different generations, classes, educational levels, and marital situations speak about themselves and one another? What kinds of forces and processes contributed to the variety of trajectories their lives took over time? Rather than test the truth or falsity of the information women recounted in interviews against some "objective" outside standard, I instead set women's accounts alongside one another to ask why and how their accounts might differ or agree. How did women of different economic means or geographic positions relate to and rely upon one another? How did related women of different generations see their own and one another's lives, and in what ways are their lives economically and emotionally interdependent? How does the advent of Western schooling affect the interpersonal relations between women in one household? My often quite intimate knowledge of the details of the lives of numerous women in one household, one neighborhood, or one extended family made it possible for me to contextualize their claims and experiences in ways no other approach to sampling would have made possible. And most important, by entering into women's lives through close friends, relatives, patrons, and the like, I gained a kind of trust and intimacy I would not have encountered had I collected a much broader random sample through the services of research assistants.

Nevertheless these conversations were neither unmediated nor unguarded. On the occasion I would like to analyze here I had been working in the mixed but heavily aristocratic neighborhood of Bagalam. I suppose that in the initial informal group meeting I did ask some general question about marriage, but I recall asking other questions as well, about the forced removal of the city from the valley in 1945, about the subsequent growth of the city and this particular

---

[7] Some 45 of my 111 informants were between 45 and 60 (qualifying them as older women, *mata*, but not as *tsofuwa*, or elderly women), while 20 were over 60 (*tsofuwa*), and 43 were under 45 years old ("young women" who are clearly of childbearing age and might be qualified as *yarinya* whether married or not). Some 20 women were between 25 and 35, and only 10 were under 25. In a region where the most recently published census suggests that close to half of the population is under the age of 15 while only 4 percent is over 60, this attention to older women reflects my concern for historical breadth as well as my introduction into the region through mature women in the A.F.N. I would have worked with a very different set of informants had I used a random sampling of the female population (République du Niger, Ministère du Plan 1985b:35).

neighborhood, about the geographical origins of my new acquaintances and how they came to be in the city, and about their participation in the *bori* spirit possession cult. Most of the questions seemed innocent enough at the time, and it was only later that I came to realize that each one was laden with local political implications. Nevertheless at the time I had not intended to convey the impression that marriage as a subject was more appropriate than, say, the forced labor of women to process peanuts grown on "government fields."

The following interview illustrates how marriage emerged, in this interview context, as both a safe and a fertile field for the exploration of Maradi's history. The interchange also dramatizes the profound differentiation among women as a group, illustrating the differing perspectives and concerns that emerged in this brief encounter between me (a youngish white American woman), Hajjiya Jeka (an elderly member of the courtly class), and Ta Kurya (a middle-aged woman of limited means). During the interview in question Ta Kurya, Hajjiya Jeka, and I were sitting in Jeka's dim but comfortable room, and Ta Kurya (a member of the AFN) was attempting to introduce me to her elderly neighbor (something of a neighborhood grandmother) whom I had already met through another contact. It was a moment of various intrusions and miscommunications, and I recall wishing that Ta Kurya would leave me alone with Hajjiya Jeka so we could get down to work my own way. What interests me here is the complex dynamic–involving perceptions of race, differential educational backgrounds and the power implications of those differences, generational and class differences, local understandings of hospitality–through which a conversation that might have moved towards an open critique of colonialism (certainly that was what I was hoping for at the time) was firmly redirected by Ta Kurya and Hajjiya Jeka towards the topic of marriage.

> Hajjiya Jeka: In the time of our parents we didn't have any experience of wars, isn't that right?
> Ta Kurya: That's right!
> Hajjiya Jeka: My mother, they took her off with her wedding gifts to Mada, she got married, she and my father. They got burned, the whites burned them when they came [*toyesu aka yi, nasara suka toye su*]. . .
> Ta Kurya: Huh?!
> Hajjiya Jeka: We had no need for fighting. . .
> Ta Kurya: Of course not!
> Hajjiya Jeka: But in our time, the things we saw! In our time we suffered greatly. Because of the coming of the whites.
> Ta Kurya: She [meaning me] asked us, if you compare marriage today, and marriage in the past, which one is better?
> Hajjiya Jeka: Oh, in the past!
> Ta Kurya: In the past is better, or now?
> Hajjiya Jeka: Today, at this point, marriage is nothing at all. Whatever you want. . . see, it's like a *faifai* (a round mat used by women to cover a dish or calabash) you can flip like this (Hajjiya Jeka, 2-12-89).

In the face of Hajjiya Jeka's emphasis upon the violence done to her family under European domination, a preoccupation with marriage appears startlingly out of place, a retreat into a safer and more innocuous topic. Earlier in the discussion Hajjiya Jeka had introduced the subject of forced labor herself, see-ing it as an important part of her past and the past of Maradi, and no doubt seeing me (a white "European/Christian") as just the sort of person who needed to hear about that past. Ta Kurya was visibly uncomfortable with Jeka's tone of remonstrance ("Hajjiya," she had retorted, "if there weren't the white people here now. . ."). Despite Ta Kurya's discomfort, I was delighted to finally find someone who could tell me more about exactly the kinds of experiences Jeka was relating. While Jeka was of an older generation who had experienced di-rectly or indirectly (through their own parents) some of the greatest abuses of the colonial period, Ta Kurya was a middle-aged woman more attuned to the perceived benefits of "the coming of the whites" such as schools, roads, con-sumer goods, and medicine. One of the most consistent observations of urban women of Ta Kurya's generation was that marriage for them was "better" than for their own mothers because the burden of pounding grain, bearing water, and collecting firewood had been alleviated somewhat with mills, water pipes, and wood vendors.

It is likely that Ta Kurya, as someone in need of patronage, felt that I should be treated with courtesy and respect, while Jeka, who was comfortably enough off to be in a position to dispense with such deference, was more concerned to set the record straight, as she saw it, about the nature of European intrusion. As the above interchange reveals, Ta Kurya abruptly directed the conversation back to the topic of marriage, a subject evidently more comfortable for her. It was also an issue that, I suspect, she was confident she could use to pressure Jeka into acknowledging that there were ways in which life had improved since "the coming of the Europeans."[8] Jeka, independent-minded as always, retorted that marriage had been better in the past, and that today marriage was fickle and unreliable. Like the proverbial two-faced *faifai* mat, contemporary mar-riage could be manipulated in a moment to adapt to every changing whim and circumstance. At the time I took her dismissal of contemporary marriage as a sign that she felt we should talk about something more substantial. Since that was how I understood her remark, I was frustrated to discover that Ta Kurya had successfully and permanently shifted the terrain of discussion. I never did succeed, in this or in subsequent interviews, in getting Jeka to return to her startling remark that "they got burned." "They" could have been either her parents or the wedding gifts, most likely the latter since her parents were alive at the time of her own first marriage. Possibly during the infamous march of the French Voulet-Chanoine expedition of 1899 the village of Mada, like many others, was burned, and Jeka's mother lost all her wedding gifts in the flames.

It was only much later that I explored the implications of the *faifai* meta-phor and came to see the seriousness of Hajjiya Jeka's observation. A *faifai* is a round mat used by women to cover calabashes and other serving dishes; women also sometimes use it, as in Photograph 1, to winnow or clean grain. It is a pre-

8   Guyer (1984:6) observes that women have often seen change in positive terms, in particular celebrating the passing of precolonial marriage systems. See also Oboler (1985:320–21).

eminently female object. Symbolically it has come to serve as an emblem of uncertainty and adaptation, and of the unpredictableness of those who do not themselves hold power directly. The following proverbs illustrate such themes: "talaka faifai ne; koina aka juya tanka'de zai yi" (the people are mere clay in the hands of the rulers); "ya sauya faifai" (he changed his tone); "sunna kallo, su ga inda faifai zai karkata" (they're "sitting on the fence"); "lokaci ya yi da za a bu'da sabam faifai" (the time has come for a change of fortune) (Abraham 1962:245, his translations). Hajjiya Jeka, in insisting that contemporary marriage is "fickle like a *faifai*," was drawing upon an image that resonated with local understandings of power, choice, fortune and most importantly, instability. The remark captures the sense that marriage has been at the heart of change in the region, and that both men and women have played upon the flexibility of marriage in order to garner power and to counter change themselves, with the end result that marriage is perceived to be the most unstable institution of all.

The issue of marriage and its history turned out to be one that women throughout my broad sample were more than happy to debate, discuss, detail, and decry. Hajjiya Jeka was an exceptional woman, both in her experiences and in her sense of herself as a person who had a history worth retelling. Many of the other women I worked with found the prospect of speaking about their past confusing, even dismaying.[9] Eventually, through much trial and error, I discovered that women did find that they had something to say on the subject of marriage. The above interchange reveals some of the reasons why marriage would emerge as a topic that most women would speak about at length, a subject they regarded as appropriate to a study of the history of women in the region. The apparent innocence of the topic put many of the women I worked with at ease–they could speak with confidence about their experiences as young brides, the shape of weddings over time, their strategies for marrying their daughters, disappointing unions, and, perhaps most important, how they managed to make ends meet in a variety of household arrangements. The seemingly apolitical nature of such conversations invited even the most cautious of my informants to speak from a position of relative safety.

This is not unimportant, for speaking openly about "political" subjects has not always proven wise in Niger's past. And of course Ta Kurya's concern that Jeka not offend me by decrying the exploitation of the colonial period must be read in light of the unequal power relations that undergird encounters between relatively privileged scholars and the disadvantaged people they frequently study. Ta Kurya, as someone with little authority, may have been fearful of the consequences of my anger if I had felt insulted. But I would insist that her actions must also be seen as part of a powerful local ethic of hospitality, an ethic that both facilitated my research (people who had little time for conversa-

---

[9]   For this reason a number of extraordinarily rich life histories of African women stand out: Mmantho Nkotsoe's interviews in Bozzoli (1991), Shostak (1981), M.F. Smith (1981), Mirza and Strobel (1989), Scheub (1988), Mbilinyi (1989), Davison with the women of Mutira (1989). It is no coincidence, I think, that some of the richest of these were collected by African women scholars.

Photo 1: "Girl sifting pounded millet" ("Niger–Jeune fille tamisant du mil pilé"). Early colonial–no date, no contributor. The round mat in the girl's hands is a faifai. Elderly informants to whom I showed this photograph laughed to recall decorating their hair in this "old-fashioned" manner. French National Archives, Centre des Archives d'Outre-mer. All rights reserved. 30F1–18 AOF.3184.

tion might indulge me out of politeness) and inhibited what my interlocutors might be willing to say for fear of offending me.

Many of my acquaintances, like Jeka, were acutely aware that marriage had undergone tremendous change in the course of their lifetimes. Marriage and wedding ritual were simultaneously the repository of "traditional" practices and relations and the locus of tremendous adaptability and uncertainty. Marriage was thus eminently suitable as a topic of history, for it fell safely under the rubric of "tradition" (after all, that is what *tarihi*, the Hausa word also used for "history," generally means in Maradi), while providing the occasion for women to relate how they themselves had experienced and negotiated rapid change. Although I sometimes chafed under this restricted definition of which subjects were suitable for discussion and which ones were not, in the end I followed my informants' lead in attending closely to how marriage had shaped and been shaped by the rapidly changing political economy of twentieth century Maradi.

Thus the seeming apolitical nature of the subject of marriage and domestic life rendered it available as a topic of conversation to me as a researcher, while its accepted status as the locus of custom and conservatism rendered it suitable as the material for "history" understood as "tradition." These myths fit well with scholarly predispositions regarding the "domestic sphere." Where Bourdieu (1977) looked to the dynamics of the domestic realm to illustrate *habitus* in operation and in so doing shed considerable light on the potential for female agency within that realm, many scholars have tended to see the operation of female power (and the taken-for-granted in general) as merely reproductive rather than transformative. The domestic sphere, Ortner insists, is that realm in which the taken-for-granted retains its fiercest grip and in which the process of ideological reproduction for the conservation of the system goes unremarked: "It is precisely in those areas of life–especially in the so-called domestic do-main–where action proceeds with little reflection, that much of the conserva-tism of a system tends to be located" (1984:150).

Ironically the assumption among scholars that the domestic sphere is the site of conservatism has occluded the ways in which the very taken-for-grantedness of that realm renders it the ideal medium through which women, in particular, can effect change. In stubbornly insisting upon marriage as a safe topic of conversation, women I worked with were seizing upon the domestic realm as the stage for their own inventiveness, agency, and subjective experi-ence. Paradoxically, they were using the signifier of tradition to point up the centrality of their experience of and contribution to change. The importance of my informants' sense of history to the direction of my own research and inter-views suggests that, however salutary the postmodernist critical re-evaluation of anthropology has been, scholars who employ anthropological methods must nevertheless attend to the ways in which the "objects" of "representation" are themselves active in shaping those representations, if only imperfectly. As Henrietta Moore and Megan Vaughan remark, "The current criticisms by an-thropologists and others of the invention of societies and cultures through the process of textualization have an important role to play both inside and out-side the discipline, but to claim that these processes float free of all the signifi-cant others involved in their production is a strange kind of inverted arro-gance" (1994:xx).

Of course women have not initiated all the changes the institution of marriage has undergone in the past century, for if the manipulation of mar-riage is useful for women, it is also at times useful for men, the state, mis-sionaries. Both women and men find the negotiation of marriage to be si-multaneously one of the primary means by which they can mediate change and the locus of tremendous instability in their own lives. Indeed it is partly because marriage is negotiable that it becomes the ground upon which change is encountered by both men and women, sometimes quite unpleas-antly. Women's attention to the subject of marriage has its own poignant urgency, however. If Hausa men have other means through which to regu-late change in their own interests, a young Hausa woman's multiple subor-dinations may leave her with few safe-houses from which to moderate and negotiate the shifting terrain of the contemporary world. Some of the in-sights and impasses James Scott uncovers in his broad exploration of counter-hegemonic culture in *Domination and the Arts of Resistance* help to make sense of why women, perhaps more than men, must rely heavily upon the double-edged weapon of marital manipulation. In explaining why his central illustrations for the workings of counter-hegemonic culture have not come primarily from gender-based studies, Scott remarks: "In the case of women, relations of subordination have typically been more personal and intimate; joint procreation and family life have meant that imagining an entirely separate existence for the subordinate group requires a more radical step than it has been for serfs or slaves" (1990:22).

In other words, where serfs, slaves, and sometimes working-class men can find spaces in which to articulate and ultimately voice their "hidden transcripts," the intimacy of female subordination within marriage often leaves women very few safe places from which to develop a counter-discourse.[10] Scott is right to note that frequently women's "resistance," if it can be so labeled, will be "hidden" more thoroughly and more ambiguously than in many of the examples he presents. Where he sees the relative choice some contemporary women experience in marriage as contributing to hegemonic incorporation, his own material suggests that women have relatively few options for developing a fully independent counter-hegemonic discourse. The question to attend to is therefore not whether women suffer from hegemonic incorporation, but whether it is possible for them to develop modes of speech and realms of mediation that are safe given the circumstances of their subordination. In fact the dynamic that seems to give rise to counter-hegemonic discourse (as Scott understands it) among men discourages its appearance among women: all of the pre-eminent spatial locations Scott offers for the most undisguised "transcripts" of the oppressed are as a rule gendered as masculine–bars, woods, markets, secluded spots at night. Indeed, although Scott does not remark upon it, women have often been stigmatized by men for their presence in just such loci of resistant culture. Women may be used to mask peasant protest, and under repressive regimes they may find ways of "clothing their defiance in hegemonic dress," nevertheless frequently the very conditions for the development of solidarity among "the oppressed" seem to require the exclusion of women.[11] It begins to appear as if women are not supposed to participate in the articulation of discourses that undermine or critique the principle of dominance. Hence, perhaps, my informants' reluctance to take part in any discussion that might appear as political in the conventional sense. Indeed it is probably no coincidence that some of the most powerful critiques of Scott's own work on Malaysia have come from scholars centrally concerned with gender, who note that subordinated populations often counter hegemony from within, inevitably becoming

---

[10] It is not surprising that the gender-related work from which Scott draws inspiration consistently is Lila Abu-Lughod's 1986 study of women's poetry among the Bedouin, highly segregated in spatial terms. Distinctive female cultural forms do seem to develope where women are highly segregated, making it more plausible to see therein a coherent "muted" culture where female solidarity can become realized. See also Pittin (1979). Abu-Lughod's subsequent work (1990), however, takes the divisions within the female sphere as one of its central problems.

[11] See Scott (1990:166n70, 150, 129) for the implicit exclusion of the wives of working-class men from their discourse.

themselves "deeply implicated in the [prevailing] religious, ethnic, and political economic hegemonies" (Ong 1995:188 note 1).

While subordinated men can sometimes find safety in their homes,[12] women's frequent subordination within the home can render the domestic sphere the most "public" and unsafe of domains. For a young Hausa woman whose husband, mother-in-law, or senior co-wife is at home, every transcript is a "public" transcript. Under such circumstances an interview with an outsider about "tradition" in which marriage becomes a central focus can serve as a profoundly political act, but one which is at the same time safe, veiled, in a word, "hidden." The most striking of the interviews I conducted were not those in which a high degree of privacy prompted my respondent to confide in me, despite my expectation that this would be the case and my staging of most of the interviews following that assumption. In fact it was in moments of agreement, debate, confrontation, and conflict occasioned by women intruding into the conversation between me and my "informant" that the most interesting material arose and that the publicness and potential political implications of the interview situation became clear. Although I lost a few informants who seemed to fear speaking at all given the likelihood, in this highly permeable spatial setting, that someone might hear and intervene, many of my informants in fact seemed to welcome the debate and conversation among women themselves made possible by my unaccustomed presence. My quest for "history-cum-tradition" became the occasion for reflections on history, authority, morality, and much else.

I would myself be quite reluctant to suggest that what develops out of such semi-veiled "transcripts" is a kind of feminist counter-hegemonic discourse. The recent "discovery" in the Western critical tradition that sex and gender are not identical is nothing new to most Africans, for whom gender is often acquired through ritual and social process rather than physiology. This modest observation has enormous implications for any theory of female culture or gender-based politics. As many scholars have noted, in much of Africa it would be inadequate to analyze patterns of authority and subordination solely or even primarily in terms of gender.[13] The importance of age in configurations of authority in Africa means that younger women are frequently *and in some situations primarily* subordinate to older women rather than to men. As Caroline Bledsoe notes, "The group that shoulders the heaviest burden of productive labor in African societies is not women, but rather the young."[14] Longstanding

---

[12] Cathar men preferred to find Cathar brides so that they would not have to be circumspect about their religion in the home (LeRoy Ladurie 1979).

[13] For a thought-provoking consideration of how differently gender and age are configured in Africa than in the West see Kopytoff (1990). For a variety of critiques of Western approaches to female subordination in Africa by African scholars see Amadiume (1987), Okonjo (1976), Oyewumi (1993), and Afonja (1981).

[14] Bledsoe (1980) provides compelling evidence for how older women can deploy "wealth in people" and the marriage system to control juniors in much the same way that men can. Oboler (1985: 202) notes the tendency on the part of informants to emphasize the division of labor by sex, obscuring the importance of junior labor.

and emerging social differentiation–possible *even within one household*–also contributes in significant ways to the forms of authority to which subordinated
women submit. The degree to which the structures of constraint and opportunity in this locale pit women against one another militates against the formation of any lasting female solidarity or unitary culture. Nevertheless, the interview situation made possible a series of dialogues and disruptions that
simultaneously surfaced and disguised the structures of domination and the
modalities of resistance or accommodation available to women differently situated within those structures. And in this sense these "hidden transcripts" might
be thought of as the practice of the kind of "infrapolitics" Scott recognizes,
through which authority, gender, age, morality, and social position might be
contested, recalibrated, and redefined.

Work in African studies has in recent decades turned its attention to how
ethnicity, kinship, and family have been negotiated and legislated (Chanock
1985, Parkin 1978), to how competing efforts to control the construction of gender have influenced economic and social policies (Hay and Wright 1982, Schmidt
1992), and to the ways in which structures of authority and seniority have been
transformed in a changing political economy (Berry 1987). Fortunately it would
no longer be accurate to observe, as Shula Marks and Richard Rathbone did in
1983, that "Historians of Africa . . . have tended to take the currency of anthropological debate–kinship–as the 'given,' unchanging category of analysis, rather
than as something itself to be analyzed and traced in its changing configuration over time" (1983:147). An attention to the changing form and contestable
nature of kinship, gender, and age have become central to recent approaches to
African history, often drawing upon the insights of work in anthropology. Two
major thrusts have become evident in such work, both of which were already
present in the broad interest in practice in anthropology in the mid-1970s. On
the one hand, scholars increasingly depict social forms as pliable institutions
structured by the day-to-day strategies and improvisations of individuals. David
Parkin and David Nyamwaya offer one formulation of such improvisation and
its implications for women: "There is . . . a certain 'play' within the structure.
And it is precisely this slack in the system, so to speak, which enables women
to initiate change" (1987:4). One strength of this approach is its willingness to
see women as agents in the construction of social forms, and feminist work
insisting on women's agency has been an element in the development of this
strand.

On the other hand, much recent work emphasizes the ways in which hegemonic representations give form to social institutions, materially shaping human lives in the realm of the taken-for-granted and the "natural." Where earlier Marxist approaches to representation tended to conflate culture with a fairly
narrow version of ideology (seeing ideology as serving primarily to mask or
justify social forms), the increasing interest in Gramsci and in feminist theory
has contributed toward seeing cultural processes as the arena in which social
and political-economic forms are defined and occasionally contested. This general approach sheds light, for example, on the "encounter" between European

notions of domesticity and African labor and kinship patterns (Hansen 1992), and has tended to cast its gaze upon the intrusions of the state into local politics and the domestic realm.

As should be clear from the discussion of my research in Maradi, my own work was shaped in part by having been brought up short by the realities of both external and self-imposed constraints to women's speech and action. This study is therefore attentive to the ways in which, given those realities, women as well as men have deployed the taken-for-granted to transformative or subversive ends. The scholarship I have found most useful in helping me to make sense of what I learned from women in Maradi has taken as its central problem the question of the relationships between individual (and more occasionally group) strategy, plastic social forms, and dominant sources of power. The central problematic then becomes the struggles of individuals and groups to define the meaning of critical institutions governing day-to-day life. We are dealing here, then, not with the conscious engineering of social institutions, but rather with gradual and unpredictable transformations emerging out of the practical choices of individuals struggling to define or redefine their terrain of action in the face of a shifting landscape of opportunity (Feierman 1990, Jean Comaroff 1985, Guyer 1984, Murray 1980, Denzer 1992). Henrietta Moore and Megan Vaughan note that what one finds, therefore, is not so much "continuity" as the reworking of familiar problems onto "a version of the past to be remade in the present." As they observe: "However 'new' a situation may be, it will have to be appropriated to a certain extent in terms of a set of practices and discourses that are already known" (1994:233).

In my own research I have found that among the Hausa of Maradi in the late nineteenth and twentieth centuries, the institution of marriage (*arme*) and a constellation of ancillary ritual and productive institutions have proven to be deceptively persistent elements in social life. I suggest that the apparent resiliency of social institutions–the *gandu/gamana* farming arrangement, the paired transfer of *sadaki* bridewealth and *kayan 'daki* "dowry" gifts, the opposition of "married woman" and "courtesan"–obscures the negotiation of markedly altered patterns of productive, domestic, and public life. Here the outward appearance of continuity has served as a kind of sanction for radical change on the part of women and men, rural farmers and urban traders, scholars and aristocrats. At the same time the rich past and the cosmopolitan present of this region have furnished actors of all kinds with an array of potent discourses upon which to draw.

I have attempted to use the turns of phrase, the terms of debate, and the occasions upon which these expressions were brought to bear as much as possible. My work attends far more to particular instances of the use of language than to "discourse" in the abstract. This is because concrete forms of language– terms used and contested, titles altered and created, expressions shared but used with different meanings–are often the specific loci of the contradictions and contestations through which, it seems to me, processual change occurs. Language permits the illusion of consensus and continuity while at the same

time opening up the possibility for conflict and change: it is at once the adhe-
sive and the lubricant of the body politic. The continued use of shared terms
retains certain possibilities while enabling a gradual shift to new arrangements.
    I do not intend through this attention to particular instances of speech to
trivialize resistance or activism as mere linguistic manipulation, however, for
not everything can be accomplished through language. A dominant code can
define the limits to what may be expressed, even within a cacophony of competing "discourses." Maradi's rich and complex history has created conditions
in which multiple ways of speaking and thinking about social forms co-exist;
however, that multiplicity has specific contours giving rise to quite particular
dynamics of possibility and constraint. Maradi differs in a number of important and striking ways from the Hausa-speaking region of northern Nigeria, a
region perhaps more familiar to most readers. In order to give the reader a
sense for the origins and complexity of these "discourses," therefore, it will be
useful to sketch out briefly the political and economic history of Niger and of
Maradi. This chronological discussion will help to frame the more thematic
treatment of Maradi history in the chapters that follow.[15] A number of themes
will have particular relevance in the ensuing discussion: the resiliency of pre-
jihad Hausa institutions, the strong military inflection of French rule in Niger,
the gradual rise of a merchant class with close ties to northern Nigeria, and the
emergence of a French-educated elite with positions of power in the government.

Background to the Political Economy of Hausa Niger

In order to make sense of the practices I shall be exploring one must begin by
noting that it was to the Maradi valley that the resistant forces of Kano, Katsina,
and Gobir retreated when forced from the Habe kingdoms by the jihad of Usman
'dan Fodio launched in 1804. The former rulers of these kingdoms combined
forces to harass and raid the emirates of the Sokoto Caliphate throughout the
nineteenth-century. Maradi became the locus of sustained resistance to Sokoto,
and in Maradi were to be found many remnants of the political culture of the
pre-jihad kingdoms. In my view it is important to emphasize that the Katsinawa
and Gobirawa aristocrats and their clients who fled the jihad regarded themselves as Muslims. At issue was not whether Islam was the true religion, but
how that religion should be interpreted, whether some kinds of concessions to
local pre-Islamic practices could be supported, and whether the local political
hierarchy should be dominated by a clerical elite. It is worth noting that debates and contradictions surrounding the role and appropriateness of pre-Is-

[15] The following discussion is intended to provide the reader with the broad contours of Nigérien
history. For more exhaustive accounts see my sources. For the political and economic history of
Niger: Fuglestad (1983), Baier (1981), Charlick (1991), Decalo (1990). For the Maradi region: David
(1964), Grégoire (1986), Nicolas (1975), Raynaut (1975), P. Roberts (1981), Souley (1987), Y.B. Usman
(1981).

lamic practices are endemic to the Muslim world (see e.g., Cassanelli 1982:119–46; Blackwood 1995), and existed within the earliest Muslim community (Peters 1994:1–59). Important Islamic principles of government make it possible to argue for the retention of some elements of local "custom" ('*urf* or '*ada* in Arabic) to supplement Islamic law or *sharia* (M.G. Smith 1965:28). Thus some Hausa customary practices, known in Hausa as *al'ada*, have long been tolerated as necessary to practical government. Obviously questions will arise as to which customary practices are to be retained, and which come into conflict with the fundamental tenets of Islam. The jihad of Usman 'dan Fodio must be read in this light. The issue of how Islam was to be interpreted and the question of the degree to which pre-Islamic practices were to be tolerated had significant implications for women.

In pre-jihad Hausaland, although stark social contrasts existed between the aristocrats of urban centers such as Katsina and Kano and the peasants and slaves of the rural areas (upon which the cities depended for food and raw materials), judicial and administrative structures nevertheless included features that could counterbalance the authority of the "king" or sarki and that served to represent the interests of the diverse population within the centralized court. A complex system of titles existed, including a number for women, and an array of members of the titled class generally acted as the electoral college that determined which of the many eligible contenders to the throne would in fact take power. In Katsina aristocratic women and members of the urban *bori* spirit possession cult were represented by the figure of the iya, a prominent woman selected from among the recently elected sarki's close family, who acted as a kind of "queen mother" figure so common in West Africa. It is possible that, as Bay (1995) suggests was the case in Dahomey, the particular woman chosen would be so favored largely because she had used her own authority within the royal family to promote the new ruler's election in the first place. The interests of the largely non-Muslim rural population were represented in the court in such figures as the durbi as rural authorities became integrated into the urban structures. The durbi oversaw the kingdom's ritual recognition of pre-existing political and spiritual powers in the realm of farming and hunting. An exhaustive treatment of the nature of pre-jihad government in Katsina is not possible here (see Usman 1981), I wish only to point out that the iya and the durbi, among others, served important ritual and judicial functions that were called into question by the interpretation of appropriate "custom" advocated by the jihadists.

Once the forces of Katsina had been routed and eventually resettled in the Maradi valley, new political formations emerged that drew partly upon Katsina's previous traditions while adapting to the new circumstances. The Katsinawa aristocracy and their allies from Gobir and Kano were invited by indigenous non-Muslims to set up camp in the valley, presumably because of the long history of mutual toleration (the valley had been a distant satellite of Katsina probably from the early eighteenth century; Usman 1981:37) and because the forces resisting the Islamic reformists were seen by the non-Muslims as the

lesser of two evils in a period of profound dislocation and warfare. The trans-
plantation of Katsina's court into a new milieu—a valley controlled by militar-
ily adept Hausa non-Muslims (known in Nigeria as Maguzawa, but referred to
in Maradi as the Arna) who dictated the terms under which the recusant kings
could rule—led to the emergence of institutions and practices whose apparent
continuity with their pre-jihad forms in the Habe kingdoms could be deceptive
(M.G. Smith 1967, David 1964). A political culture emerged that retained features of pre-jihad Katsina while integrating new practices recognizing more
local nodes of authority. The titled position of the *maradi* entered into court
culture, indigenous religious specialists known as *sarkin arna* developed to set
forth local ritual practice and reinterpret it for the urban court setting, and the
bori cult adapted to this new spiritual milieu with new or reinterpreted spirits.
In short Maradi continued the process of integration and internalization of social cleavages into the fabric of urban and court life.

Significantly for women, aristocratic women retained certain titled positions dating to the pre-jihad era, including the title of iya. The *bori* spirit possession cult so important to women was not only practiced openly but was an
important element in establishing and sustaining the legitimacy of the rulers.
And finally, the majority of women continued to farm[16] and to go about their
lives unsecluded as they had prior to the jihad. By contrast, in territories conquered by the jihadists (largely in what was to become northern Nigeria), secluded marriage has gradually become the norm, the spirit cult was discouraged (but not eliminated) by the Fulani rulers, and even rural women have
almost entirely retired from farming to perform other kinds of economic activities in seclusion.

Since the Maradi region fell largely under French colonial jurisdiction while
much of the territory under the jihadists fell to the British, in the late nineteenth and early twentieth centuries, the tensions between France to Britain
seemed to reiterate the hostility between Maradi and northern Nigeria. The
French did not gain definitive claim to the Maradi region until 1907, and the
regional post was not consistently staffed until the mid-1920s. Hence early
French intrusion could often be evaded by local populations simply by moving
out of the reach of the colonial administration, and the urban center of Maradi
suffered from depopulation in the early decades of French rule.

Differing French and British styles of colonization and administration also
left profound marks on the character of Maradi as opposed to, for example,
Kano and Katsina. While one can overstate the implications of the French policy
of direct rule as opposed to British indirect rule, certainly indigenous Hausa/

---

[16] In sharp contrast with women in northern Nigeria, Hausa women in the Maradi region of Niger
have played and continue to play a significant role in agriculture. A study conducted in northern
Nigeria in the late 1970s illustrates this difference strikingly. Women in the study contributed less
than 2 percent of peak agricultural season family labor as against 11 percent by children and 16
percent by hired labor (Norman et al. 1979). By contrast a 1978 study in *Matan Niger* of women's
role in production in Maradi Department estimated that female *gamana* production alone represented 35 percent of the millet crop, not counting their contribution to labor on the *gandu* plot.
(PM/Issa 1981:6).

Fulani political and judicial structures were integrated into the British colonial structures of Northern Nigeria to a much greater degree than parallel Hausa structures were in Niger as Maradi became subsumed into the French colony.[17] Furthermore differences in the wealth and perceived potential of the two regions led to increasing differentiation between them. While roads, schools, and hospitals were gradually introduced into Northern Nigeria–Britain's paradigm of indirect rule–the French permitted Maradi to languish as a neglected backwater in a peripheral colony, where infrastructure developed fitfully if at all.[18] Thus the economic boom launched in the nineteenth century in the Sokoto and Gwandu caliphates was carried on into the early colonial period in Nigeria, despite increasing polarization within the population and heavy demands upon the local economy to fill colonial coffers. In Maradi, on the other hand, significant economic gains dating from early in the colonial period resulted, tellingly, from the completion of the rail line to Kano by the British.

With an outlet for local agricultural and pastoral produce via the rail from about 1914, the Maradi economy began to shift from its dependence on warfare, regional trade in high-value crops such as tobacco, and links to the dying trans-Saharan commerce towards the production of peanuts for export for the global market. European demand for oil bearing plants was high, so that although the French were originally attempting to promote cotton production, local farmers instead seized upon the market and outlet for peanuts.[19] French colonial exactions in the form of taxes were notoriously high in the Hausa-speaking region, and as the administrative grip on the region gradually tightened farmers in Maradi had to expand production phenomenally, particularly after 1925 when the tax burden doubled (Fuglestad 1983:127). In addition to the heavy tax burden, farmers found particularly onerous the requirement that they devote large portions of their crops to *greniers de réserve* after the famine of 1930–31. These reserve granaries were created and controlled by the French administration in order to forestall the perceived "improvidence of the native" to which colonial officers attributed the famine in the west of Niger. The famine might with greater justice have been attributed to the erosion of traditional mechanisms for surviving occasional drought years resulting from colonial requisitions and tax demands (Egg et al. 1975).

A number of interrelated processes developed in this early period of the colonial era. The local population consistently deployed the option of simply migrating to evade French controls, often into areas that had not been farmed previously or into British Nigeria. Nevertheless, the urban center of Maradi was at the same time becoming a stronger and stronger pole of attraction. The

---

[17] For a full study of differences between Hausaland in Niger and Nigeria, see Miles (1994).

[18] I am speaking in relative terms here; one of the implications of British indirect rule was that the "Islamic values" of the north were ostensibly respected and missionary intrusion into the region was systematically discouraged, with the result that compared to southern Nigeria, the emirates received an underdeveloped educational infrastructure.

[19] For fuller discussions of the rise of peanut production in Niger see Grégoire (1986), Collion (1982), Roberts (1981), Péhaut (1970), Raynaut (1975).

city took on new importance as the commercial and administrative center of the region, particularly after Maradi became an administrative *cercle* in 1926. Women discovered new income-earning options there and occasionally sought judicial fora more sympathetic to their marital woes than were to be found in their marital villages. Accordingly the documents of the period sketch a picture of intense mobility on the part of the population, a mobility that the colonial administration found both puzzling and frustrating.

The farming economy was undergoing a radical transformation as production patterns, crop mixes, and distribution patterns adjusted to the demands of expanded peanut cropping. However in the pre-war period farmers never neglected their balance between millet, beans, and peanuts, keeping a wary eye on a shifting market, alert to the danger of declining prices for cash crops. The development of peanut farming was fitful. The advent of the Depression had temporarily halted the expansion of peanut production for cash. Furthermore French colonial attitudes towards the growing commercial links between Nigeria and Niger were ambivalent, and the French administration periodically set up customs barriers or closed the border altogether, precipitating economic crises and migration into Nigeria. Incipient commercial linkages and a shared sense of embattlement among Hausa speakers on either side of the border fostered the increasing integration of the two previously warring regions; the acceleration of contacts among Hausa speakers on either side of the border contributed to gradually increasing cultural integration, particularly in the idiom of Islam.[20] By 1940 or so the tide of migration into Nigeria had been largely stemmed, and farmers were returning to migrate instead into more northerly zones of the region traditionally devoted to pastoral activities.

The implications of colonial rule for the chiefs and the court were complex. On the one hand succession was more settled than it had been in many years, for the squabbling among varying contenders to the throne that had marred the history of the region from 1890 to 1907 was put to rest, more or less, with the French administration's arrogation of the right to assign successors to the throne. On the other hand, the colonial administration's divide-and-rule strategy, coupled with its tenuous understanding of local politics and its impetuous tendency to depose rulers at will, meant that the tenure of successive rulers remained quite insecure. Indirect rule in this region bore a strong authoritarian and military stamp, embodied for the local population in the *indigénat* law code permitting the local administrators to impose penalties upon subjects without any judicial procedure. French attitudes and policy in this period regarding indigenous political structures vacillated between an avowed devotion to direct rule and a practical need to make use of indigenous rulers. In Maradi the relative strength of the court structures in the precolonial era meant that colonial administration tended, on the whole, to employ these preexisting structures rather than effectively erase them. However the powers of the local sarkis were redirected towards tax collection, eroding other strands of

---

[20]   For a rich analysis of the rise of the merchant class see Grégoire (1986).

their authority and shifting some of the resentment for colonial impositions upon local rulers, whose insecurity of tenure and insulation from traditional sanctions invited them to make the most of their positions while they could. The local population simultaneously resented indigenous authorities for their implication in colonial domination and turned to them in preference to the more formal institutions of direct rule represented by the French *commandant de cercle*. Consequently many of the practices and institutions of the Katsinawa and Gobirawa aristocracy continued to have relevance, particularly in the judicial realm.[21]

World War II was experienced by the people of Maradi primarily as a period in which trade was hampered by the closure of the border with Nigeria under the Vichy government of the AOF, and in which black market trade across the border nevertheless flourished as the two colonial governments competed for control of the peanut oil so vital to wartime needs. Conditions eased somewhat with the take-over of the Gaullists in 1944 (Fuglestad 1983:141), however in 1945 a serious flood damaged much of the city, which had been nestled in the river valley of the Gulbin Maradi for reasons of military defense since the mid-nineteenth century. The barricades and waterworks that had in the past protected the city from occasional flooding had been neglected as a result of heavy colonial demands upon local labor for other projects. The city was moved forcibly from the valley to the sandy plateau above the Gulbin Maradi, significantly altering the character of the urban center (David 1964). The new location, set on an open plain, made possible the expansion of the city in three directions, an extension that had not been possible in the protective confines of the valley location.

By the interwar years European trade houses had begun setting up in Maradi, promoting intricate networks of local petty traders selling imported consumer goods such as European and American cloth and kerosene lamps. Such networks eventually also serviced the peanut trade, and as peanut production took off after World War II, the two trades were so intimately linked to one another that trade houses sometimes paid for peanuts with *bons d'achat* that could only be used to purchase goods–notably cloth–from the company store (Grégoire 1986:74n1). This early trade fostered a cadre of local Hausa traders (largely male) who were shut out of the larger wholesale market, but who became extremely skilled and knowledgeable about how to buy and sell retail, particularly in rural areas where customers had little access to the urban trade stores.

The expansion of commerce in the city provided trade opportunities for women as well, particularly selling cooked food to the expanding population of wage laborers and peddling cloth door-to-door with the aid of their young daughters. Prior to about 1930 most women's primary source of income came from sales of handspun cotton thread, which was produced exclusively by women and was, in a sense, monopolized by them. The relentless expansion of

---

[21] My emphasis on the continuing importance of the chiefs, unlike Miles (1994), is shared by Abba (1990) at a rather different level of analysis.

trade in prestigious imported cotton cloth, facilitated in important ways by women themselves, gradually eroded the local cloth industry. In order to continue to gain prestige by giving cloth to others women, by the 1940s, had to scramble to earn income through petty trade in food or imported goods rather than by participating directly in local cloth production (Cooper 1993).

With the ending of the war and the reopening of the border, Maradi experienced a boom period. Peanut production expanded phenomenally with higher producer prices, and construction in the city gave rise to new neighborhoods, such as Sabon Gari, into which the urban population swelled. After the forced transfer of the city to the plateau and with the easing of unpopular colonial exactions as the *indigénat* was abolished after the war, the population of the city expanded rapidly. In rural areas the peanut boom generated increasing conflict between farmers and pastoralists over land, particularly in the north. By 1954 the government began to attempt to stem the expansion of agriculture into the pastoral zone, to little effect. The government also attempted to redirect the flow of peanuts away from the Nigerian rail route by evacuating them by air in "Operation Hirondelle" to the rail line in Dahomey. The attempt was, not surprisingly, quite unsuccessful, and the commercial and cultural integration of Hausa Niger and Fulani/Hausa Nigeria continued to grow stronger.

More successful was the fostering of an urban bourgeoisie to serve as the bureaucratic political class who would take the reigns of power upon France's inevitable withdrawal from the colony. The period between 1945 and Niger's independence in 1960 was marked by the increasing salience of an educated elite dependent upon the state for salaries and deeply invested in the urban bureaucracy. Because the capital of the colony had, from 1922, been located at Niamey in the Zerma-speaking region, and because the French mistrusted the Hausa for their deep ties with the Hausa-speaking population in rival Nigeria, Hausa speakers were in general disadvantaged in terms of access to education and experience in the political idiom of the French. Despite their numerical majority and their importance to the economy, the Hausa came to be politically dominated by Zerma speakers under Diori Hamani at independence in 1960. While the transition to independence gave rise to numerous political parties and a great deal of competition among members of the educated elite, for most farmers in Maradi the early years of the postcolonial period were in many ways indistinguishable from the late colonial period. A bureaucracy dominated by Frenchmen and Dahomeans gradually shifted to one dominated by Zerma speakers, while Hausa farmers and petty traders continued their work as before. However as the new state attempted to shift control over the peanut and import trades away from European commercial firms and towards local traders who served as buyers and distributors for the state's monopoly organisms, a few experienced Maradi traders who had served European firms managed to gain a far more important position within the networks of exchange. As the importance of the peanut revenues and the profits from transit trade with Nigeria increased, the state bureaucracy and the burgeoning merchant class entered into subdued but growing competition with one another (Grégoire 1986:102–103), a competition tempered by their dependence upon one another (Grégoire 1990).

A period of unusually high rainfall encouraged the expansion of farming into zones that had previously been regarded as suitable only for pastoralism; peanut production soared at the expense of food crops. By the mid-1960s the region was no longer self-sufficient in staple food crops such as millet, and many farmers were relying upon sales of peanuts to purchase food crops. The illusion that such expansion of the peanut economy could be sustained was abruptly and tragically burst with the Sahel Drought of 1968–1974. Farmers who had expanded beyond the traditional farming zone could no longer produce a harvest, and many migrated in search of relief food. The Tuareg and Fulani pastoralists were hardest hit, however: pressed into increasingly arid territories as agriculture expanded, many lost entire herds through starvation and livestock sales to purchase staple foods whose cost had skyrocketed. By 1973 farmers in Maradi had shifted from peanuts to focus once again on high-value staple food crops and the agricultural economy began a slow and unsteady recovery. The minority population of nomadic pastoralists, perennially marginalized by territorially based governments in which French education is indispensable, have been even slower to recover their footing.[22]

Nevertheless this crisis period, combined with the Nigerian civil war in Biafra, contributed to the prosperity and power of the emerging second generation of merchants in the urban center of Maradi, traders who capitalized upon the high value of grain they stockpiled and who provisioned Nigeria during the war. The ravages of the drought (caused to a very large degree by the overemphasis in the economy upon peanut production), therefore, contributed to increasing differentiation between the urban center (dependent upon trade) and rural areas (dependent upon agropastoral production). This merchant class has come to be known as the *alhazai*, a plural form of Al Hajj, the honorific for a man who has made the pilgrimage to Mecca. The local term for these merchants reveals the deep connections between religious identity and class formation in this situation, as the increasingly close ties between these men and their patrons and creditors in northern Nigeria have promoted, ironically, the more conservative Nigerian vision of Islam that the founders of the Maradi kingdom had so long resisted (Grégoire 1986).

The trauma of the drought also contributed to the fall from power of the Diori Hamani regime in 1974, as Diori's preoccupation with international affairs and his cynical mishandling of drought relief prompted a coup d'état.[23] The military government under Seyni Kountché enjoyed tremendous popular-

---

[22] Bourgeot argues that the disastrous effects of the droughts of 1969–1973 and 1984–1986 were symptomatic of broader processes rather than the cause of the pastoralists' decline. Among the relevant factors would be: the expansion of cultivation into the pastoral zone, the establishment of international boundaries, the decline of the trans-Saharan trade, and the weakening of social control over space (1990:70n7).

[23] Raynaut and Abba (1990:11) suggest that anxiety among the military about potential disruptions from a congress called by Diori in order to gain the upper hand in internal rivalry within the PPN also contributed to the coup. They also point out the importance of the educated intelligentsia in articulating discontentment immediately prior to the coup. For another full study see Fuglestad and Higott (1975).

ity at first, buoyed by short-lived prosperity due to the newly developing export of uranium at a time when prices were high. The state invested heavily in
the agricultural sector, and used the new income to expand the construction of
roads and schools. For the first time the Maradi region began to have access to
educational facilities on a scale in keeping with its population. The state expanded its bureaucracy enormously, hiring teachers, clerks, and medical pro-
fessionals. For a brief period literate Hausa from Maradi were able to earn positions as state functionaries. The increased access to schooling, in turn,
generated growing numbers of school leavers who anticipated white collar work
in government employment and who were poorly prepared and little inclined
to enter the agropastoral sector.

This moment of prosperity ended, however, with the collapse of the price of
uranium in 1985. The sudden constriction on state revenues coincided, in Maradi,
with the closure of the border with Nigeria, as Nigeria's own financial troubles
prompted an insular impulse. The merchant class was pressured to buy up failing state enterprises and Maradi's fledgling import substitution industry wasted
away. With the death of Kountché in 1987, his military successor Ali Saibou inherited an extremely weak economy and an increasingly restless populace: the
growing numbers of unemployed school leavers in urban centers such as Niamey
wanted and felt entitled to positions in a state bureaucracy that could no longer
sustain expansion; farmers felt the pinch as state investment in the rural sector
retracted while the cost of consumer goods increased; the civilian elite was increasingly resentful of austerity measures under military rule and unimpressed
with the Supreme Military Council's efforts to rectify the problems with the
economy.[24] Saibou attempted to forestall the growing murmurs of dissent by staging a relaxation of military rule in the guise of a new party, the National Movement of the Society for Development (MNSD) and by continuing a now-familiar
state strategy of co-opting the various nodes of authority within the country (the
Islamic leaders, the youth movement, the traditional rulers, the cooperatives). In
principle the "movement" was to pave the way for civilian elections, yet in private Nigériens were quietly skeptical, aware that the elections would leave power
in the hands of the military, even if a civilian were elected as president. Once the
new constitution, which in principle codified a shift from arbitrary rule (*régime
d'exception*) to the rule of law, was passed, heralding in the "Second Republic,"
civilian skepticism quickly proved well-founded.

Nigérien popular resentment of the continuing reality of military rule came
to a head in 1990: the army fired upon student protesters in Niamey in February and news reports emerged alleging that hundreds of Tuaregs had been
killed, arrested, or tortured in retaliation for an armed attack on the Tchin-
Tabaraden sous-préfecture in May. As Pearl Robinson observes, "within less
than a year, the use of military might against student demonstrators and innocent civilians stripped the thin veneer of legitimacy from the Second Republic"
(1994a). Popular discontent over the attacks upon the Tuaregs, the shooting of

---

[24]   For a study of the crises leading to Niger's structural adjustment program and a frank look at
policies and their outcomes under Kountché and Saibou see Tinguiri (1990).

students in Niamey, and austerity measures crystallized in a coalition between students and labor unions, who joined together to use strikes to pressure the Saibou regime to initiate a national conference for constitutional reform and to arrange multiparty elections. The national conference phenomenon drew upon the "script" for regime change embedded in the French discourse of Republican rule of law and popular sovereignty, a familiar discourse for francophone Africans and one given heightened saliency in the wake of the bicentennial of the French Revolution.[25] The national conference "script" was partially rehearsed in Benin in 1990, and was consciously mimicked by Nigérien intellectuals (Robinson 1994:596). The MNSD candidate was defeated in multiparty elections held early in 1993, bringing a coalition government to power under President Mahamane Ousmane, a Hausa statistician from Zinder: a civilian coup had been effected.

If French Republican discourse had the potential to create a mobilizing and structuring "script" for this civilian coup, such discourse was not, unfortunately, the only legacy of French political and colonial influence. The coalition government was fraught with competition among diverse party interests and individual leaders, and that competition came to a head in tensions between the president and his prime minister, Hama Amadou. The two politicians' ability to work out an arrangement of "cohabitation" after the French parliamentary model was hindered by the postcolonial reality that domestic and international matters are inextricably linked in the questions of international aid and the role of the military. Some have argued that the French dual presidency model is inappropriate for Africa, and has led to other, similar, crises (*West Africa*, 5–11 Feb. 1996a:168). Indeed debates about how to handle the relationship between the *président de la République* and the *président du Conseil* have a long history in France itself (see e.g. Shennan 1989:106–40). Ultimately competition between the two figures precipitated a constitutional crisis, which many international and national figures attempted to resolve, to little effect. At length the crisis served as justification for a military coup under Lieutenant-Colonel Ibrahim Bare Mainassara on January 27, 1996. The equally potent colonial legacy of paternalist military intervention in the name of a "responsibility" to safeguard an ostensibly powerless populace once again surfaced (Ola-Davies 1996:177), setting an unwelcome precedent in a region where a number of francophone countries are attempting to make a transition to some form of multi-party democracy.

The constitutional crisis alone did not lead to the fragility of the fledgling civilian government, however. Opposition from the MNSD party, whose members are often public figures who built strong personal followings under military rule, continued to be vocal. The government inherited unresolved crises that have only deepened since 1993: a Tuareg rebellion in the north that crosses

---

[25] I am here summarizing Pearl Robinson's insightful analysis of the Niger conference in the context of numerous factors, including the bicentennial of the French Revolution, the release of Nelson Mandela, and the emergence of the broader national conference phenomenon in francophone Africa (1994).

international boundaries, has no single leadership, and lacks clear objectives;[26] unrest and protest in the capital generated by students and unemployed school leavers clamoring for scholarships and employment with the state; a debt in excess of $1.5 billion generating debt service obligations that have thrown the Nigérien budget into a cycle of seemingly unending deficit (McCarus 1993b, Gervais 1995); pressure for politically impractical austerity measures from international lenders helping Niger meet its debt service obligations; and a civil servant class that has struggled to get by with unreliable and inadequate pay at a time when inflation is at 80 percent (Ola-Davies 1996:179). Social services have deteriorated as a result of the state's inability to provide medical, educational, and agricultural materials in the wake of Structural Adjustment. These difficulties have been compounded immeasurably by France's devaluation of the West African franc in January of 1994. The devaluation has been disastrous for the Maradi region, where prosperity has largely been based upon traders' ability to take advantage of price and currency differences on either side of the border. It eradicated overnight the one asset of the Nigérien economy relative to that of Nigeria, namely the strength and stability of its currency. It is difficult to imagine how any government, civilian or military, will be able to sustain popular support for long under such circumstances.

Contesting Hegemony, Contending Discourses

As the foregoing account suggests, competitive social relations and economic tensions in the Maradi region have only increased as the century has progressed. In attempting to hold their own in this unstable environment, individuals have drawn upon the existing repertoire of mutable idioms, social patterns, and productive elements through which they could adapt to change. The complex history of the region offers individuals a multitude of rich discourses from which to draw. Some of the resident competing discourses include: the ideology of the Katsinawa aristocratic class (itself highly textured with accretions from pre-jihad Katsina, from Maradi's Arna traditions, and from the *bori* traditions of the urban setting), the ideology imbued with Nigerian Islamist values characteristic of the merchant class (an increasingly variegated terrain where adherence to different Islamic brotherhoods and movements serves to create distinctions within this class as it expands),[27] the "Westernized" ideology of the bureaucratic elite (an ideology, however, that is not reducible in any simple way to French culture), and the contradictory and opportunistic discourses on motherhood, female independence, and modernity

---

[26] The Tuareg revolt is complicated by the "Libyan factor": Qaddafi has played Nigérien dissent movements to his advantage for decades. See Raynaut and Abba (1990:22–23). For a study of the rebellion in Mali which sheds light on the geography and internal differentiation of the dissident movement see Klute (1995).

[27] In this work I shall generally refer to the practices of this relatively restrictive and occasionally anti-Western brand of Islam as "Islamist" rather than "Islamic" in order to stress that this is only one strand of Islam and to remind the reader that other interpretations of Islam are possible.

fostered by the single-party state under Diori, Kountché, and Saibou. Thus women in Maradi might choose in one moment to favor an Islamist discourse in order to promote their legal rights and to secure their maintenance as wives; they might borrow from the rhetoric of female independence proffered by the party in power by using the women's association to state visually their right to public space and political representation; they might adopt the perspective of the Katsinawa aristocracy which guarantees certain women spiritual and political powers in titled positions or in the *bori* spirit cult. But this does not mean that all discourses are available or functional within this milieu: as we shall see, the terms of debate familiar to academic feminists (from second wave equal-rights feminism, to third-wave "womanism," to postmodern "cyborg" hybridities) are stunningly absent here. While the cultural forms that mold women's experiences can be stretched and redefined, there are limits to how and when this change through praxis can be brought about. In what follows I have attempted to set out some of the critical moments and key cultural terms that both define and have been defined by women in the Maradi region over the course of the twentieth century as actors of all kinds have sought to mediate broader political, economic, and cultural change through the flexible articulating institution of marriage.

This renegotiation of the lived content of seemingly persistent institutional forms frequently comes about not only through the plasticity of language but also, and importantly, by means of the praxis of the body: the active reformation and redefinition of the spaces to which women have access. Accordingly, I have looked to actual spatial practices rather than simply to "discourse" in the narrower verbal sense in order to locate the arenas in which contestations over meaning occur. In a region characterized by a high degree of spatial segregation between men and women, I found that in order to make sense of how marriage, marriage ritual, and the routines of everyday life within marriage had been transformed over time it was critical that I make note of how familiar spatio-temporal patterns were altered and by what means.

In considering these questions I found myself faced constantly with the conundrum of how to come to terms with the cumbersome and problematic domestic/public dichotomy. Work in feminist studies has long attended to how space is implicated in power relations as an important element in the production and reproduction of gender difference and sexual stratification (Ardener 1981). Such work has tended to become mired in debates about the origins, character, and validity of a binary opposition between "domestic" and "public" spheres, setting up a dichotomy between a domesticized female "space" and the "space" of male public power.[28] Because of the often metaphorical character of this theoretical use of "space" or "domain," the domestic/public binary readily stands in for other, often naturalized, dichotomies (nature/culture, reproduction/production, private/politico-jural, profane/sacred, practice/symbol). It is partly because of this pernicious ten-

---

[28] Of enduring significance in this debate have been Rosaldo (1974) and Ortner (1974). For useful overviews of this literature see John Comaroff (1987) and Yanagisako and Collier (1990).

dency that the domestic/public binary has rightly been critiqued.[29] Nevertheless many who do work in societies in which male and female spaces are sharply differentiated are reluctant to abandon the analysis of gendered spaces altogether.

My own resolution of the problem of how to attend to the relationship between gendered spaces and the options and constraints women have experienced has been to ask not whether male and female spaces can be characterized as "public" and "domestic" respectively, but rather to take note of the ways in which both women and men transform and redefine the spaces available to them in order to gain access to previously excluded options. In this work I suggest, for example, that women have found ways to break down the expected barriers to women's entry into "public" life and the broader market by effectively transforming the "interior" spaces of their homes into spaces that are well known outside the home, in effect creating "public" spaces from within seclusion. While this occurs most clearly in women's development of house trades and in their attempts to obtain real estate they can use and define as they please, it can occur in more subtle ways as well. As I have suggested above, by taking part in discussions of "tradition" and marriage with me women were sometimes deliberately rupturing the purported intimacy of the domestic realm, drawing upon the very "publicness" of this permeable arena in order to air grievances, enter into debates, and prompt the renegotiation of domestic life. Similarly, ongoing contests over women's dress and veiling reflect the importance of such transformational strategies on the part of women, for by taking on *hijab* women, ironically, increase their mobility into the spaces hitherto reserved for men. In redefining their interior and bodily spaces through dress and decor, ritual and performance, women redefine their options in marriage, the nature of respectability, and their claim to a range of forms of capital. These contests frequently occur in extremely concrete spatialized arenas: in rural women's struggles to retain access to the "wife's field;" in urban women's investment in housing and rural farmland; in divorced and widowed women's movement into open or "external" market spaces; and in women's generalized efforts to earn the title "Hajjiya" by performing the pilgrimage to Mecca.

Summary of the Chapters

This book opens in **Chapter 1** with a discussion of the uneven and unpredictable efforts of the colonial state to act as "emancipator," first of slaves and later of women. While the state has had a profound influence upon the shape of marriage in Maradi, that influence has been neither direct nor intentional. The abolition of slavery set in train a series of redefinitions of marriage as slave-

---

[29] In an important contribution to the debate Sudarkasa (1986) points out that the binary automatically implies a dual stratification and argues that "female" and "male" are not two ranked statuses but rather autonomous and unranked clusters of statuses which are not directly congruent with gender.

owning families attempted to recast master/slave relations onto the intra-household hierarchies of women.[30] This projection of servitude onto marriage protected the prerogatives of wealthy men and women, but was not foreseen by the colonial state.[31] Once this reformulation of marriage had been effected, any attempt to regulate women's rights in marriage would threaten the principles structuring the social order as a whole, undermining existing patterns of production and accumulation. The growth of Maradi as an urban center under colonial rule provided women with experiences and options previously unavailable, options that potentially undercut male authority. The colonial state, torn between its republican impulse to advance the interests of women and its imperial imperative to maintain social order, mouthed an intention to advance protections for women while actively promoting the interests of senior men and women by assisting in controlling women and turning a blind eye to de facto domestic slavery. The colonial and postcolonial states have moved gingerly in attempting to legislate reforms to marriage for fear of provoking large-scale social and economic disruption. Thus while the availability of legal and judicial structures put in place by the colonial regime could reasonably be expected to have served as one of the most powerful forces available to women in reshaping marriage, presenting as it did the potential for women to use the courts to protect them in marriage, in practice, French legislation and the formal court system never effectively supplanted indigenous fora for arbitrating disputes in Maradi.

Rather than regularizing or concretizing one version of "tradition," or imposing a Victorian vision of marriage, the colonial Tribunal instead introduced a further element of uncertainty into an already unstable situation.[32] As a consequence most people in Maradi have avoided the formal courts, preferring other forms of mediation instead.[33] However the existence of the formal courts altered the legal/jural field and the nature of debate over "tradition" considerably. In **Chapter 2** I explore a number of cases adjudicated in a variety of judicial settings to demonstrate the incapacity of even more local mediators to fully control the men and women they serve. These disputes will stage in advance

---

[30] Work on other regions of Africa suggests that occasionally marriage could shade into servitude under the pressures and inequities of the global market. Guyer provides studies of two Beti chiefs who expanded food production through their control of the labor of hundreds of wives (1984:38–42). Wright's studies of the life stories of women in East and Central Africa give startling evidence of the vulnerability of unprotected women, whose "marriages" could dissolve into slavery almost without warning (1993).

[31] The growing literature on the implications of the abolition of slavery in general (Miers and Roberts 1988, Lovejoy and Hogendorn 1993) shows that the institution of marriage (conflated with concubinage by colonial authorities) frequently facilitated the persistence of female slavery long after most forms of male enslavement had been eliminated or radically transformed.

[32] Berry argues that colonial regimes were unable to impose any fixed version of law on indigenous societies: "colonial 'inventions' of African tradition served not so much to define the shape of the colonial social order as to provoke a series of debates over the meaning and application of tradition, which in turn shaped struggles over authority and access to resources" (1993:24).

[33] For a wonderful study of how and why a marital dispute might be handled outside the courts see Mann (1982).

some of the nodes of conflict, idioms of debate, and processes in play to be explored in subsequent chapters.

Chapter 3 explores how changes in land access in conjunction with a growing need for cash gave rise to a redefinition of the uses of married women's fields and to corollary shifts in male rights and responsibilities in marriage. By reading marriage in the Maradi region in light of how changing demands upon the local productive system positioned women and men over time I have attempted to see productive and social processes as mutually determining, while understanding developments within the urban and rural areas as interwoven. Women and men both attempt to draw upon available discourses concerning marriage to redefine the terms of their access to land, one another's labor and capital, and to gain purchase on cultural capital resident in particular versions of marriage. In rural areas women seized upon the Islamic ideology of female dependence in marriage to lay claim to the right to dispose of the entire *gamana* crop as they chose. Men could use the same ideology to claim greater control of women's labor on the *gandu* fields and, more recently, to withdraw married women's rights to *gamana* land in usufruct altogether.

The transfer of the city of Maradi to the plateau in 1945 contributed to the growth of a market in urban real estate. **Chapter 4** explores the circumstances under which women began to acquire property through inheritance and purchase, dramatically altering their options in marriage. Both women in "soldier marriages" and women married to "strangers" (non-Hausa traders and ex-soldiers) have invested disproportionately in urban housing. Their exposure to travel, to the workings of the state, and to the advantages of independent housing prompted many such women to invest in urban land. Access to housing has made it possible for them to remain independent of their husbands in times of stress, to use their houses as bases from which to operate trades, and to build ties with their male children, who in the past had relied upon male kin for access to housing. Women's acquisition of land and houses has helped to shape the urban landscape both physically and socially, for by investing in rental housing they have made it possible for other women to find housing and to remain outside of marriage without entering into prostitution.[34]

In both rural and urban settings this remolding of marriage has been played out in shifts in the rituals and material goods associated with weddings. Both men and women use the wedding ceremony itself as a medium for setting out differing interpretations of the respective duties of men and women in marriage. In **Chapter 5** I argue that marriage ritual reflects and enacts an ongoing struggle among the various participants in weddings to define marriage and to evaluate women's worth and roles. Where most studies of African marriage interpret wedding gift exchange as a series of material exchanges that compensate parties for the loss of various rights, I see wedding exchange in Maradi as

---

[34] The centrality of urban property in the literature on women in Africa (White 1990, Robertson 1990, Bledsoe 1980) suggests that we need to explore more fully the relationships between property, residency, women's economic and political options, and the means through which they define themselves and the social landscape around them (Barnes 1990).

a dialogue in which women take an active role in defining their own worth, thereby setting the terms of their own marriages and those of their junior female kin. Women have responded to servitude in marriage by staging ceremonials that publicly state that a formal bridewealth marriage has been transacted implying a series of rights and protections for women in marriage. Wedding celebrations also serve to display the worth and social network of the bride and her mother. These ritual statements involve, significantly, large quantities of "gifts for the room" that women use to decorate the interior spaces of their homes. Women's ritual performance of free status is memorialized and quantified in vast numbers of material goods they later continue to use to define themselves in the interior spaces of their homes.[35]

The growing importance of both "Western" and Islamic discourses in the region in this century has contributed to ambiguities surrounding the interpretation and expectations of men and women in marriage. These contending discourses are embodied institutionally in competing Koranic and Western schooling, the implications of which I discuss in **Chapter 6**. The recent expansion of Islamic schooling has been in part in reaction to the intrusion of Western education and the contradictory opportunities it offers women: monogamous, companionate marriage at one extreme, and independent wage-earning "outside marriage" at the other. The growth of the *alhazai* class, by contrast, has coincided with the increasing incidence of polygynous secluded marriage. While Western and Islamist ideologies in some respects clash, both colonial education and *alhazai* ideology have promoted an ideal of leisured female domesticity. And both Western and Islamic education, paradoxically, offer educated women opportunities to redefine their roles in the local economy and provide a language in which to contest dominant interpretations of female respectability. The discourses of female domesticity, on the one hand, and of prosperity through knowledge, on the other, alternately clash and resonate with one another in local understandings of wealth and femininity.

The proliferation of images and discourses surrounding marriage gives rise to tremendous uncertainty in marriage. Men and women may, indeed, have fundamentally different perceptions about the nature of marriage and about their respective rights and duties. In **Chapter 7** I argue that residual Hausa culture offers women a relatively organic understanding of marriage, reflected in the rituals central to women. For Hausa men marriage can appear to have a strictly contractual nature since marriage is contracted and broken at will by men according to Islamic law. Women, however, often speak of marriage as a living thing that grows and dies, and that must be nurtured to succeed. Women's processual and organic model retains key elements of ambiguity, making it possible for women to withdraw from a marriage at various stages and to gain symbolic advantage over their spouses in view of their roles as mothers and cultivators. However, women themselves have made use of the male contractual

---

[35] A similar process may account for Phokeng women's entry into waged work in order to purchase household furnishings (Bozzoli 1991).

model of marriage in insisting that their husbands meet their "promise" to maintain their wives as dependents. Women's organic model stands in more and more radical disjunction with the realities of marriage in the region as wealth is increasingly derived not from organic processes, but from access to cash. Women must, therefore, work from within the contractual paradigm to protect their interests. They can do this by keeping bridewealth payments low so that the *sadaki* can be returned should the expectations of the two spouses differ enough for a woman to be prompted to provoke a divorce. Alternatively, elite women may insist upon high bridewealth to state symbolically their own worth and education in an effort to gain the cultural capital necessary for their own interpretation of marriage to prevail.

The book closes in **Chapter 8** with a discussion of how the debates surrounding the nature of marriage and the role of women have been played out at one intersection of national and local interests, namely the various national governments' attempts to create a local "women's movement" to bolster the political party in power. The existence of national women's associations in the Maradi region has generated interesting schisms within the feminine community, and made possible a kind of visual/spatial and terminological debate about whether women in general should have a public role in politics. Political spectacle prompted debate about whether and how married women, non-married women, and as-yet-unmarried women should be seen in public and how such public activity should be interpreted. As seclusion has become associated with Islamic virtue, and as public mobility has been seen as a sign of promiscuity, the public appearances of the Association of Nigérien Women in the late 1980s simultaneously catalyzed a debate about marriage and non-marriage and created a kind of social space in which that debate could be carried out visually. In prompting such debate the AFN helped pave the way for women's increasingly visible participation in politics since 1991. The **Conclusion** reflects upon the implications of the importance of gender, marriage, and cultural change in the region of Maradi for the understanding of history more broadly. Throughout the major processes the region has undergone in this century–the abolition of slavery, the emergence of new productive arrangements, the transformation of wealth and power, and the reshaping of the urban landscape–marriage, whether fickle or merely flexible, has served as a central institutional and discursive locus for the mediation of change.

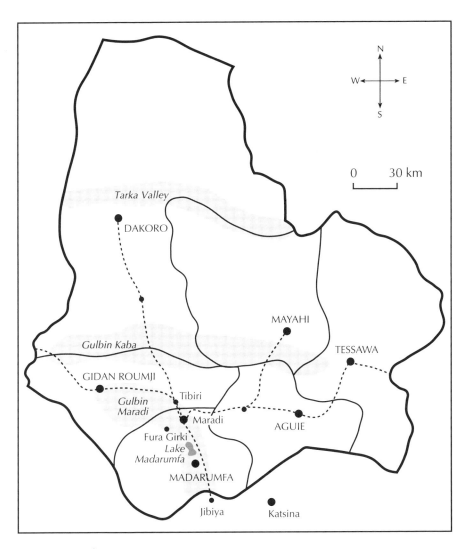

Map 2. Maradi Department

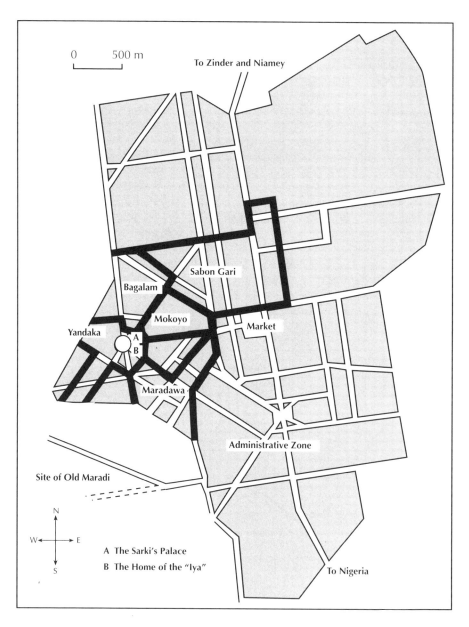

Map 1. The City of Maradi

1

Unpredictable Interventions: Emancipating Slaves and Regulating Marriage

In this chapter I shall explore how the decline of slavery affected the nature of marriage in the Maradi region, and why the state's efforts to mold marital practice more deliberately through legislation have for the most part failed. This chapter highlights, then, the unpredictableness of state interventions, for antislavery provisions were never formulated with a view to modifying marriage practices, while interventions directly targeting marriage practices have belied rather stunningly the all-encompassing power of the state. I choose to begin with this theme as a palliative to any assumption that the shape of marriage in this region can be viewed as the product of colonial Victorian ideals promulgated unproblematically by the state to shape a malleable populace. Marriage practice in Maradi is, rather, the outcome of complex and contradictory negotiations on the part of Nigérien men and women to clear sufficient social and cultural space in which to take advantage of new opportunities while forestalling disadvantageous constraints. "External ideological influences," as Bledsoe and Pison note, "ironically appear less to have constrained choices or eliminated ambiguity than to have added yet more idioms for rationalizing action" (1994:5).

Recent studies of the decline of slavery, rich through they have been, have not generally addressed the question of how abolition affected the definition of marriage and the nature of family life. The intent of antislavery legislation in the colonies was not, as a rule, to alter other institutions governing social life: to the contrary, it was hoped that slavery could be done away with without seriously altering the foundations of local systems of authority controlling juniors and women. My study of Maradi suggests that such a hope was illusory, for only by translating the slave/free hierarchy into some other familiar hierarchy could existing patterns of production and accumulation be protected.

1

By drawing upon traditional intrahousehold hierarchies among women in marriage dominant men and women in the region could maintain their productive enterprises and retain the social capital that inheres in control of persons and labor. Wealthy senior women, in particular, stood to gain from this remapping of master/slave relations onto relations between senior women (mothers-in-law or senior wives) and the junior wives of a household, for the preponderance of slaves in the region were female slaves serving wealthy urban households. Such slaves made it possible for women of wealthier families to devote their leisure time to overseeing the production of the cotton thread so critical to the accumulation of social, symbolic, and economic capital. The shock of abolition was absorbed by such households through the acquisition of junior "wives" whose labor could "replace" that of slave women. Thus today senior women in Maradi remark of new brides entering the household they preside over, "we married her," meaning that not only the groom or the male members of the family have taken in a subordinate, but that senior women of the lineage themselves have access to her labor. Such senior women have a strong voice in the disposition of a junior wife's children, and may, indeed, be instrumental in negotiations for the marriage itself.

The implications of abolition for intrahousehold hierarchies in marriage were, then, largely unforeseen. The efforts of the state to effect intentional changes in the practice of marriage through legislation failed, on the other hand, because any legislation that might prove disruptive of the social order was in no danger of being implemented at the local level. Just as the abolition of slavery potentially threatened existing structures of authority governing production and the maintenance of order, any assault on marriage practices could undermine the principles regulating family life. Having projected master/slave relations onto intrahousehold relations, the elite of Maradi could ill afford to dismantle the newly heightened differentials between men and women in marriage and between wives of different status. It was because of the predictable upheaval any serious attempt to revise marriage practice would produce that the state broached the topic gingerly, often retracting or failing to enforce what little legislation it did pass. While it was convenient to mouth an interest in promoting women, in practice neither the colonial nor the postcolonial state has had an interest in pursuing women's "emancipation" to its logical outcome, namely dismantling the gender and age principles undergirding the social order. Any such dismantling would have to be carried out at the local level through a much subtler process of redefinition and negotiation.

Slavery in Precolonial Maradi

Much work has been devoted recently to the question of how the ending of slavery affected African societies.[1] Paul Lovejoy and Jan Hogendorn have shown

---

[1] For an excellent review of the state of the literature on this subject see Roberts and Miers (1988).

in detail that the ending of slavery in Northern Nigeria was a deliberately gradual process completed over several decades. Colonial policies protected slave owners from the disruptions the loss of slave labor might have caused and placed the economic burden of emancipation upon the slaves themselves. British officials were prepared to turn a blind eye to female slavery, viewing women in general as dependants of men regardless of their status (Lovejoy and Hogendorn 1993). Nevertheless colonial conquest and the impending decline of slavery produced major disruptions in the routines of life for slave owners, as an anonymous Hausa poem indicates:

I have no slave, I am not able to practice purdah,
I have no slave girl who shall fetch water,
Who will go to the bush and fetch me a little wood.[2]

While Lovejoy and Hogendorn do not make the character of marriage a central focus of their excellent study, the poem suggests that in Northern Nigeria the demise of slavery was to have implications for female labor more generally and for the seclusion ensuring the leisure of women in slave-owning families. M.G. Smith suggests that it was the decline of slavery that in fact precipitated the growth of seclusion in northern Nigeria (1981:22–23), a suggestion somewhat at odds with the anonymous poet's view, and one which, in any case, begs the question of how such a radical restructuring of marriage might have been orchestrated and by whom. In order to make sense of the complex and contradictory relationship between slavery and seclusion we must begin by looking more closely at the nature of slavery in the precolonial period.

The precolonial pattern of indigenous slave use in the Maradi region is one of the most striking ways in which the Maradi region differed from the regions conquered by Usman 'dan Fodio and his allies in the first half of the nineteenth century. Most of Hausaland experienced an economic boom in the latter half of that century, as the cohesion and consolidation of the Sokoto Caliphate created an enlarged internal market. The decline of the slave trade and the growth of agricultural exports led to a redirection of slaves into internal activities rather than export. Slaves in the Caliphate were used for large-scale labor-intensive enterprises including agricultural production on plantations, mining, crafts, and commerce (Lovejoy 1978). The central regions of the Caliphate in particular experienced dramatic growth in the textile industry, leather manufacturing, iron production, and livestock production, and benefited from increased demand outside the Caliphate for Hausa products (Lovejoy 1978:347, Adamu 1978: 185–86). By contrast, in Maradi large slave-holding enterprises seem to have been the exception rather than the rule.

Where the theocratic emirates promoted the Islamic ideal of seclusion of women in the home, and were able to replace female farm labor with the labor

---

[2] Lovejoy and Hogendorn (1993:54), citing from from Mervyn Hiskett, "Hausa Islamic Verse: Its Sources and Development Prior to 1920" (Ph.D. thesis, University of London, 1969), 462.

of captured peoples, in Maradi the majority of the farming population consisted of free non-Muslim or semi-Muslim Arna, Hausa-speaking peoples whose
highly localized religion was intimately tied to their agricultural and hunting
activities. Immigrants from the kingdoms of Gobir and Katsina defined themselves in opposition to the emirates, and were more interested in regaining
their lost territory than in building a new agricultural base in the Maradi valley. Consequently neither agricultural slavery nor female seclusion ever had
very wide currency in the precolonial Maradi kingdom.

Certainly the military of Maradi engaged in slave raiding during their
numerous expeditions into emirate territories; however, the slaves taken
seem not to have been destined for plantation farming such as that promoted in the *ribats* (military outposts) and *rimjis* (slave villages) of the Sokoto
Caliphate.[3] Rather, slave raiders from Maradi had a reputation for seizing
slaves in order to hold them for ransom. Raiding served largely as a source
of goods for exchange rather than for production.[4] While this limited the
incidence of slavery in the kingdom, it also meant that since the nobility
did not have a productive base for their income, they relied heavily upon
taxes and arbitrary seizures of grain and other goods from the farming population in order to subsist. The lack of a productive base also meant that
continued raids and incursions into enemy territory for booty were necessary for the maintenance of the aristocratic class, engaging the region in a
continuous cycle of raids and counter-raids which made agricultural settlements at any distance from the fortified city of Maradi highly insecure (M.G.
Smith 1967:118, Landeroin, 1911:536).[5]

While it was possible for commoners to obtain slaves either through purchase or as part of spoils from raids, the slaves retained seem to have been
primarily female slaves who worked alongside free women in local farming
households and communities. This form of slavery would have been quite different in character from the plantation slavery of the Sokoto Caliphate, as the
slaves could be assimilated into the local community over time and were understood to be "kin" and neighbors of their owners (Hill 1985).[6] Thus while

[3] Informants in Maradi associated slavery with warfare (Hajjiya Rabe, 2-1-89); although the aristocratic class did have farm slaves (Hajjiya Jeka, 2-14-89), most captives seem to have been absorbed into the administration. Commoner women were often seized at will by aristocratic war-
riors in their own territories as well as in enemy territories (Hajjiya Indo, 10-25-89; Fatchima, 2-5-89).

[4] Thus Baba remarks that, unlike some other slave raiders, the Maradawa gave up slaves for
ransom (Mary Smith 1981:47, 38–39, 46–47). Landeroin emphasizes that domestic slaves were better integrated into the household than trade slaves, but also notes that prior to the French occupation the court dignitaries who had greatest access to slaves took little interest in agriculture or
commerce (1911:518, 536). Périé noted the high value of slaves on the market, especially women
(1939:394–95). Hamani suggests that in Adar a similar phenomenon obtained: slaves were easily
ransomed, and the slave population was concentrated among the Tuareg. Some slaves were to be
found in the homes of the aristocracy, but in general slaves made up only a small percentage of the
sedentary population (1975:227–28).

[5] For similar processes elsewhere see Latour (1982).

[6] Slave use patterns in Maradi probably resembled those in Borno; see Nachtigal in Fisher
(1991:125).

slave-holding was possible at all levels of Maradi society (as in Borno), the character of that slavery seems to have been quite different from that which obtained in much of the Sokoto Caliphate. Because a limited number of slaves lived and worked alongside their owners, no clear association between slavery and agricultural labor emerged. In the city female slaves were taken as concubines and domestic workers, while male slaves seem to have been retained only by the wealthiest aristocrats and were used primarily to fill administrative positions controlled by the ruling class.[7]

The Hausa-speaking areas north of the Caliphate differed from both the Zerma region to the west and Damagaram to the east, each of which relied upon much larger and more conspicuous populations of slaves in farming and industry.[8] These regions today differ from the Maradi region in the division of labor by sex (in neither region are women active in agriculture)[9] and in the kinds of technologies adopted (both regions use the *iler* hoe, which is not commonly used in Maradi) (Raulin 1984, Raynaut 1984). One might hypothesize that because local norms in these regions did not encourage free women's participation in agriculture, women could not readily be induced to make up the loss of slave labor with the abolition of slavery. Free men had to take over the majority of the agricultural tasks formerly performed by slaves and consequently such men adopted the *iler*, a technology that made extensive, low-labor-intensity farming possible. By contrast, the limited slave use in agriculture in Maradi made possible women's continued (and indeed intensified) role in agriculture after the decline of slavery, in combination with local norms encouraging free commoner women's participation in farm activities. Thus the labor-intensive *haiwa* hoe is more commonly in use in Maradi than the *iler*, and women continue to be highly visible in agriculture.

The evidently limited incidence of rural slavery in both Adar and Maradi suggests that the assumption in much of the literature on the Hausa that widespread agricultural slavery and slave villages or *rimjis* existed among the Hausa-speaking populations of the pre-jihad kingdoms may be

---

[7] Guy Nicolas reports that among the non-aristocratic farmers of the valley there still exist joking relations between the lineages of former slaves and their former masters; among the "dynastic" urban class the evidence of former slave ownership even among commoners persists in the memory of female ancestors who had been taken into the homes of urban dwellers as concubines (1975: 77, 179, 213).

[8] Raulin argues that the Zerma used slaves in agriculture to a higher degree than the Hausa of Niger, who were less averse to performing physical labor (1964:98–99). Slaves played a significant role in the administration, military, mining, trade, and agriculture of nineteenth-century Damagaram (Salifou 1971). Landeroin also noted that there seemed to be more slaves in the Kanuri area of Damagaram than in the Hausa-speaking areas of the Niger territory (1911:522). For a full discussion of slavery in Damagaram see Dunbar (1977).

[9] Women in the Zerma-speaking west may help at planting but do not grow their own millet; they may produce some condiments or vegetables (Diarra 1971:104). Similarly women in the Hausa-Kanuri region of Damagaram do not hoe, but may help at planting and harvest, and may have small gardens plots; however Saunders suggests that women may have hoed in the recent past (1978:7–8).

overgeneralized.[10] As long as the slave trade continued, some Hausa king-doms may have found it advantageous to export the majority of the slaves they captured. The aristocratic class would have retained some concubines and eunuchs for domestic and administrative purposes; slaves procured by the peasant population would have been gradually absorbed into the house-hold or community of their masters. The Sokoto Caliphate, on the other hand, found itself faced with the dual tasks of absorbing and acculturating a large conquered population while meeting defense needs. Slave settlements strategically placed along defensive borders could be used to answer both needs at once and could be patterned after the slave villages established by Fulani herders.[11]

Without the use of slave labor to replace women in agriculture in the Maradi region, free women's contribution to the agricultural labor force would have been absolutely critical. In the Caliphate, one way in which individuals could mark their status as Muslims and loyalists was to remove their wives and daugh-ters from agriculture and replace them with slaves. Thus in Nigeria seclusion became associated with free-born status, and agriculture with slavery. In the Maradi region, the Katsinawa immigrants insisted upon their Muslim status prior to the jihad, and were disinclined to be bullied into mimicking the be-havior of the jihadists with regard to female dress and labor, just as the Mus-lim women of Borno described by Humphrey Fisher were unwilling to adhere to strict seclusion when it was thrust upon them by Muslim reformists. As Fisher observes, "If we are to weigh up, in a balanced and reasonably complete fashion, the various factors determining the subsequent shape of a society, we need to include, alongside secular and environmental elements, also religious standards, and the resonance which these call forth (or do not call forth, as the case may be) in the hearts and minds of local men and women" (1990:132–33). In the Maradi region to use slaves in order to promote seclusion and the fe-male dress associated with it would be to capitulate to the jihadists whom the residents of the valley had so long resisted.

The Arna farmers of the Maradi valley, for their part, initially took little interest in Islam one way or another, relying instead upon the favors of local divinities associated with the earth, rain, and hunting. Since the Katsinawa

---

[10] Hiskett argues from evidence in the mid-nineteenth century and from the poetry of the Fulani reformers that pre-jihad society practiced plantation slavery, despite citing Polly Hill's objections to generalizations that plantation farming was widespread in Hausaland (1984:97–100). He uses the Kano Chronicle to argue for the existence of slave villages in pre-jihad Hausaland, but this source on its own is not very compelling evidence as it reflects post-jihad inventions (1985:107).

[11] The word *rimji*, which is used in Hausa to refer to slave village/plantations, is originally Fulani in origin. The *rimji* is set in contrast to the *ruma*, or the Fulani master's cattle encampment, as in the proverb: "Sai ruga ta kwana lafiya, rimji ke kwana lafiya" (Only when the master sleeps well does the slave sleep well, Abraham 1962: 84, 742). Hogendorn (1977:382) cites a slave song which reconfirms the association of *rimji* slavery with the Fulani. Hill emphasizes the difference between the "Hausa" form of farm slavery, in which private farmers own and work alongside a small num-ber of slaves, and the more "Fulani" system of large plantations owned by absentee aristocrat and merchant farmers, and shows that the vocabulary of the *rimji* form comes primarily from Fulfulde (1985:36, 40).

immigrants were reliant upon the good will of the Arna for their security in the valley, wholesale enslavement of this local population was out of the question (even though as "pagans" they were legally enslaveable). In Maradi agricultural labor came to be closely associated by both rural and urban populations with animism and commoner status rather than with slavery.[12] However, the frequent and close interaction of the farmers of the valley with the nobles, traders, and artisans of the city meant that over time the Arna assimilated many features of Islam into their religious practice. Today both urban and rural practices are highly syncretic, rural dwellers invoking Allah and recognizing Muslim spirits, and urban dwellers turning to spirits and Arna priests for intervention in their affairs, particularly those related to love and agriculture.

It is thus entirely possible to be a devout male Muslim farmer in Maradi today while permitting one's wives to participate in agriculture, or to be a devout female while publicly taking part in farming. Rural women who disdain agriculture today do so not on religious grounds, but because they dislike the arduous labor it entails and its association with low status. Where according to M. G. Smith newly freed Hausa women in Nigeria emphasized and capitalized upon their new status by entering into seclusion in the early decades of the century, Hausa women in Niger, as we shall see in a moment, have been retiring from agriculture in emulation of the merchant class much more recently. The abolition of slavery had very little immediate effect in this region, and did not provide a major watershed in reducing labor demands upon women or reducing female vulnerability to servile status more generally–to the contrary, evidence suggests that abolition and colonial rule may have exacerbated the demands upon women whether former slaves or free women.

Marriage Practices, Slavery and the State

In the early years of colonial administration, the status of women and the status of domestic slaves were in many ways similar, and arguments for moving cautiously in emancipating slaves were quite similar to those advanced somewhat later concerning the emancipation of women. This is no coincidence, for as many scholars have noted, large proportions of the slaves in Africa were in fact women (Robertson and Klein 1983, Roberts and Miers 1988). Like wives, farm slaves in Maradi worked four days a week for the "master" in the field; like women they did not pay taxes (Landeroin 1911:518). Domestic "house" slaves were seen by the French as being well treated "family members," and as being able to buy their freedom if they so desired. The lieutenant governor of the Sudan territories, referring to domestic slaves as the "unfree," argued in 1899 that freeing the slaves would

---

[12] Today in Maradi small rural farmers speak of farming as their "heritage" (*gado*) and may remark with some pride that all they know is farming, while larger urban farmers see farming as only part of a diversified range of income-generating activities. For a comparative discussion of Arna and Katsinawa understandings of farming see G. Nicolas (1975:279–99, 413–18).

lead to massive social disorder, and that since the trade in slaves had effectively ended, the government should turn a blind eye to domestic slavery (AOM/200Mi 1191 K15).[13]

The administration found it convenient, however, to tax "unfree" and free individuals alike by 1901, and in doing so promoted the erosion of indigenous social categories (AOM/200Mi 1191 K15). The elimination of domestic slavery in the Sudan territories was nevertheless hampered by promises that had been made to local rulers in various treaties not to disturb local "usages and customs." Furthermore the administration's reliance upon local notables (likely slave owners themselves) in the court systems made it unlikely that the courts would truly ignore differences between the free and the servile, an outcome the colonial administration itself anticipated (AOM/200Mi 1191 K16). In effect, French legislation freed domestic slaves without in any way enforcing their freedom, knowing that with the passage of time domestic slavery would die out with the new generation of free-born children. However as one prescient administrator remarked, "The entire burden of slavery, once abolition is complete, will fall directly onto the shoulders of indigenous women," who had no protections and limited means of supporting themselves (AOM/200Mi 1192 K17).

The slaves scattered widely through Maradi's urban families in the precolonial period had been numerous enough to assume much of the burden of heavy chores (such as pounding grain, getting water, bearing crops from the fields to the granary, and collecting wood). With the end of slavery those chores would increasingly become the duty of the "wife." In rural areas, where a limited number of slaves had farmed alongside freeborn household members, free married women also farmed, and the duties of wives and slaves were probably indistinguishable.[14] Where the high incidence of relatively exploitative *rimji* type slavery in northern Nigeria and in the French Soudan seems to account for the exodus of slaves out of these regions in the aftermath of abolition (Roberts 1988, Lovejoy and Hogendorn 1991), in Maradi abolition probably had little immediate effect on most of the rural population, whether slave or free, since the conditions of life for commoners and slaves did not differ a great deal. Slave women and free women in the same rural communities would not have been easily distinguished visually, as neither slave nor free women were veiled or secluded. Where in the former Caliphate newly freed *rimji* slaves might choose to mark their equality with their freeborn masters by taking on the seclusion and

---

[13] The French were not alone in fearing catastrophe if emancipation were to proceed too quickly. Lugard and his successors in Northern Nigeria used legal and tax reforms to eliminate slavery gradually rather than eradicate it immediately (Lovejoy and Hogendorn 1993).

[14] Rural wives were expected to perform all the arduous tasks of a slave, and issues of control of labor probably centered less on slave versus free status than upon men's control of women as wives. Thus on the eve of colonial rule in the region Landeroin would report the response of a local dignitary to the suggestion that mills would one day reduce the labor of women, "A woman who works has neither the time nor the desire to cheat on her husband" ("La femme qui travaille n'a pas le temps ni le désir de tromper son époux!", Landeroin 1911:474 [face]).

veiling of that class, in Maradi such visual distinctions did not exist. Because, unlike Northern Nigeria, the administration never used restrictions on access to land as a means to keep ex-slaves in the service of their masters, former slave populations simply set up farms alongside their former masters, and were absorbed relatively quietly into the rural population.[15]

In the city, however, slave and free women were more readily distinguishable, not primarily because of veiling, but because of their different duties and because of substantial differences in wealth. The leisure made possible by the use of female slaves enabled aristocratic women to spin cotton thread, a significant source of income and prestige. Hajjiya Malaya, a daughter of Sarki Kure (who ruled from c.1890 to 1920), describes the shifts that occurred in aristocratic households as slavery was gradually abolished:

> BMC: When you were little were there still slaves?
> Malaya: No, by then, by the time we came along, there weren't slaves. But our older brothers and sisters, they were given slaves, yes. I think that during my father's time the Europeans came and they forbade slavery. Back then, all of the children of the Sarki, when they were married, they would go off with slaves to do work for them. They would leave the house (at marriage) with slaves. But in our time there were no slaves, they had been forbidden. And there were no more wars, we never saw any wars, since the Europeans had forbidden that too. . . . It was in wars that they had gotten slaves to bring back home (Hajjiya Malaya, 9-4-89).

Aristocratic urban women therefore had to find ways to retain or replace the captive domestic labor that had freed them from onerous household duties in the past. The simplest solution, of course, would simply be to redefine the slave women as concubines and junior wives, women whose labor could then be controlled by senior aristocratic women as senior wives and mothers-in-law. Malaya elaborates on the organization of labor in her first marriage in the 1920s, when she was herself still very young: "Even though when we were married off we didn't bring slaves with us, still when I was taken from my father's house to my first husband's it was two years before I was old enough to have sense, and for those two years my co-wife cooked and pounded. It was only after I was older that I started to help make our husband's food . . ." This strategy of shifting the burdens of domestic slavery onto junior wives from less prominent families suited the assumptions of the French colonial officers, who regarded domestic slavery as a benign form of kinship to begin with.

The replacement of unfree labor with that of junior "wives" and captive concubines depended upon a conceptual fuzziness between marriage and en-

---

[15] The earliest stages of British conquest in Northern Nigeria resulted in a massive slave exodus, which the British quelled by making it virtually impossible for former slaves to farm independently. As a result, many *rimji* slaves ended up sharecropping their former masters' lands. The *gandu* slaves of smaller farmers were less likely to gain access to land where landholdings were too small to divide up, and probably left their masters in larger proportions than *rimji* slaves. In such cases slave-owners' wives were likely to pick up the slack once the slaves had departed (Lovejoy and Hogendorn 1993:232, citing Hill 1972:43).

slavement, a fuzziness that certainly existed and could be exploited.[16] Before the "tying of the wedding," the Muslim ceremony in which senior males of both the bride and the groom's families met to pray and in which the bridewealth was publicly given by the groom's representative to that of the bride, there was a sometimes lengthy period of betrothal. Once the groom had made his interest known and the bride's family had accepted his proposal, a ceremonial exchange known as the *ba-iko*–the giving of power–took place. The groom gave the bride's father a gift to signify the beginning of transfer of power over the bride from the father to the groom (G. Nicolas 1986:47).

The word *baiko* was interchangeable with the word *baiwa* which meant both "gift" and "betrothal," and differed only slightly in tone from the word for "female slave," *baiwa*. One might say "an yi masa baiwar da ke," meaning "they made him a gift of you" or "they made him a betrothal of you." A girl given in marriage without a bridewealth payment was known as *baiwar Allah*, "slave of God" (Abraham 1962:59–60). The kinship of language for marriage and for slavery was more than merely superficial; for example the primary image of marriage in Hausaland as in the West is "tying the knot," and the "rope" to tie the knot of marriage is the *igiyar aure* (the thread of the marriage) or bridewealth payment. When a marriage was broken, the payment had to be returned. But the image of the rope applied equally to slavery: a slave woman could (at least in theory) "cut the rope of her slavery" and earn her eventual freedom by bearing her master a child or by paying him a redemption fee (Abraham 1962:947).

All of these expressions are consistent with the hypothesis that with the decline of slavery alternative forms of "marriage" could become a means whereby men (and through them senior aristocratic women) could continue to control the labor of women who were now nominally "free" in status. The exchange of gifts in marriage created ties, ties that linked together the couple and the two families, but also ties intended to control the bride. It was the transfer of the bridewealth payment that distinguished a legitimate marriage from a less formal union, and a "free" wife from a woman whose labor could be controlled through the idiom of marriage, but there were many stages to a marriage, and there was much room for ambiguity. Both the legitimate wife and the concubine were understood to be "tied" in a sense to their "husband."

The ambiguity surrounding the distinctions between wife and concubine, and concubine and slave, made it possible for wealthy and sizeable households in the early decades of colonial rule to maintain concubines as "extra wives" to perform the burdensome labor of maintaining the household well after slavery had been abolished. As colonial rule continued and access to slaves from elsewhere declined, evidence suggests that issues surrounding the con-

---

[16]   The conceptual and functional kinship of marriage and enslavement has been remarked upon by others and arises in part because men of limited means could marry by obtaining a slave as wife, and because captive women and their offspring were often integrated into households as the wives and children of the owner (Kopytoff and Miers 1977:65–67). In Borno slaves served as wives to men without the social and monetary means to obtain a full wife (Fisher 1991:128).

trol of women became more acute, and were expressed in terms of differences between "legitimate" wives and concubines, and between "Muslim" and non-Muslim women. In an attempt to get a firm grasp on "local custom" the French compiled a series of "Grands coutumiers" throughout their territories in which local "law" would be recorded in fixed form as presented by local elders (Coquery-Vidrovitch 1994:111–12). Thus the 1933 *coutumier juridique* for the Maradi region reports:

> A legitimate wife must obey her husband. A Muslim [husband] may administer light physical correction, but if she is the daughter of the chief or the Al'kali he may not. Animist men have no right to use corporal punishment, however light, upon their wives. . . . A concubine must also obey the household head. She is considered to be a captive, and he has the right to beat her. . . . A legitimate wife must cook, wash clothes and clean the home of her husband. But her husband may not force her to work the fields or to collect water. A concubine, since she is treated as a captive, may be required to carry out any labor the household head requires of her. . . . A "head wife" is the woman who has been married longest of the married women. She can command the other women if her husband authorizes her to do so. She may be in charge of the distribution of grain and food to the other wives. . . . The captives or concubines of the husband are not required to obey his wives other than those who have children ("Coutumes haoussa et peul" 1939:281–83).

It is difficult to assess the precise nature of the information reported here. The unknown author presents it as "Hausa custom" which seems to him to be growing in influence in the district even among the Fulani, and which "rules the majority of natives in this subdivision" ("Coutumes" 1939:263). It is likely that it is information provided by local notables (the relevant elders) to the local administrator and one must be aware that those notables had an interest in establishing for the record their idealized sense of how women in a household *should* be controlled and ordered rather than how they in fact were ordered at that time or in the past. The caveat that although Muslim wives could be beaten, the daughters of the two officials most likely to have contributed to the document could not, would seem to underscore that likelihood.

Other evidence suggests that the 1933 document codifying local custom in fact proposed powers over women far in excess of those actually witnessed in Maradi in the first two decades of French presence in the region. In 1907 Landeroin (the historian for the Tilho-O'Shee Mission) reported that a man whose wife committed adultery could repudiate her and reclaim his bridewealth payment, or beat her and retain her as his wife (Landeroin 1911:515), and in 1913 the administrator Villomé reported from his observations of local practice that in general one could avoid any physical punishment by paying a fine, and that adultery was punished by a fine for the man involved and "exposure to public ridicule" for the woman (ANN/14.1.12). By contrast the 1933 report on Hausa custom claims:

A) Among Muslims: When a woman betrays her husband with a lover both are condemned to death. The execution takes place in a public place in the following way: the two lovers are buried alive up to their waists and the children of the village stone them. The woman's execution may be delayed if she is pregnant. Then she will be executed after the child is weaned. The child, considered a bastard, is turned over to the maternal family. . . .

Among animists: The husband has the right, without taking his case to court, to kill his wife's lover. . . . He may repudiate his wife or keep her. . . . If a child is born the lover may recognize it and the child becomes his own legitimate son ("Coutumes" 1939:292).

What this document and interviews suggest is that with the decline of slavery and the rise of the potential influence of the French administration over local practices, senior males struggled to claim for themselves powers and sanctions they had not had in the past concerning the marriages, labor, and sexuality of nominally free junior women. Men's right to provide "physical correction" for their wives, to beat captive concubines, and to seek capital punishment for illicit sexual alliances would serve to limit women's ability to resist the labor and sexual demands of their masters and husbands and would make it more difficult for women to seek protection and redress with their own kin or with the courts. Catherine Coquery-Vidrovitch remarks of this process throughout French West Africa: "With the suppression of slavery chiefs observed with unease women's initiatives threatening chiefly authority. The chiefs contrived, therefore, to rework to their own advantage customs and prerogatives which in the past had often been more flexible. 'Customary law' was a reworked and rigidified law" (1994:112).

At the same time senior men attempted to secure protections and powers for senior aristocratic ("Muslim") women that were not expressed in any of the earlier discussions or observations of local law. The labor duties of senior legitimate wives are clearly set out (cooking, washing, and cleaning the home), their seniority over childless women and concubines is affirmed, and their control of food distribution is established. Where even today rural Muslim women are in fact frequently called upon by their husbands to perform farm labor, the 1933 report attempts to protect urban Muslim women from such heavy labor in the context of colonial labor exactions and the rapid extension of agriculture. It is a protection that could only be enforced by an influential family in which women had never been called upon to farm in the past. Senior women, understood as older married women with children, as well as women from aristocratic families more generally, could thus control junior female labor, which was to include both junior wives and "captive" concubines: women taken into households in informal marriages who had no male kin to establish and protect their marital rights. Thus while the French had a de jure policy of abolishing slavery, their understanding of local marriage did not distinguish slave women from wives, and in their efforts to minimize the dislocation resulting from the abolition of slavery they consistently turned a blind eye to domestic servitude so long as it concerned only women–women who could be distinguished from, but at the same time assimilated to, wives.[17]

With the replacement of slave labor with the labor of junior wives between c.1920 and 1945, tensions between wives within a household probably increased as the social order as a whole reformulated what was in the past a distinction between free and unfree classes into naturalized intrahousehold hierarchies of women. The ranking of wives could mask the friction generated by an unequal division of labor as rivalry between women, seen throughout Hausaland as inherently contentious, deceitful, and "jealous."[18] While the ranking of wives has had a long history in the Hausa kingdoms, in the early decades of this century such intrahousehold ranking facilitated the transformation of junior female wives into labor to meet the needs of senior women as wives and mothers-in-law.[19]

Thus where in Nigeria the abolition of slavery meant among other things that some women may have chosen to take on the seclusion of free Muslim women, in Maradi, where slavery was limited to small-scale holdings in rural areas but could be significant in the households of urban families, the loss of access to slave women meant in effect that many "married" women found themselves in ambiguous polygynous marriages, subject to the commands of other women, and burdened with the tasks of former slaves. One indirect consequence, therefore, of the abolition of slavery in this region may have been a climate in which polygyny became more important to male status. In the times of Sarki Kure and Sarki Kollodo (from 1900 to 1946) the numbers of women in the royal household approached the hundreds. Sarki Labo of Tibiri had twenty-five wives at the time of his death in 1963 (Hajjiya Jeka, 2-12-89). With the growth of the economy and the increasing prestige associated with Islamic polygyny, what had in the early decades of the century been interpreted as rights to limitless polygyny among the aristocracy shifted to successive Islamic polygyny among a broader segment of the population than simply the aristocratic class: many wealthy male traders in the city of Maradi from the 1930s to the 1950s reputedly began taking numerous wives over their lifetimes in sets of four in a kind of inflated serial polygyny.[20]

---

[17] Complicity between the colonial administration and the male aristocracy concerning female slavery occurred in northern Nigeria as well; see Lovejoy (1988:145–46). For a slightly different reading see Christelow (1991) as well as Jumare (1994). On marriage as a cover for illicit trade in girls for prostitution see Coquery-Vidrovitch (1994:205–206).

[18] The words for "co-wife" and "jealous rivalry" are the same–*'kishiya*–and Hausa folklore depicts co-wives as irrational and violent, and women generally as naturally divisive and cunning. Stories from B.L. Edgar's (1924) collection of Hausa Folktales echo these beliefs about women: co-wives regularly attack one another irrationally, often with magic (I: Nos. 10, 30); they are a constant source of trouble between men (I: Nos. 40, 67, 148); the quality of jealousy in a wife is worse than stealing or unbridled sexuality (I: No. 120).

[19] Usman 'dan Fodio's followers, who had no quarrel with slavery itself, cited this ranking of wives as evidence of the non-Islamic nature of the Hausa kingdoms (Hiskett 1960:567, 578). However, circumstances since the *jihad* have not tended to eliminate it either in northern Nigeria or in Niger.

[20] Where none of my oldest informants mentioned any problems concerning serial polygyny, women who married from about 1945 on often described marriages that ended because their husbands divorced one of his four wives in order to marry a new bride. In rural areas serial polygamy following the more familiar pattern of successive monogamous marriages occasionally occurs.

With the increasing incidence of ambiguous and semi-legitimate marriages prior to about 1945, women could assert their status as legitimate wives rather than concubines or de facto captives through a variety of means. As I discuss in detail in Chapter 5, women could use the ceremonial gift exchanges surrounding weddings to stage the formal marital status of the bride and the wealth of the bride and her mother. As the century progressed another means through which women could assert their status as legitimate wives was to counter their reduced status in polygynous marriages by asserting visually their seniority and authority by donning the clothing of secluded aristocratic women. This sartorial strategy was inextricably linked to a complex dynamic promoting the rise of seclusion in the urban center, discussed in Chapter 6. Today, while the rate of polygyny in the Maradi region is well below that of northern Nigeria, it is the highest in Niger and is by all accounts increasing.[21] This is in contrast with the situation in the region surrounding Niamey, where polygyny appears to be declining. This difference may be associated with the higher educational levels and access to state employment in Niamey (Pool 1972:249) on the one hand, and to the low levels of education and proximity to Nigeria in Maradi on the other. In sum, the state's move to abolish slavery precipitated a series of redefinitions of marriage and female status that is still in process today.

Emancipating Women: "The Idea of Freedom in Marriage"

While both the colonial and postcolonial governments have occasionally expressed an interest in protecting women and promoting their interests, on the whole the state has had little direct and deliberate impact upon the institution of marriage. Just as the colonial government was faced with the contradictions of its republican impulse to protect slaves and its imperial imperative to avoid undermining the local authority so essential to administering the colonies, so also did it find itself alternately mouthing an interest in uplifting the condition of women and upholding the principle of paternal authority. In the first of many such gestures, the lieutenant governor of Haute Volta called for the uplifting of indigenous women in March of 1920, only to be restricted in October of 1920 when the governor-general of French West Africa responded with a circular emphasizing that local institutions must be respected and the authority of the head of family must not be weakened *"en émancipant la femme"* because to do so would be to "undermine the entire indigenous society based

---

[21] According to the 1977 census, men with more than one wife represented 27.8 percent of all married men in Maradi department, compared to 6 percent in Agades and 17 percent in Diffa (République du Niger:1985b:99). In urban and semi-urban areas the figure would be much higher, since polygamy is relatively limited in rural areas. Raynaut (1971:136) found that in the village of Sumarana on the outskirts of Maradi, 25 percent of all men had more than one wife, although most had only two. The 1992 demographic study suggests that 50.2 percent of all women in the region are in polygynous marriages, the highest incidence of polygyny in the country. The study once again finds that urban areas have higher polygyny rates than rural (République du Niger 1992:63).

upon that authority" (Robert 1955:86). Justice in the French colonial system was contradictory and difficult for the central colonial government to control effectively: administrators were distant from the administrative centers in Dakar and Brazzaville (and therefore left very much to their own devices except on paper) (Fuglestad 1983:81–82); local administrators were assisted and advised by various interested notables (in Maradi the al'kali or qadi and the durbi were for a time part of the colonial court system);[22] and the Republican values of *liberté, égalité, fraternité* justifying colonialism were in conflict with the *Indigénat* law code through which colonial domination was maintained.[23]

Thus, when in 1934 legislation was passed by the governing body of French West Africa protecting girls from being married before puberty and requiring the consent of both husband and wife, the legislation was impossible to enforce locally. By 1937 another circular was sent out reiterating the importance of respecting local custom and urging a gradual promotion of the principle of consent. However the issue would not die; once again in 1939 a law was passed in the French Chamber nullifying marriages of girls before the age of puberty. As the law was never passed in the Senate due to the outbreak of World War II, the text was promulgated instead as a decree, known as the *décret Mandel*. During the war enforcement of the decree was neglected, so in order to underscore the seriousness of the offense, the postwar colonial administration added a new article stipulating that "any marriage contracted in violation of these dispositions will be considered enslavement," implying, of course, severe consequences. But as historian Andre Robert remarks, it would be difficult to find another law so draconian in language and so ineffective in its practical application (1955:86–88).[24]

Finally, the 1944 Conference at Brazzaville sponsored by de Gaulle and the Free French made what seemed to be rather radical recommendations as part of social and economic reforms proposed in recognition of the contribution of Africa in the liberation of France, declaring that:

> If the Black family represents an element of stability in the social order which it would be unwise to undermine, it seems nevertheless possible and desireable to introduce henceforth the idea of freedom in marriage, which is properly the freedom of women (Robert 1954:89).

---

[22] According to French administrator Paul Marty (1930:428) the local al'kali was absorbed into the tribunes in Niger as judges by the late 1920s. G. Nicolas reports that the durbi was somewhat bitter that he was so infrequently consulted at the Tribunal during Nicolas' research in the 1960s (1975:198). During my research the durbi stood outside the Tribune in Maradi ready to give advice on questions of local and Islamic law, but he was so little recognized that the presiding judge didn't know his name or title.

[23] From 1904 to 1946 "subjects" of France (which included the indigenous peoples of Niger, or *indigènes*) had no constitutional rights and were subject to a law code permitting immediate trial and sentencing by the local civil or military administrator for offenses such as refusal to carry out an order, failure to pay a tax or fine, or showing disrespect. With the end of World War II the *Indigénat* was revoked and judges replaced the administrators in the courts (Fuglestad 1983:80, David 1964:128).

[24] The law on the books dated December 12, 1905, punished enslavement with 2–5 years imprisonment and a fine of 500–5,000 Fr. (AOM/200 Mi 1194 K24).

However in the postwar period this "idea" could only be introduced through indigenous judicial authorities, who had no immediate interest in doing so. The administration was preoccupied with developing and monitoring the new electoral apparatus and in truth took little interest in social reform. Furthermore the postwar abolition of the *Indigénat* impeded the imposition of sanctions of all kinds, including those implied by the *décret Mandel*. With the abolition of the *Indigénat*, Nigérien men were given the status of French citizens, which the French administration assumed would be received with enthusiasm; elite men in Maradi were ambivalent, wondering whether their new status would affect their rights to polygyny or the prerogatives the *sarauta* class had established for itself under colonialism (ANN/14.2.8).

Most of the legislation passed that directly touched upon women did little to promote their welfare and may in fact have merely contributed to the uncertain status of many women's marriages. For example, the effort to promote marriage registration in order to enforce the *décret Mandel* created new ambiguities (Phillips and Morris 1971:112): was an unregistered marriage not a marriage? What if the couple failed to notify the authorities prior to the marriage, as was stipulated in Arreté Général No. 973, of 13 December 1940? And was a marriage that was registered but not recognized by the bride's relatives a valid marriage in local eyes?

Regulating Bridewealth

Beyond the issue of consent, the matter of greatest interest to both the French colonial and postcolonial governments after 1945 was that of the high cost of marriage. The colonial government saw high bridewealth as a cause of "social disequilibrium" and in 1951 attempted to regulate it through the Jacquinot decree. The decree had little efficacy, however, because as a regulation governing all the French colonial territories it failed to take into account enormous local variations in the amount, contents, and significance of bridewealth. It fixed the age of majority for women absurdly high at 21, when all women in Maradi would already have been married at least once, and set a maximum for the bridewealth when in practice it could vary enormously depending on the age, status, and wealth of the bride and her family. But ultimately the decree was to fail because it looked to local notables to enforce a decree that was against their own interests as heads of family (Robert 1955:91). Senior men had an interest in controlling younger men (and their labor) by limiting their ability to marry and form new households without the aid of their elders; they also had an interest in gaining as large a *sadaki* bridewealth payment for their maiden daughters as was reasonable according to local norms. Rising bridewealth seems to have been a phenomenon born out of the conjuncture of the need to control junior labor (both male and female), the increasing value of young wives as labor with the end of slavery, and the impulse to find a means of tapping the income of junior males entering the new wage economy.

In the immediate postindependence years other matters were of greater concern to both the French and the newly independent government and the regulation of marriage was temporarily forgotten–by male legislators at any rate. The Union de Femmes du Niger (UFN), the women's branch of President Diori's RDA party, urged several reforms in the early independence period, among them the reduction of the "dowry" (the French misnomer for the *sadaki* bridewealth payment) and the suppression of polygyny (Clair 1965:134, 137). Women in general have an interest in keeping *sadaki* bridewealth payments low, for they tend to have little access to that portion of the marriage gift transactions. Since the payment must be returned to the husband if the woman initiates a divorce, high bridewealth can thwart women's efforts to sever a union, for their kin may be unwilling or unable to return it. The UFN also urged the adoption of a family code that would protect women's rights to their children upon divorce and prevent repudiation without the woman's consent. The family code was the subject of tremendous debate and was never completed.

The Sahel Drought of 1968–1974 precipitated a coup d'état in 1974 because of widespread disillusionment with Diori Hamani's regime, in power since independence. The military regime that came into power under Seyni Kountché saw the interests of rural areas and rural women as more urgent in the context of the drought than those of a vocal minority of urban women. The now obvious fragility of the Nigérien economy and the need for investment in rural development created an environment in which large and conspicuous expenditures for marriages were seen as being against the national interest. Kountché attempted to place an upper limit on the bridewealth and outlawed the conspicuous display of the *he!* wedding ceremony which directly concerned women (Hajjiya Indo, 10-25-89).[25]

The perennially resuscitated family code debate, however, has yet to yield a reform in family law, governed (in principle) at the moment by Maliki Islamic law. The predominance of Islam in Niger brings any attempts at family reform directly up against entrenched interpretations of Islamic family law guaranteeing a man's right to four wives, his custody of children upon divorce, and his right to repudiate his wives at will. The women's association had all but dropped the issue of the family code by the late 1980s, believing it to be too volatile an issue to win as Islamist sentiment from Nigeria spread into Niger. The issue has recently been revived under civilian rule as groups devoted to women's issues have proliferated with multiparty politics; Niger's other pressing problems make it unlikely that any substantial reform will be effected soon, however.

Efforts of postcolonial Nigérien governments to limit bridewealth and require the consent of those to be married have faced the same kinds of enforce-

---

[25] According to G. Nicolas the *he!* had been discouraged under Diori as well, and limitations were placed upon the size of various wedding transactions, but because the party could benefit monetarily from its "monitoring" of these transactions, the decrees were counter-productive (1986:108).

ment problems as colonial efforts to regulate marriage.[26] As Éliane de Latour observes, "the state attempts regularly to intervene to 'moralize' the matrimonial economy, but decrees and grand pronouncements have little power against the symbolic burden of a marital alliance: the union of two families must be manifested in ostentation, the display of united powers" (1992:71). Fear of the consequences of breaking the regulations under Kountché and Saibou's military regimes seemed nevertheless to have some effect in keeping conspicuous display in wedding ceremonies in check in the 1980s. The issue of women's consent in marriage has been more difficult to control. I know of no cases of girls married off before puberty in recent years, while many women over fifty (particularly of the *sarauta* class) were given in their first marriages well before puberty: there does seem today to be a consensus that girls under thirteen should not be married. But girls who are not in school are regularly married as soon as their breasts form, when they are too young to resist their parents' wishes. If asked whether they chose their husband they are likely to respond that they "agreed to the marriage." As in the past, a young woman's first marriage is extremely fragile and often ends before the year is up. As the foregoing discussion would suggest, young women's reasons for leaving such marriages often center as much around conflicts with their co-wives as around their dislike for their actual marriage partner.

Education and Marriage Age

The increasing percentage of girls being sent to school appears to have contributed to new marital patterns. Maradi's Hausa families seem to adhere to the following principle: so long as a girl is succeeding in school, she will not be married off, but once she has passed puberty, if she fails in school she is to be married immediately. Husbands almost never allow their bride to remain in school, so if a family believes that the girl can finish enough schooling to qualify for a good job they will postpone marriage for her unless she has a promising suitor who is very insistent. This creates several peaks in marriage age, one at thirteen, when most girls reach puberty, and another at about fifteen, when girls who are not going to make it into *lycée* fail the entry exam. Once a young woman has passed the age of fifteen she is likely to marry a man of her own choice whom she has met in school or at her job in her late teens or early twenties. Girls who are married because they have failed their exams do sometimes marry schoolmates of their own choice. However, Western schooling is not a guarantee that a girl will have choice in her first marriage.

One must not exaggerate the numerical importance of this shift in marriage age, as the change is very clearly related to schooling, and in the most recent census figures available (1977), only 3.5 percent of girls in the department of Maradi under the age of fifteen had received any education, and only

---

[26] Legislation touching on marital practice in Africa is in general contradictory and difficult to enforce, see Ngondo a Pitshandenge (1994).

.52 percent of all girls from ten to twenty had succeeded in continuing on to secondary school, while 97 percent of all women over the age of ten had had no schooling whatsoever (République du Niger 1985a:23, Table 2.01). Marriage continues to be arranged by a young girl's parents, and she continues to be in the unenviable position of providing labor for her senior co-wives while becoming at the same time an object of resentment because she competes for limited resources and favors.

Conclusion

In the end it has not been prescriptive legislation or the intervention of French courts in the realm of marriage proper that have most influenced the nature of marriage in the region, as we shall see, but rather a series of local contests over the meaning of marriage itself precipitated by the decline of slavery, new commercial patterns, changes in uses and access to land, the rise of the *alhazai* merchant class and the expansion of education. In particular the nature of marriage has been disputed, contested, and renegotiated in moments when production politics and family politics have overlapped: when peanut cropping, for example, demands greater control of family labor on the part of the household head just as subordinate members of the household themselves hope to capitalize on a shifting economy, or when education and infrastructure offer women opportunities in the economy that conflict with the cultural capital the merchant class earns through wife seclusion. Precisely because production and accumulation in this setting occur primarily through the idiom of the family, any major shift in the political economy entails a recalibration of family relations. As Judith Carney and Michael Watts observe, "the complex resistances which emerge from the conflation of household and production politics are fought out on the terrain of cultural representations and struggles over meaning" (1990:211). Let us turn, then, to the more local fora for negotiating the meaning of marriage and to the most intimate foci of contestation to see how the distant influences of the colonial and postcolonial state and the global market have in fact impinged upon the lives of men and women in Maradi.

2

Mediating Marriage: State Intrusion and Local Dispute Settlement

With rising polygyny and a perilous economy, tensions within a household over who is to perform what labor, who controls household resources, and which women have authority over other women are acute in Maradi society today. Both the domestic hierarchy and marriages themselves are subject to constant debate and negotiation, and many women feel extremely insecure about their marriages. Although most failed marriages are ended by the husband with little or no formality, only rarely do marital and household conflicts in Maradi erupt in the form of confrontations between husbands and wives or men and women, but rather they crystalize in battles between co-wives and female in-laws. This pattern emerges elsewhere in Hausa Niger: "Female jealousy is our heritage," remarks the chief of the canton of Tibiri to Éliane de Latour as he determines fault in a marital dispute (1992:50–51).

Marital conflict is not simply a question of incompatibility between spouses, but represents the working out of a complex series of issues: control of junior labor, both male and female, at a moment when education offers youth sources of income outside the domestic group; polygyny as an institution in a context where women have access to alternative models of marriage; the rights of wives according to Islam in a region where the nature of Islam has historically been hotly contested; and the distribution of resources within and between households in one of the most densely populated regions of Niger. These issues are complicated even further by the growth of seclusion in both rural and urban areas at the very moment when some women are beginning to gain greater public mobility than in the past with the growth of public education, markets, and infrastructure. As one might imagine, therefore, debates over women's rights to choose their sexual partners, to contract their own marriages, and to negotiate the terms of those marriages are volatile, not only between women and men, but between junior and senior women as well.

This chapter will explore some of the loci of marital and domestic mediation in order to set out some of the critical nodes of conflict that have emerged over the century since French conquest. My purpose in exploring marital conflict in the present is in part to suggest that recent work on the law and gender in Africa, although it has been extremely fruitful and thought-provoking, may overdraw the importance of formal institutions of mediation such as colonial courts in recasting the nature of marriage and gender in Africa. Too great an emphasis on customary law and the courts introduced in the colonial period can lead to an overestimation of the power of the state and "patriarchy" to the neglect of the profound and continuing importance of more local mediational domains in the negotiation of marriage, gender, and family life. It is in these more local structures that one gets a sense for how fluid and uncontainable the definition of local practice can in fact be, and the ways in which both women and men deploy a range of discourses about gender, family, and marriage. This is not to suggest that the existence of formal judicial settings does not impinge upon local mediational structures. However, the ability of either the state or local patriarchal structures either to capture "customary law" in any fixed form or to impose any major reform of local practices through new laws is limited by the unpredictability of encounters in the formal courts, by the continuing existence of alternative mediational domains, and by the ambiguities created by the state courts themselves. Indeed, far from fixing local practice according to a reworked "traditional" or an imposed "liberal" order, colonial intervention probably interjected yet a further element of instability into what was already a dynamic landscape. As Sara Berry remarks, "Colonial officials certainly tried to govern according to fixed rules and procedures which were based on what they imagined to be the stable political and jural systems of the African past, but they rarely exercised enough effective control to accomplish exactly what they set out to do" (1993:25). The effect of both the colonial and postcolonial states has been, in her words, "intrusive rather than hegemonic" (1993:20). Debating just what constitutes "tradition" has become one of the means by which individuals negotiate access to resources and wealth. Rather than fixing "customary law," the state has in effect merely institutionalized a certain kind of instability. As we shall see in the following chapters, that instability causes both men and women to devote tremendous amounts of time, energy, and capital to negotiating and moderating the interpretation of their social position in order to gain control over their own and others' capital, land, and persons.

The Limits of Formal Institutions

If the state has had little ability to control marital practice directly, what have been the primary influences upon marriage, and how have women responded? Most influences, like the abolition of slavery discussed in Chapter 1, have been indirect, unpredictable, and have had differential impact upon women of dif-

ferent backgrounds (elite versus commoner and urban versus rural). The following discussion of marriage dispute mediation will shed light on some of
the trends that have affected marriage and some of the causes of marital instability, setting the stage for a more detailed presentation of those processes in
the following chapters. While the institutions sketched out here exist to mediate disputes, they have not by and large actually been able to alter marriage
patterns in and of themselves. Rather, local adjudicators have been faced with
the increasingly difficult task of regulating marriages while the institution of
marriage itself is undergoing change and as guidelines for determining how to
rule on a given issue are unclear and contradictory. For example, if the local
understanding of Islam increasingly stipulates that a woman should be secluded,
local norms offer strong protections to a married woman's right to farm her
own *gamana* plot. All of the "arbiters" I shall present below found marriage
disputes (and the regulation of inheritance, a related issue concerning women
and their children) to be tiresome and frustrating. As the al'kali (the qadi) remarked to me in exasperation, "there are never any papers, no evidence, nothing, it's all *jahilci* [ignorance, particularly of Islamic practice]."

    Marital disputes can be handled through a variety of means which, like
successive courts of appeal, can be turned to progressively as previous attempts
fail to yield the desired outcome. As Périé noted during his tenure as an administrator in the region prior to World War II, justice in Maradi is "the justice
of arbitration" (Périé 1939:394). The first and simplest method of dealing with
a problem is to air it openly to friends, kin, and neighbors in an attempt to
gain as many supporters as possible. The following incident, reconstructed from
my field notes, illustrates this approach and, significantly, occurred in the poor-
est of the neighborhoods I worked in, Maradawa, where none of the participants had the "greeting money" necessary to bring a grievance before a more
formal authority. I had gone to visit Buga, a poor woman who had recently
moved into a small rented room in a mud building. Her neighbors were a young
couple with small children, who were also tenants. She did not know them
well, and was in some ways as much an observer as I was.

The Neighborhood Forum

    I went down to Maradawa to see Buga. Just as I arrived a voluble
    argument erupted, attracting a large number of neighborhood women
    and children. As I arrived on the scene an old woman was screaming
    into the doorway of the room next to Buga's, and as Buga and I sat in
    the shade of one tree other women loitered under another one. Chil-
    dren shamelessly peered into the room.
        According to Buga the young woman who is her neighbor had just
    sent her husband to get her younger brother out of the hospital. Be-
    cause she was busy at the house with her baby and was making fura
    (millet porridge), in the presence of her mother and her mother's older
    sister she had given her husband 550 CFA to pay the outstanding medi-
    cal bill. She later discovered that she had not owed any money at all
    and that her husband had secretly spent the money on something else.

The old woman screaming into the doorway was the young woman's mother, who was roundly abusing her son-in-law, while making public the event, her witnessing of the transaction, and the failure of her daughter's husband to return the money. The daughter was crying and noisily stacking her pots and pans in the courtyard, signalling her intention to leave her husband. The clatter brought the son-in-law out of the room to defend himself publicly, saying the whole thing was a lie, he never had the money. So the mother marched off noisily and returned with another old woman, her sister, who also proceeded to abuse him roundly. The wife stomped about angrily with her infant, bitter but silent. The woman's aunt and the young man argued noisily before a scandalized neighborhood.

Buga reproached the old women quietly, saying that since they were old they should be trying to reconcile the couple, not break them up. The old aunt descended upon Buga saying that she had repaired this marriage three times already and she had had enough. What was the point, she asked? The son-in-law, silenced, slunk off with his prayerbeads. When he was gone his wife offered a soliloquy to the crowd, asking, "How can we all three be lying?" Again thinking out loud, she remarked that she was not going to run off after all (and end up having to pay back the bridewealth), he would just have to divorce her himself. Neighbors urged patience and offered sympathy. A young Koranic scholar walking by the compound looked over the stalk fence and urged her to be patient but did not seem to have the temerity to enter the compound buzzing with neighborhood women. Little by little things calmed down, people went off to do their own work, and the wife sat disconsolately on a broken stool nursing her baby. Her husband crept back in to carry off his fura, neither of them looked at one another or spoke.

The purpose of such a public display seems to be to air grievances, garner support for one's position, and ultimately to pressure one's adversary into concessions of some kind. The couple in question did remain together, and this particular conflict was finally resolved to the satisfaction of the wife who, having convinced the neighborhood that she had been wronged, managed to compel her husband to repay her with a gift of equal value. The role of seniors in these conflicts is somewhat contradictory: on the one hand, as experienced and wise arbiters they are expected (as Buga observed) to mend the marriages of the young. On the other, it was the vociferous support of the wife's mother and aunt that made the husband finally give in, and therefore it is not sufficient simply to have seniors present urging patience. Note that in all of this a direct confrontation between husband and wife was avoided, and the wife maintained her image of reserve and deference to her husband by leaving the argument up to her mother. Young women are not supposed to be vocal. One consequence of this is that frequently discontent is not expressed until the situation has deteriorated so far that the woman has decided to leave in earnest.[1]

---

[1]   First marriages in Hausaland are extremely fragile, as they are in a number of other Muslim societies in sub-Saharan Africa. See Coquery-Vidrovitch (1994:339–44).

Women who leave their husbands generally go to stay with kin they believe will be sympathetic to their plight. However a rural woman's marital home is likely to be within a limited geographical range of her paternal home, and her husband may have strong ties to her own kin (particularly if it is a marriage between cousins, as is common in rural areas). She may find that to break away from her marriage she must go to the city to live on her own. One consequence of this pattern is that rural marriages appear at first glance to be far more stable than urban marriages: of twenty-five rural women informants over the age of thirty, only two had had more than two marriages and both cases were anomalous (one woman was divorced and then remarried the same man, so the intervening marriage was simply a legal device to permit her and her first husband to remarry; the other woman had been widowed twice). Where in the city roughly one out of three women I worked with had contracted three or more marriages, among women remaining in rural areas only one in ten had contracted more than two marriages. While rural mores will permit a young woman to leave her first marriage, which is often contracted without her consent when she is very young, they are less permissive when it comes to leaving a second marriage. This does not mean that rural marriages are happier or more successful than urban marriages, but rather that rural women who are unhappy with their second marriage must often move to the city if they are to improve their marital situation.[2] One could argue that one consequence of unhappy rural marriages is the gradual migration of a portion of the female population to the city. Of the women I worked with in the city of Maradi, roughly a quarter came to the city after a rural marriage and before remarrying someone from within the urban milieu.

This phenomenon is probably very recent, rising dramatically since World War II and in particular since independence, for while in the nineteenth century the fortified city of Maradi represented a pole of attraction for rural populations (both male and female) fleeing raids from the Caliphate, from 1900 to 1945 urban centers in general suffered from out-migration rather than immigration due to local displeasure with colonial policies and control.[3] Prior to the mid-1940s aristocratic families may have brought young rural women to the city in "marriage" to gain access to their labor. This did not represent the voluntary immigration of non-married women resisting rural marriage, but rather

---

[2]   G. Nicolas observed in the late 1960s that marriages of rural non-Muslims seemed to be more stable than urban Muslim marriages, partly because of the high incidence of kin marriage, but he then went on to remark that the influence of urban norms has resulted in greater independence for women, who now marry and divorce frequently. He seems to assume that such women inevitably enter into prostitution, which is not bourn out by the life histories of rural women in my sample who move to the city, although *karuwanci* may be an option (1975:93, 180).

[3]   Spittler (1977) argues that it has only been since the fifties that most urban centers in Niger have grown at a more rapid pace than the population as a whole, but treats Maradi as an exception which grew earlier. Judging from the timing of the growth of neighborhoods in Maradi and from aerial photographs of the city I suspect that Spittler has exaggerated the growth of Maradi prior to 1950. Grégoire's estimation of population growth in the city shows rapid population increase only after 1950, and particularly since 1965 (1986:25).

the involuntary marriage of young girls into aristocratic families.[4] The option for women to come to the urban center to resist rural marriage and to arrange an urban marriage of their own choosing represents one of the most powerful forces altering marriage in the region, probably beginning in the 1930s.

When these women come to Maradi they may have no kin to help them, and when this is the case it is often to the home of the iya that they turn. Iya is the title of the senior woman of the aristocratic class, who is often the sister or aunt of the traditional ruler of Maradi, the sarki. Mediating for rural women is an extension of the iya's traditional judicial function as arbiter between women of the *sarauta* class and as judge in disputes between the primarily rural members of the *bori* cult.[5] Thus one of the functions of the iya is to act as an arbiter in rural marriages, a function which is probably more important today than it was in the past, as the city acts increasingly as a center of gravity towards which rural women migrate.[6] The limited opportunities available to a rural woman who comes to the city make it likely that the iya will urge her to remain in her rural marriage, particularly if she has suffered no material or physical abuse, as the following incident shows.

The Iya's Home

I went down to visit Iya Wandara at about 5:00, and on the way into her room I passed a young woman of about nineteen sitting on the mat out in the courtyard; she seemed astonished to see me. Iya was inside chatting with her husband who was visiting from Niamey. . . . We spoke for a while and then she explained that she had to regulate something outside, so she went out into the courtyard and I followed.

Outside a number of people had gathered. The young woman was still there, nursing her baby. A well-dressed man of about forty had come, accompanied by an older man referred to as Al Hajj. An old woman wearing the red beads of a Hajjiya (a woman who has completed the pilgrimage) had also arrived. They began discussing a marriage dispute. The young woman explained that she no longer wanted her marriage. She didn't like being secluded, she wanted a room of her own, and she wanted a field of her own to work. She remarked that she could not live her life talking to no one but her co-wife.

[4] Hajjiya Hasiya's mother is probably a good example of this phenomenon: she was taken by force around 1915 by the sarkin Filani, Hajjiya's father, when he was out collecting the cattle tax from Fulani herders near Da'din Kowa. As Hasiya remarks, "Back then the people with power, if they wanted something they just took it" (Hajjiya Hasiya, 10-27-89). Hajjiya was not raised by this woman, but was given to her father's sister to be raised, and has been treated as a full member of the *sarauta* class. Her mother was eventually divorced, and Hasiya has retained close enough ties to her maternal kin to obtain foster children from them.

[5] The iya traditionally had a significant role in other disputes as well: along with the members of the electoral college she had the power to intervene and prevent the death penalty and to provide sanctuary (David 1964:125–26n2; M.G. Smith 1967:117).

[6] Coquery-Vidrovitch (1994:140–41) notes that the relatively recent migration of women from rural areas to cities tends to be more permanent than male migration, and is often linked to their subordinate status in their villages: "Le rejet du milieu rural, quel qu'en soit l'origine, est definitif."

The younger man, who was her husband, then said that she had not told him any of this. None of the other wives had their own fields, why should she? She had never lacked for anything. Had she ever gone hungry or thirsty?, he asked rhetorically. Everyone looked at her pointedly. The wife continued to nurse her infant sullenly.

The old woman, who was the young woman's mother, proved to be an unsympathetic representative. She told the young woman that this marriage was not "dead," and proceeded to give her a lecture on her foolishness. "You must be patient, you have no sense, you don't know what the future will bring," she declared. Iya then agreed with the mother, remarking that she had herself been married to her own husband for many, many years. The husband then expressed a desire to repair the damage, and he, his representative, and the young woman's mother worked out an agreement. He would give the wife 2,000 CFA and a bolt of cloth. He also gave them money to get back to the village. Before leaving, he and his representative gave the iya a small gift of money as well.

The young woman was clearly not content with this arrangement, her jaw tightened with anger. She said to the women, who had remained after the departure of the men, "I don't have permission to talk to anyone but my co-wife, I can't live like that." The two older women told her she must be patient and think of the children.

The final outcome of this particular dispute is not clear, at best the young woman has aired her discontent and made it clear to her husband why she is unhappy. Even so she has no one who is willing to support her in her dispute. Discontentment because of seclusion in a region where many rural women are overburdened with chores and risk food insecurity does not seem to be a legitimate grievance to the senior kin around her, or to the iya, whom she had probably hoped might be more sympathetic than her mother. The longer-standing practice of seclusion in the urban center and the increasingly unstable rural economy contribute to the reluctance of the iya to promote the dissolution of a marriage on the grounds that seclusion is unreasonable. Both of the older women regarded the fact that the wife has at least one child in this marriage as a serious reason for urging reconciliation. Her husband's relative success and wealth made it hard for the young woman to argue that she was not sufficiently provided for, yet it was also his wealth which made seclusion of his wives possible and desirable as a sign of status. What this young woman suffers from, in the minds of the older women, is the "discontentment of youth," and both older women were no doubt painfully aware that despite the younger woman's unhappiness, she could easily find herself in a far less desirable situation. In the following chapter I shall discuss in greater detail some of the processes that have contributed to the instability of women's access to the farmland this young woman is attempting to claim, and to the parallel growth of seclusion in rural areas in recent years.

In order to appreciate the ramifications of the resolution of this particular conflict, one must realize that although the iya urges reconciliation in this case, her own marital history tells a rather different story. She was married to a cousin in a "marriage of kinship" as a young girl, and disliked the marriage so much that she provoked a divorce after only nine months. She lived unmarried for many years and chose her current husband herself. They have a very satisfactory arrangement whereby he lives in Niamey and visits occasionally, and she lives in her own home in Maradi. Clearly Iya as an individual has been perfectly willing to break a marriage and to choose what is in many ways a rather unconventional lifestyle. But as an institutional figure in the titled position of iya, she urges patience and promotes the fiction that she has been married to the same man since she was a young woman. While the spirit possession cult that the iya commands does have unmarried women as members, the iya does not promote divorce as a rule. Iya has been unsuccessful in having children of her own, which has contributed in a sense to her independence. But given a choice between remaining single without children or enduring marriage for the sake of the children, Iya in her institutional role seems in this case to be urging the latter.

Much of the literature on the figure of the iya in Hausa culture has assumed an automatic association of the iya with *karuwanci* (or courtesanship) and unmarried women,[7] an association that seems to have resulted from the degeneration of the office of iya to a kind of representative of karuwai in post-jihad northern Nigeria. With the elimination of many titled positions of political power for women in the emirates, the single female office was often retained only to provide a liaison between the authorities and the karuwa population, for whom bori provides community, spiritual support, and material resources, and who often use bori dancing as a form of entertainment.[8] In Maradi there is not now nor was there in the past any automatic association of the iya with women who practice karuwanci; in fact it was another titled woman, the magajiya, who was in charge of the courtesans (Hajjiya Jeka, 4-13-89).[9] The iya was only indirectly associated with them because bori cult members could also practice karuwanci on the side. A few rural women who prefer to remain unmarried for a time have nevertheless been housed and protected by the iya over the years particularly if they are already members of the bori cult towards whom she has a special responsibility.

---

[7]   M.G. Smith, probably following administrator Jean Périé and then historian Philippe David, states that one of the iya's functions was to head the local prostitutes (1967:108). I have seen no evidence that this is an accurate depiction of the office in Maradi. To the contrary the title is directly tied to *bori* and a separate title (which otherwise would be meaningless) is tied to *karuwai* (Périé 1939:389, David, 1964:84).

[8]   See for example Baba's accounts of *bori* dancing and prostitutes in Nigeria (Mary F. Smith 1981:64, 224, 230; see also M.G. Smith's note on the title magajiya in the same volume, note 10 to page 63).

[9]   Landeroin (1911:532) makes no mention of prostitutes when discussing the female leaders of the *bori* cult. With the duplication of the office of magajiya in the PPN–RDA party and later in the Samariya Youth Organization, the *sarauta* title has lost much of its importance in Maradi and now signifies primarily that the holder is a likely successor to the iya. It is possible that the confusion in the literature over the role of the iya is due in part to the exceptional powers of the corresponding office of inna in Gobir, who, through close association with the party in the post-colonial period, seems to have managed to co-opt the powers of the magajiya under the office of the iya/inna (G. Nicolas 1986:75).

This preference for reconciliation rather than divorce (and temporary single status) seems to be equally true of the three other institutional fora for regulating dispute in the region, namely the court of the sarki, the home of the al'kali, and the Tribunal magistrate's court initiated under colonial rule. While the iya's home seems to have become a forum to which rural women who are thinking of leaving their husbands appeal, the sarki's court tends to be used to pressure one of the parties in a marriage to make some change or to meet some obligation. Should the parties resist the attempts of the intermediaries to work out a reconciliation, they run the risk of losing access to that forum as a source of mediation altogether, as this incident in the court of the sarki illustrates.

The Sarki's Court

A young man entered dressed in Western slacks and a shirt, his head uncovered, unlike those of all of the older turbaned notables of the court. He was ushered in with his two wives, one a brash young woman who looked about the court eagerly, the other a thin, dour older woman carrying a child on her back. The younger of the two women had brought a complaint against her husband and the older wife on the grounds that whenever there was a disagreement between the two wives the husband only listened to the first wife, which was unfair.

She proceeded to tell her story, which was told with great conviction and righteousness and little regard for the usual formalities of speech that characterize court appearances before the sarki. According to her the friction between her and her co-wife had reached such heights that the older woman was attempting to kill her. She whipped her shirt up to show that her co-wife had bitten her on her chest. As evidence that her co-wife had now turned to magic to kill her she recounted incoherently various incidents in which objects were misplaced; the story culminated with the older woman hiding a chicken which she clearly intended to use in her magic. The younger woman had stolen the key to the older wife's room so that she could not get the chicken hidden there out and do any damage.

The older woman, who had remained quiet and deferential throughout, at this point began to laugh and attempted to interrupt. The sarki told her to be quiet and wait for her turn. When at length she was allowed to speak she said that if the younger wife hadn't brought suit she would have herself, because of the theft of her key and the accusations that she, who had never tried to do magic on anyone, was engaging in such behavior. By now, however, the older wife had angered the sarki with her attempts to interrupt the younger wife and her failure to account for the bite on her co-wife's chest.

The husband had little to add, explaining rather lamely that because his work kept him on the road a great deal he didn't really know exactly what was going on, which made it hard to mediate between the wives, and that was why it was better if someone else mediated. The sarki informed him that it was a husband's job to mediate and to know what was going on, wryly remarking, "If you have a hat, do you leave it at home and not wear it?" The rebuke provoked considerable amusement among the men in the court.

The sarki then gave the older wife a long lecture, clearly regarding all of this confusion as being initiated by her. The older wife eventually exploded, saying that if they were all going to blame it on her, well then they could just give her her divorce papers right now, she was not going to sit around when people were accusing her of doing magic. This outburst angered the sarki, who told the man to take his wives and leave, if they could not listen to him it was not in his hands. The three got up to leave, the young man utterly at a loss, the younger woman disappointed, and the older woman triumphant.

While the sarki may be brought into serious disputes, there is not much anyone can do if the parties involved are resistant to outside attempts to work out some resolution. The real loser in this case is the husband, who not only failed to win peace in his household, but also revealed himself publicly to be unable to control his wives. The sarki's remark about owning a hat but not wearing it was a very pointed criticism: the young man's right to have more than one wife is one of his prerogatives as a Muslim male, but that right comes with important responsibilities, and a man who cannot be troubled to wear the responsibilities of the head of household should not have more than one wife. The association of the wearing of a hat with one's identity as a Muslim also meant that in a sense the sarki was questioning the young man's adherence to his faith, arriving in court without a headcovering and failing in his duties as a husband to treat his wives fairly and to protect them from danger. Note, however, that while the husband is humiliated, it is the older wife who is blamed for the *fitina* or discord.

The younger wife had succeeded in airing her grievances but had not managed to remedy the situation, which, however unlikely her witchcraft accusation, was clearly destructive to her physically as well as emotionally. The older wife had managed to thwart the younger woman's attempt to provoke a settlement in her own favor, but had not cleared herself of a witchcraft accusation, which she had legitimate reason to be angry about if the accusation were unfounded. It is hard to imagine how this particular household can remain intact, and the failure of the younger woman to win the day through the court means that it is unlikely that she will remain with her husband unless they have children. On the other hand he may decide to repudiate the older wife to end the disturbance. The older woman made a point of arriving in court with a baby on her back, however, making it unlikely that she can be dismissed easily, and explaining visually why she has put up with what seems to be an impossible situation. As we shall see in a moment, now that the man and his wives no longer have access to the sarki in their dispute, they have lost the most important milieu for arranging a settlement.

When a marriage seems impossible to repair, the next step is to begin formal actions to make a divorce. For a man this is a relatively simple affair: he can simply state before witnesses that he has undone the three "threads of the marriage." This is the Hausa equivalent of stating the Islamic formula, "I divorce thee, I divorce thee, I divorce thee." As we shall see in Chapter 5, the "threads of marriage" are understood quite literally and are part of a broader cultural understanding of the ties between individuals and families created and maintained through marriage. When a man pronounces his repudiation of a wife in this manner (that is, definitively stating that all three renunciations have been made), he can make no claims upon the bridewealth payment he made to her kin at the time of their marriage and he cannot remarry her until she has married and divorced another man.

More commonly, however, the breaking or "death" of the marriage occurs more gradually than this and may result from a number of successive incidents that have been aired before the Muslim legal scholar (the al'kali), or before the sarki. If a man and a woman come before the al'kali prepared to divorce, he will tell them to go home and "cool off" for two weeks and then to come back. Sometimes they never reappear, having reconciled their differences. But they may come back after the two weeks are up and each side will explain who is at fault, bringing friends to bear witness. The al'kali will decide who seems to be at fault and give him or her "a talking to" in the presence of the other and tell the injured party to be patient. They may go off and be reconciled. But if this is repeated three times, the al'kali will decide that the three "threads of the marriage" have been broken and will declare the couple divorced, in which case they cannot remarry unless she marries and divorces another man in the interim. If it is the woman who has brought the case forward, as is generally the case (since a man who wants a divorce needs only to make a verbal repudiation), she must return the bridewealth payment to her husband unless the sarki or al'kali determines that the husband has been at fault. The following incident illustrates how the office of the al'kali figures in most attempts to end an unwanted marriage.

"The House of the Al'kali"

As we were talking a young woman came in to get an official *takarda* paper formalizing her divorce. Her husband had written one in Hausa, which she had taken to the sarki, who sent her to the home of the al'kali to have an official one written out in Arabic script and officially stamped. "This woman is sensible," the qadi remarked, "she came to get a witness and to make sure the paper would be official. Other women aren't so clever, and when some other man comes to marry them their former husband comes forward and claims that he never made a full repudiation and that he still wants her." The note her husband had written read: "I, Hamsu, released the three threads on Sunday." The al'kali had his secretary write out a new note with the man's full name, the woman's full name, and declared the date of the beginning of Idda (a period of separation and seclusion of the woman) and the end date. He also noted the amount of child support the sarki had set, which was 3,000 CFA per month for the child she had with her. She was to leave her other child with her husband. He then gave her the *takarda*, telling her it was to show her next husband, and that she should keep the other note written by her ex-husband as a "remedy against forgetfulness" should he claim never to have written any such document. The Idda was set to start the following day; the original date written by her husband was irrelevant.

This case is fairly typical, because in fact it has only been very rarely that anyone in Maradi has turned to the al'kali as anything other than a record-keeper. It is the sarki who has the influence to urge a reconciliation or to determine which party is at fault, and it is the sarki who has staff to compel a man to meet his child support obligations or shame him publicly. The legal niceties of divorce are ironed out by the al'kali, but the rough outline of a divorce proceeding transpires elsewhere. The general contours of Islamic practice touching on marriage in this region are quite clear, and are readily summarized. As a rule the woman is permitted to retain her sons until they are seven years old, when her husband may claim them. The daughters generally remain with their mother or with other female kin until they are married. If the father feels that his ex-wife has been behaving in an unseemly manner, he may claim the children back early, but she has undisputed custody until they are weaned at about two years old. When women remarry they must negotiate with their new husbands whether they will bring their children to the new home and whether he is to be in any way responsible for them. In theory the children's biological father is responsible for their upkeep wherever they live, but in practice it is frequently the mother and/or her new husband who must bear the cost of raising them.[10] Thus the al'kali is only brought into most cases as the repository of the details of Maliki Islamic law and of records of earlier proceedings.

"The House of the Judge"

The only other local court in which marriage disputes can be aired is the Tribunal de Première Instance, the magistrate's court established under French rule. This court is locally referred as the "house of the judge" as opposed to the "house of the al'kali." Very few marital disputes are ever referred to this court, since it is Islamic law and local norms that rule in divorces, and men and women who hope to continue to live in Maradi must have local sanction for their behavior or risk alienation. However, occasionally a woman who cannot convince the sarki and al'kali to give her a divorce may appeal to the justice of the peace. As the judge there remarks, "If someone wants a divorce, you can't really tell her 'no.'" Generally the woman comes in and tells her story and the judge sends out a subpoena to the husband. When the husband appears the judge arranges a period of formal separation, which if the woman is pregnant will be until she has given birth. When the separation is up there will be a three-month Idda, after which the woman is free to remarry. Thus the same pattern of setting a period in which the couple can be reconciled followed by Idda and divorce is adopted here as in the other settings, although the woman can initiate

---

[10] Conversations with the Al'kali and Magatakarda, Gidan Al'kali, Oct. 17, 1989.

Chart 1
Marriages and Divorces Registered,
Tribunal de Première Instance–Maradi, October 1985–September 1989

Period	Marriage	Divorce*	Repudiation
10/85–9/86	228	18	67
1/86–12/86	232	20	65
1/87–12/88	192	20	69
1/88–12/88	243	38	104
10/88–9/89	250	43	92
Total	**1,145**	**139**	**397**

* "Divorce" is defined by record keepers in Maradi as an action brought by a woman, "Repudiation" as an action brought by a man.

Source: Tribunal de Première Instance, Maradi, "Relevé du Registre des Jugements supplétifs, du Registre des jugements de divorce, du Registre des actes de Répudiation, Conseil de Famille, Reconnaissance d'enfants, et Autres," 1985, 1986, 1987, 1988, 1989.

it herself and does not have to wait through three separate meetings with the judge, as she would with the sarki or the al'kali. When the husband comes in to announce that he wants to repudiate his wife, the judge attempts to repeat a similar pattern by calling in the wife to formalize it in her presence, which is not necessary in cases taken by a man before the al'kali or sarki.

The clientele of this court is varied: sometimes poor farmers who don't have the "greeting money" expected by the sarki and al'kali will come to the court because it is free; government functionaries who require documentation of all major life events invariably appeal to this more formal court; and ironically, the sarki's close kin, who may feel they can't get a fair hearing in his court, often bring plaints here.[11] Nevertheless the number of cases handled in this setting is very small and the judge himself remarks that in practice the sarki handles the vast majority of divorces as well as most inheritance disputes (although formally he is not supposed to regulate inheritance).[12]

In five years the average number of "divorces" initiated and registered by women before the magistrate's court over a twelve-month period is about thirty-five. The average number of cases of repudiation brought by men is much higher, at ninety-nine.[13] However, for a city as large as Maradi and for a region where divorce is very common, the numbers brought before this court each

---

[11] Compare Latour (1992:91).

[12] Information on the Tribunal was collected in visits to the Palais de Justice and a discussion with the Justice de la Paix, Abdou Mondanchirou, Nov. 9, 1989.

[13] An average was taken rather than a total because the time periods for which records were available are not consistent and sometimes overlap; it was possible only to figure the number of cases recorded in each twelve- month period.

year are quite small, suggesting that while some individuals, particularly government functionaries, see the court as an important source of mediation and a repository of legal records in cases of divorce, the majority of the population has little use for the formal court.

As a fairly loose but suggestive indicator of this phenomenon of high divorce rates in the region of Maradi, out of 212 marriages contracted by 105 women I worked with (82 urban and 23 rural),[14] 51 percent of all marriages ended in divorce as opposed to only 18.8 percent ending in death. Some 54.2 percent of these women's first marriages ended in divorce, 49.2 percent of their second marriages ended in divorce, 51.7 percent of their third marriages ended in divorce, and 50. percent of their fourth marriages ended in divorce. Thus while first marriages appear slightly less stable than later marriages, as a rule of thumb all marriages seem to have about a 50/50 chance of surviving. Rural marriages appear slightly more stable than urban marriages: of the 23 first marriages, 12 are still viable and of the 11 second marriages, 3 ended in death, 1 ended in divorce, and 7 are still viable. The numbers are too small to be conclusive, but roughly six in ten rural second marriages continued, as against five in ten urban second marriages. As I have argued above, however, the probability that a rural woman who is unhappy in marriage will leave her village to go to the city means that the impression that rural marriages are more stable is somewhat misleading. This sketch of my informants' marital experiences is consonant with Raynaut's finding in the early 1970s that approximately 55 percent of both men and women of the village of Sumarana in the Maradi region had been divorced one or more times (Raynaut 1971:136). Among the rural and urban women I worked with more recently the figure is even higher, at 60 percent.[15]

The cases presented above shed light on some of the sources of marital instability. The limitations of the rural economy and women's increasingly disadvantaged position within it, which I set out more fully in Chapter 3, make city life and urban marriage very appealing to rural women. The rise of seclusion increases the likelihood that a woman will lose access to an independent income, provoking rural women to leave their marriages and move to the city, as in the case brought before the iya. At the same time the increasing incidence of polygyny means that friction between co-wives can become a source of conflict, as we saw in the sarki's court, particularly if the husband is not wealthy enough to provide well for his wives, and if he is not diplomatic in his dealings with them. Finally, the stresses within the economy as a whole create enormous competition for cash and valuable goods, and the clear division of property between husbands and wives which has long been a feature of Hausa

---

[14] Out of my total of 111 informants, I had reliable marriage and divorce information on 105, which I have used here.

[15] The stability of marriage in Mirria, a Hausa village in the Zinder region where Margaret Saunders worked in the late 1970s, seems to have been much higher; she found that 72 percent of the marriages registered in the 1968 census were still together in 1974 and that of those which had ended, only 59 percent had ended in divorce rather than death (1978:259).

marriage can become a source of conflict if a husband does not respect a woman's right to her property, if he does not provide her with her upkeep from his own income according to Islamic norms, or if he uses household income to bring a new wife home to compete for limited resources. In the dispute in Maradawa, competition over control of cash resources in a very poor household led to marital conflict. While the courts may discourage rural-to-urban migration, arbitrate between co-wives, and recognize or fail to recognize women's rights to certain kinds of property, they do not in themselves either create these conflicts or eliminate them. If the woman who came before the iya fails to gain land and continues to be unhappy, she will inevitably come to the city, regardless of what the court has to say about it. The courts neither promote nor eliminate polygyny, seclusion, or competition for cash–these trends are created out of numerous instances of individual choice effected in unremarkable day-to-day settings. In the end, the courts have been little able to control either marriage or women. The only issue touching upon women and their marriages that the courts have affected, again indirectly rather than directly, seems to have been their access to landed property, which I shall discuss in greater detail in Chapter 4.

Sources of Change in Marriage: Potential and Actual

While the French legal court is not often used by women, it does represent a kind of potential that could be tapped more frequently if women so desired. One might ask why it is that so few women avail themselves of divorce in this new institution. I believe there are a number of reasons. First, while women sometimes do hope to end a marriage, often what they want is recognition of a legitimate grievance followed by social pressure resulting in some modification of the behavior of their husband or co-wives rather than divorce per se. In the first incident recounted above, the wife made a gesture of moving her belongings outside as if to leave her husband, when what she wanted more immediately was simply the return of her money and an assurance of his respect for her property. This assessment is consistent with the findings of historians of colonial law and women's marital rights elsewhere: women may avoid the formal courts because those courts focus less upon reconciliation and social sanctions against unacceptable behavior than upon punishment and the relatively unimpeded breaking of ties.[16]

Contrary to what one might suppose, it is not entirely in women's interests for divorce to be made more simple than it already is. In fact, most women in Maradi who want a divorce will at length get one, despite resistance from

---

[16] For another study of women's use of the colonial courts, see Mann (1982) and other studies in the same volume. In a similar vein, the judge in Maradi remarked to me that although women have a legal right to pursue child support cases in the court they rarely do so since the failure to provide such support is a punishable offense and women do not want their ex-husbands to be imprisoned, but only to exert pressure upon them to provide money for the children.

their husbands. Husbands in Maradi will occasionally thwart their wives' desire to instigate a divorce by refusing to give them a divorce paper, or by making them wait long periods of time before granting one. But this tactic, which serves primarily to humiliate and frustrate the woman, is a double edged sword, for a man who seems unwilling to give up a headstrong wife may seem to have been "mastered" by her, and will lose face if he holds out too long.[17] The most common method by which a woman can provoke a divorce is to go to her parental home for a visit and simply not return. In order to get her back the husband will have to come and get her, which will mean facing all of the kin she has managed to win over to her position. If he truly wants to make the marriage last he will have to make some kind of concessions. If he doesn't want to then he will be compelled to repudiate her himself, saving her the trouble and expense of taking the matter to the Al'kali and losing the sadaki. Women are often extremely offended if their husbands do not come to get them when they run home: the point is not to leave permanently, but to compel the husband to make concessions. If a woman runs home repeatedly then the marriage will be ended, either at the husband's behest or her kin's.

Thus the colonial court system does not in reality provide women with any power they do not already have, and can have a number of undesirable side effects, one of which, as I have said, is a dissolution of the marriage without any real effort at reconciliation. Another effect of resorting to unprecedented means to end a marriage is that one may lose the support of one's kin in later disputes or difficulties, which would not be in most women's interests. If the al'kali and sarki aren't willing to support a divorce, why should a woman's friends and kin? Resorting to colonial or postcolonial state structures is perceived to be dangerous and unpredictable, the outcome of which may be undesirable. National laws are not clearly promulgated and court procedures are mysterious to the majority of the population. The following story illustrates the risks entailed in appealing to an authority that is "foreign" and unknown.

Rabe is a commoner woman in her early sixties who was born in a rural farming village. This account of her first two marriages in the early 1940s at the time of the Vichy government's control of French West Africa highlights how new institutions made possible by the colonial situation could become elements in struggles to control marriage and women, but it also shows that those institutions could have an unexpected life of their own. In this case the structure is the judicial precursor of the "House of the Judge," for prior to 1946 court cases brought before the colonial authorities were handled by the military officer or administrator of the district rather than by a trained civilian judge.

---

[17] Thus Fatchima's husband made her wait for a year before bothering to deliver a *takarda* to her, and Zuera's husband made her wait about six months before finally giving her a *takarda*. But both women did eventually win out, showing that the virtue of "patience" can work against a marriage as well as for it. One iconoclastic commoner woman never got a formal *takarda* from her first husband in a rural marriage, and remarried twice in the city anyway. When her first husband visited her during my research and told her that even after all these years their marriage was not "dead" she retorted, "It's not over? I'm old, and you're old, what are you looking for?" (Zule, 3-9-89).

Appealing to Colonial Judicial Structures

BMC: So your first marriage was to a Koranic student?

Rabe: Yes, Sale. We lived in Karamne, where my mother lived. My father was a Muslim scholar, he would gather together students, and so they brought this Saidu to my father, and he taught him. He lived with my father until I grew up, and when I grew up [to puberty] my paternal uncle said "let's give her [to Sale] in a marriage of alms." So they washed me, and gave me to that student as alms. I stayed there one year! And then I said I didn't like it. I refused. So I ran off, I ran and ran, I set out, there was a rocky hillside way out there in the bush, there were hyenas and I don't know what else! So that's where I went.

BMC: So you didn't go to your father's house.

Rabe: That's right. I ran off, I ran off and kept going.

BMC: Did you go to your grandparents?

Rabe: Right, in another town. That was that. When I went off, there was tension between Niger and Nigeria,[18] like they might go to war, and they sent lots of soldiers along the border between Niger and Nigeria, they sent them there and had them wait. So anyway, they sent off a message to that town, back then they talked using drums, there weren't telephones. We didn't know what the tension was about, we were just village people, just that they had sent all these soldiers to the village I ran off to. And they sent my second husband there, the one I stayed with for many years.

BMC: So he was a soldier?

Rabe: Yes, he was a soldier. There we were, they sent a message that there was a young girl who had run off, and that they should take hold of me and bring me back. So, there we were, they [the military] called us in. I was shaking, I was so scared! And my maternal grandfather, whose house I had run to, he was shaking too! And they said, "Come, you are called, and bring the girl who came to stay with you." There we were, so we went to his [the military administrator's] house, and when we got to his house, he said, "Is this the girl who ran off to stay with you?" And my grandfather said yes, he was the village head then; he said, "She's the one who ran off and came to stay with us because they made her a marriage she didn't like, and she's my granddaughter, I'm her mother's father." Well, so he [the military administrator] said "Is that right? Why did they make her a marriage she didn't like?" So he said, "Well, she said she didn't like it, and they said, if she didn't accept this marriage, they would kill her." And so he [the soldier] said, "Well, will you give her to me in marriage?" And [my grandfather] said, "Yes, I will give her to you."

And that was that, so he climbed up on his horse, and he put me behind him, and we went off with the village head to my parents' village. And he said to them, "This girl, since you made her marry someone she didn't like, now I will marry her." He scared them! [She laughs.] Because he was a soldier. That was that, so they said, "Fine, since that's

---

[18]   The brief period of Vichy rule of French West Africa occasioned considerable tension between Niger and Nigeria, which as a British colony sympathetic to the Free French was enemy territory.

what you say, and she doesn't like her marriage, we drop the matter."
So he said, "So you are giving her to me [in marriage]?" And they
said, "Yes, we give her to you."
Mariama: [Rabe's co-wife, who was listening in] They gave you?! They
were really scared!
Rabe: So they said, "After three months, come and we'll do the wedding." And after three months he came back with money, and he
showed them his money, and they said "Oh no," because back then
when you did a wedding you didn't spend so much money, they didn't
take the money. So he said, "Well how much sadaki do you want?"
And they asked my father, and he said, "50 francs." So, I swear, they
did it for 50 francs! And I stayed with him for 19 years until we broke
up when they sent the troops back to their home countries at independence (Rabe, 1-21-89).[19]

What makes this a striking story, aside from Rabe's riveting storytelling
style, is the spectacle of her paternal kin trying to manipulate the power made
available by the colonial military court only to find that that power had interests of its own in the affair. This is a clear case of an attempt to manipulate a
new power to create new rights for senior males over junior females, but in
this case it backfired. Rabe was at the time a girl of perhaps fourteen, and as
young women of that age are apt to do, she decided that she was not going to
remain in a marriage to someone she did not like. Since the marriage had been
arranged by her paternal kin, she could not turn to her uncles for help. But she
could hope that her mother's senior male kin might help her, and so she set off
impetuously through what was probably very dangerous terrain to find them,
and once she got there they were indeed sympathetic. Her running off to maternal kin was socially acceptable behavior,[20] and the proper response of her
husband and father would have been to come themselves or send a representative to get her and to face the kin she had managed to win over to her side. But
her father decided instead to try to use the legal and policing infrastructure of
the colonial administration and its support for paternal control over women to
get her back, even if it meant angering or endangering his in-laws. Normal
reconciliation by coming to get a runaway wife is known as *bi'ko*; colonial structures in Nigeria as well as Niger presented senior males with a new solution,
bi'kon soji, "reconciliation through soldiers," in which the woman was returned
by force (Abraham 1962:100).

Little did her father know that young soldiers (who were often Africans
brought in from other territories), stranded as they were in strange lands with

---

[19] Prior to the 1956 *Loi-Cadre*, troops and administration in the French West African territories
were pooled. With the *Loi-Cadre* Overseas Reform Act the colonies had internal self-rule and were
more clearly differentiated, so that by the time of independence many troops from other territories
had returned home.

[20] Moroccan women may run away from their first marriages as well. Mernissi also notes a phenomenon I observed often in Maradi, namely that a woman may "forget" her first marriage altogether when recounting her life. Mernissi sees this amnesia as symptomatic of trauma (1987:112). A
rather different way to account for this, in Maradi, might be to note that such unions may have
had little significance for the bride herself, particularly given their short duration.

no kin or ties to arrange marriages for them, could use the same structures for
their own ends. Rabe's future husband was a native of Chad who, on the pretext of defending the rights of a girl married against her will, ensured that he
himself could marry.[21] Conspicuously absent in her narrative is any query from
any of the male figures as to whether she herself was interested in this new
marriage, which nevertheless proved to be a very happy one. She had as little
choice in her second marriage as in her first, just better luck. To her paternal
kin's credit, however, despite their fear they insisted upon a formal divorce
and remarriage, and rather than accept an unusually high sum of money as
her bridewealth (which might have been difficult to repay had she attempted
to divorce her Chadian husband later, and which might have suggested slavery) they ensured that the sum was reasonable by local standards. The incident damaged her relations with her paternal kin permanently, but she retained
ties with her maternal kin, who came to live with her later when she lived
alone in Maradi in the house which her soldier husband provided for her before returning to his homeland. One can well understand why most men and
women have tended to prefer more familiar mediational institutions, whatever
they may feel about the traditional authorities such as the sarki and al'kali
personally.

Miles has recently argued that "In French Hausaland, colonial administrators assumed much of the onus of meting out justice themselves, with the corresponding denigration of the indigenous judicial system. The Napoleonic code
prevailed over Koranic shari'a" (Miles 1994:289). This assessment seems, at the
very least, to be an overstatement, and one that obscures the complexity of
actual judicial practice in the Maradi region. Certainly Miles is correct that in
British Nigeria shari'a courts were quite deliberately recognized and employed
within the colonial structure. In French West Africa administrators were, as I
shall argue more fully in Chapter 4, alternately seduced and repulsed by Islamic law. While the existence of the colonial court certainly altered the judicial terrain, it neither fully eliminated Islamic judicial practices nor entirely
supplanted other fora for mediating disputes. To the contrary, I would argue
that French intrusions into the judicial realm had in fact a number of quite
different, and unexpected consequences. Because most Hausa encountered
French law first and foremost through the indigénat code which, as Jean Suret-
Canale observes, "consisted of giving the administrative authorities the right
to impose penalties on subjects without having to justify their action before
any judicial authority" (1971:331), the local population had a poor opinion of
French "law" in general. Consequently rather than replace or eliminate local
judicial authorities and legal discourses, the excesses of French intrusion in
fact guaranteed that such indigenous authorities would continue to be important as an alternative (even resistant) locus for dispute mediation. Furthermore
the preference for codified law among French administrators tended to shift

---

[21] Because Hausa peasants avoided military recruitment by crossing the border into Nigeria, military recruiters in the Maradi region often signed "Nigérien" recruits who were in fact Sara peasants from Chad (Echenberg 1991:75).

the legal discourse of the region not towards the Napoleonic code but rather towards the Maliki law already available as a resource. French rule thus neither eliminated the salience of indigenous judicial practices nor replaced local judicial discourses altogether. Rather than reducing law to one codified form, colonial intrusion in fact contributed to the uncertainty and instability of judicial understandings of marriage by generating new loci of dispute resolution and by recognizing Maliki law, the Napoleonic code, and uncodified *justice indigène* all as potential discursive resources for defining local practice.

Marriage in Maradi has been altered less by direct colonial imposition than by a number of processes set in train by colonial rule and the intrusions of the international economy. The growth of the cash crop economy, the subsequent rise of a powerful merchant class, and the development of education, transport, and marketing infrastructure have played a much more significant role in the shaping of marriage practices in the region. The state's intrusions into the judicial realm did, indeed, contribute to unpredictable transformations of marriage, however it was in the domain of land transfers and inheritance governed by Maliki law (rather than marriage law proper) that colonial rule had important and quite unintended implications for marriage, as we shall see in Chapter 4. More common than such state-initiated transformations have been adjustments to marriage made by the men and women of Maradi themselves as they struggle to accommodate the demands of a rapidly changing political economy by moulding the understanding of marriage to meet the new needs, constraints, and opportunities of the productive arena. Such adaptive transformations have tended to amplify and reinterpret features of the discursive terrain that were already available in some residual or emergent form, features that had not been emphasized in the recent past. Thus, as we shall see in the following chapter, an understanding of female dependency in marriage resident in Maliki law and implicit in Katsinawa marriage practices enabled the relatively recently Islamized rural population to meet the growing demands upon the agricultural economy. By embracing this ideology, husbands could accommodate the demands of new cropping patterns and wives could seize upon new commercial opportunities. The implications of invoking female dependency have been, as one might expect, highly contradictory for women.

3

Ambiguities of Dependency: Negotiating Land and Labor in a Shifting Agricultural Economy

Much of the literature on farming among the Hausa focuses on the *gandu* as a means of recruiting, organizing, and controlling dependent male labor. The term *gandu* has been used by researchers and development specialists to refer both to a relationship of dependency between individuals (whether junior males to senior males, slaves to owners, or peasants to aristocrats) and to the farm production unit in which such individuals are assumed to work, live, and eat. These usages are not entirely inconsistent with Hausa expression in Maradi, for a young man, particularly in the first half of this century, might often be said to be "in *gandu*" with his father, meaning that he worked his father's land under his father's supervision, while a large farm enterprise was, at least until recently, referred to as "so-and-so's *gandu*." However as Christine Wallace pointed out in her classic critique of the literature on *gandu*, the precise relationships between labor and land, production and consumption have not been sufficiently explored:

> Smith says a *gandu* is a production unit and also a consumption unit, Norman assumes all consumption units are production units. Hill separates the two units but does not explore the relationship between the two. Goddard says a *gandu* may or may not be a consumption unit. These assumptions have meant that most research has failed even to ask the question about the relationship between production and consumption in Hausa society (1978:140).

Wallace goes on to point out the practical implications of this lack of clarity about how actual farm units operate; who performs what labor; how land is acquired, named, and distributed; and how labor is compensated. She finds that, contrary to the expectations of the planners of the Kano River Project, senior men do not have automatic access to large quantities of family labor, and may have to hire junior male labor.

In a subtle and perceptive study of the transformation of the production system in Maradi, Claude Raynaut (1976) traces the shifting senses of the word *gandu*. For a variety of reasons the collective *gandu* field once farmed by members of an extended household under a senior male (the *mai gida*) has ceased to be a collective field for the entire household, while the household itself has become a smaller unit under a single married man, his wives, and their children. Where once the *gandu* field would have contributed to the needs of several married men and their respective wives and children under a single *mai gandu*, today virtually every married man is the head of his own *gandu* to meet the tax and subsistence needs of his immediate family. Emphasizing the rise of commercial transactions involving goods, labor, and land, and pointing to the impoverishment of the rural productive base as urban entrepreneurs with greater access to cash intervene in the production system, Raynaut (like Christine Wallace) notes the growing importance of hired labor as senior males lose control of junior male labor. In Raynaut's analysis global forces external to local configurations of power and culture serve as the primary mechanisms prompting social transformation. As he himself observes, his analysis does not make clear whether or how the transformation he describes can also be seen to be driven by forces and stresses intrinsic to the local productive system. Only analysis on this level, he suggests, could account for the striking recurrence of gender issues in his discussion of the family and village economy (1976:306).

In this chapter I will address not the familiar, if important, relationship between *gandu* and junior male labor; rather I will discuss how the changing uses of *gandu* and *gamana* plots in the Maradi region reflect renegotiations of female labor, female access to land, and the obligations of marriage. Focusing on how men and women have been differently situated within a shifting political economy helps to shed light on both the question of the relationship between production and consumption in the *gandu* and on the problem of why male/female relations figure so prominently in local level conflicts. In nineteenth-century Maradi, *gandu* land was used to meet taxes, rainy season seed and food needs, security reserves, and exchange needs of the entire farming household. Women were responsible for meeting the dry-season subsistence needs of the household sub-units through family *gamana* plots. Under French colonial rule the increasing demands upon the product of the *gandu* plot controlled by the senior male of the household led to the growth of peanut cropping and the expansion of the area under cultivation in the region. The product of the *gandu* field came to be used not only for the many cash needs of the household, but also for the food needs of the farm unit throughout the year.

Increased female labor upon these "communal" lands was justified through an ideology of female dependency in marriage reflecting spreading northern Nigerian understandings of Islam. In this new formulation it was the duty of

Photo 2: "A young Hausa woman bringing her husband his meal" ("Jeune femme Haoussa allant porter son repas à son mari"). Late colonial–no date, no contributor. Courtesy of the French National Archives, Centre des Archives d'Outre-mer. 31F12S (60.3)

the Muslim husband to provide the food needs of his wife throughout the year. Thus her contribution to the *gandu* fields was entirely at his disposition, while the product of the *gamana* plot was entirely at her own disposition. With increasing fragmentation of farm units, the *gandu* plot has come to be understood not as a communal plot, but as the plot controlled by the male household head, while *gamana* plots are seen as the private enterprises of wives and dependents. This arrangement has had ambiguous consequences for women: by entering into marriages that define them as dependents, women have gained access to independent sources of income; but they have at the same time undermined the key justification for female access to land–women's role in feeding their families. As a consequence women's access to land in the region is becoming highly contested on precisely those grounds which gave women control of the *gamana* product in the first place, namely female dependency in marriage.[1]

The Normative Farming Household: *Gandu* and *Gamana*

The precolonial farming pattern in the valley is difficult to reconstruct, for there are few references to agriculture in the available sources. What one can reconstruct is what I shall call the "Normative Farming Arrangement," namely the system as described by early ethnographers and elderly informants: a kind of ideal type that purportedly obtained at the turn of the century and against which current farming arrangements are measured. This then is the system recorded by Guy Nicolas, an anthropologist who first worked in the Maradi region in the 1960s.[2] Elderly women who farmed in the early decades of this century describe agricultural production in this period in terms very close to Nicolas's, and there is no apparent reason to assume that they are incorrect (Atu, 8-29-89; 'Yar Fatake, 8-30-89; Zule, 3-9-89; Hajjiya Gaba, 3-10-89; Hajjiya Mai Gobarci, 11-16-89).

The "normative" structure of the farming unit was that of an extended family, with the head of the farm, or *mai gandu*, presiding over several junior adult males and their wives and children. One large *gandu* field was farmed by all the adult labor (male and female) of the household and the harvest was stored to ensure the subsistence of the unit during the follow-

---

[1]   Coquery-Vidrovitch points out that Akan women's willingness to press men to take responsibility for their biological children as dependents (contrary to matrilineal principles) has had similar costs: shifting the burden to their spouses has threatened married women's autonomy (1994:145). See also Robertson (1984). The temptation to place the responsibility for family expenses upon men creates interesting contradictions for Muslim women elsewhere in Africa; see Callaway and Creevey (1994:83–84).

[2]   While G. Nicolas describes in great detail the world of the Arna in the ethnographic present, it is clear from his occasional remarks that much of what he describes no longer held true at the time he was writing, in the late 1960s and early 1970s (1975:93–96). See also PM/PDRM 1986:63. These descriptions accord fairly well with J. Greenburg's findings on the Maguzawa, the non-Muslim farming population of northern Nigeria (1966:17–18).

ing agricultural season. The *gandu* granary provided the seed and the food
necessary to maintain the household during the following rains, although
part might be sold to meet the *ku'din kai* head tax to be paid to the aristocratic class. It also served as the security reserve should there be a crop
failure in the following season. The *gandu* head (*mai gandu*) would also allot
each of the sons or junior males (which in a relatively prosperous farming
unit might presumably include male slaves) a field with which to feed his
wives and children during the non-agricultural season, fields known as
gamana. Sometimes the son, younger brother, or slave might allot his wife a
small plot within his own so that she could grow something for her own
purposes. This was known as a *gamana*-within-the-*gamana*. The four days
allotted each week for communal labor on the *gandu* field were known as
kwanakin maza or "men's days," and the three days remaining for working
the *gamana* were known as *kwanakin mata*, or "women's days," since it was
primarily the wife's labor (and one would suppose female slave labor, although Nicolas and others leave slaves entirely out of the account) that ensured the *gamana* production (G. Nicolas 1975:93, 232, 292).

Such, then, is the account of turn-of-the-century farming arrangements
in Maradi commonly provided in secondary sources today and ratified by
the remarks of older women. This normative *gandu* organization is found
only rarely today in Maradi and it is difficult to know to what degree it was
actually followed in the past. All that can be said with any certainty is that
today farming units tend to consist of a husband, his wives, and their unmarried children in something close to a nuclear family structure.[3] There is
a widespread perception as well as strong supporting evidence that both
farm land and farming units are becoming more fragmented and individu-
alized over time. Because today more individuals may make claims upon
that land, the number of individual parcels increases, and the size of each
parcel diminishes. While prior to the 1970s the assumption of unchanging
area of land over time would be unrealistic because it was possible for
nuclear sub-units to clear new land for themselves, today the degree of saturation of the arable land is very high and clearing new land is no longer
possible. Instead households increase the available land area by reducing
or eliminating fallow periods on older land.[4]

The *gandu*, which in normative terms ensured household reproduction
during the rainy season and in times of food shortage, is today regarded as the
husband's field. Current norms insist that the husband is responsible for feeding and clothing his wives and children; consequently, the *gandu* production is
expected to meet the needs of the household throughout the entire year and

---

[3]   See for example Raynaut's observations of the village of Serkin Haoussa in the late 1970s (PM/
Raynaut 1977:413).

[4]   Of course the degree of saturation of the land in the region varies greatly within the Maradi
department and particularly according to soil type. All of the best *jigawa* land in the Maradi region
is occupied at a rate of 70 percent or higher. Researchers at the Projet Maradi found that where
rates of occupation were lower the soils were unsuitable for agriculture (PM/G.R.I.D 1988:71, see
also 33–41, and Map 14 on p. 72).

not simply during the agricultural season (Steverlynck 1984:5). As a result the *gamana* fields, which are now regarded primarily as women's fields (although unmarried junior males also occasionally farm a *gamana* plot), are in theory wholly at the disposition of the wife. The *gandu* production frequently cannot meet the needs of the household throughout the year and, as a result, the *gamana* production must be called upon to meet subsistence needs. Nonetheless women generally regard the *gamana* product as their own to be used for whatever purposes seem best to them.

With the greater demands upon the *gandu* product–not only to ensure reproduction during the rainy season but during the rest of the year as well, to meet the taxes of all the members of the household, and to provide the husband with his own personal income–the competition between individuals in a household over land and the income to be derived from its product is likely to be intense. The greater demands upon the *gandu* product are, however, counterbalanced in part by a greater emphasis on that field in terms of days collectively labored on it and by its greater area and quality relative to the female *gamana* plots. Thus while normatively the number of "men's days" is four and the number of "women's days" is three (numbers associated with gender and of broader cultural significance), in practice today the number of days worked on the respective fields varies enormously, and may not be set out in any systematic way.[5]

The altered farming arrangement visible today presents us with a number of questions. Why has there been a tendency towards land fragmentation? Why and how have women come to have control of the *gamana* product? And finally, given the French administration's general lack of interest in the details of local productive practices, is it plausible that these shifts have been engineered "from above?" In order to address these questions we need to set out the conditions of life for farmers under colonial rule, particularly the rise in tax and labor exactions and the characteristics of colonial law.

The remainder of this chapter will be devoted to setting out how these shifts in structure have emerged in conjunction with a redefinition of the rights and obligations of men and women in marriage. While no single cause can be adduced to account for the changing production pattern and the correlative recasting of marital relations, a number of interrelated phenomena seem to have contributed to the emergence of the current arrangement, including changing inheritance patterns under Katsinawa and colonial rule, the rapid growth of commercialization of peanuts and other crops beginning under French colonial rule, and opportunities for women to take advantage of the increasingly monetized economy.

---

[5] PM/PDRM 1986:47; PM/Issa 1981:5; PM/de Miranda 1979:72. Discussions with women from throughout the Maradi region who farmed between 1930 and the present suggest that the division of the week varied regionally and with the size of the household: thus I found that by the late 1950s in villages south of Maradi, a large household close to the normative structure might adhere to a division of 4 days *gandu*, 2 days male *gamana*, 1 day female *gamana*, where in a smaller household in the same region the division might be 4 days male *gandu*, 3 days female *gamana* (Hajjiya Indo, 11-14-88; Zule, 3-9-89).

Colonial and Postcolonial Exactions

The heavy obligation endured by the peasants in French territory is a
consistent theme in Fuglestad's history of colonial Niger. . . . The poll
tax seems to have doubled in one year (1914–15) and tripled in the
decade from 1906 to 1916. It doubled again in the second half of the
1920s, rose 60 percent during the Vichy regime (with further increases
after the Gaullists assumed power), and skyrocketed sevenfold between
1946 and 1951. Not only was the postwar tax rate higher in Niger than
elsewhere in French West Africa, but even within Niger tax rates were
consistently and significantly higher in Hausaland than elsewhere in
the colony (Miles 1994:193).

The heavy burden of colonial taxation for the Hausa in Niger has, as Miles
nicely summarizes, been amply demonstrated. While the British in Nigeria were
largely content to leave peasants to raise cash through cash cropping on their
own farms, the French intruded into the local economy far more forcefully by
setting up obligatory peanut production on "government fields" through forced
labor (Miles 1994:185), by insisting that local farmers contribute large portions
of their crop to *greniers de reserve* (reserve granaries), and by requisitioning crops
and labor arbitrarily (Roberts 1981:201; APM/"Rapport annuel, Cercle de
Maradi, 1947"; APM/ "Rapport économique, Cercle de Maradi, 1948"; Hajjiya
Indo, 11-14-88). One feature of the taxation system was particularly burdensome: unlike peasant farmers in Nigeria, the male household head in Niger
had to pay head taxes for his wives and male children (Miles 1994:191). While
the French administration tended to read the severe famines that resulted from
its disastrous policies in 1913–14 and again in 1931 as evidence of the "improvidence of the natives," in fact colonial policy consistently undermined local drought management practices (AOM/200 Mi 1698 2G22:16; Grégoire
1986:131; J. Egg et al. 1975:33; Raynaut 1975:12, Roberts, 1981:199). Local farmers had to be resourceful to find ways to minimize the demands upon them for
cash, particularly taxes, while maximizing their access to labor to meet their
tax needs. The fragmentation of landholdings resulted, thus, in part from a
strategy on the part of household heads to reduce the tax burden they faced to
pay the taxes of their junior male dependents. By permitting younger men to
set up independent households on family land, older men could shift tax burdens to juniors. For their part junior men may have preferred such an arrangement, for it would have enabled them to benefit individually from the growth
of the agricultural economy so long as good land remained.

The increasing cash demands placed upon the local population to meet
colonial taxes could only be met through increased sales of agricultural products. While at first the government promoted cotton, by 1922 the administration had begun promoting improved peanut seed. Some trade firms began to
take an interest in the region in the early 1920s; between 1934 and 1937 three
large European commercial houses had set up in Maradi to export peanuts and
to import consumption goods such as processed foods and cloth (Grégoire
1986:60). Peanut prices fluctuated in the following decades, dropping during

the Depression until 1932, when government protective measures bolstered the peanut market and production become once again profitable in the region (ANN/14.2.3; AOM/FOM 141/98; Collion 1982:294–97). The market stagnated during World War II, and farmers returned to millet, because, as one farmer explained to the local administrator on tourney, "you can always sell millet. If you can't sell it, it's never a loss, since it's our main food" (ANN/14.3.59). However the Vichy government and later de Gaulle's AOF forced increases in production of both peanuts and millet (Collion 1982:298; Campbell 1975). It is probably at this time that the expressions *gonan gwammnetti* (the government's field) and *gonan l'impot* (the tax field) emerged to describe peanut fields grown to meet government demands.[6]

With the boom in peanut production, Maradi became deficient in grain beginning in 1960 (Raynaut 1975:16; Péhaut 1970:37). While the price of millet stagnated from 1948 to 1970, producer prices for peanuts were relatively high until the 1960s when they began to drop progressively (Roberts 1981:204; Grégoire 1986:92-94). With increasing tax demands and dropping crop prices, the amount of peanuts an individual farmer had to sell to meet taxes alone rose progressively from 17 kg in 1948, to 27 in 1959, to 90 kg in 1971 (PM/ Brasset et al. 1984). Increased production was effected by increasing the area under peanuts, reducing millet production, and extending cultivation into previously pastoral zones which under ordinary rainfall conditions could not have been cultivated. The expansion into such areas contributed to agricultural failure during the disastrous Sahel Drought of 1968–1974.

Very little concrete evidence on how women participated in farming prior to World War II remains, since the colonial administrators, preoccupied as they were with problems extracting taxes while preventing out-migration from the region, took little interest in the actual organization of production. Although the documents tell us little about how production was organized, they do carp on the difficulty of preventing Hausa speakers in Niger from escaping tax and labor exactions by slipping over the border into Nigeria. The theme of migration suggests that Maradi's farmers resisted the demands of the state and that those demands resulted in a heightened need for female labor for state projects and to meet tax needs. Nigerian officials documented this movement with a more sympathetic eye than their counterparts in Niger, noting the evidence that women, in particular, were being used for forced labor: "It is alleged that they [the migrants] are dissatisfied because of demands made on them for labor, particularly the seizing of their women folk at Maradi" (Miles 1994:80). A popular song cited by Miles evokes this aspect of colonial rule:

The whiteman said, "Even the Arab, the learned man, the soldier,
The soldiers' wives, married women (what an infidel!)
Tell them that they are not exceptions."

---

[6] Women who were children during the war often recalled being hidden from administrators and soldiers by their elders so they couldn't be taken off to do forced labor. Attempts to meet heavy demands for peanuts and other crops caused the clearing of new land, and children were given small hoes to help weed the fields (Dije Mai Waina, 8-29-89).

Young girls selling snacks, butchers, peddlars,
Cripples and blind men and lepers,
Even the old woman selling groundnuts,
Baudot [Bordeaux] would not spare (Miles 1994:103).[7]

However, the demand for female labor came not simply from the colonial state, but from male heads of household facing increasingly onerous tax demands, a burden that could only be met through sales of the principal cash crop, peanuts. Men sought therefore to gain as much control of family labor as possible, while simultaneously working to reduce their tax responsibilities. The outcome was a pattern of fragmentation of holdings combined with increasing demands upon the labor of wives.

Women and the Distribution of Farm Labor and Produce

The new pattern of distribution and demands upon the *gandu* and *gamana* product over the course of the year appears to be a hybrid of Islamic and Arna norms. Like the alteration in inheritance norms to be discussed in the following chapter, this shift resulted partly from the growing adoption of the household arrangements of the Katsinawa urban elite (further promoted by the emphasis of the French upon regularized Maliki law to govern disputes), and partly from the emulation of successful Muslim merchants in the urban centers of southern Niger and northern Nigeria. In the normative Arna model, the *gandu* product serves as reserve and sustains the household during the agricultural season. It is the *gamana* that is expected to feed the nuclear sub-units of the household during the dry season. With the increasing influence in Niger of the regularized Maliki norms common in northern Nigeria, men are expected to provide their wives' subsistence and clothing throughout the year, failure to do so constituting grounds for divorce.[8] Thus, while women may still have access to a *gamana* plot, their husbands are expected to provide the full year's subsistence through the *gandu* product.[9] The following response by one rural woman in her mid-fifties to my question "Is the *gandu* crop used to feed the family during the agricultural season?" shows how closely the use of the crops is tied to current understandings of the obligations of marriage and suggests that those obligations may be differently interpreted by different men:

---

[7]   Bordeaux was the French commandant in Zinder.

[8]   Thus in the *coutumier juridique* of 1933, a Muslim man is reportedly expected to feed and cloth his wife, and cannot obligate her to work fields or to draw water; neglect of these obligations would then theoretically be grounds for a woman to request a divorce before the sarki or the native court ("Coutumes haoussa et Peul" 1939:281–82, 290). In reality this characterization of local law touching on female labor represents an extreme that was probably rarely enforced until the mid-1970s. The requirement that a husband meet his wife's food needs has probably been enforced far longer, since the early 1940s.

[9]   Collion remarks that this places agriculture in Niger in a transitional stage between Maguzawa [Arna] patterns and the Muslim patterns in northern Nigeria (1982:201–202).

It depends on the household head, one might just feed you during the agricultural season, another would give his wives grain to look after to feed her children and he'd set aside the agricultural season grain separately. It's all a matter of effort and will! One husband will really take his responsibility seriously. You see, marriage is like a promise that you make with the [woman's] parents, right? One man, he makes a promise he can keep, that he really wants to keep, he will keep his promise and another, well, he won't keep it. If he keeps it, then they [the wives] can go and make use of [their own crop] for their own needs, for a celebration, or some expense, or to go to see a relative or friends, or to welcome a guest. That's how you do it (Cimma, Fura Girki, 10-15-89).

In practice the *gandu* crop is not often adequate to meet all the household's cash and food needs, and the woman's *gamana* production may be called upon to meet the deficit. Nevertheless a woman will expect to have free disposition of the *gamana* product and any cash derived from it and she may legitimately lend her husband the grain or cash needed to meet household needs at high rates of interest (Raynaut 1972:47n25). Increasingly, particularly among wealthy households or households where the husband wants to retain control over the entire product of the household land, a man may decide to seclude his wives according to Nigerian Muslim norms, as in the dispute brought before the iya described in Chapter 2. In such a case the bride and her kin will nevertheless expect him to provide his wife with an income of her own explicitly understood to be the equivalent to her potential *gamana* production (G. Nicolas and Mainet 1964:83–84; G. Nicolas 1975:417n1). An intermediate form of seclusion eliminates the woman's obligation to work the *gandu*, but she may still work a *gamana* for herself (Lévy-Luxereau 1983:40).[10] The woman quoted above no longer worked the *gandu* land at all, which her sons worked with her husband, but she continued to work her own *gamana*.

While it is clear that the shift in the use of the *gamana* crop is related to changing understandings of the marital obligations of men, it is less clear why these changes might have come about. An examination of how men and women have farmed their respective plots with the rise in colonial exactions and the growth of the peanut trade may help to explain why a change in the definition of marital obligations might have served both parties. Interviews with older women in the city of Maradi proper suggest that in the early decades of the century women's participation in agriculture varied enormously regionally and between social groups. Women born into the Gobirawa and Katsinawa aristocracy did not generally perform farm labor, although they might have had other activities through which they earned their own income, and some may have managed agricultural land (Hajjiya Gaba, 4-25-89, Mariama, 8-29-89, Hajjiya Jeka, 2-14-89, Hajjiya Aisha, 2-28-

---

[10] For example, in her first marriage c. 1955 to a *mallam*, Mariama had her own *gamana*, but did not farm his *gandu* land (2-29-89).

89, Aisha Labo, 2-1-89, Maskomi, 8-20-89, Ta Kurya, 2-18-89).[11] Women of the commoner class or living in rural villages did farm both *gandu* land and their own *gamanas* and were far more likely to suffer from the demand for female labor under colonial rule.[12]

Occasional remarks in colonial reports confirm the existence of female fields and suggest that certain crops, such as Bambara groundnuts, corn, and gourds were exclusively female crops (AOM/FOM 141/98). Women's plots probably fell into two categories, which the colonial administrators did not recognize, namely *gamana* plots used for rainy season agriculture, and less formal vegetable plots around the house used to grow crops such as corn and gourds that require manure and watering. My informants insisted that the crops grown on the *gamana* land were always identical to those grown on the male *gandu* farms, but were simply more limited in area.[13] Men might specialize in certain crops on the clay soils of the *fadama* valley land to which women were rarely given access. Crops which could be grown on this land tended to be high value non-food crops, such as tobacco, henna, indigo, and cotton. Unlike Mauri women to the west (C. Piault 1965:25, 43–45), women in Maradi seem not to have had a crop, such as Bambara groundnuts or tigernut, which was considered to be primarily female.[14] Their informal vegetable plots could nevertheless contain a wide array of crops for domestic use such as peppers, corn, and gourds grown on a very small scale next to the house. Women tended not to mention these crops unless specifically asked, since the scale of production was very limited. The corn was grown "to make the children happy," and wasn't thought of as a staple food crop.

---

[11] The one exception to this rule is rather telling: 'Yar Fatake's mother farmed land her own mother had inherited as an only child and used the produce for her fried bean cake trade (8-30-89).

[12] Thus the relevant distinction here seems not to be whether the women were "Muslim" or not, but rather where they were married. Ta Kurya's own mother lived in Maradi and did not farm, but she was raised by a paternal aunt who farmed in the rural village of Kurya (2-18-89).

[13] Women emphasized that what made male and female agriculture different was not the crop planted, but the size of their respective plots and the uses to which the harvests were put ('Yar Fatake and A'isha, 8-30-89). "If a man planted ten containers of seed, you might plant say three," (Hajjiya Ta Dogo, 2-18-89). "You would plant what you could work in your two days, it wouldn't even be half of what a man would plant" (Asabe Hassan, 8-14-89). "You just used the seeds of the household head" (Cimma and Amina, Fura Girki, 10-15-89).

[14] The comments of two non-aristocratic urban women suggest that occasionally when urban women had access to land near ponds in the valley they grew rice; when the course of the Gulbin Maradi shifted after the 1945 flood most of the ponds were "swallowed up" and the land reverted to *fadama* land worked by men (Hajjiya Ta Abu, 8-31-89; Hajjiya Ta Dogo, 2-18-89). Certain crops were understood to be male crops, perhaps because of their association with *fadama* land, particularly cotton, tree crops and root crops ("Sarkin Gobir" Fura Girki, 10-15-89; Asabe Hassan, 8-14-89). Women's memories of crops planted on the gandu in the 1940s and '50s suggest that men as well as women grew Bambara groundnuts (Atu, 8-29-89; Zule, 3-9-89). The brief spurt in their production in the early 1930s, like that of manioc, seems to have been associated with a period of heavy attacks by crickets–because Bambara groundnuts mature underground, they would have been protected (AOM/FOM 141/98). As a rule women in Maradi planted only small quantities of this crop because it wasn't very reliable (Mai Muni, 4-25-89).

Women's lack of access to the valuable clay soils of the river bed excluded them from the production of tobacco and henna, the major cash crops prior to the advent of peanut production and the later rise in commercialization of the millet and sorghum crops. If, as Guy Nicolas suggests (1975:279), the *fadama* land was little used prior to the arrival of the Katsinawa, and if the Katsinawa elite tended to exclude their women from agriculture, the pattern of male use of *fadama* land is easily understood, and it is possible that as the practice of exploiting the land spread the Katsinawa division of labor was adopted by Arna villages as well.[15] Women's exclusion from access to the *fadama* land meant that in order to earn their own income they had to process those products to which they did have access: cotton (which they spun into thread), peanuts (which they processed into cakes and oil), and grains (which was processed into cooked meals).

The most significant source of female income in Maradi in this century, as in most Hausa-speaking regions, has been the sale of processed foods in the form of meals and snacks. It is unlikely that women's sales of cooked foods is a new phenomenon, since Barth noted the sale of ready cooked foods in markets from Kano to Tessawa in the mid-nineteenth century and the earliest French administrator in the region also noted such sales at the turn of the century (Barth 1857:I:438, 532; APM/Brantonne, "Histoire, Poste El Hassan, 1901."). Nevertheless, year-round sales of cooked food call for a market center of some kind and sufficient cash or exchange within the immediate economy to warrant attempts to sell food. Consequently, women in relatively well-established and well populated villages are more likely to have success in selling food than women in more remote, cash-poor communities. In a study of women's income sources in rural areas of the Department in the late 1970s, women in the newer grain-producing villages in the north and northeast did not participate in trade in cooked foods, in contrast with women in the central peanut producing areas near Maradi and Madarumfa, where the practice "dominates overwhelmingly" (PM/Grégoire and Raynaut 1980:137). In farming communities where women take part in most aspects of the farming cycle, food sales by some women during the rainy season alleviate demands upon other women's time devoted to cooking and gathering fuel (G. Nicolas and Mainet 1964:78, 223).

Because in the late nineteenth and early twentieth centuries men could meet their cash needs through *fadama* crops in areas where such soil was available, sales of grain were resorted to only by those without access to such soil (Raynaut 1975:14). Women, perennially excluded from *fadama* production, were therefore more likely than men to rely upon sales of part of their grain crop–in either threshed or in cooked forms–to meet their cash or exchange needs. Although today women may in fact sell part of their agricultural production unprocessed, women in the past probably only sold that

---

[15]   In the Mauri case men also controlled all of the *fadama* crops, which explains somewhat women's specialization there in two crops that could be grown on *jigawa* land: Bambara groundnuts, and tigernut (Piault 1965:44).

produce once it had been transformed in some way, thus evading the stigma
attached to grain sales per se.[16] From the 1950s through the early 1970s,
with the rise in peanut production on the sandy plateau land previously
used for grain production, the possibility emerged for women to take part
in peanut production as a cash crop. However because women have been at
the periphery of networks for the distribution of new agricultural inputs
and techniques, they were far less able than men to take advantage of the
peanut trade at its peak. It continued to be the case in the late 1980s that
women sold a larger proportion of their grain crop than men, and that those
sales represented a larger proportion of their overall income than grain sales
did for men.[17] Because men have greater access to income from outside agriculture through trade and crafts than rural women, the percentage of a
male household head's total income derived from agriculture is considerably less than that for women.[18]

   The new pattern of land use whereby men control the *gandu* crop (now
responsible for feeding the family throughout the year as well as meeting the
household needs in cash to pay taxes and purchase commodities) and women
control a *gamana* plot for their own-account farming seems therefore to have
emerged out of a combination of factors. Economic pressures focused upon the
male household head from the beginning of the colonial era made the male
household head's increasing control of the *gandu* product necessary. At the same
time women's interest in farming on their own account grew as it became more
possible for them to commercialize a portion of their peanut and millet crops.
When women's *gamana* production was used to feed the entire family during
the non-farming season, women could not use that crop to sell for themselves–
they could only use their spun cotton to earn income and build social ties. Men
could not easily justify increasing the demands upon women's labor in the
gandu fields when women were already responsible for family subsistence for
much of the year.

   The adoption of a new understanding of marital obligations through a
particular reading of Islam and of female dependence therefore provided both
men and women with justification for adjusting the agricultural pattern to new

---

[16] My older informants insisted that they did not sell grain, repeating the adage "Ba a saida hatsi ba" ("One never sells grain"), but allowed that they did sell cooked food, and circulated food and threshed grain as gifts (Fatchima, 2-1-89; Ta Kurya, 2-18-89; Hajjiya Ta Dogo, 2-18-89).

[17] This picture may be changing with the rise in men's commercial grain production since the mid-1970s, increasing the relative importance of grain production and sales to men's income, how-ever I have no specific data on the subject. Raynaut suggested in 1977 that women produced 24 percent of the total millet production, but that earlier studies in 1970–71 had placed their percent-age of the overall crop higher at close to 35 percent (PM/Raynaut 1977:25). By 1979 the Service de Plan placed the percentage at slightly over 20 percent (République du Niger 1979:2,4). Neverthe-less, because rural women's income is far more closely tied to sales of agricultural produce than is men's, it is probably still true that women sell a larger proportion of their own crop, and that those sales represent a larger part of their overall income than for men (PM/PDRM 1986:66).

[18] Thus in the village of Gouraje the percentage of a woman's income derived from agriculture in 1978–79 was 29.9 percent, where for male household heads it represented only 9.6 percent (PM/PDRM 1986:67).

circumstances. While on the one hand the belief that it is the husband's responsibility to feed his wife would seem to make women more dependent upon men, paradoxically this ideology permitted women of the valley to farm on their own accounts, probably for the first time, beginning in the early 1930s. Their ability to use their farm produce for their own purposes became all the more important as their control of locally produced cotton thread and cloth declined and disappeared during the same period (Cooper 1993). The social ties that cloth could generate for them could now only be created through cloth purchased with cash on the market.

This ideology made it possible for men to emphasize the importance of the *gandu* crop, while at the same time maintaining strict control over it. The dependency of women implied their subordination to the male household head, making it more possible for him to control and redirect their labor as well as that of junior male members of the farming unit. Far from eliminating women from participation in farming, this ideology made it possible for them to participate in the economy in a new manner. As we shall see in the following chapter, women began to gain greater access to land through inheritance and purchase under colonial rule. Their new claims to farmland increased the number of claimants to the land just as the demand for land in order to meet cash needs was rising, contributing to the saturation of the arable land in the region. With increased competition for land it is becoming more likely that more men will push the ideology of female dependence in marriage to its logical extreme, placing rural women in seclusion and eliminating them from access to farm land altogether.

Despite women's significant inroads into the male economy through food sales, through their control of the *gamana* crop, and through their access to purchased and inherited land, women's control of their own labor and the product of that labor is threatened by the increasing competition for land, land fragmentation, and rising cash needs. Today, despite the prevailing Islamic norms, the degree to which a woman can control the product of her *gamana* varies enormously with the stability of the household as a whole–the poorer the household, the more likely it is that her production will be used for subsistence.[19] In a moderately well-off household, she will assist in the *gandu* production, but if her husband's granaries are adequately filled, or if he has income from outside agriculture, the *gamana* production will be hers to use as she pleases. In the wealthiest households she may not take part in the *gandu* at all and may work her own *gamana* exclusively (Lévy-Luxereau 1983:40). The *gamana* crop is highly contested and women in troubled marriages are sometimes anxious at the close of the agricultural season that their husbands will divorce them and they will lose their harvest (Steverlynck 1984:25, n. 1; Interview with the Justice of the Peace of Maradi, Abdou Mondachirou, 11-9-89). The more marginal the household, the more critical the woman's production will become to her own and

---

[19] Women prefer not to sell the entirety of their crop all at once, but to sell a little at a time as they need cash, so that they will have food supplies if they need them (Malaya, 9-4-89; Hajjiya Ta Dogo, 2-18-89).

her children's survival and the more likely it is that she will lose control of it and of her direct access to land.

The Domestication of the Female Farmer:
Subordination for Development

From the 1930s to independence various agencies have promoted new techniques that in principle might relieve women of some of the demands upon their labor and increase the productivity of the relatively small plots they tend to farm. However the efforts of the Service de l'Agriculture, the cotton industry, the cooperatives set up upon independence, and the Protestant Sudan Interior Mission were all largely unsuccessful up until the mid-1970s due to the high cost of the inputs and the failure of promoters to adapt the inputs and techniques to local conditions. It was not until the establishment of the Projet de Développement Rural du Département de Maradi in 1976 that efforts to promote the new techniques met with appreciable success due to the favorable conjuncture of lower taxes and state subsidies to new inputs, which improved the terms of trade for agriculture (PM/Grégoire and Raynaut 1980:44-45).

Far from representing a countervailing force securing women's farming enterprises and female access to land, however, the Projet Maradi (as it was known locally) contributed to the redefinition of women's rights to land through marriage, increased differentials between the rewards to men and women in farming, and supported dynamics that discouraged women's investment in improvements to their land. The aims of the Projet Maradi were multiple: to augment the productivity of the rainfed cereal crops and peanuts (to improve rural income and to keep urban food cheap); to reconstruct the herds decimated in the Sahel drought; to set up infrastructure from roads to cooperatives (to help eliminate intermediaries between producers and consumers); and to provide training in improved agricultural techniques, health and literacy (PM/Issa 1981; PM/Grégoire and Raynaut 1980). At the heart of the project were numerous "Centres de Promotion Rurale," or CPRs, which were to provide training in new techniques to villagers sent from the target communities for a nine-month training course. The CPRs were the portion of the project most likely to have an impact on the female farmer, as they were the only element bringing women directly into contact with trainers.

By 1981 the project had established twenty CPRs closely associated with cooperatives set up in the headquarters for each arrondissement. Each took in twenty couples per year, and the husband and wife were to receive training separately in men's and women's classes. The couple sent from each village was chosen by the village "assembly." Since women are not as a rule consulted for village decisions, in practice the village delegated a particular man, and his wife was sent along obligatorily. It is hardly surprising, therefore, that the women seem to have resented the increased labor burden entailed by domestic duties in a foreign setting without the help of their established food and labor exchange networks (Steverlynck 1984:13–14). While the wives of the male trainees worked fewer hours in the fields than they would have at home, they had no *gamana* of their own and they worked more hours per day than they had in the villages, and more hours than the men. Where the men sent tended to have had some primary schooling and their literacy skills improved with the training, their relatively young wives had not and they showed little improvement (PM/PDRM 1983; PM/Issa 1981:15). Men were in the classroom longer, since they did not have domestic duties. Additional training in health and hygiene intended for the women probably occurred only sporadically.[20] When the successful trainees returned to their home communities with their new ox-plow equipment provided on credit, a follow-up study revealed that the women used neither the new techniques nor the new equipment consistently on their *gamanas* and that the training they received was not passed on to other women in the villages, as had been intended (PM/Issa 1981). The study failed to reflect upon the limitations upon women's access to the new equipment and to the cooperatives through which new inputs could be purchased (Steverlynck 1984:22).

After several years of operation the project conducted a self-evaluation in 1983 and found that the CPR training was ineffective. More research was needed to adapt the equipment and techniques to local conditions, particularly to intercropping, and to the specific seed preferences of local farmers (PM/PDRM 1983). Despite the self-conscious efforts of the project to keep a close watch on how the programs were progressing, to adjust the research to meet changing priorities, and to conduct careful follow-up studies, problems with women's participation persisted. Of all fields in a household, women's *gamanas* were consistently least affected by the new techniques, and women trained in the CPRs regarded the training and equipment as being for the men (PM/PDRM 1984:53; PDRM/LeGal 1984:57). As one 1986 study remarked, "There is a lack of fit between the place women hold in agriculture and livestock raising, and their lack of participation in development efforts" (PM/U.S.E. 1986:51). The CPR training never included a *gamana* plot for each woman, which would have linked the new training clearly to the women's own farming and would have created a precedent for cooperation in the use of equipment and inputs between husbands and wives. Instead, after 1981 women were given 20 percent of the husband's share of the crop produced, a quantity intended to be the equivalent of women's *gamana* production. The implicit suggestion here was that men should take over the land women had used for the *gamana* and offer her a portion of the *gandu* crop instead. Such an arrangement would have been very much in line with the growing tendency of men to exclude women from control of family farmland altogether, while still making use of their labor.

---

[20] Even the enthusiastic supporter of CPR training, Guy Belloncle, admitted that the training for women was less than ideal and questioned why women should have been targeted for traditional home economics material when their role in production is so important. According to Belloncle, men felt that they had learned most about techniques and equipment, and literacy, while women felt they had learned most about hygiene and literacy (1984:146–47).

Women did take an interest in and employ certain portions of the training they received.[21] However, because the equipment was given to the male trainee and because the project promoted oxen (associated with men) over donkeys (which are smaller, easier to handle, and are not so closely associated with men), women assumed the equipment did not belong to them and was not relevant to their work on their own fields. Furthermore the emphasis on single cropping in the training left out women's fields, which were invariably inter-cropped.[22]

The numerous studies done by the project in the Maradi region reveal several patterns emerging in agriculture today. Farmland around villages in the region tends to fall in concentric bands around the village proper. The circle closest to the center contains the best land and the majority of the *gandu* land farmed by senior adult males in prosperous families, and is cropped intensively with little fallow; manure or fertilizer is applied wherever possible. Further out are the more extensively farmed *gamana* lands belonging to both junior men and to women, and these farms are of poorer quality and rarely receive manure despite the overwhelming tendency for the animals to belong to women (PM/U.S.E. 1986:14, 16; PM/PDRM 1986:37; Steverlynck 1984:25).[23] Men's *gandu* fields are far more likely to be single cropped than are women's fields (PM/PDRM 1986:31; PM/U.S.E. 1986). Improved seeds for peanuts and millet are limited to men's *gandu* and male *gamana* fields (PM/LeGal 1984:56). Women's parcels are rarely fertilized and are rarely worked with the new equipment. They are, therefore, more poorly maintained than men's fields, whether *gandu* or male *gamana* (PM/U.S.E. 1986:16, 19). While the labor bottleneck at planting time is met by the cooperation of everyone in the community–men help plant women's fields, and women help plant men's–the critical bottleneck at weeding is not dealt with in the same manner. Women help men in the *gandu*, but men do not necessarily help their wives with their *gamanas*; since the greatest advantage of the new animal-drawn equipment lies in its adaptation to local weeding needs, women enjoy little benefit from the new techniques if their husbands do not help them at weeding time.[24] Harvest is staggered among crops that

---

[21] Women trainees had a tendency to adhere to the suggested planting distances better than men, about 25 percent made use of fertilizer, and about 16 percent had access to the new equipment (ox-plows, seeders, and weeders for the most part) because their husbands helped them on their fields (PM/PDRM 1984:109). Women seem to have used fungicide almost as frequently as men do, partly because it is inexpensive (PM/U.S.E. 1986:24).

[22] Even urban women who otherwise seem to adopt many of the techniques available through new equipment and inputs don't seem to be interested in monocropping. Successful female urban farmers seem to use those techniques they find useful, and ignore others incompatible with inter-cropping, so they may use equipment for weeding but not for harvesting.

[23] For a similar pattern among a variety of ethnic groups in Senegal see Callaway and Creevey (1994:128).

[24] As one study notes, "the use of animal traction falls into the domain of the men, who own the equipment and apear little inclined to work their wives' plots" (PM/U.S.E. 1986:30, my translation). In general *gandu* heads work only the *gandu*, while women work both *gandu* and *gamana* (PM/LeGal 1985:25).

mature at different rates, and it therefore rarely presents significant problems; men and women often cooperate in getting the crops in. Pepe Roberts reports that women's differential access to labor has resulted in different farming practices from men, and there is "intense struggle going on between husbands and wives, household heads and subordinate labor, over the allocation of labor between household fields and women's private plots" (1988:102). Overall LeGal's observation that the means of production are increasingly concentrated in the hands of male household heads seems inescapable:

> The concentration of the means of production on plots controlled by men is obvious, leaving 15–30 percent of the land and an entire social group outside of the improvements in production. The manner of disseminating materials and training, the limited role or absence of women in development structures (the village council and the cooperatives), and their position in household production, have all eliminated women from the general trend in technical innovation (PM/LeGal, 1984:64).

However despite their near-monopoly on the new equipment and techniques, not all men are necessarily benefitting from their access to new equipment. The ownership of equipment is on the surface a sign of access of capital and credit and tends to reflect existing inequalities rather than to create new ones. On the other hand, for a farm enterprise without sufficient land to make the new techniques cost-effective, "the use of animal traction as it is currently disseminated can represent a heavy expense rather than a source of profit" (PM/G.R.I.D, 1988:155). Close examination of Projet Maradi studies suggests that a very high proportion of households that purchased the ox-drawn equipment did not have sufficient land to use it effectively.[25] Under the circumstances the failure to use the equipment on women's land is striking and dramatizes the failure on the part of both households and communities to promote rural women's interests to the benefit of the community at large. It also shows the logical outcome of the separation of women's *gamana* plots from the collective food production enterprise. Men may choose to rent out their animals and equipment on the land of other men rather than use it without remuneration on their wives' fields.

Given the expense and questionable suitableness of ox-drawn agriculture to the small plots of the region, the more relevant issues affecting women are probably their exclusion from structures of access to fertilizer, improved seeds, and training, and the monopolization of the household manure by the male *gandu* head. Women's land, since it is often already marginal, needs inputs to maintain its fertility as fallow periods are reduced. Efforts at *"animation femi-*

---

[25] Some 20 percent of the units were owned by households under the 5–10 hectare threshold at which the unit is useful, and even at 5–10 ha the units are "marginal at best" (PM/PDRM 1986). Given the failure of men to use the equipment on their wives' portion of the household land, the percentage of households underutilizing the equipment is probably even higher. The promotion of ox-drawn equipment may be inappropriate for the region in general, since 54.1 percent of all farm units have less than 5 ha of land (République du Niger 1980b).

nine" have consistently emphasized health and hygiene to the exclusion of more relevant training in agriculture and livestock raising.[26] Women's own priorities for training and development interventions are quite different from those assumed to be appropriate for them, generally reflecting women's desire to reduce the increasingly burdensome labor-time they must devote to simply reproducing the household daily: firewood is lacking in the region and women express interest in (and are willing to devote precious time to) forestry projects to grow more wood; they also want means of reducing their labor devoted to pounding grain and collecting water. Women in the Sahel are also interested in improving agricultural and livestock production (Steverlynck 1984:2; Cloud 1986:44–47; Monimart 1989:122–24). They are aware of the danger of soil deterioration, and are interested in access to improved seeds, fertilizer, and better techniques for intercropped fields.[27]

Female farmers I spoke with were very conscious of reduced yields for their crops which they attribute to soil deterioration: two women, when I asked how farming today is different from in their mothers' time or their early marriages responded:

> You grow food! But what you used to get, how could you get it today?! You don't! In the past you got what you needed to eat, but now, these days, the land is spoiled.
> Back then, you'd get 150 bundles of grain, now you only get 40, or 30. Only someone who Allah looks out for gets 50. The difference is now the yield is very small (Hajjiya Habi and Saude, Fura Girki, 10-15-89).

One might be tempted to interpret these remarks as simply nostalgia for a mythical golden era were they not reinforced by shifting cropping patterns from one generation of women to the next, as this conversation between me and two women in Fura Girki who are in their late 50s and early 60s reveals:

> BMC: What did your mother plant in her *gamana*?
> Salla: Millet, and then sorghum. Then she'd put in beans, and peanuts, and she'd plant tamso, and sorrel, and tigernut...
> BMC: Goodness, she planted a lot. Were those to sell?
> Salla: [She sold] even sesame.
> Friend: Some people still plant that, some people can get that to grow still.
> BMC: The land here must be good [strong]!
> Salla: Well, she was strong! She'd cut the sorghum, and she'd thresh it herself.
> BMC: What do you plant yourself these days?

[26] See G. Belloncle's reflections on the training for employees of animation feminine from 1973 on in administration and health rather than in agriculture and livestock raising (1980:53–54).
[27] Steverlynck 1984:17–21. Kathleen Cloud's survey of women's groups throughout the Sahel suggests that rural women and women who work for *animation féminine* in Niger communicate well, but that the women agents do not always themselves have the clout or training to effect changes in policy (Cloud 1986:45–47).

Salla: Me! I plant those things too. I plant millet, and peanuts, and sorghum.
Friend: That's not true, you don't plant aya, or tamso, like she did, you wouldn't!
Salla: Well, that's true, I don't plant those, I just plant beans, and sorrel, and sorghum, and millet.
BMC: So you don't plant sesame...
Salla: Just peanuts. Our time isn't like theirs, you know, our time has changed. Back then, whatever you planted, it would grow well. For us, now, farming has no strength, the land is spoiled now, it's lost its strength (Salla, Fura Girki, 10-15-89).

The problem for women is not simply that yields are down, but that the range of crops they can grow on the land available to them has declined. While Salla's mother, who farmed in the same village in the 1940s and '50s, could grow tamso, tigernut, and sesame to supplement the staple foodcrops of millet, sorghum, beans, and sorrel, Salla herself can only grow the staple crops (as another women cited remarked–"We grow food!") and occasionally peanuts, which eliminates the possibility of earning income from the supplemental crops and places a greater burden upon the food crop as a source of cash. Salla politely refrains from contradicting my statement that the land must be "strong" by suggesting that it was her mother who was "strong," and only a little later does she come out openly to state that the land itself has lost its strength.

Women at the time of my research particularly emphasized the drop in peanut yields, and many had given up peanuts altogether, because the fertilizers necessary for a good yield were too expensive.[28] Many were discouraged with bean production, as yields were very low with regular seed, and they didn't have access to improved varieties or the insecticides needed to protect the crop. However without crop rotation, fertilizer, or fallow periods, it is critical that women retain a variety of crops and in particular a nitrogen-fixing crop in their crop mix. These dilemmas are typical of the problems women farmers face: they are disadvantaged in terms of access to productive land, and lack the resources necessary to improve or even maintain the land to which they do have access. Despite the rhetoric of female dependency in marriage, such women frequently find themselves bearing much of the burden of feeding themselves and their children. The precarious position of women in Maradi's agricultural economy may partially account for an alarming pattern of unusually poor nutrition, growth, and health among mothers and children in the region.[29]

---

[28] Hajjiya Rabe, 2-1-89; Hajjiya Asma'u, 10-24-89. Women in Fura Girki had virtually all given up peanut production, with the exception of one woman whose brother works for the Service de l'Agriculture and who may therefore have inputs other women do not have.

[29] The poor health status of women and children in the Maradi region stands out in the 1990 demographic survey: 43 percent of children under five are underweight, and 18 percent show signs of chronic undernutrition. The region has the highest infant and child mortality rates in the country. Indices of maternal nutritional status in Maradi are not reassuring. Maternal mortality rates are, in general, extremely high in Niger relative to other African countries. République du Niger 1992:124–27, 139, 130, 153.

Given their tenuous control over land, rural women may have less interest in investing their limited capital in agricultural production than men or urban women. On the whole rural Hausa women have little interest in investing their meager income in forms over which they have little control and which are less profitable and more laborious than food transformation enterprises, as ethnozoologist Anne Lévy-Luxereau observes:

> Acquiring expensive materials and learning complex new techniques to be put to use on tiny little plots of land which, on top of everything else, belong to someone else, in order to enhance income which can be increased more effectively through food transformation–this is what seems to be embedded in women's remarks that they "don't have the money" to invest in agriculture (1983:41).

It is not that women are not interested in productive investment or in the welfare of the rural community, but rather that women, because of the fragility of their control of land, are loath to invest their income and time in forms that can be lost should their husbands divorce them or simply deny them access to *gamana* land. Women are most interested in development interventions that "they themselves can organize and manage without the intervention of men" (Steverlynck 1984:25).

While rural women may have little interest in using their income to invest in intensive agriculture, urban women seem to take an increasing interest in just such investments. Urban women who gain access to land tend to use it in much the same way that urban men do, hiring labor and purchasing inputs. Urban women, ironically, are in a better position to use their full harvest for consumption, because they have other sources of cash income and can therefore use their harvest to protect themselves from price swings in grain.[30] Rural women's limited sources of cash places a much higher burden upon their harvest as a source of income. For the rural economy as a whole, it has only been through access to income from outside agriculture that it has been possible to invest in agriculture (PM/PDRM 1986:73). The following example, admittedly an exceptional one, illustrates how a successful urban woman takes part in the rural economy:

> Hajjiya Asma'u is a well known peanut oil producer in Maradi in her sixties. She was raised in the city of Maradi by her paternal aunt after her parents divorced when she was small. Although she visited her mother, who remarried and farmed in the nearby village of Garin Mokoyo, she herself did not take part in agriculture. In her first and second marriages in the city she used her peanut oil trade to earn money, and was very successful. In the late 1950s when her mother died, she renewed her ties with her half-brother in Garin Mokoyo, and he began to provide her with peanuts for her oil production. Her second husband's resistance to her taking up farming in her half-brother's

---

[30] Urban women who manage farms often mention the high cost of purchasing grain; in a sense farming is a way of retaining a greater portion of their income from other sources by eliminating the need to purchase grain (Hajjiya Aisha, 2-28-89; Asabe Hassan, 1-21-89).

village contributed to their divorce in 1961. "My younger brother kept saying to me, Hajjiya, why don't you buy some farm land to use, since you use peanuts? And so I had them look around for me for someone who would sell to me." Today she has three fields of her own she purchased, one lent to her *aro* by her older brother, and seven she uses in exchange for *jingina* loans. She intercrops millet, beans, peanuts, and sorghum. She has invested some of her oil income in farm equipment and animals, and owns two vehicles to transport herself, her sons and workers, and her crops from village to town. She uses the peanuts for her production, sells the beans, and uses the grain to feed her numerous sons and their wives, who work for her in her various enterprises. Her younger brother clearly benefits from her access to labor and cash, while she benefits from his presence in the village and his access to the local cooperative.

Clearly Hajjiya Asma'u, thanks to her access to non-farm income, has an ability to farm in ways which many rural woman cannot. She also has control over a very sizeable labor force because of her ability to treat her numerous sons as clients rather than to be a dependent herself. By means of her extensive holdings and farming enterprise, Hajjiya Asma'u emulates male urban farmers, and it is possible that aside from any other profit she obtains from this farming, her status as a "big woman farmer" alone would make farming worthwhile since it places her on a par with successful male traders in the city. The ways in which she can farm and her motives for doing so contrast sharply with those of most rural women. The diversity of her income-generating enterprises buffers from the vagaries of both the urban and the rural economies. She has used her investments to place her brother and sons in a subordinate position, and it is she who is responsible for providing for them, rather than vice-versa. This ambitious enterprise is possible because she has taken advantage of the new availability of land through purchase, and has been successful in defining her relations with rural kin in such a way as to gain access to family land through them. As a married woman she is, in principle, the dependent of her scholarly husband, a man of rather modest means who confesses readily that it was his wife who financed his trip to Mecca. In practice, obviously, it is Hajjiya Asma'u herself who acts as the "masculine" *mai gida* or household head in this marriage, unlike most Maradi women, who are dependents in their husbands' homes. While Hajjiya has enjoyed unusual success, some of the strategies she has pursued, particularly the acquisition of real property, have been common to many urban women. In the following chapter we shall explore how and why women have come to gain access to land in freehold, and the implications of emerging land tenure arrangements for gender and marriage.

4

From Migrant to Mai Gida

Women as Perennial Migrants

It is paradoxical that in a society in which women's mobility is so strictly controlled by seclusion, women are, in a way, permanent migrants. This is necessarily the case, given the fact that marriage is virilocal (Pittin 1984:1298).

A girl should sit quietly, talk softly, cover her head, and never disagree with a male. "Ba ki gani ke mace ce, she [sic] namiji ne," meaning "Can't you see you are a woman while he is a man?" (and thus superior) is a refrain repeated to her from her earliest years. She will also hear "Ke mace ce, gidan wani zaki" ("After all, you are a woman and you are going to someone else's house"), or "Komai abinki, gidan wani zaki" ("No matter what you do you are going to someone else's house"). (Callaway 1987:29–31)

Postmodern theory with its emphasis on the dislocation of the contemporary subject loses sight, at times, of the ways in which some subjects (notably slaves, traders, and women in virilocal marriages) have been constituted in dislocation well before the present moment. In a sense, the inherited location of most Hausa women has for centuries been a state of perennial dislocation.[1] Women's life histories, today as in the past, are often geosocial maps of their marital careers, for with each new marriage a woman moves into an entirely new household, and it that new locale largely defines the parameters of her social, economic, and spiritual world.[2] A girl moves from the home of her parent or guardian to her marital home at puberty, usually between thirteen and fifteen years old. She will remain in that home until she is divorced, widowed, or dies; the fragility of Hausa marriage generally ensures that she will be divorced at least once before she is too old to remarry. If she is divorced or widowed she will

---

[1]   Echard (1991:210) refers to Hausa women in Adar as "transients." Schmidt points out that the subordination of young wives in Shona marriage in the nineteenth century was closely linked to their status as outsiders (1992:16–19).

[2]   Deborah Pellow (1991) illustrates how important a shift in milieu can be for a woman's experience of marriage and work.

return temporarily to her paternal or maternal kin while awaiting a new marriage, and once remarried she will move into her new husband's home.

A Hausa woman has no permanent claim to a place in her father's home, and will be pressured to remarry as soon as a suitor can be found. A woman may chose to live among other women in a "House of Women" as a *karuwa* (courtesan/prostitute), but until recently the option of living on one's own outside marriage without the temporary but very real stigma of courtesanship was unavailable. Before about 1945 most Hausa women in the Maradi region moved through life dwelling in the homes of male kin or affines in arrangements of greater or lesser durability, and while a woman might enter into courtesanship temporarily between marriages, marriage was considered the normal state for a woman. Without an original or final "home," women are in a sense condemned to perpetual motion, for their primary means to advance their social position, as Renée Pittin argues (1979), is their movement into and out of different marriages: marriage and divorce then become a kind of ongoing career through which women progressively negotiate better material and social conditions.[3]

This is necessary because women have until recently only rarely succeeded in becoming the "owners" or "masters" of the compounds in which they reside. For a man full adult status is achieved when he becomes the "master of the house," or *mai gida*, and one might remark: "an yi masa gida" ("they built him a house") to mean "he has recently been married." The corresponding expression for the recent marriage of a woman, "an yi mata mahalli" ("they made a place of residence for her"), underscores her provisional membership in the household. Most women can expect only to be mistresses of the rooms in which they store their wedding gifts and sleep. Because this small female space (the *'daki*) within a larger male space (the *gida*) is the only locale in which a wife in such a household has any real claim to privacy and self-expression, women devote enormous quantities of time, money, and energy to creating pleasing and impressive "homes" within these residences.[4]

The warmth and wealth revealed in this room through the display of many and various wedding gifts serves to remind a woman's co-wives that she is loved by others and is as worthy of respect as they. It invites the bride's husband to spend time with her while demonstrating to him visually her ties to others outside the *gida* should he be tempted to mistreat her. This impressive display of "things for the room" is the bride's to keep if the marriage should break up, often constituting a woman's most significant store of wealth. Women

---

[3]   Seeing movement into and out of marriage as a kind of career vitiates assumptions that the marriage system itself automatically relegates women to subordination and inactivity. Compare Callaway and Creevey, *Heritage of Islam*, 99.

[4]   The importance of women's spaces to their self-definition in marriage may account for the importance of women's decorative arts elsewhere. See Coquery-Vidrovitch (1994:347). For a fuller descriptive study of Hausa women's decorative arts in Niger see Fala (1988). I must thank Alice Burmeister for this reference; I look forward to her own study of Hausa women's wealth display with anticipation.

rely upon this moveable property to carry them over during times of stress and homelessness, particularly between marriages. By selling this "dowry" women can generate capital to invest in some form of income-producing activity or simply to live on in case of widowhood or divorce. As Enid Schildkrout has noted, the "things for the room" is "a form of exclusively female property which constitutes capital, savings, and insurance for women in a male-dominated society" (1982:64).

While the creation of a female "room" through the giving of gifts has a long history in this region, the contents and form of that gift exchange have of necessity shifted over time. As we shall see in the following chapter, over the course of this century women have been caught up in a scramble to earn cash income in order to continue furnishing the "things for the room" and other gifts. The value of the gifts and their social significance must keep pace with the market and the evolving sense of what constitutes wealth in a changing world. Today a woman's room is decorated with imported goods and an array of icons of modernity, from clocks to televisions, all of which bespeak her own and her mother's ability to earn cash income.

The control of "dowry" helps women maintain links with the world outside the *gida* through trade and gift exchange, enabling women to sustain the network of social relations necessary to protect them both within and outside of marriage. The vast majority of a woman's "things" are given to her by her mother and other female friends and kin, and the bride herself has usually worked assiduously throughout her childhood to help earn the money to buy and save her own dowry. Once she is married the fruits of her childhood labor transform her marital home, her internal domestic space, into an internal public space with links with the world beyond the *gida*. As a woman matures and has children of her own, those children serve as the intermediaries between her and other spaces. Children buy the inputs she needs for her enterprise (often selling cooked food), and then sell the finished products outside the home, either in the marketplace or door to door. Thus while a woman may remain in her marital home, her children—her daughters in particular—connect her with the market and with information networks outside her marital home. She and her children transform some of her "things" into working capital, which in turn generates income for immediate purchases, for investment in gifts to maintain ties with friends and kin, and for investment in the girls' own dowry. The maintenance of this gift exchange is a critical means by which women breach the spatial limitations of virilocal marriage, transforming their productive ability into social assets that can protect them in times of stress.[5] By converting their assets into social ties women can renegotiate the significance of the boundaries (both spatial and social) that surround them. These "things," serving as insurance, capital, and savings, are critical to women in the Hausaphone region largely because marriage is so fragile.

---

[5] For a fuller historical discussion of women's gift giving and the importance of the social ties it creates, see Cooper (1993).

Fickle Marriage: Marriage as Career

Women's perception of the fragility and unpredictability of marriage is captured in Hajjiya Jeka's observation, discussed in the Introduction, that today marriage is "like a *faifai*," fickle and changeable. Jeka's condemnation of this changeableness is somewhat ironic since she herself went through four marriages, only one of which ended with her husband's death. The *faifai* is the quintessential female implement, covering over the calabash so important in turn-of-the-century female gift exchange. Together the *faifai* and calabash evoke the closure of the womb and the abundance of food produced by women: the internal business of production and reproduction made external in consumption and public display. Appropriately, women's powers are resident in the symbol of the *faifai*, for women (including Jeka) have been active participants in the shaping of marriage in Maradi. It will be useful here to set out Jeka's marital history to illustrate some of the changes in marriage practices during this century and some female attitudes and beliefs about marriage. Like most women, Jeka's marital history is intimately related to her income generating history.

In her first marriage at age twelve Jeka was married to an urban merchant-farmer, with whom she had four children while conducting a trade in cooked food from within seclusion. After about ten years, however, she found that the marriage was "failing to take hold," so she left to go live with her older sister, and in the meantime her husband (who was elderly) died.

While she was living with her older sister, a customs officer saw her and asked to marry her. She married him and travelled about the country with him as he was transferred for his work. While she characterizes her first marriage as one contracted with cowry shells, her second marriage was a "paper" marriage, one formally recognized in the French courts. She remained with this "soldier" for four years, but became increasingly concerned about the health of her young children from her first marriage, who lived in Maradi with their paternal kin. So the customs officer granted her a divorce and she returned to Maradi. Unfortunately her two sons nevertheless died, and only her two daughters lived.

While she was living with kin in Tibiri, Sarki Labo (the traditional ruler of Tibiri) approached her father, a minor notable in the court of Maradi, and requested that she become his *jekadiya*, or court messenger. Her father refused, saying that she had just come back from much travelling, and that it would be improper for her to move about since she was unmarried. The sarki agreed, saying that he too felt that she should be married, and proposed that he marry her to his *yari*, an important notable in Tibiri in charge of the prison. Her father agreed, and she worked as the *jekadiya* in the court of Gobir for almost fifteen years, until Sarki Labo died.

When the sarki died she declined to continue as jekadiya under his successor, and returned to Maradi, where "Allah brought her together" with an elderly Kanuri man from Bornu whose livelihood comes from grain given to him by virtue of his status as a "Sheribu," or descendant of the Prophet Mohammed. She refers to this as a marriage of "the thread of Allah." She and the Sherif see one another only rarely when he stays with her in the house given to her by her kin in Maradi. She herself is too old to conduct any large trade, and is supported by her two daughters and their children.

The range of marriages Jeka has experienced over the course of her life reflects shifting options in marriage both as a result of colonial rule and as a result of her changing status over the course of her life cycle. In her first marriage, contracted when she was quite young, she had little choice in her partner, who was considerably older than she was. She remained in that marriage long enough to please her kin and to have her four children, but left it as soon as she could do so without offending anyone. That marriage, contracted with cowry shells, followed very much the traditional pattern appropriate to women of her aristocratic status: she spun thread and sold food from within seclusion. Her second marriage reflects the impact upon marriage of the large numbers of soldiers, police, and customs officers which the colonial regime required to maintain its control of the military territory of Niger. She married a "soldier" and, like other women who contracted such marriages, she experienced a lifestyle entirely unlike anything their mothers had experienced.[6] These marriages came to be known as *armen soji*, a kind of marriage distinctive enough to have earned its own name. Women who have been married to soldiers often repeat the formula, "There is no place we didn't live," because soldiers were moved about frequently and brought their wives with them. Their interactions with other peoples and places often make these women more cosmopolitan in outlook than other women, which may explain in part why Sarki Labo felt that Hajjiya would be a suitable woman to become his jekadiya. Marriages to soldiers and other state employees began to be formalized through registration at the justice of the peace or the mayor's office, and we shall examine some of the evidence provided by marriage registrations such as these in Chapter 7. This formal "paper marriage" has provided women whose husbands were employed by the state with protections and options unavailable to women in unregistered unions.

Jeka suffered emotional turmoil in her second marriage, however, because her children had been retained by their paternal kin, and they were not doing well. Women often find it difficult to manage the separation from their children that occurs when they remarry. Women who remain unmarried after a divorce or being widowed may retain their children, but often when they remarry they lose control of them, particularly if their previous husband has died and his kin are anxious to see that the children are protected. A woman whose previous marriage ended because of the death of the husband is far less likely to remarry than a woman who is simply divorced, for divorced women may be

---

[6]   All men in any way associated with military power are referred to by women locally as "soldiers," and women in military marriages often have only a very vague notion of what their husband's exact duties were or are.

able to negotiate with their former husbands to keep some of the children, and have no immediate worries about their children's access to inheritance. Widowed women, on the other hand, usually lose both their children and control of their children's inheritance if they remarry.[7] Jeka's choice to remarry was short-lived, and after only four years she returned to look after her children herself, even if she had to remain unmarried to do so. It was only after her two sons had died that she again remarried. There is no way of knowing why they died, but Jeka certainly feels that their ill health was due in part to their having been taken from her, a sentiment echoed in Hausa proverbs such as, "The mother is the medicine for a child's tears," and "Cut off the mother and you cut off the child."[8]

Hajjiya's experience and family background led to her third marriage and the position of jekadiya. Where in northern Nigeria the position of jekadiya seems to have degenerated into a form of concubinage after the Sokoto jihad,[9] the original position as understood in Hausa kingdoms unaffected by the jihad was quite different. When Sokoto captured Jekadiya Iyargurma Fatima of Gobir during one of Bello's raids on the recusant forces of Maradi, she owned forty slaves of her own and was a valued messenger for Sarkin Gobir Yunfa. Her skills were recognized in Sokoto and she became a messenger between Bello and his vizier (Last 1967:92).[10] In nineteenth-century Damagaram, the jekafadu (as the title was referred to there) had "the delicate role of acting as intermediary between the Sultan and his wives," whose marriages were part of his means of building political support (Salifou 1971:120). In Ader in the eighteenth century the jekadiya announced important visitors, maintained the fire in the sarki's entryway where men gathered, and was sent on special diplomatic missions (Hamani 1975:110). Jeka's father's concern that she be married if she took the position seems to reflect a fear that the sarki might intend to use the position as a form of concubinage, as was done in Nigeria, and he was reassured when the sarki agreed that she should marry a notable. Jeka acted as intermediary between the sarki and his numerous wives, introduced visitors, and acted as the eyes and ears of the sarki, a task she was well positioned to perform objectively since she was not in the center of the Tibiri royal family. As historian Philippe David observes, the position of jekadiya is one of the few traditional positions that has lost none of its usefulness in modern Maradi (David 1964:77).

---

[7] Out of the 41 marriages my informants contracted that ended in widowhood, only 24 resulted in remarriage (58.5 percent). By contrast of the 171 marriages that ended in divorce, 128 resulted in remarriage (74.8 percent). This is not a function of old age—to the contrary, the younger women whose husbands die have a greater interest in remaining unmarried because their children are still dependent. Older women whose children have grown often express an interest in remarrying once again.

[8] "Uwa ita take maganin kukan 'danta; Yankan uwa ya isa ma 'da."

[9] See Baba's remarks on the various jekadiya of Fagaci, only one of whom seems to have functioned as a real messenger; the others were taken as concubines outside marriage (Mary Smith 1981:147, 235).

[10] It is probable that the woman referred to as Tallé by Urvoy in his story of the intermediary between Sarkin Katsina 'dan Kassawa and the animist population of Maradi valley was his jekadiya (1938:281).

In fact one might argue that as competition between co-wives becomes more intense and as marriage itself becomes more conflictual, the role of jekadiya as a sort of internal diplomat in the sarki's court may have taken on even greater importance. The wives of the sarki of Maradi today come from all over the region and reflect ties with strategic interest groups: maintaining those marriages and ties is an important part of maintaining his support more generally.

Jeka's decision to leave her position as jekadiya was in effect a decision to leave the marriage arranged so that she could take the position. She and the yari were divorced and she entered into her final marriage, "the marriage of the thread of Allah." Because women are in the local understanding of Islam inferior and impure creatures, their access to Paradise after death is seen to be subject to their having a marital tie, a literal thread to a man who has the "pull" to get them into heaven through prayer.[11] Older pious women will go to great pains to arrange a nominal marriage to a Muslim man so that they do not lose their links with Allah when they die. Often these marriages are not co-residential and the couple make no sexual claims upon one another. As another elderly aristocratic woman who is hoping to remarry explains:

> Well, the reason you will try to get another marriage, it's not out of any sexual desire or love. It's for the thread, so that you can go to Paradise in the afterlife. It's because of Islam that you want a marriage. You know, for us [old women], we can't really do any "farming," it's to please Allah. It's that with Islam, if the marriage takes, and then if you die, then your husband will pull for you, he'll look out for you and have them do prayers, he'll ask that you be forgiven, and then the forgiveness will be granted to you. . . . Without prayers you will have no happiness in the afterlife (Maskomi, 8-20-89).

Thus Hajjiya's final marriage is a kind of religious convenience, and neither she nor her husband have any strong emotional ties to one another. However sometimes such elderly couples, perhaps because their demands upon one another are so limited, have very companionable relationships and find in old age "chatting partners" they never could have had when the woman was younger and such intimacy was deemed inappropriate.[12]

It is worth wondering what psychological trauma this belief regarding the afterlife causes older women when they cannot find marriage partners to "pull" for them in their old age because they are physically unable to bear children and are in little demand as partners. A small hint of that emotional pain is to be found in the distress one elderly woman in such a marriage felt when her

---

[11] As Guy Nicolas reports, "It is said that the husband 'saves' the wife, and that a pious woman married to a sinful or 'pagan' man has little chance of entering Paradise" ("On dit même que c'est l'époux qui 'sauve' l'épouse, et qu'une femme pieuse mariée à un homme pecheur ou 'païen' a peu de chance à accéder au paradis," 1975:323). The image probably derives from the Koranic injunction to "cling to the rope that binds you" to God. The symbolism thus reiterates the notion of salvation through dependence resident in the "rope of slavery" tying a slave woman to her Muslim owner. I am indebted to an anonymous reader for Heinemann for this observation.

[12] The iya and her husband are such a couple, as well as Hajjiya Adama and her husband. Hajjiya Adama, 3-1-89.

husband failed to come to her and to pray when her only daughter (from another marriage) died: she was deeply hurt and felt betrayed and ended the marriage immediately, even though she has little prospect of remarriage (Fatchima, 2-5-89). The husband she had was clearly not someone who would "pull" for her.

Soldier Marriage

Jeka has experienced over her lifetime a full range of marriage possibilities, from seclusion to a very public position, from traditional office to modern "soldier marriage," and ending with a marriage honoring Islam's preference for marriage. The rise of the military presence in the region has had a striking effect upon the lives of women marrying from about 1930 on. Jeka chose to enter into a marriage that broadened her horizons and provided her with experiences that shaped her later life. While Hausa women in the nineteenth century and earlier sometimes accompanied Hausa traders on their caravans, they remained together in Hausa settlements that often became small Hausa communities outside foreign cities (Lovejoy 1980:29). The rise of the military, and later the rise of public employment in a broader range of positions, has linked women to the state and to new ideas and ways of life more directly and thoroughly than the court system or *fatauci* trade. Women in such "soldier" marriages experienced the world in a new way, since they were often housed in neighborhoods together, found that they had to communicate in other languages (usually French and Zerma), and developed a culture all their own.

Miles points out that from the outset, French colonial rule bore a distinctly military stamp, such that "government in Niger remained permeated by a military culture. . . . Even in the villages, the image of *soji* (soldier) evokes reactions of varying intensity, from the serious to the humorous" (1994:111).[13] This powerful authoritarian heritage accounts for the Hausa attribution of *mulkin zafi* (hot rule) to the Nigérien state. Unlike the British, the French relied upon conscription for military recruitment, fostering deep resentment among the Hausa of Niger. To stave off Hausa emigration to Nigeria the French colonial government kept enlistment quotas low for the Maradi region, and conscripted heavily to the west instead (Echenberg 1991:50, Figure 4.1). The military in Niger came to be dominated by the Zerma, contributing to the political subordination of the Nigérien Hausa despite their numerical superiority (Miles 1994:136). Because so few Hausa men entered the military, Hausa women in military marriages tended to have married "stranger husbands" who had been stationed temporarily in the Hausa region.

---

[13] The *soji* captured the imagination of the Hausa, who incorporated military figures into the spirit possession cult pantheon. White spirits known as Babule appeared speaking "French," bearing arms, performing mock military exercises, and, for a time, fomenting unrest in what became known as the Hauka movement. See Latour 1992:39–40; Fuglestad 1983:129–31.

Military life, even from the earliest days of the *Tirailleurs Sénégalais*, demanded that women play an important role in the maintenance of a sense
of community. Soldiers' wives had to learn new languages and customs and
to adapt to alien surroundings. Because of the mobility of the troops, women
were responsible for creating and recreating home life under the most demanding conditions, providing food and shelter, training the children, and
occasionally acting as carriers in battle. By acting as companions and enter-
tainers they provided pleasure and stability in an otherwise difficult life.
As Myron Echenberg points out, "The French military encouraged family
life in the camps, seeing in women and children a force for stability and a
situation much preferred to the problems presented by prostitution and camp
followers" (1991:23). Military women identified so deeply with military life
and their husbands' positions that they even occasionally felt empowered
to bring grievances against French officers whom them felt to have abused
them and their "rank."

While military life was difficult, there were a number of important benefits accruing to soldiers and their families that had profound implications
for marriage. The soldier and his family were exempt from head taxes so
long as he was in the service, making it possible, at least in principle, for
soldiers and their wives to build up significant savings in cash for investment once they had quit military service. From 1904 on soldiers were also
provided with a pension after they had served fifteen years in the army,
providing some soldiers and their wives or widows with a form of security
in old age hitherto unheard of in the region (Echenberg 1991:24).

Echenberg's evidence suggests that soldiers often did not return to their
rural villages, but used their capital and pensions to establish themselves in
larger urban centers (1991:82), a finding consistent with my observation that
most of the veterans who settled in Maradi were originally from other parts
of West Africa. While his study shows that the majority of veterans did not
use their capital to accumulate land or to embark on a business enterprise,
subsisting instead off their pensions (1991:138), a minority of them clearly
did invest, including some of the veterans who built houses in Sabon Gari
in Maradi.[14] My own research suggests that, while the soldiers themselves
may have come to look upon entrepreneurial activity as beneath them, their
Hausa wives endeavored to continue their income-earning enterprises despite the difficulty of conducting trade among "strangers." Once these wives
returned to their homelands they brought with them new ideas about how
to invest capital, and became enthusiastic purchasers of land. Hence the
growth of the military contributed to the flow of population to urban centers, to shifting patterns of absorption of "stranger" populations, and to the
shape of cities as newcomers and their Hausa wives built homes for themselves with their savings.

---

[14] Latour (1992:177) also found that in Niger returning soldiers invested in land and home construction.

Beyond these material advantages, military life also gave rise to a definitive military culture, a culture that women in Maradi referred to as "soldier marriage." For the most part this culture emerged out of the difficult conditions of military life: constant movement, dislocation from familiar languages and cultural practices, adaptation to the opportunities and demands of urban centers and military camps. However by the late 1950s the army itself promoted a vision of "modern" family life for the more elite soldier and his family, partly to combat the hostility of African intellectuals towards military service:

> Calling their new program *la promotion africaine*, the army issued glossy new magazines . . . showing the modern social and civil role African army officers could play in their society. . . . for example under the rubric of "habits of Modern life," an African officer, his wife, son, and daughter, all in European dress, were depicted eating a French meal complete with a bottle of Evian at their table. Another photograph portrayed an African sergeant teaching his son to read . . . Still another photographic article emphasized . . . opportunities for the wives of African officers, which included a variety of functions from sewing classes to adult literacy courses (Echenberg 1991:121).

While it is unlikely that African soldiers or their wives received this propaganda without some humor and suspicion, military life clearly exposed soldiers to consumption patterns, social forms, and familial and gender ideals emanating from France. Members of the military adopted these influences in their own ways and to their own ends. The outcome was a social form and cultural milieu unique to the military of French West Africa.

Thus when I showed women in Maradi a colonial-era photograph purporting to show the ethnic "types" through three young Hausa, Zerma, and Bella women, my informants could not in fact distinguish the women by ethnicity, but did state with confidence that judging from their hairstyles, ornaments, and dress, they must be the wives of soldiers. Evidently a colonial ethnographer had found several women from among the wives of soldiers in Niamey or Zinder and had assumed that because they were of different ethnic origins they could be used to show ethnic differences. What mature women in Maradi remarked upon was what they had in common: *armen soji*. The unique military culture of these African women was invisible to the French photographer, who saw only "natives" who could by typologized. Ironically, having created the conditions for the emergence of a culture that transcended (however partially) ethnicity, the French colonialists were blind to that culture.

Beyond forging a culture of their own, these women also gained access to state resources that women in non-registered marriages did not have. Women whose husbands had been employed by the state began to have access to pension money, insurance money, and child support if their husbands died and their marriage had been registered. Thus, while the French court was not appealed to often for divorce, a growing number of couples have had their mar-

Photo 3: "Typical young women, from left to right: Zerma, Hausa, Bella" ("Types de jeunes filles de gauche à droit: Djerma, Haoussa, Bella"). Early colonial–no date, no contributor. The difference between the caption provided by whomever contributed the photograph and Maradi women's comments upon it was striking: where the photographer saw ethnic/racial "types," women saw wives sharing the culture of *armen soji* or soldier marriage. French National Archives, Centre des Archives d'Outre-mer. All rights reserved. 30F1.23.AOF.3269.

riages registered both there and at the Mairie.[15] Because registration is not practiced as a matter of course, and state employees may fear (incorrectly) that
polygynous marriages are not covered, the three wives of a customs officer
had quite different experiences when their husband died recently, for he had
registered the marriage of only one of the women, and as a consequence only
the registered wife and her children have had access to insurance and child
support money since his death (Kande, 11-15-88; 1-18-89).

"Today the Land Is an Old Wife:" The Emergence of Freehold Tenure

Women who have been exposed to soldier marriage have gained an understanding of how the state works and have been more likely than other women
to invest in urban real estate and licenses.[16] Commoner women seem to have
been exposed to *armen soji* more often than women of the aristocratic class,
who tend to marry notables, traders, and Koranic scholars. Aristocratic women
and women of the merchant class have increasingly gained control of urban
property through inheritance or gifts, however, so that these women often have
houses of their own as well.[17] The increasing tendency for women to be included in inheritance is a striking and unexpected outcome of French colonial
intrusion in the judicial domain. Prior to about 1945, women were systematically excluded from the inheritance of houses and land. It was only with the
rebuilding of the city on the plateau and the influence of the colonial courts
that women began to have access to land through inheritance. While it is commonly assumed in studies of French colonial rule that the Napoleonic code
prevailed, eliminating women and wives from property ownership (Coquery-
Vidrovitch 1994:111–12; Miles 1994:288; Latour 1992:128), in fact, in Maradi at
least, women's property rights were bolstered rather than undermined. Women's

---

[15] I have full figures only for the Mairie: from only 21 marriages registered in 1956 the numbers
grew rapidly to 70 in 1965, and 137 marriages in 1985. The registrations in the Palais de Justice are
usually made after the fact, and can be quite numerous; in 1987, for example, 167 couples recorded
their marriages belatedly, as against 25 who did so at the time of the marriage ceremony, suggesting that registrations are made as couples learn of the benefits available because of it and need
some form of documentation.

[16] All of the women I worked with who had been in *armen soji* except Jeka owned houses through
purchase rather than inheritance. Examples of women who own houses they did not inherit include Hajjiya Halima (her husband had worked for the Department of Agriculture–she also owned
a licensed bar and had an import license), Hajjiya Sa'a (who had married a soldier), Kande (whose
husband was a customs officer), and Asabe Hassan (whose husband was a state-employed well-
digger). Three women who had been *karuwai* but had never been married to a state employee own
houses, two women who came to Maradi after the 1984 drought built mud houses on small plots at
the edge of the river valley, and the successful trader, Hajjiya Asma'u bought a house from the
sarki.

[17] Women of the aristocratic or courtly class who own houses of their own through inheritance or
as gifts from the sarki or other men include Hajjiya Aisha and her co-wives, Hajjiya Zabaya, Hajjiya
Hasiya, Hajjiya Larewa, Maskomi, Malaya, and each of the sarki's wives. Merchant-class women
such as Hajjiya Adama and Hajjiya Gaba also own houses.

rights to property were already strongly embedded in Islamic law (Ahmed 1992:110–12), and it was the enhancement of the status of Islamic law under colonial rule that promoted women's access to land. This promotion of Islam under colonial rule was largely unintended and was in fact a matter of considerable contention among French administrators and scholars (Harrison 1988).

With the reorganization of legal structures in French West Africa, in principle local judicial structures and practices were to be replaced by a three-tiered system of law. The most local courts, the *tribunaux de village*, were to arbitrate in civil and commercial matters; the next tier up, the *tribunaux de subdivision*, could handle penal offenses as well as civil and commercial cases. Finally, the *tribunaux de cercle* handled criminal cases and acted as the court of appeal for the lower courts of the subdivision. All cases were adjudicated by the military personnel or by career administrators in place: it was only in 1946 that the civilian *justice de paix*, or professional judge trained in law, was introduced with the abolition of the indigénat (David 1964:128). Prior to 1946, any African *"sujet"* was governed by administrative decrees emanating from the French president. To be a *sujet* was to be subject to trial without notice by the local French administrator and sentenced to a maximum of fifteen days' imprisonment and fifty francs in fines for any of twenty-six offenses. Among those offenses were the refusal or reluctance to carry out requisitions, nonpayment of taxes, disrespect towards the administrators or the French in general, and a non-collaborative attitude (Fuglestad 1983:81).[18] The French *commandant* was assisted by two native assessors who were to advise him on local customary law: in Maradi these were the durbi, a Katsinawa functionary who had represented the interests of the Arna animists in the court, and the al'kali (the local Muslim judge, or qadi).

As seems to have been the case elsewhere in French West Africa, administrators in Maradi evidently found it convenient to apply Islamic law uniformly throughout the population despite the complex judicial traditions of the region.[19] Maliki law had the appeal of offering beleaguered administrators a familiar understanding of land as a heritable form of wealth that could be sold. Furthermore Islamic practices regarding women and inheritance may have fit well with contemporary notions of the ranking of "civilizations" according to the "position of women" within them. These remarks on practices regarding women at the Niger bend show how even one of the most "liberal" of colonial administrator/scholars, Paul Marty, could see Islamic practices as superior to "pagan" practices when women's treatment was at issue:

> Islam gives her [women of an Islamicized population] a certain personality, thanks to which she can acquire, possess and sell [material goods] . . . to a certain extent govern her own life and, above all else,

---

[18] As an example of how broad these powers could be, Mallam Mijinyawa of Maradi was sentenced to three years in prison followed by exile for composing a song in Arabic ridiculing the sarki's willingness to follow the French command to move the city from the valley to the plateau in 1945 (David 1964:161–66).

[19] See Marty's criticisms of this practice in Harrison (1988:136).

she may pray. The fetishist women, similar to the woman of pagan antiquity, takes no part in religion . . . and if she is reasonably free physically to come and go as she pleases she is not by any means her own mistress (Harrison 1988:132).

Thus the predilections of French administrators in Maradi, as elsewhere, had the effect of promoting Islamic law, particularly as it touched on women, despite the deep controversies surrounding this issue in debates among French administrators and scholars (Harrison 1988:94-117).

In fact, it was in an effort to balance the tendency of French rule to promote the advance of Islam that the *Coutumiers juridiques* were originally collected: "French knowledge of indigenous customs derived principally from studies commissioned for legal purposes, that is studies that were intended to provide French administrators with a corpus of customary law that was more suitable than either the Code Napoléon or the *sharia*" (Harrison 1988:129). If the motivation for collecting a corpus of customary law was to counter the unsuitability of French law and the "dangers" of Islamic law, the effort in fact failed, for the Coutumiers in effect recorded as law the preferences of those notables who had most interest in advancing their own vision of the social order, preferences that accorded well with the prejudices of administrators accustomed to French law.

The Coutumier for the Maradi region is a peculiar and contradictory document, offering brief statements about "Muslim" practice, followed by even briefer addenda suggesting that "animist" practice could often differ considerably. The assumption of the document, namely that the population was unambiguously divided between animists and Muslims, belied the complexity of the history of settlement and religion in the region. It also glossed over the power issues that must have come into play any time an "animist" entered a court dominated by Muslim notables (for both the durbi and al'kali were Muslim Katsinawa members of the sarki's court). Thus the Coutumier asserts: "Among Muslims farmland and urban concessions have a value and can be sold, rented, or mortgaged. Among animists land can never be sold; only the harvest has value, not land itself" ("Coutumes haousa et peul" 1939:294). The document suggests alternately that law is handled by the qadi and that the sarki rules through local custom.

While the durbi was present at the Tribunal and the Coutumier made a gesture towards recording Arna customs, in practice Arna usages were largely disregarded. This disregard is reflected in administrators' accounts of precolonial Maradi, as historian Philippe David observes:

The Maradi region has too many ties with the animist world for its political, judicial, and social life to be systematically reduced to Islam and the Qur'an. This misconception was nevertheless so common among the few European soldiers and functionaries who troubled to even collect information [on the region] that we know almost nothing about Arna justice, despite the fact that [in the precolonial era] the sarki did not have exclusive or total jurisdiction over all of his subjects (1964:124).

While in theory even under colonial rule the Arna benefitted from the presence of the durbi and "customary law" as institutionalized in the court system, in practice the residents of the valley greatly preferred to turn to the sarki and other Muslim scholars for arbitration. In his study of the region, Marty remarks that "all sorts of agreements are regulated by the literate class, although the indigenous people know very well that the justice of the Whites is free" (1930:427). When locals did turn to the Tribunal, they tended to claim Muslim status rather than Arna status before the court. Guy Nicolas accounts for the tendency of the Arna to claim Muslim status for judicial purposes by noting the contempt of urban functionaries for non-Muslims and the association of prestige with Islam (1975:198, 204, 382, 509). However the notable appointed the title of durbi–one of the Katsinawa elite–was just as much an outsider to the people of the Maradi valley as was the sarki or the French administrator and it seems probable that the appointed notable's understanding of local practices was arbitrary and his application of sanctions draconian, with the overall effect that he imposed a uniform "code" upon a highly localized and diverse population.[20]

Furthermore there were advantages to individuals in making use of Islamic law through the court rather than observing practices that had evolved to protect the broader Arna communities. For example, under Arna land distribution norms, when a head of household died, the household land was managed by the next senior male, who might be an eldest son, a younger brother, or simply an older man in the community. This pattern protected the larger community's control over the land in question, since the holding was understood to be for the use of a household and not of individuals. The land was not divided among the remaining children unless one of the sons or brothers wanted to set up a new household on his own, which he could have done in the past by clearing new land for himself. Women were given part of the household land to farm or helped their husbands with his *gamana* plot. Over time, women (particularly older women) seem to have enjoyed uncontested usufruct rights to land provided by their husbands, although the land available may have been poor in quality and of limited in area. However under Maliki law, which has increasingly become the norm governing inheritance, when a man dies his land and property may be divided among the children, sons receiving twice the share of daughters. One of Éliane de Latour's informants captures the qualitative shifts in land law in Hausa Niger in a striking metaphor:

> You see, twenty years ago the land was like a young woman, all the boys could visit her. Today she has become an old wife, no one else can come on her and you are obligated to finish out your days with her (1992:45).

While Latour sees this shift as resulting primarily from the French "Republican" vision of law (1992:128), the debates within the French adminis-

---

[20] Trial by ordeal seems to have been preferred by the durbi, whereas reconciliation and fines were the norm with the sarki and al'kali (ANN/14.1.12).

tration about the role of Islam in local law suggest that such an outcome was far from guaranteed. In fact local Africans also had a great deal to do with the transformation of land law, as the elite Katsinawa attempted to gain greater controls through the judicial system in the moment of recording "local custom," as local agriculturalists resisted the deformation of their practices by claiming Muslim status over Arna, and as juniors and women seized upon the potential for land ownership presented in the newly simplified "Muslim" code.

By preferring Katsinawa norms of inheritance in the nineteenth century and Maliki law increasingly under French rule in this century, individuals in the valley could gain control of land which in the period prior to the arrival of the Katsinawa would have been available to them only in usufruct. Such control became more desirable as access to bush and fallow land declined. Appealing to colonial courts in matters pertaining to marriage could prove disadvantageous, as we have seen, and did not confer on either men or women options they did not already possess. By contrast, by taking advantage of the courts in issues related to land inheritance individuals gained entirely new options, options worth risking the ire of their kin and the cupidity of the court. In practice this potential to inherit land only benefitted men in the nineteenth century and in the early decades of the twentieth, for Katsinawa norms preferred that daughters receive their share of an inheritance in livestock, cloth, or cash, rather than in land or property: "it is the man who inherits the *gida* [household, house, family, clan, heritage]" (Hajjiya Jeka, 4-13-89). Muslim clerics overseeing the division of inheritance felt that it was inappropriate for women to inherit even a house, since:

> If you gave the house to a woman, or so people thought back then, if you divided things up and gave her the house, then she would sell it, and then some prostitute would buy it and come live in it. Back then we thought–or anyway the Imam would say–that a woman shouldn't take her father's house, only a man could inherit . . . Every woman is part of someone else's house [because she leaves her paternal household to live with her husband when she is married]. When she marries, if she isn't happy she will just keep divorcing, so well then, where is the *gida* in that? When a person dies and he has no sons, it is as if that house had died with him, because if a woman inherits, she will just sell it and go off to her marriage. That's why you didn't give a woman a farm or a house. That was the father's heritage. Back then, whatever your father did, that's what you did (Hajjiya Jeka, 4-13-89).

The close cultural association of maleness with the continuation of the family heritage, and of that heritage with land and real estate, effectively eliminated women from the inheritance of one of the most important factors of production. However under colonial rule this understanding of inheritance began to shift with the more literal application of Maliki law, and it became possible for women to inherit fairly regularly according to the proportions set out in the Koran, although there is still today a preference for sons to inherit farmland.

These shifts in inheritance practice are best understood as the outcome of a combination of adjustments to both urban and rural practice, as the above quote would suggest.

Women and Access to Land in Maradi

The practice of counting women into the distribution of inheritance opens up the possibility for a woman to inherit land in her own right, particularly if she is the only remaining child.[21] It also ensures that any land her mother inherited or purchased can pass to her as well, and makes individual sales and purchase of land possible. Because Hausa women do participate in agriculture, unlike women in the Zerma west of the county, women's success in enforcing these claims to land is far higher than in other parts of the country (Raulin 1964:107, 129). A woman may successfully lay claim to a portion of the family land, and then leave the land in the hands of her brothers for their use in an arrangement known as *aro*, a kind of rent-free loan. The brothers then provide the woman with a portion of the crop in recognition of her ownership. By maintaining ties with their villages of origin in this manner, women can ensure that their access to land is not entirely lost, and can benefit from the security and access to staple foods that the maintenance of their ties to the land can provide.

Conversely, making a claim to a portion of the family harvest is a way a woman can assert her rights to a portion of the family land. This possibility provides women with options that would not otherwise have been available to them when their access to land depended upon the maintenance of their marital or widowed status. The following cases give some idea of how women have gained access to land in the past several decades, the high degree of conflict their land access can occasion, and the variety of ways they have participated in agriculture even from within the urban economy. Just as the state's attempts to regulate marriage tended to introduce a further element of uncertainty into the determination of whether a union was formalized or not, the regularization of Maliki norms had the effect–not of finally fixing property rights through a clear code–but rather of generating greater and greater conflict over how to define particular pieces of land and particular transactions. As Carney and Watts point out (1990:210), the interpellation of the state's production paradigm into family politics is likely to give rise to "an internalization of small-arms warfare within the household, articulated as struggles over access to and control over land, and interpretive conflicts over the naming and classification of property." Maradi women's ability to win these definitional battles is undermined by virilocal marriage and their mobility for trade: because rural women move to live with their husbands upon marriage, they are often absent from their natal communities. Several of these women were in fact living in the city of Maradi at the time of my research.

[21] "Coutumes haoussa et peul" 1939:286. After asserting that "the fields are automatically passed on to the sons; daughters can't inherit anything except livestock," the study goes on to cite practice in the case where a man dies without sons, leaving everything to his only daughter.

Case 1: Buga was born in a small village south of Maradi, and in her second marriage to a man who was a driver in the city, her father allowed her to farm a portion of his land since her own husband had none. She farmed that land for ten years from 1959 to 1969, and had several sons by her husband. When that marriage ended in divorce, she married again, this time to a "stranger" from Gaya in Benin. She and her new husband moved to Gaya with her sons, and lived together until his death in 1986. Before his death he urged her to return to Maradi with her sons, fearing that his own kin would not be supportive of them as outsiders once he had died. She returned to Maradi expecting to use the land her father had left to her, only to find that her brother had sold all of the family land in her absence. Today she and her sons lead a very marginal existence in Maradi, where she works as a cook to earn money (Buga, 4-14-89).

Case 2: Mariama was born in the city of Maradi, but her father as a Muslim scholar was given land in a nearby village, Fura Girki, and had *fadama* land in Maradi. Like many commoner women of the city, she had never farmed the land herself. When her father died her older brother was stationed in Agades as a soldier, and was not interested in farming. Her younger brothers were still too young to farm. So she was offered the *jigawa* land for her husband, a landless blacksmith, to farm. Her husband Ma'keri farmed the land for twenty years, from 1964 to 1984, at which time her younger brother claimed it for himself. Ma'keri discovered that because the brother's crop failed in the drought of 1984, he had not even bothered to use the land for two years. So Ma'keri began to use the land again, only to have his crop ruined by Mariama's brother's cattle, which had been set loose to graze on the field. The conflict threatened to become violent, and Mariama was afraid that it would end her marriage, her third, and one which had made her very happy. She convinced her husband to leave the land for her brother, and instead she redeemed her father's *fadama* land, which her father had pawned *jingina* many years previously. She is confident that it would be difficult for her brother to claim the land which she herself had redeemed at 50,000 CFA (about $160, a considerable sum for a poor woman). She has decided not to take the issue of the *jigawa* land to court, since he is a full brother and in her view open disputes between such close kin are to be avoided at all cost (Mariama, 8-29-89, 10-11-89).

Case 3: Maskomi is a titled daughter of Sarki 'dan Kollodo, and as such occupies a privileged position in Maradi society. When her father died a large portion of his land had been given out *aro* for various people to use, and her older brother, a diplomat, managed to reclaim most of the land for himself and his siblings. Today 'dan Kollodo's *gandu* is in a sense still intact, since although each of the siblings owns a portion of it to farm, they have found ways to cooperate with one another. Maskomi owns a part of it, and she uses hired workers to do most of the work on it. She has used her income from trade and her position within the *bori* spirit possession cult to invest in farm animals and equipment. In exchange for sharing her equipment with her broth-

ers, they help her manage her farm, which helps to prevent any conflicts that might have arisen between them (Maskomi, 8-20-89, 10-8-
89).

Case 4: Mairi is a young woman about thirty years old who was born
in the village of 'Ya 'Daya and who is now married in nearby Fura
Girki. When she was small she did not farm, but when she was married at about fourteen her husband showed her how to farm so she
could help him on his land. Because he only has one field, and she
and her co-wife both have several children, it recently became clear to
Mairi that more land was needed to feed her children. So she went to
her older brother in her home village and asked if she could clear some
of her father's old land. Now she only helps her husband on his field
at planting and harvest time, the rest of her time she devotes to her
"inherited land" which she and her brother now farm together. She
contributes manure from her household in Fura Girki to help improve
the land in 'Ya 'Daya.

These cases reflect how land use and inheritance in the region have shifted
since the 1950s. By the late 1950s and early 1960s women seem to have earned
a clear right to inherit a portion of their father's land, which might be given to
them to use before his death (as in Buga's case) or after (as in Mariama's). In
the 1960s and 1970s there seems to have been little difficulty in women's use
and retention of this land; by the 1980s, however, competition for land had
increased, brothers occasionally selling the valuable land or claiming it for themselves. Conflicts over whether land was to be used for farming or pasture increased, and the importance of inputs such as manure and fertilizer grew. Most
recently the high value of vegetables grown on the clay soils of the river valley,
known as *fadama*, has caused greater competition for that land as well. A few
women, like Mariama, have managed to find means of getting access to *fadama*
land, which in the past had been the exclusive province of men.

As Paul Ross (1987) found in the Kano close settled zone in Nigeria, women
who inherit land do not tend to sell it as the Muslim clerics had predicted;
rather, like Buga they hope to save it for their own sons, since with growing
land scarcity and competition women cannot always count on their husbands'
ability to look out for their children.[22] Land can also be important to maintain
social ties, for the "ownership" of land that women may not themselves work
provides them with a claim to part of the family harvest and support from
male kin, as Maskomi's farming arrangements reveal. Furthermore, by making
a public claim to a portion of the family land—whether they farm it themselves
or not—women reinforce their membership in both a community and a family.
The reinforcement of those ties is one way in which women can, to borrow
Ross' formulation, "foster the maintenance of preexisting responsibilities and

---

[22] None of the women I worked with made reference to selling land themselves, although women
often referred to giving out their land *aro* or pawning it *jingina* when they did not use it themselves. Pawning land is in general preferable to selling it since one always retains the right to
reclaim it. When asked why they keep land they don't use women usually reply, "Don't I have
children?"

obligations in the face of resource scarcity and increased consumer needs" (1987:224). As needs in cash increase, and as grain in particular becomes scarce, women may find themselves excluded from the protections normally afforded them as members of a family, particularly if they have moved away from their village of birth. Women who have fostered linkages through their insistence upon a share of the land, which they may then permit male kin to farm, can later use the *zummunci* or kinship so underscored to appeal for help when grain prices are high.

In Mairie's case she has managed to build upon her ties with her older brother and to make a substantial claim to the land he inherited by contributing her labor and a very valuable input, manure, to the farm. In return she has secured part of the harvest and it is likely that her own children will be in a position to petition their uncle for land if necessary in the future. She and her brother are fortunate, since the fallow land she reclaimed could be supplemented with manure, which is not always possible.

Women's access to land, however, is fragile and can be difficult to secure, particularly as women are highly mobile and may move about with successive marriages or because of trade. Women are therefore not always present to maintain their claim to the land. Women sometimes receive land from their fathers as a kind of pre-mortem inheritance, as Buga did, and such land is often referred to as *kyauta*–a gift (Raynaut 1972:35n13). But as she found, land that a woman understood to be part of her inheritance may at a later time be proclaimed by other male kin to have simply been an *aro* loan. Terminological difficulties in naming women's land reflect the conflict over their control over it: the most common terms for different kinds of farms, *gandu* and *gamana*, are inappropriate for a plot a woman has purchased or inherited, for she is not the male household head of a *gandu* farming arrangement, neither has she been given the plot in usufruct as is the case with *gamana* land (Raynaut 1972:35). Women tend to refer to their plots as *gona* (a field) or as *gonar gado* (an inherited field). Woman's mobility makes control of the terms used to refer to their land difficult and their maintenance of their claims to land often hinges upon how that land is understood and referred to locally. Thus Mairie's brother may refer to his land as *gandu,* suggesting in effect that her use of part of it is akin to *gamana*. She, on the other hand, refers to her land in 'Ya Daya as *gonar gado*, suggesting that she has a right to it by way of inheritance, which is not strictly speaking accurate, since it was her brother who inherited it. Women as well as men can manipulate these terms: no doubt the family from whom Mariama redeemed the land used by them for several decades were dismayed to lose it. Out of twelve urban women who had inherited land from their fathers, five lost that land when someone sold it without their permission, usually because they had left it in an *aro* arrangement with their brothers.[23] One gave her brothers the land outright because she had no sons at that time,

---

[23] Laure, 8-29-89; Zuera Abdu, 8-29-89; Buga, 4-14-89; Mai Buhu, 2-21-89; Mariama, 8-29-89. Other women expressed worries about leaving their land *aro*, Ta Durbawa and Hajjiya Hasiya, 9-4-89.

and one got *jigawa* land but was excluded from the valuable *fadama* valley land owned by the family (Magajiya, 1-17-89; Asabe Hassan, 1-21-89).

Rural women who remain in stable marriages sometimes have more secure access to land through their husbands and fathers than urban women, since they are present to work the land and to keep up the social ties necessary to renew and define their claims upon it. Of the twenty-five women I worked with who live in rural villages, all but two very young wives farm some land on their own account. Eighteen have access to land through their husbands, and five have access to land through inheritance or purchase, and all still use their land. However even for urban women who risk losing land they inherit when they lend it out, the benefits to be reaped from staking a claim in family land and then permitting male kin to use their portion can be quite significant, as Maskomi's case shows—she not only has access to the product of that land, but by participating in her father's *gandu* she reinforces her status as one of the children of Sarki 'dan Kollodo, a status crucial to maintaining her standing and title in the urban community.

Houses of Their Own: Women and Urban Property

As paternal inheritance set the way for women to inherit real estate, inheritance between spouses began to shift as well. Today urban women tend, when they inherit property, to inherit a house from their husband, which they hold in a sense for their children by him. It is not clear how this shift occurred, but it may be partly due to a construction boom in Maradi after the city moved to the plateau in 1945. Where in the cramped "old city," it would have been impossible for each wife to have her own house, in the new town there was a great deal of room to expand. When a husband died each wife was left to hold "her" house for her children, unless she remarried. Since each of these households needed to support itself, each wife managed a certain amount of her dead husband's land for her children by him, and the land was "hers" unless she remarried, when it would revert to a senior male in the husband's family. In practice a large number of women in Maradi manage farms left by their husbands, to be worked through hired labor or through their own networks of kin.[24] This land is not referred to as *gamana* (or women's usufruct plots) but rather as *gona*, fields and farms managed and used in the same manner as fields owned by men.

The phenomenon of *sarauta* and merchant-class women gaining houses is, unexpectedly, also related to the phenomenon of serial polygyny. It is not uncommon that a woman in Maradi who is to be repudiated by her husband, even though she has done nothing wrong and has borne children for her husband, be given a house (or capital to buy a house) in recognition of her services and as a kind of pre-mortem inheritance for her children. This custom

---

[24]   Mariama, 1-21-89; Ibida, 11-17-88; Hajjiya Aisha and her co-wives, 2-28-89; Hajjiya Larewa, 9-4-89.

seems to apply only to women divorced because the husband needs to divorce one of his four wives to take a new one; it is not officially sanctioned, but is common enough that women of the merchant and aristocratic class expect it and a man may be criticized for failing to fulfil what is now seen as an obligation.[25]

Yet urban women have acquired houses through their own strategies of investment as well as through the reinterpretation of inheritance rules. This account concerning the house of Hajjiya Sa'a, a woman from a merchant class family in her mid-fifties, illuminates women's investment in housing:

> In her first marriage Sa'a was married off by her parents to an old merchant in the city of Maradi. She disliked this marriage a great deal and would sneak out at night to visit her girlfriends. She managed to provoke a divorce with her behavior and then married the young man she had been in love with. This marriage did not work out either, however, although it produced one son, and she divorced again and remarried, this time to a soldier. They lived for many years in Niamey, where she often baby-sat for the French officer's children, and picked up a smattering of French and Zerma. She had a second son with this husband, but she and the soldier fought frequently, and at length she left him and returned to Maradi.
>
> When she returned she went to her father's house, and found that he, a notorious serial polygynist, had divorced her mother and could not even tell Sa'a where to find her. She visited various kin until she found her mother, and was so angered and distressed by her mother's situation that she sold much of her dowry to buy a plot of land in Sabon Gari where she and her mother could live. She states that she never again visited or spoke to her father.
>
> She bought the land in the late 1950s at a time when a plot in Sabon Gari could be bought for about 5,000 CFA. Because she did not have a great deal of money to build, she and her mother lived at first in a small round hut made of sorghum stalks and thatching. As her son grew older and became a trader based in Niamey he occasionally provided her with money, and she used it to build a two-room mud house.
>
> She eventually remarried, this time to a moderately successful Maradi trader, Al Hajj, with whom her second son had close trade ties in the late 1960s. This marriage was reasonably happy, as she lived with her husband in Sabon Gari very close to her house and her mother, and she could continue to provide for her mother until her death. However as she herself began to age, Sa'a became anxious about the stability of her marriage, and quietly had a wall built around her plot. When the wall was completed she began to have a better house made of cement-plastered mud built in the compound. She used capital provided by her son to have cloth bought for her, which she resold from within seclusion to other women. This very limited trade was sufficient to build the new house gradually. The mud house still stands next to it.

---

[25] Conversation with the al'kali and Magatakarda, 10-17-89.

Her fears proved well-founded, and her husband Al Hajj divorced her five years ago to take a young girl as his fourth wife. Part of the reason for the divorce may have been his anger over her secrecy; however, she claims that she saw the writing on the wall. In any case, she now lives on her own land, and with the help of her now-successful second son has built a third house on the plot, this one a well-constructed house in concrete with a tin roof, fans, a shower, and storage rooms.

She rents out rooms in the other two houses. Her remarkably unsuccessful first son, whom she does not particularly like and did not raise, lived in one of those rooms with his wife for most of my research, but was eventually forced to move out after a conflict between Sa'a and his wife.

Sa'a and her ex-husband Al Hajj are in fact still fairly close and he occasionally gives her gifts of grain and cloth, which occasions some scandal in the neighborhood, as many women claim that she is in effect a fifth wife. Their continued intimacy has hindered her attempts to remarry.

Sa'a's compound stands as a kind of material history of how her land was developed over time. She is not a particularly successful businesswoman because she considers it inappropriate for women to trade publicly, and she would not have been able to build without the help of her son. But she has been quite shrewd in choosing what form his help should take: she has been to Mecca twice at her son's expense, but when he offered to send her a third time she insisted that they use the money instead to build the third house, a very comfortable concrete building, freeing up the plastered house for renters. Other women who learn of her house and visit her are often startled and impressed that she has managed to acquire such a fine house. I think it is likely that she was so traumatized by her mother's experience that she became much more entrepreneurial than she would have been otherwise and her building in secrecy reflects her expectation, based on her mother's fate, that she might have to fend for herself in old age.

Caroline Bledsoe's observation concerning the Kpelle holds equally for the people of Maradi: "Owning a house is an indicator of wealth and independence for both men and women. Behind almost every Kpelle adult I found a house story: people with houses were proud to relate at great length how they acquired them. . . " (1980:128–29). The tales of other women reveal that many who have been successful in trade have built their houses entirely on their own. Some who inherit land may use their own income and cash from their children to improve their houses. Women who are public employees often prefer to invest in housing rather than farmland or animals, which require more expertise and attention (Hamsatu and Rahama, 8-20-89).

Female ownership of urban real estate is not an entirely new phenomenon. "Houses of women," houses belonging to prostitutes where other prostitutes may live and gather, have probably always existed in a limited way in Maradi, and their existence is part of the reason why males prior to 1945 attempted to prevent women from inheriting houses. Since the move of the city to the plateau in 1946, however, it has become impossible to control the transfer of urban land as the city expands, or to monitor the construction on that land by women.[26] The regimes in power since independence have had no consistent interest in thwarting the activities and interests of "free women," and this may have contributed to women's ability to acquire real estate. The opening up of this possibility for women has indeed made it possible for some women to acquire houses for *karuwanci*, but it has also made it possible for many women to choose to remain unmarried without entering into prostitution, or to dictate the terms of their remarriage because of their spatial autonomy. Residential autonomy gives women flexibility both within traditional polygynous marriage and in less formal "outside" unions (Karanja 1994). As Thérèse Locoh discovered in Lomé, "Men and women appear to use the diversity of residence situations to bring about new forms of unions to minimize the tensions between their lineage and the urban culture, thus creating types of households that are particular to the new culture of African cities" (Locoh 1994:228).

Income from renters, a space from which to conduct trade, and enhanced ties to children (particularly sons) and other kin through the provision of housing are some of the reasons why house ownership appeals to women who are not necessarily too old to remarry.[27] Women with houses can live in their own space and avoid pressures to remarry, and are left with a reputable place to live should they decide not to remarry. Land can serve as collateral, opening the way for women to gain access to venture capital beyond what they accrued in the past through rotating credit associations (Coquery-Vidrovitch 1994:143, Maher 1974:69). They can also marry on their own terms, and frequently women who have their own houses choose to live in them and have their husband visit from time to time, so that it is their husband who is the guest rather than the reverse.[28]

By acquiring her own home, and by becoming a patron to others through the provision of housing, a woman positions herself as a *mai gida*, someone who is master of a house, like a man. This gives her authority over a series of potential dependents, including sons and daughters, sons- and daughters-in-law, foster children, clients, and renters.[29] Such patronage in turn may provide her with access to labor that otherwise would not have been available, and

---

[26] This is in striking contrast with the situation Callaway describes in Kano, where a house built by an aristocratic woman was razed by the city because authorities claimed that "no house built by a woman could be safe" (1987:46).

[27] Of the 32 women I worked with who own houses only 3 could be unambiguously characterized as *karuwai*; 15 are unmarried but are considered for the most part to be respectable; 14 are married (7 to the sarki). Many of these women have strengthened ties with their married sons by providing housing: Hajjiya Indo, Hajjiya Asma'u, Hajjiya Halima.

[28] Such is the case with Iya Wandara, Hajjiya Hasiya, Hajjiya Ta Dogo, Magajiya, Asabe Hassan, and Hajjiya Asma'u.

[29] Bledsoe argued that among the Kpelle home ownership gave women the ability to remain unmarried, to take lovers, and to accumulate and redistribute dependents (1980:128–31).

may free up her own time to take advantage of the most lucrative opportunities in the market, such as longer distance trade in goods from Nigeria. Home ownership facilitates her economic enterprises (every taxi driver in Maradi, for example, knows where to find the house of Hajjiya, "The Milk Woman") and can provide income from rent, presenting the possibility of investment capital of a different order from that which other women acquire through petty trade. Construction is, in Maradi, a highly public and masculine means of making visible wealth and social ties. While Muslim men may debate whether building schools or mosques is more beneficial to the community, conspicuous construction is nevertheless the emblem of the successful merchant (Grégoire 1993:112). In building homes women intrude into a masculine realm of display, one that projects them into the community outside the home and the female room.[30]

House ownership provides women with membership in neighborhoods and communities on terms closer to those of men: women homeowners may legitimately claim an interest in a neighborhood meeting, or a debate on taxes levied from each household, or the location of a market. They may become members of local associations, be called upon to mediate disputes, and establish ties of patronage or clientage with others in that community. In other words, as Sandra Barnes cogently argues, access to such space alters the "structure of opportunity" women encounter:

> Property frees the owner from subordinating herself to the authority of another person in domestic matters. It places her in a position of authority over others and in a position to form social relationships in the wider community that are politically significant. Property owning legitimates her entry into the public domain. Indeed, being the head of a self-owned domestic domain virtually necessitates a woman's entry into the public domain (1990:275).

For these reasons significant female investment in real property has been documented across Africa in the present century.[31] Property is crucial to women not simply as a material asset, but because it creates, defines, and facilitates social relations.

The availability of housing in newer neighborhoods has also made it possible for many "outsiders" to settle in Maradi, primarily Yoruba traders from Nigeria, and Zerma or Fulani traders from the west of Niger. Some of these are ex-soldiers who decided to settle in Maradi. Hausa proverbs and stories discourage young men and women from marrying strangers through predictions of strange and terrible outcomes (Edgar 1924:Nos. 11, 26, 91, 64). Women who enter into marriages with these "stranger" men in fact may experience liberties

---

[30]   Construction also links the human and spirit worlds; *bori* practitioners in Dogondoutchi build houses for their spirits in "an objectification of the interconnection of human and spirit worlds," Masquelier (1993:25).

[31]   White (1990); Parpart (1986), Mann (1991), MacGaffey (1988:164), Oppong (1981:120); Coquery-Vidrovitch (1994:200, 205, 277 n29), Callaway and Creevey (1994:135).

that are not often granted to them by Hausa husbands, who must satisfy their family's standards of respectability, and who are not compelled by their need to retain ties in a foreign setting to compromise in marriage arrangements. Some of the strongest marriages I encountered, both in terms of length of duration and in terms of intimacy and cooperation between the partners, were marriages in Sabon Gari between Hausa women and "stranger" men. Because most of these men are traders, they often have been able to assist their wives in setting up a trade, and have given them the freedom of movement to conduct that trade outside the home.[32]

Finally, the availability of rental housing made possible by women's investment in housing means that women who wish to live alone but cannot afford a house can today rent a room in a house, and not necessarily resort to renting in the home of a *karuwa*. When men invest in housing to rent out they usually build a "villa," an elaborate house after the European model, surrounded by a wall and garden. These are rented by European development workers or by government employees (Grégoire 1986:144). It is women who use their more limited capital to build rental housing in units small enough for unmarried women and junior men to afford them. Thus Atu, a woman who was divorced from a court notable who wanted to take a different fourth wife, was eventually able to rent a room on her own rather than live with *karuwai* or remarry. When she was first divorced she immediately remarried, but she was so unhappy not being able to see her children, who were retained by the notable, that she obtained a divorce and has since managed to rent a room opposite the notable's residence in a house owned by an old woman. In this manner she has been able to remain close to her children (who can spend the day with her and whom she feeds and gives gifts) as well as provide discipline and supervision to see that they go to school and dress respectably. As she states concerning her current situation, "I'm not a *karuwa*, I wouldn't be able to, it wouldn't suit my heart. And I wouldn't want anyone to shame my children because of it" (Atu, 10-7-89). She sells fried millet cakes outside her house to meet her expenses.

One consequence of her new independence and visibility was that she had joined the AFN, the national women's association founded under Kountché. Here is her account of how she came to join:

BMC: Before you and your husband divorced were you in the women's association?
Atu: Oh, no! I didn't even go out of the house! I would have felt ashamed, and frightened!
BMC: So it has only been since you've been staying here. . . .

---

[32] Women in Sabon Gari with marriages that can be characterized in this way include Rabe and Mariama (co-wives), Hajjiya Indo, and Hajjiya Ta Abu. Asabe Hassan, in Maradawa, has a similar non-married arrangement with an ex-soldier. "Soldier marriages" in which women do not live in Maradi close to their own kin, on the other hand, often render women more vulnerable to abuse, as was the case with Hajjiya Gobarci and Hajjiya Sa'a.

Atu: Yes, I was sitting here [we were sitting outside while she worked] and I saw some women, they kept on walking by. So I said, "If you go off to watch [political gatherings], they don't chase you away?" And they said to me, "No! If they see that you can go out, then they write your name down, and then you can dance, we do traditional dances, like this. . . ." So they wrote me down, over there in the Maison des Jeunes. And that was the beginning of my joining the women's association and even now we are still going. To help develop the country (Atu, 10-7-89).

Atu was quite active in the association, assisting the neighborhood president as a kind of factotum.

One should not underestimate the importance of women's mere presence in an external public space as a force for change: it was only because she was outdoors and chatting with women she had come to know through her trade that Atu gained the confidence to enter a political domain and become involved in the association. Women secluded from the time of their first marriages often state that they would be frightened to go out, and feel physical symptoms such as "heaviness" and "shaking" when they enter public spaces.[33] The opening-up of urban housing to women's control is creating situations that may help women break out of their fear and ignorance of external spaces. Older women who have not been out frequently may experience real discomfort and may need to be taught by other women how to use transport, how to go to market, and how to begin to build a more public trade. Hajjiya Adama, who now has a house of her own (since her husband's death), is being trained by Hajjiya Ta Dogo, who also has a house of her own. They use their houses to store goods they buy in Jibiya, Nigeria. Ta Dogo sells her goods from a stall in the market, but Adama is still too "ashamed" to sell publicly, and sells from her house in very small quantities. Both women are married, but their husbands only visit infrequently. These women are no longer perennial migrants; their residential stability has profoundly altered what is possible for them in terms of constructing social ties, negotiating marriages, and building trade.

Ownership and control of urban housing, then, has enabled women to define themselves as fully adult heads-of-household and has provided them with access to the spaces often seen as "public" and "masculine." However if women's ownership of, presence in, and movement through urban property is one way they can stake a claim, quite literally, to public life, women's worth and wealth has not been solely defined through fixed property. If immovable wealth enables women to secure ties with their sons in particular, the means through which women forge lasting bonds with daughters have been rather different. Daughters' mobility in marriage requires that mothers employ other means to forge social bonds with them. Other–moveable–forms of wealth will

---

[33] Beik (1991:235) notes that the feeling of *kunya* (shame, embarrassment) women experience in public is one of the main obstacles to their performance in Hausa theater.

be necessary to ensure their daughters' future well-being. In the following chapter I discuss how women have used ritual gift exchange at marriage to secure social ties and to make manifest wealth in people and things at a time when the means of securing wealth has undergone tremendous change. Much is at stake here, for the performance of wedding gift exchange, I will argue, determines the nature of the bride's marital union, her own and her mother's social worth, and the bride's longer-term security through the social ties she herself creates.

5

Women's Worth and Wedding Gift Exchange

Weddings and the gift exchanges they entail represent a key intersection of the material and emotional dimensions of social life, for the transfer of wealth in material goods creates other values: cultural capital, affective ties, and individual self-worth. At the same time the material goods in and of themselves embody the local culture in the sense that they carry a wealth of cultural associations that can have important implications for the practice of marriage and the evaluation of women. As the material contents of gift exchange shift with the changing sociopolitical economy, so also do the implications of the transfer of those gifts shift. The evaluative propensities of the gifts change with any alteration in the gifts themselves, even when the ritualized transfer of those gifts adheres to a familiar and seemingly unchanged cultural idiom.

In this chapter I explore how the shifts in the material contents of wedding gifts exchanged in the Maradi region in the late nineteenth and early twentieth centuries have affected the evaluation of women. I will consider changes in bridewealth to show that far from representing a moment in which a calculable loss to one family is materially recompensed through a "payment" by another, the act of transferring bridewealth in fact establishes the "worth" of the bride and her kin, expresses and creates social difference, and brings into being social relations that had previously been only potential.

Existing literature on gift exchange in African marriage has tended to focus heavily upon the "brideprice" paid by the groom's family to the bride's family. Attempts to understand brideprice have run the theoretical gamut from structural-functionalism to structuralism to marxism to more recent processual approaches.[1] Literature on Hausa marriage more particularly has focussed instead upon the "dowry" a bride brings to her marriage. This work sometimes decries women's preoccupation with earning cash to invest in their *kayan 'daki*

---

[1] For an insightful summary of the range of approaches taken to the analysis of marriage payments, see John Comaroff (1980); the edited volume in which it appears offers examples of processual approaches to the question.

or "things for the room": this investment is seen as unproductive or even counter-productive, since it diverts scarce capital from other kinds of invest-ment and in effect causes women to invest in the very marriage system that constrains their income generating options.[2] Neither of these two sets of litera-ture addresses how women themselves, who are after all at the center of all these transactions, view and understand them.

I argue that Hausa marriage payments must be understood as a broad ar-ray of gifts and counter gifts, a range of prestations in which women have taken an extremely active part. To analyze any one segment of this array of gifts in isolation from others is to lose sight of the essential discursive charac-ter of gift exchange. In other words, I see Hausa wedding gift exchange as an ongoing dialogue between crosscutting groups: women and men, kin of the bride and kin of the groom, seniors and juniors. The dialogue concerns (among other things) the status and worth of the bride and her kin, and in it women are energetic participants. By exploring the evolution of the material contents of these gift exchanges I shall show how women themselves have contributed to their self-definition through the discursive medium of gift exchange while they have participated in and responded to a changing political economy.

Women have been able to do so not simply because the material goods embody metaphorical statements about women and marriage (certainly wed-ding gifts can echo dominant images and metaphors of marriage), but also because the giving of gifts creates social debt, and that social debt will vary with the character of the material goods that created it. A debt, for example, created through a gift of agricultural produce is not the same as a debt created through cash or trade goods. Gifts provide a measure of the productive and redistributive capabilities of the giver, and this measure will vary with the quali-ties of the material goods given. Mauss was certainly correct that the gift itself has a kind of power over the recipient (1967:8-10, 40-3), however the character of that power is resident not in any sacred quality in the gift, but rather in the particular social context out of which the material goods emerged. By studying the changing contents of gift exchange we can therefore trace out changes in how women have been "valued" and in how they have created value them-selves.

Weddings at the Turn of the Century

To a masculine viewer the most prominent of the gifts exchanged on the occa-sion of a wedding at the turn of the century in Maradi was probably the *sadaki* bridewealth payment. This payment was transferred publicly from the family of the groom to that of the bride during a Muslim rite known as the "tying of the marriage." Often in rural unions the *sadaki* consisted either of a cow, goat, or camel, or of a sum of money equivalent to the price of such an animal. The

---

[2]   Callaway (1987:69–70), Schildkrout (1982:74). For a provocative view of how women's food trade can be seen as "unproductive" see Raynaut (1977).

animal was generally considered to be the property of the bride rather than
her kin in keeping with Muslim prescriptions that the bride receive the
bridewealth so that the transaction should not be thought of as a "sale." Oddly,
in urban areas (which in theory would have been more Islamicized) the *sadaki*
payment was generally made in cash and a young bride not only did not receive it herself, but almost universally had no notion of how much it was. When
the *sadaki* was an animal, it served as both a symbol and source of *arziki* (fortune, prosperity, and divine favor) by producing wealth in the form of offspring for the bride: "They would look for a cow to buy, and that would be
your *arziki*. When you had it for a while it would give birth, and then the
offspring was yours as well. You wouldn't slaughter it."[3]

In the city of Maradi the *sadaki* was usually paid in cowries, and the amount
to be paid could vary from only 20 to 20,000 cowries depending upon the status of the bride and her family. Often the quantity was based upon an equiva-
lence with the market value of the animal it stood in for. The emotional and
symbolic resonances of cowries can be seen in the many uses to which they are
still put: they are used in *bori* divination and sewn in rows on the costumes
worn by *bori* adepts, they are mimicked in costumes of the Samarya youth
organization as tokens of "tradition," they serve as counters for gamblers. In
the early decades of the century their uses were even more varied: they were
used for jewelry, and were tokens of affection a woman would receive from a
suitor and figured in wedding songs and games, and they were used in all the
transactions women took part in from day to day. The cowry was likened to
the female genitals, and was associated with pregnancy because of its rounded
shape. It was also called an "eye," through which one could read the future (G.
Nicolas 1986:126). Thus cowries were commonly associated with female sexuality and fertility, fate and luck, wealth built in small increments, beauty, affection, and the supernatural. "With these we would do our work," Hajjiya Jeka
remarked nostalgically (2-14-89).

Before the actual "tying of the wedding" there might be a lengthy period
of betrothal during which the groom's control over the bride was gradually
made public. As I argued in the opening chapter, with the decline of slavery at
turn of the century alternative forms of "marriage" could become a means
whereby senior men and women could control the labor of junior women. Gift
exchange created ties linking together the couple and the two families, ties that
were also intended to control the bride. Through the formal transfer of a *sadaki*
bridewealth payment a legitimate marriage could be distinguished from a less
formal union, and a "free" wife from a woman whose labor could be controlled
through the idiom of marriage.[4]

The gifts offered in marriage reflected symbolically the creation of ties and
the notion of control of the bride. Woven cloth made from thread spun by

---

[3]   Tanin, 3-15-89; other women from rural areas spoke in very much the same terms: Asabe Hassan,
3-9-89; Hajjiya Akbar, 2-19-89; Hajjiya Fati, 11-17-88.

[4]   In Morocco as well the *sdaq* served to establish the wife's free status; it became, therefore, associated with Arab identity (Maher 1974:216).

women made up an important part of the gifts exchanged. The husband would henceforth be responsible for seeing that the wife was properly fed and clothed and that she have cloth to "tie" herself with (or the cotton to produce such cloth herself); failure to "provide for" her in this way could be grounds for divorce. Thus rope, thread and the image of tying figure prominently in marriage ceremonies.[5]

The bridewealth itself, however, was not the most significant portion of the gifts transacted in monetary terms, in contrast with the Zerma region around Niamey in the same period, where the equivalent payment could range from 25,000 to 50,000 cowries and represented the single largest expense incurred by the groom's family (Diarra 1971:303). One consequence of the relatively low *sadaki* is that Hausa women in general, and certainly in the Maradi region, enjoyed (and still enjoy today) a high degree of freedom in leaving their marriages, since the payment has not generally been so high that it could not at length be returned to the groom's family. It is partly in the interests of Hausa women to keep the sadaki bridewealth payment manageable in the event that they or their kin must return it due to divorce. At the same time the *sadaki* needed to be significant enough to establish the social value of the bride and her male kin.

An account of local wedding customs collected in 1907 suggests that the *sadaki* was only one of many expenses a groom incurred when seeking a bride. The groom had first to announce his interest in the bride with a gift of 1,000 cowries to her father "to buy wood." Later the man would send the bride gifts including several new mats, a basket, two new pairs of sandals, assorted body cloths, cotton bands to use in making new clothes, and henna. The mother of the bride was given a traditional gift of two mats and two blocks of salt. The "tying" ceremony itself called for cola nuts, 1,000 cowries to pay the Muslim scholar and another 100 to pay praise singers. Another block of salt was divided up and distributed to the musicians, the paternal and maternal kin of the bride, and a portion was kept for the new household. After the ceremony the groom paid the bride's friends 1,000 cowries to bring the bride out of hiding (Landeroin 1911:513–14).

As this rather idealized picture reveals, marriage could be an expensive affair, one that would call for either the assistance of many members of one's family or the financial independence of an established senior male. In meeting these prestations the groom created or reinforced links between himself and a constellation of individuals in the bride's and his own family, both by giving gifts, and by becoming indebted to various contributors to the wedding. Most young men would have had to call upon the assistance of numerous kin, both male and female, to meet the demands of the bride's family, and in rural areas would have had to seek the help of young male friends to work the in-laws' fields. Senior males would be solicited for cash and for items purchased with cash like the traditional blocks of salt, for only they would have access to large

---

[5] For a more extended discussion of the importance of thread and cloth in Maradi, see Cooper (1993).

sums of cash from sales of surplus *gandu* grain or from titled positions. Other kinds of marriage goods, such as cloth, would be obtained as *gudummawa*, or "help" and "reinforcements" from kin. Older male kin might contribute grain to the new household, while older women, who set aside cloth from their spinning for such occasions, might provide the marriage clothing, surplus from their granaries, or decorative calabashes.

However, the emphasis upon gifts from the groom in the early historical documents on the region obscures somewhat the equally important gifts from the bride's family to the bride, the groom, and the groom's kin. The array of gifts offered by the groom were to be met or surpassed by counter-prestations from the bride's family. The bride's family and in particular the bride's mother presented counter gifts to the bride and to the groom which could equal or exceed the value of the groom's prestations. The celebrations surrounding a wedding are known in a general way as *biki* and, today as in the past, the bride's kin sponsor various *biki* events during the course of the wedding. In the late nineteenth and early twentieth century, when the bride had been taken from the home of her paternal kin to that of her new groom her female kin formed a procession to bear on their heads the large number of gifts known as *kan kaya* ("bearing the things"). The image conveyed in the term for the ritual was literally one of headbourne wealth, or in more economic parlance, moveable property. In this early period, however, it was the public act of bearing that was a more important indicator or wealth (wealth in people) than the actual objects being bourne. Among these "things" were items a woman uses to perform her household duties (pounding grain, cooking and washing), farming implements, and items to decorate her room or hut. A young woman therefore brought to her marriage a set of goods essential to the running of the household, and these goods were hers to keep should the marriage break up.

However of greater importance than the practical utensils in the memories and imaginations of the women I interviewed about their own weddings prior to 1945 were the numerous gifts "for the room" brought as part of the *kan kaya*:

> They brought us things back then, at that time it was just calabashes, you would harden them up, and you'd wash them...and you'd decorate them with chalk, and you'd carry them and line them all up before the house. That's what you'd take. Back then there weren't enamel bowls, just calabashes. You'd line them up, line them up in piles of say eight or nine, each pile with its calabashes.... Here in town you would line them all up, and you'd parade around the town with them, to take them to the bride's new home (Hajjiya Malaya, 9-4-89).
>
> After the money [for the *sadaki*] was brought, then we would arrange the *kan kaya*. Calabashes–you'd line them up, line them up–we didn't know about these enamel bowls then.... You do it for decoration, you carve them, and you wash them and put on chalk, and then you carry them and line them all up (Hajjiya Jeka, 2-12-89).
>
> We'd take calabashes, and turn them upside down like this, and we'd place a plate on top, and then put another calabash on that, and so on, and we'd stick them together in the [bride's] room like that (Hajjiya Indo, 11-14-88).

The element of display, both in parading the gifts and in providing the bride with goods to show off in her home, was clearly very important. The calabashes were far too numerous to be of practical use in daily needs of the family; women consistently described them as being "for decoration:"

> What is the use of ... the calabashes? Well, that's [our] history, the traditional kind. The calabash, you'd rub it with chalk so it would be beautiful! Even the black bowls, you'd line them all up together. They were stored like that, you had different ones for food. These were for decoration (Hajjiya Indo, 11-14-88).

The success of a mother and the nubility of a bride were both suggested by the multiplication of similar objects, which were to be displayed in rows. In an image to describe the beauty of such an array of marriage goods for her friend Adama, Baba of Karo reveals the probable origin and cultural foundation for this association of the multiplication of objects in rows with prosperity and good fortune among the Hausa: "We had set out her dowry in rows in the bride's hut, like the ridges on a farm" (Mary Smith 1981:175). The rows of gifts, like ridges on a farm, bespoke of future fertility and wealth earned through the work of creating and nurturing social ties. Rows of identical ridges, and row upon row of harvested grain, both images of agricultural fertility, are suggested in the rows of similar objects presented upon marriage.

Where in the West a bride would be disappointed to discover that each of her guests had brought the same gift, in Maradi and Hausaland more generally the repetition of similar objects is associated with *arziki*, or prosperity.[6] The quantity of the gifts served as a measure of the breadth of the social network of bride and her mother, for the mother's *biki* exchange partners would provide gifts of cash or goods, which would then be assembled by the mother and joined into the goods she herself had provided for the *kan kaya*. The more abundant the gifts brought to the bride, the greater the social network of her mother. The calabashes (whether decorative or not) also suggested the generous quantities of food that the bride would be able to provide to many people in *biki* gift exchanges for weddings and births in the future. Food containers in abundance suggested that food could be made available in abundance and that the bride would have an abundance of friends and kin whom she would feed in the future. Thus when guests or rivals visited a woman's "room" they would encounter a material measure of her worth and standing in the household and in the community. The numerous "things for the room" served as an indicator of how many friends and kin she and her mother could turn to for support should the bride need help, and of how many she in turn could be called upon to support in the future.

It is striking that in contrast with many of the other gifts exchanged by male parties to the wedding, from animals and money to luxury goods like

---

[6] This prosperity was also reflected in gifts from the groom's female kin who brought the *tuwon jere*—the "porridge to be all lined up" and offered to members of the bride's family (Mary Smith 1984:114–15).

salt, the calabashes which were so important in the *kayan 'daki* gifts to the bride were often collected, carved, and decorated by the women themselves, and consequently reflected their own labor and interest in providing a beautiful gift, rather than having a clear market value in themselves. Women I spoke with never mentioned buying or selling these calabashes, and women of all classes and origins, both rural and urban, seem to have given and received calabashes as wedding gifts at this time. Since they were locally grown and carved by women themselves, the quality of the individual calabash did not serve to distinguish the wealth of one woman from another, but rather reflected the skill of the woman who made it. It was the quantity of calabashes rather than the quality of the individual calabash that served to differentiate women from one another. The calabashes represented ties to individuals rather than links to the market. As such they served not as a measure of material wealth, for they had little market value in themselves, but as a symbol of wealth in people, *arzikin mutane*.

While the audience for the *kan kaya* seems primarily to have been the women of the bride's new household, who would see her "things" in her room and be reminded that the bride was someone with backers who should not be taken for granted or abused, other prestations from the bride's kin were directed to a male audience. The most conspicuous counter gift from the bride's family to the groom was the *gara*, or "increase," which might equal and then exceed the prestations of the groom. The *gara* was given by the mother of the bride to the groom, sometimes with the assistance of her kin, and might include a horse, money, quantities of traditional woven cloth, grain, and oil (Hajjiya Aisha, 2-28-89). Typically large quantities of grain and food to feed the new conjugal unit made up the largest part of the *gara*. The food was intended to feed both the bride and the groom, but as it is among the marital responsibilities of the husband to feed the bride, the *gara* can be seen as a gift to help the groom meet his responsibilities in the early months of marriage. The *gara* might also include livestock both for immediate slaughter and as gifts to swell the family herd (Aisha Labo, 2-1-89).

In rural areas the *gara* was known as the *kan kwarya*, a term blending the image of headbourne wealth of the *kan kaya* with a more agricultural image of "overflowing calabashes" filled with grain. The ceremony called for special drumming outside the home of the groom, along with praise singers to make known to the community the generosity of the bride's mother. Where in urban areas the *kan kaya* to bring the bride her "things for the room" was probably the centerpiece of the women's wedding celebrations, in rural areas the *kan kwarya* became the focal point of women's attentions during a wedding, combining the transfer of the *gara* gifts with the display of the "things for the room." Women often call this ceremony the *he!*, "you there!," a bold call to get the attention and respect of the new son-in-law and of the community as a whole: "You'd take the gifts and put them on your head and go *eidireidireidir!* [ululating]. And you'd take them to the bride's [new] home and bang on the door and cry 'Hey! Where's the bridegroom!? Here is some money for you to buy cola nuts!'" (Hajjiya Gaba, 3-16-89). A woman who provided her daughter with an impressive array of marital gifts and dazzled her son-in-law with a generous *gara* counter gift could earn for her daughter the title of "Tambara" in a rural community, a title that served to enhance her daughter's status and set her apart from other women (Raynaut 1972:85). An older bride might throw a *kan kwarya* to earn the title of "Tambara" for herself, providing the gifts directly to her husband and displaying thereby her own ability to produce grain and her own network of friends and kin (G. Nicolas 1975:190). Like the "gifts for the room," the *gara* or *he!* invoked images of plenty, fertility, and the ability to feed many people.

The display of such gifts did not serve simply to enhance the reputation of the bride's mother, who usually staged the event and provided most of the gifts through her own savings, labor, and social networks. It was an important signal to the community as a whole concerning the status of the bride as well. Women who had *not* been given a *kan kwarya* celebration were marked socially and could not participate in the dances held at subsequent *kan kwarya* celebrations. As we shall see in a moment, the failure to perform a *kan kwarya* counter-prestation ceremony suggested that the initial transfer of a *sadaki* payment had never transpired, and that therefore the marriage was either not entirely legitimate or had been a "marriage of alms" in which the bride was given away without *sadaki*. Thus the celebration of dances at the *kan kwarya* set women whose marriages were unambiguous apart from those who could be treated as captives or concubines, and those with considerable social ties from those whose kin were either absent or lacking in productive ability and social ties. The *kan kwarya* celebration continues to be important to women in rural areas today, and serves to launch the young bride into the social world of adult women. Here is how Buga explained its significance when I asked whether her own mother had performed the "bringing of things" (*kan kaya*) for her in her wedding c. 1955:

> She brought things! My mother ... you know, they call it a *kan kwarya*! That's when you take wealth and divide it all up among people, that's what she did for me. The reason you do that, is to keep you from feeling ashamed when you are set alongside other women. If they do the kind of drumming for a "Tambara," and you're sitting there with your head in your hands because you can't dance ... you know, then you feel bad. But if your mother took away all your shame, then if they drum you can join in the dance.... If you can't dance people will abuse you and your mother verbally, but if your mother placed you in *arziki*, there you are, you give your husband gifts, and there is a praise singer to praise you, and people clap for you. That makes you happy, and your mother happy, right? We are all "Tambara," she didn't allow any of us [Buga and her sisters] to be left feeling ashamed (Buga, 4-14-89).

Thus while the gifts to the bride and her new husband could enhance the status of the giver, they also publicly announced the wealth, value, and *arziki* of the bride. She would be seen as someone whose kin were industrious and were interested in looking out for her, someone who was in no sense being "sold" or given away, who could distribute wealth herself and was valued by her own kin and friends.

With the increase in attempts to use less formal marriage as a means of gaining control of female labor as slave labor declined and as the need for agricultural labor increased with growing taxation, this ceremony gained in importance as a means by which women could publicly display their worth, their social ties, and make clear that this was a marriage in which a *sadaki* payment had been made. Women today are offended at the suggestion that there might have been no *sadaki* in their marriages, and when Buga details the kind of abuse a woman who had not been given a *kan kwarya* might suffer, among the most important is that people might say, "May the person who loaned you out be forgiven," and "Well, there's nothing wrong with giving a daughter as alms, there's some reward in that" (Buga, 4-14-89). Anthropologist Guy Nicolas noted that in the 1960s women who had not had such a ceremony were belittled as *buzu*, the slave caste of the Tuareg, whereas women who had had a *kan kwarya* ceremony were known by the aristocratic Tuareg title, "Tambara" (1986:89, 136).[7] It was the mother who took a special interest in ensuring that there be no ambiguity in her daughter's status, and that her own motives in permitting the marriage be understood to be honorable.

Where for a senior male arranging a "marriage of alms" or *auren sadaka* for his daughter or niece might bring honor and divine reward, from the point of view of women the arrangement smacked of servility and humiliation. The *kan kwarya*, as Guy Nicolas suggests, was a means whereby a bride and her mother could assert the bride's value regardless of what the men might have arranged among themselves; it established the bride as more than a "dependant," but rather as an autonomous, independent and "masculine" giver. This was a message both for the groom–who was to understand that the bride was not indebted to him–and the bride's father–who was to be reminded of the bride's value and that it was the mother who was truly responsible for the bride (G. Nicolas 1986:141–42). Because a new bride spent much of her time in the company of other women in her new household, this message was also directed towards the women in the bride's new home. It would be her senior co-wives and mother-in-law who would be most likely to make demands on her labor or treat her as a subordinate. Nicolas associates the prominence of the *kan kwarya* ceremony in the Maradi valley with the rise of women's wealth in the nineteenth century through cotton spinning (1986:220), a wealth that made it possible for women to assert their economic independence relative to men at the very moment when their personal autonomy and safety was becoming increasingly vulnerable with rampant slave raiding. With the decline of the slave trade and the manipulation of marriage to control female labor, women could con-

---

[7] The humiliation implied is amplified by using Tuareg social categories since, as Nicolas notes, the social distance between the noble Tuareg and their slaves was generally greater than that between the Hausa and their slaves.

tinue to use the *kan kwarya* to set forth publicly their status and social ties. The more valuable the gifts offered, the better they served as measures of the abilities and wealth of the bride and her maternal kin. At the turn of the century providing the groom with a horse, which could only be obtained through raiding or through long distance trade, would have been the most startling and impressive of the *kan kwarya* gifts. The woman who could provide her son-in-law or husband with such a gift could demonstrate not only the strength of her female network, but the support of her own male kin, whose help she would probably need to acquire such a gift.

Clearly wedding gift exchange served not only to state publicly the *arziki* of the bride, but also to show that of her mother and senior female kin. Women on both the bride's and the groom's side of the family made sizeable and conspicuous contributions to the gift exchanges, and because it was women who controlled much of the local cloth production and distribution prior to about 1945 (when local cloth production collapsed), the many symbolically significant gifts of cloth throughout the wedding ceremonies stood in for the wealth and redistributive abilities of female kin on both sides of the new conjugal unit.[8] Women contributed conspicuous gifts of calabashes and grain as well, and while the Muslim "tying of the marriage" was dominated by men, all of the succeeding gift exchanges involved women visibly and symbolically.

The Changing Content and
Implications of Wedding Gift Exchange

Under French colonial rule the economy of the Maradi valley shifted away from an emphasis on grain production and regional trade and towards the production and export of peanuts for the international market to meet the rising colonial tax burden and the cash requirements of an increasingly commoditized economy. Peanut exports began c.1913 with the completion of the rail to Kano in Nigeria, and grew throughout the colonial period, particularly after about 1950, peaking shortly after independence in 1960. Since the ravages of the Sahel drought in the early 1970s and the drought of 1984 that the trend has been reversed and grain production has surpassed peanut production as the greatest source of agricultural income in the region. Even today some farmers continue to grow peanuts for the market, although many have shifted to beans in their crop mixes to replace peanuts.

As the regional economy was transformed by the expansion of peanut production, the arrival of international commercial trading houses, and the development of market and transport infrastructure, the material contents of wedding gift exchange began to shift. Certainly marriage customs in the valley had

---

[8]   Women's labor would have been resident in the cloth a suitor brought to the bride and her family before the ceremony and in the cloth the groom provided the bride after her ceremonial washing. Women's control of cloth production would also have been evidenced in the *kan kaya* and *gara* gifts.

never been static: the presence of the Islamicized Katsinawa and Gobirawa beginning in the first quarter of the nineteenth century introduced new customs and profoundly altered marriage and wedding ritual in the region. As the region became more closely integrated into the trade routes linking Hausaland with north Africa and the Atlantic coastal regions the use of cowries as a currency increased, reflected in the use of cowries for the *sadaki* payment in urban areas at the turn of the century. And as Guy Nicolas suggests, the growth of textile production in the late nineteenth century in the region enabled women to add a new form to the constellation of wedding rituals through the elaboration of the *kan kwarya* ceremony.

However the pace of change introduced into the region with colonial rule and independence has been breathless, and residents in the valley, both men and women, associate that change with the rapid commercialization and monetization of the economy, characterizing the era initiated with the peanut boom of the 1950s and 1960s as the "time of searching for money" [*zamanin neman ku'di*]. In a somewhat nostalgic evocation of an earlier period when there was little to buy, but cowry money was plentiful, elderly women refer to their childhoods as the "time of cowries" [*zamanin biringizau*]. Marriage before c.1935 was embodied in a set of symbols that suggested wealth and value through fertility, natural increase, and productive labor: the cowry and livestock offered as *sadaki* betokened the future fertility and *arziki* of the bride; calabashes provided for a woman's *kan kaya* through the labor and productivity of her friends and kin conjured images of her wealth in people, *arzikin mutane*, and foretold of the bride's ability to share her own wealth and productivity with others; locally produced cloth simultaneously created and made visible "ties" between the bride and groom and between the new couple and the female kin who had spun the thread from locally grown cotton; and finally grain and other goods in the *gara* or *kan kwarya* summoned the groom and his kin to acknowledge publicly the wealth and free status of the bride by partaking of the food and goods produced through her skills and those of her supporters.

The images of *arziki* based largely on organic production competed, even in the nineteenth century, with other symbols that show the importance of market exchanges in the Maradi economy. Some goods, such as the salt a groom was to provide to the kin of the bride, or the horse a bride's mother might provide for the groom, reflect the region's involvement in the trans-Saharan trade and broader regional trade. Locally produced wealth could be transformed into forms of wealth brought in through trade, from horses to luxury cloth to livestock. It was not trade, however, that gave rise to wealth in Maradi but success in agriculture or, in the nineteenth century, success in warfare and raiding. Unlike the commercial centers of Zinder to the east or Kano to the south, Maradi had been in the nineteenth primarily a base of operations for resistance to the Sokoto Caliphate and an agricultural center exporting grain and tobacco within the region. It was only under colonial rule that Maradi became an important commercial center.

With the growth of transport, markets, and links with European trade houses, gifts purchased through the market began to replace gifts produced through the labor of the giver, and cash became a more significant part of the wedding transactions. Cowries have been replaced by various French-issued currencies in the *sadaki* payment. The close association of the peanut trade with imports of cotton cloth eventually led to the decline of local textile production, and locally produced cloth has gradually been replaced by imported cloth in wedding gift exchange. Women's preference for the more prestigious imported cloth in their own gift exchanges contributed to the demise of the local textile industry.

Just as woven cloth was replaced by imported cloth, so the calabashes grown, produced, and decorated locally by women were gradually replaced by the metal bowls offered for sale in the trade stores.[9] Urban women in their fifties today say that when they were married in the 1950s they were given many enamel pots and bowls, which were stacked to line the walls of a bride's room in much the same way that the calabashes had been "lined up" in the past.[10] Guy Nicolas and Guy Mainet, who performed an ethnographic study of the Maradi Valley in the early 1960s, found that women at that time decorated their homes with:

> enameled plates bought on the market and attached to the wall. Most women accumulate in this way significant quantities of these dishes with the sole end of decorating their rooms. The value of these decorations is generally on the order of thousands of francs (1964:247).

The *kan kaya* has undergone yet another change in the past twenty years or so, as the enamel bowls give way to pyrex and porcelain goods which are displayed in a cupboard, itself an expensive and cumbersome part of the dowry.[11] Once again the gifts are "lined up," sometimes across the headboard of the bed as well. The sleeping mat and wooden bed have been replaced by ornate metal beds decorated with embroidered bedspreads and pillows.[12] Many young women today have two beds, one metal canopy bed and another "formica" bed, made of pressed wood covered with formica and featuring numerous storage and display compartments for their enamel and pyrex "things." This furniture represents a very substantial portion of a mother's expenses for her daughter's wedding. Where the calabashes given in the early decades of the century did not in themselves show the wealth of the bride or her kin, these

---

[9] The earliest metal bowls were known as "Amerika" and could be purchased from French traders women knew by local nicknames such as "The one who breaks bottles" and "The one who has sheep" (Hajjiya Ta Abu, 8-31-89).

[10] In the mid 1950s there might be separate rows set up of calabashes and enamel bowls (Aisha Labo 2-1-89).

[11] This phenomenon occurred in Nigeria as well, see Pittin (1979:398).

[12] Hajjiya Gaba claims to be the first woman in Maradi to have received a metal camp bed in the mid 1940s, which she still owns and points to as evidence of the wealth of the grandmother who raised her, 3-10-89.

expensive gifts reflect the different social status of various women: a woman from a relatively poor background might have only enamel dishes, where the daughter of a wealthy trader might have pyrex, porcelain, and furniture to "decorate" her room.

Similarly the goods provided in the *gara* and *kan kwarya* have shifted. As the *sadaki* came increasingly to be paid in French currency it altered the character of other gift transactions. It was difficult for the bride's mother to make a counter-prestation of equal value given her limited access to cash. A'i, a rural woman whose first marriage was in 1950, describes her mother's reaction to the *sadaki* of 1,500 CFA that the men had agreed upon:

> When I think back on it! That money! At that time they had begun to "break" one another–if someone gave some money, say they did the wedding with 1,500 CFA, then you would return [a *gara* gift equal to] 1,500 CFA. Then my mother said she would not give cash! [She laughs.] People said, "why not?!" She said there was no way she could give that kind of cash. So she gave grain, she gave ten matting sacks of millet and five guineacorn dishes. But she didn't give him very much money. She said, "If I give that much money, my daughter's marriage will be spoiled. I don't have that kind of money. If he chased her back to me, then I would suffer a big loss. I don't have 1,500 CFA" (A'i Mai Muni, 4-25-89).

By returning a *gara* in kind A'i's mother could buffer herself against a sizeable loss in the event that the new marriage failed, but the significance of the gift as a statement of the mother and daughter's independence and wealth would be undermined, as A'i's account of the surprise and dismay of others at the time of her marriage conveys. Her mother's failure to make a counter-prestation in keeping with the cash gift from the groom's side signalled her mother's relatively weak position in the economy, and A'i's correspondingly weakened position within the new conjugal unit. A'i's subsequent life trajectory reflects the weakness of her social position: she eventually left her husband because he repeatedly beat her. She was in such a precarious position during the Sahel drought that she migrated to the city of Maradi and was taken in by the Christian community of the Sudan Interior Mission. A'i's weak social position was in a sense foreshadowed in the dialectic of gift exchange, and one could argue that her mother's failure to satisfactorily state her daughter's social worth at the moment of her marriage and to generate the social ties necessary to protect her in moments of stress such as the drought contributed to her entry into one of the most marginalized communities in this overwhelmingly Muslim region. In the absence of strong kinship and affinal ties both revealed and generated through wedding gift exchange, A'i had to find some other source of security, which she eventually did find in the small but active Protestant community of the city.

In order for the significance of women's prestations to keep pace with an increasingly monetized economy, then, the content of the gifts had to change as well. They had to reflect women's increased participation in the cash economy.

Gifts given by the bride's mother to the groom increasingly came to consist of purchased goods, from woven tapestries to lamps, lanterns, and gasoline, as well as cash (G. Nicolas 1986:50). All of these new items must be purchased on the market and cannot be produced by women themselves as could the calabashes, cloth and grain given as gifts in the early decades of the century. Despite this financial burden, women see their contributions to their daughters' "dowry" and *gara* as a matter of honor. As one woman explained to me:

> For my daughter I gathered together things and I brought them to her. What my mother brought to me, I also brought to her. I brought her every little thing, her room was all fixed up, she was brought a *gara* of millet and oil, all that was done for her. Someone did that for you, mustn't you do the same for her? You understand? You dress up her room, you do dishes, you do plates, all of that you put there to fix up the room, so it will be pretty, and so everyone will come and see it. That's what you do (Hajjiya Hasiya, 9-4-89).

That "what my mother brought me" is not literally what a woman in fact brings to her daughter seems to be unimportant. Gift exchange in Maradi today gives the outward appearance of continuity with the past: most exchanges called for in a wedding bear the same names as they did at the turn of the century and often the transfer of those gifts follows the same form as was observed at the turn of the century. The perception of continuity and reproduction is an important part of the transactions, partly because what is being reproduced is not the material goods per se, but the social ties and debts that they create and imply. The giving of the gifts creates not so much material wealth as social capital: the recognition of worth and value, dependency and patronage.

Nevertheless, as the goods and the means by which they are acquired change, the symbolic resonances they carry change as well. Where the cowry and brideprice animal once evoked *arziki* through production and organic increase, the cash used in *sadaki* payments today is associated with market exchange. The calabashes, cloth, and grain women once contributed to gift exchange served as measures of their productive ability in an agricultural economy; the imported goods that they now provide prove the business and trade acumen of the giver, or her ability to tap into the wealth of male kin. The lifestyle evoked by such gifts is that of the wealthy merchant or functionary rather than the successful farmer.

The decline of cotton spinning and local textile production has eliminated one important source of wealth that women in the late nineteenth and early twentieth century used to make public their own productive abilities and to establish the worth of their daughters. Women began to tap into the cash circulating with the rise of the peanut economy by selling processed foods and conducting other kinds of petty trade, often with the help of their daughters. By 1945 or so many urban women had abandoned spinning in favor of more lucrative trades, and their access to cash made it possible for them to replace calabashes with enamel bowls, and locally woven cloth with imported cloth. Women's preference for these trades, however, gradually eliminated the possi-

104   Marriage in Maradi

Photo 4: "The merchant of cloth and enamelware" ("Le marchand de tissus et de plats émaillés"). Dogondoutchi, March 1955, donated by M. Jacques Alluson–Admin. FOM. While this was taken in a Hausa-speaking region to the west of Maradi, the market goods available are characteristic of the period: enamelware, soap, and imported cloth. The stall is not all that different from a market stall today, except that now there would be likely to be more plastic, Pyrex, and porcelain goods. Note that men and boys comprise the traders and the curious crowd. French National Archives, Centre des Archives d'Outre-mer. All rights reserved. 30F1.AOF.5933.

bility of providing cloth without the intervention of the market, and thus women's continued engagement in gift exchange became contingent upon their participation in trade.

One subtle dimension of wedding gift exchange that has been lost as access to gifts has become tied to the market is the link between the ability to give and the ability to produce/reproduce. In giving grain they produced themselves on their own plots, calabashes they themselves carved, or cloth made from cotton they themselves had spun, women exhibited their productive abilities even as they evoked images of fertility and reproduction with row upon row of calabashes, cloth, and grain. The images of organic reproduction implied in the calabashes, traditional cloth, and locally produced grain women contributed to gift exchange at the turn of the century have been replaced with images that lead to the market place. Pyrex dishes, wax print cloth, macaroni and canned tomato, all gifts that can replace the locally produced gifts of the past, demonstrate one's ability to tap into the market and to acquire cash. With an eye for the exquisite irony of some of these gifts, Éliane de Latour describes some of the icons of modernity now dominating the ceremony:

> Today on the wedding day a mother will be bursting with pride if, beyond the usual utensils, her daughter can display a metal bed with mattress, enamel basins, framed pictures of Chinese babies dressed in pink layettes with pompoms, porcelaine figures of dogs and blond princesses, Jex tampons, and acrylic wall murals of Mecca or of wolves in the snow.[13]

The change in the significance of the gifts is most evident in the case of the "things for the room." Where at the turn of the century these gifts had little or no market value, beginning in the late 1940s the "things" acquired through the market began to take on a different role in women's lives than simple "decoration." Certainly they still marked out a space in the bride's new home that was emphatically hers and that served visually to remind others in the home of her many supporters. However the objects themselves began to serve as material repositories of market value: the goods could be sold in an emergency, and thus have become, as others have observed (Callaway 1987:70), a form of female savings and insurance. In a sense the importance of the actual public "bearing" of the gifts on the heads of many supporters, kin, and patrons has been superceded by the value resident in the moveable property itself. In other words, they have come not simply to embody and generate "wealth in people," but also occasionally to compensate for women's loss of productive ability and to substitute for the security of wealth in people. This shift in the significance of the counter-gifts to the bride may account for the increasing tendency in other parts of Africa to see education as part of a woman's "dowry," for it this intangible that will serve as her security rather than her kin or her "things."[14] Maradi Hausa women's relative disadvantage in the realm of education, then, heightens the importance of having a tangible repository of wealth, drawing women and their daughters into a frenzied cycle of small-scale trade in processed foods in particular. This trade makes it possible to earn the money to buy and store "things" which then will serve as the daughter's security net in her marriage. The monetary importance of the "things for the room" is a significant departure from the past, and suggests that the social ties that wedding gifts embody and create are not always in themselves sufficient "insurance" for a young bride in a cash dominated economy.

While cash income has grown in importance, and the means of access to such income have become diversified, women have in many ways been marginalized by the growth of the cash economy, which circulates in circuits

---

[13] Latour (1992:52). Oboler points up the importance of the ultimate icon of modernity–the car–in Christian marriage among the Nandi (1985:113).

[14] In northern Nigeria a girl's education is increasingly seen as part of her "dowry," further linking gift exchange and social position. See Callaway and Creevey (1994:104). In Iboland female education and the appropriate dowry of household goods educated marriage entails has driven up the cost of brideprice and contributed to a rise in the age of first marriage, see Isiugo-Abanihe (1994).

from which women are largely excluded. Despite, or rather because of, their relatively disadvantaged position within the agricultural economy and in the emerging trade and bureaucratic economies, women's access to independent income is key to their long term security. For it is through trade that women can create the reserves of value and the social ties which will protect them and their children in the likely event that they are divorced and lose the support of their husbands. The networks and linkages created and reinforced through gift exchange can help women to retain access to disputed resources such as land, the labor of juniors, and capital: a woman's demonstrated ability to make good use of land, her ability to provide for others, and her visible wealth in people who support her facilitate her access to such resources. Participation in gift exchange with the purpose of creating and maintaining social ties simulta-neously draws women into their desperate "search for money," and makes it possible for them to continue to engage in income generating activities.

Conclusion

Far from representing a moment in which a pre-determined and calculable loss to one family is materially recompensed through a "payment" by another, the act of transferring bridewealth in fact establishes the "worth" of the bride, ex-presses and creates social difference, and brings into being social relations that had previously been only potential. The "family" that emerges out of the wed-ding ceremony is not a pre-existing descent group, but rather a collection of friends and kin whose individuated ties to the mother and father of the bride and groom crystallize into a network of "kinship" centering around the new couple over the course of the wedding. As John Comaroff observes, "the mobi-lization, alienation and distribution of prestations... may represent a generative mechanism whereby social units, roles, and relationships are actualized, trans-formed and given their manifest content" (1980:33).

Women have participated in and been affected by this evaluative and creative process in a number of ways. Because the decline in slavery at the close of the nineteenth century produced a crisis in domestic labor, infor-mal marriage became a means through which the labor of junior women could be used in urban households and for rural farm labor. These informal marriages, in which a formal *sadaki* bridewealth payment had not been trans-ferred, created a context in which the rights and responsibilities of all wives were called into question, for both formal and informal wives were "tied" to the master of the house. Thus women began to use their wealth from cotton thread production to stage a number of highly visible public ceremo-nies that established the worth and standing of the bride. The *kan kaya* pro-cession, in which the female kin of the bride presented her with useful house-hold implements as well as an impressive array of "things for the room," asserted the bride's worth by: creating a personalized and comfortable space over which she, and not the male household head, was mistress; suggesting the wealth of her ties to other people through the number of goods brought to her by her kin; and metaphorically asserting her fertility and ability to feed others. Similarly the *gara* counter-prestation offered by the bride's mother to the groom asserted publicly that a *sadaki* had been paid, and that the bride should be seen not as a passive dependant but as someone with many social ties and an ability to distribute wealth among others. The performance of a *kan kwarya* ceremony was an explicit denial of servile status, a public event through which women could respond to any implication that anything other than a legitimate marriage had occurred.

By contributing to these ceremonies women created, reinforced, and nurtured social ties to one another and to junior male kin. These social ties emerged from the acceptance of social debt: younger men and women accepted the gifts of older women in order to complete the marriage ritual, so that in effect the marriage ceremonies also made public social ties between the younger generation and older women, and probably between older women and their own patrons and supporters as well. It was primarily through gifts of cloth that women could create such social alliances, for women controlled the disposition of much of the local cloth production through their control of cotton thread up to the late 1950s. However as local cloth production declined with the growth of peanut cropping and the associated sales of imported cloth, women simply made good their responsibility to provide wedding cloth by participating more actively in the market. Where at the turn of the century a gift of cloth bespoke of a woman's industriousness in spinning, today such a gift generally reflects a woman's skill in trade.

Thus marriage ceremonies and the gifts they entail have been important means through which women in the Maradi region have participated in defining marriage and in defining the standing of brides and the senior female kin of both bride and groom. As the material contents of wedding exchanges have shifted, so also have the local associations with those gifts. With Maradi's energetic entry into a transit trade economy, gifts that at the turn of the century reflected an economy and values centered on agro-pastoral production, by the 1950s reflected an economy in which self-worth was increasingly defined in terms of an ability to trade successfully. While the outward form of the ceremonies has remained the same, the changing contents of the gifts exchanged embody new understandings of *arziki* as well as new aspirations among those taking part in the ceremonies. The imported cloth, dishes, containers, and foods that have entered into gift exchange reflect an understanding of wealth and fortune that is tied to success in state employment and international trade (domains in which men have a clear advantage over women) rather than in local agro-pastoral production. Women, whose ability to participate directly in production has been eroded since the turn of the century, must now scramble to generate cash through small-scale trading activities. Much of this cash is then reinvested into the gift exchange through which women continue to create social ties and to "invent" themselves, defining their own worth in a society and economy in which they must actively resist marginalization and devaluation.

If the giving of the gifts has symbolically and socially reproduced inter-generational linkages and created social personhood for both the bride and her mother, the changing context in which the gifts have been acquired has altered the significance of those gifts considerably. Where in the past women could acquire appropriate gifts through their own productive labor and through the mobilization of social networks, today women struggle to earn cash to acquire such gifts. On one level this shift does not appear to be particularly startling: gifts once provided through farming and spinning have been replaced by gifts provided through trade. A closer examination of the terms on which women gain access to cash reveals, however, that women's disadvantaged position within the commercial trade economy amplifies the importance of their invest-ment in gifts and social ties, in turn making their acquisition of cash for gifts all the more urgent. Women are trapped in a frenzied cycle of petty trade to earn cash to invest in gifts to create the social ties and repositories of wealth which will then protect them at times when they can no longer gain access to cash. They find themselves in such a cycle precisely because cash is necessary to day to day survival, yet women are severely limited in their access to cash, and must accordingly find ways to ensure their longer term security in a vola-tile economy and a brittle marriage system.

While women have indeed succeeded in continuing to provide gifts which bespeak female worth, the outward appearance of continuity with the past masks profound changes in the day to day means through which women earn income, and disguises the urgency of investment in wedding gifts and social ties as mere "tradition." As women's purchase upon the local economy dete-riorates due to the erosion of women's rights to land in usufruct, rising de-mands on their labor, and their exclusion from access to key resources (educa-tion, information, credit, Islamic cultural capital), their ability to retain access to land, labor and capital through the nurturing of social ties becomes all the more important. Ironically, as women's ability to earn cash income becomes more and more tenuous, the importance of goods purchased with cash increases, for these goods are essential for the maintenance of the social ties and social worth which can guarantee a woman's future access to contested resources. Furthermore as their security within the economy erodes, women become more and more reliant upon the potential exchange value of the wedding gifts they store as a form of female insurance and savings. Accordingly women find them-selves caught up in a desperate "search for money" to feed the very social networks (wealth in people) and repositories of value (wealth in things) which serve as bulwarks against the depredations of an increasingly male-dominated economy.

Throughout these transformations of wedding gift exchange local under-standings of wealth have been simultaneously created and contested. Chang-ing sources and perceptions of wealth–so evident in shifting gift exchange–have been accompanied by new discourses concerning the nature and origins of prosperity and domesticity. With the increasing importance of commercial transactions in the region the meaning of wealth, as we have seen, has been radically redefined. However it has not been trade alone that has contributed to this shift in the meaning of wealth and prosperity. With the rising importance of Maradi as an administrative and commercial center the region has been increasingly exposed to Western bourgeois ideology, on the one hand, and Nigerian Islamist discourse, on the other. These competing discourses have played out their differences on the shared but contested ground of a reverence for learning and a preference for female domesticity. Both Western bourgeois domesticity (embodied in the Western education offered for girls in the region beginning in the 1950s) and Islamic seclusion (the prerogative of the *alhazai* class) have served as means to distinguish the prosperous elite from the less favored classes. In both ideologies the figure of the respectable home-bound matron marks the literate status and class pretentions of the husband. Women have not been passive pawns in such ideological battles, however, and in the following chapters we shall explore the emergence and implications of these discourses as well as how women themselves have drawn upon and spoken back to them.

6

Wealth and Learning: Discourses on Prosperity and Domesticity

The population of contemporary Maradi consists of distinct, if imbricated, social groupings: the elite educated functionary class, the wealthy male traders known locally as *alhazai*, the traditional aristocracy long known in Hausa as the *sarauta* class, and the mass of workers, farmers, scholars, unemployed youth, and petty traders who, in a moment of self-deprecation, might refer to themselves as *tallakawa*, or commoners. The quality of *arziki* that both constitutes and promotes the prosperity of the merchant class is evidenced in the success of their trade, in their good health, and in the numerousness of their offspring and wives. The prosperity of the elite educated class, on the other hand, is seen as arising out of their special *ilimi*, or knowledge, which through medicine, education, and technology has contributed to improving the standard of living of Nigériens. This *ilimi* has earned for the educated the privileges of state employment and a relatively comfortable and salubrious lifestyle. Both of these enviable and successful social groupings are therefore blessed with the favor of Allah, or *albarka*.

Women, as we shall see, associate *albarka* with the expansion of education and with the success of the merchant and civil servant classes. Both merchants and the elite enjoy *arziki*, a kind of prosperity and good fortune. *Arziki* is a quality of having good luck, luck that is itself a sign of divine election and favor. *Arziki* is also a quality which can be earned and passed on to others, and as such is closely associated with *ilimi*. Both *arziki* and *albarka* are evidence of a divinely sanctioned productive, generative force that brings growth and that multiplies offspring, crops, money, and trade (G. Nicolas 1975:147, 192, 237, 251, 390).[1] Hence achieving a state

---

[1] Women will say, for example, that their marriage is a successful one if it has shown itself to have *arziki* through the production of children (Mariama, 10-11-89).

110

of health and prosperity is often associated with education. As one woman, who herself comes from a modest family of Muslim scholars, explained when I asked what hopes she has for her children:

> Me, I hope Allah will give my children schooling [*karatu*: both Western and Islamic schooling]. If he gives them schooling then he will give them *arziki*, so they will be happy. I don't want them to have any trouble or worries. . . . I hope they will settle into their studies and get *ilimi*, so that *arziki* will come upon them. Then even if I die they can look after themselves. If you have *ilimi*, then *arziki* comes to you easily, Allah will open doors for you and you will succeed. So you can look after yourself and others. . . . That's what I hope for them (Kande, 11-15-88).

The ideals of both the merchant and elite classes find sanction in local ideology, yet the outward expression of the success of these two classes varies tremendously. The merchant class emulates the polygyny and seclusion of Islamic northern Nigeria; the functionary class emulates, at least on the surface, the lifestyle of the Western nuclear household, tolerating a relatively high degree of mobility and visibility for educated women as wage laborers (if not always for women as wives). The coexistence of two such different discourses of prosperity and domesticity in one setting makes for complex combinations and contradictions, presenting women with options for different forms of marriage and work, and with quandaries about how to define themselves, their labor, and their marriages. In this chapter I shall explore some of the origins and implications of these simultaneously consonant and dissonant ideologies.

Female Schooling and the French Domestic Ideal

The earliest schools in Niger were established to train Africans to become clerks, teachers, and minor administrators, but because Niger was "pacified" later than France's coastal colonies her school system always lagged well behind those of colonies such as Dahomey and Senegal. Rather than build a comprehensive school system in Niger, the French relied upon educated labor imported from other colonies, exporting Niger's secondary school students elsewhere for their higher schooling.[2]

The French found, as the British had in Nigeria, that in order to administer their territory cheaply with representatives whose authority was locally recognized they had to rely upon a system of de facto semi-indirect rule, absorbing traditional leaders into the colonial bureaucracy, and superimposing the colonial administration upon political structures already in place.[3] Rather than re-

---

[2]   Where all of the other French West African colonies except Mauritania had primary schools and middle schools by the 1920s, Niger with under 1,000 students in the entire colony had only a very few primary schools, and the majority of the students were concentrated in the capital, originally in Zinder and after 1927, in Niamey (Manning 1988:101).

[3]   However for an engaging account of the differences between colonial rule in Nigeria and Niger and of how they have been carried into the present see Miles (1994).

place "unenlightened native rulers" with colonial officers, the French retained local offices but appointed rulers for their usefulness and loyalty to the French administration (occasionally creating "traditional" rulers where they were needed but did not yet exist). The effect upon the local rulers was to make them at once more authoritarian (because they were no longer accountable to local norms and local modes of removal from office) and less autonomous (because their continuation in power depended upon their subordination to the French colonial hierarchy).[4] In this context schools were explicitly intended for the children of local aristocrats: Western education would make them better and more useful liaisons between the local communities and the French administration.

The first school in Maradi was in the open air, and in 1911 included fifteen "sons of chiefs and notables" (APM/ "Histoire politique, Subdivision de Maradi" [c. 1923]). The first teacher was an African named Lobit in service as a government translator. Later one of the sons of Sarki Kure, 'Dan Baskore, taught in the school. When the administrative post closed down in 1920 for lack of personnel, the school closed with it. It was only after 1927 that French teachers were brought in to run the school and it was kept open continuously under a consistent staff. Thus, where in Niamey the primary school population had by 1931 grown large enough to justify the opening of an École Primaire Superieur for the Zerma and Songhai population, in Maradi the primary school was still only barely functioning after decades of French rule (Fuglestad 1983:121). Those students who were in the school in Maradi were ideally to be the children of the aristocracy: as a 1933 report notes, "particular attention was given to obtaining a majority of sons and nephews of chiefs and notables among the students to enter in September" (APM/"Rapport politique, Cercle de Maradi, 1933"). As a result the small literate class in Niger has strong antecedents in traditional aristocracies.[5]

The French preoccupation with a possible resurgence of Islamic resistance among the conquered population created enormous hesitancy to promote any educational effort that might be interpreted as undermining the Muslim faith, thereby providing a rallying point for dissident factions. Missionary groups were consistently discouraged from setting up primary schooling and were later forbidden to provide schooling in local languages when the French began to consolidate the school system. By 1956 less than 2 percent of the school age population in Niger as a whole was in school (Charlick 1991:36–37).

As one might expect, only a select number of the students who successfully completed their schooling were women. Few girls were offered entry and even fewer were permitted to finish school by their kin. Hajjiya Ta Abu's recollections give a sense of the origins of the most elite members of Nigérien soci-

[4]   Charlick (1991:35). While Maradi's rulers could and did lose their positions under colonial rule, on the whole reigns and tenures of office were far longer and more stable than in the twenty years preceding colonial rule.
[5]   Latour found that forty-six of the fifty-five functionaries in the canton of Tibiri came from three royal linages (1992:176), figures consistent with my own less systematic soundings in Maradi.

ety today and illustrate how unlikely it was, prior to independence, that a girl would successfully complete her schooling:

> Hajjiya Ta Abu: We went to Koranic school, we went to Mallam Na Aya's school in the old town [before Maradi was moved to the plateau late in 1945]. And we also started the European school. Our grandparents, back then they would run off when they saw the Europeans, they were frightened of them, they took us out of school and took us to the bush and hid us.
>
> BMC: So you didn't stay in school very long?
> Hajjiya: No, I didn't stay long. Back then they didn't do it like they do now, back then it was in Hausa.
> BMC: Who taught you?
> Hajjiya: The one who taught us was Monsieur Lobit, he was a man people used to call Mai Lebi. . . . Anywhere you go in town people will tell you about him. He's the one we all knew, he started the thing [the school] here. After him there was Lamine. But I think Lobit was Bambara, he still has children who live here. They all married here, some here and some in Tahoua, two wives in Tahoua and three in Maradi.
> BMC: He must have had a lot of wives.
> Hajjiya: Well! He had ten wives! [She laughs] Children and grandchildren, some in Tahoua, some here. They're all government employees now. They're in the customs office, some are Prefects, some are army Commandants–goodness! Well, blessings from Allah [*barka Allah*], he had children!
> BMC: And you, were you afraid when they sent you off to European school?
> Hajjiya: No! We weren't frightened because our parents were in the military. They were the ones who had taken us, and then when they were off in the bush on their horses doing their work our grandparents came and seized us . . .
> BMC: So they're the ones who didn't like it?
> Hajjiya: They fought and fought about it. They would say the children shouldn't be put in that heathen thing [*abin kafir*], back then they didn't know it was a good thing [*abin da'di*, "a thing of happiness"], so they took us away and kept us from school.
> BMC: So your parents and grandparents couldn't agree about it.
> Hajjiya: Oh, back then they didn't agree at all.
> BMC: When you were in school, you were with the children of your father and mother?
> Hajjiya: Oh, there were lots of us. Out of those who were there and are still alive, some are in the gendarmes and some are in the police. Of the ones who stayed in–but that was all men! All the boys continued in school, it was the girls they pulled out, at least in my neighborhood, but all the boys, look at them now! Some of them here, some of them there, and their children, they're all happy. And they all had lots of children.
> BMC: Well, when they hid you out in the villages, what did you do then?

Hajjiya: Oh, we just went about our affairs! We'd stay with our kin in
the village, and when they were finished collecting [*'dauka*] for school,
then we'd come home and wander about peddling things as before,
since they had finished taking children (Hajjiya Ta Abu, 8-31-89).

Hajjiya Ta Abu is unusual in that she is the only woman of her age I encountered who had had any brush with Western schooling prior to 1945 other
than a few métisse women. Her parentage accounts in part for this: her father
was a soldier in the French army who would have had a clear sense of how
useful a Western education could be. Thus another effect of the military on
women has been the greater probability that the girls of educated soldiers would
be sent to school.[6] Her father and his brothers attempted to place all of their
children–both boys and girls–in the new school. But her father's parents, from
the powerful and intensely Muslim clan heading the settled Fulani population,
would not permit the children to continue, seeing the schooling as tainted by
Christianity and therefore dangerous, particularly for the girls. The Fulani clerical heritage of respect for learning made it possible for the younger generation
to envisage Western education as a virtue for all the children; the same powerful Muslim heritage, however, inclined the older generation to discourage girls,
understood as weaker and more easily swayed by falsehood, from taking advantage of the new education.[7] Although Hajjiya Ta Abu was raised in a Hausa-
speaking household and is unambiguously integrated into the Hausa aristocratic milieu, her family's special origins presented her with a brief opportunity
that most other women of her generation did not experience.[8]

The language Hajjiya and others use to describe the recruitment of children in the early schools suggests that the taking of children for the schools
was locally regarded as yet another in a long series of taxes: like taxes, forced
labor, and later contributions to the reserve granaries, children were "taken
up" [*'dauka*] during specific periods of the year, and parents hid them to protect them just as they would hide their sons and daughters to keep them from
being pressed into forced labor. The language is also similar to that used to
describe how girls and women were seized at will by marauders in the
precolonial period to be taken as wives or enslaved. With such powerfully negative associations it is not surprising that school recruitment was resisted and
that girls in particular were seen as vulnerable and in need of protection. As
occurred in many other regions of Africa, aristocratic parents in Maradi sometimes circumvented this new imposition by sending the children of slaves or of

---

[6] See also Coles (1991:186), Coquery-Vidrovitch (1994:240).

[7] As Pittin observes for similar women in northern Nigeria, "historically, gender and class were
prime determinants in limiting women's educational opportunities, with ideology concurrently
providing bases both to support such education and to limit it" (1990:10).

[8] Some 93.8 percent of all females in Maradi of school age or above have had no exposure to
schooling whatsoever, compared with 80.2 percent of men. Only 5.4 percent of women have had
any primary schooling and .6 percent have achieved any secondary schooling. At the same time,
16.1 percent of Maradi's school age or older males have had some primary schooling, while 2.5
percent have gone on to acquire some secondary schooling. (République du Niger 1992:16–17).

poor clients instead of the "sons and nephews" desired by the administration (Malaya, 9-4-89; Magajiya, 11-15-88; Rabe, 11-17-88). As Hajjiya Malaya, one of Sarki Kure's elderly daughters, remarked:

> Our children didn't go to school, not one went to school at that time [when she was bearing children, from about 1920 to 1935, when Hajjiya Ta Abu was a child]. One day the white man came to our father, the sarki, and said, "You are biting your own hand! We ask you to bring schoolchildren and you brought the children of commoners!" And see us today, Safiya [my nickname in Maradi], what he said came true! Now we send all the children to school . . . Only one of our brothers went to school, Sarki Mohammed, he became Sarki, but he died. The other one who did school is 'dan Dukku, he works in Niamey now (Hajjiya Malaya, 9-4-89).

In general, because the labor of girls was important to the older women in a household, boys could be spared more readily and therefore their schooling was resisted less tenaciously. As Hajjiya Ta Abu explained, once the school recruitment was over she went about her normal work of peddling in the street for her grandmother.

Older women who were deprived of the opportunity to go to school and now see the successful careers of their literate brothers are openly envious and dismayed (Hajjiya Malaya, 9-4-89; Hajjiya Gaba, 3-10-89), as can be seen in Hajjiya Ta Abu's remarks about the success of her brothers. In her case not only did her brothers manage to get coveted jobs in government, but they have been blessed with numerous children: her own failure to have children seems to be associated in her mind with her failure to finish school. Her brothers have *albarka*, a condition of being blessed and rewarded by Allah, just as her teacher Lobit was rewarded with many successful children. Western education introduced new forms of prosperity and new understandings of knowledge, wealth, and success. Women like Hajjiya have had to watch helplessly from the sidelines as others gained access to this new *albarka*; their sense of failure and feeling of having been passed by is mingled at times with resentment at having missed out on schooling while others benefitted from it. Rather than expressing anger at the ideological, economic, and social structures that caused them to be disadvantaged, older women often internalize the source of their failure, seeing it as coming from some lack in themselves. For Hajjiya Ta Abu, the fact that her only child is a crippled girl unable to go to Western school seems to underscore her own personal failure, despite her own prestige among women in Maradi and her daughter's remarkable success in Koranic study.

Those families that benefited from education early have continued to reap the benefits of that advantage even as the number of openings for educated individuals declines relative to the total number of educated people in the country. Mechanisms placing educated aristocratic men in power and educated commoner men in trade have not tended, however, to favor the inclusion of Hausa women in significant positions. Women have been limited to trade in the informal sector and have not managed to build large, diversified commercial enter-

prises like men of the *alhazai* merchant class. Although traditional titled positions for women were, as we shall see in the final chapter, co-opted by
postcolonial governments for the purposes of mobilizing female support, it has
been educated women who have been drawn into the most public positions of
political power. Because Hausa women in Maradi have lagged behind other
women in Niger in access to education, those coveted positions have gone overwhelmingly to non-Hausa women, diminishing the importance of the titled
positions available to aristocratic Hausa women and aggravating differences
between women of different backgrounds and origins. The rise of education in
the region has had little direct effect on the lives of the majority of women
through schooling proper. Rather, as we shall see in a moment, with the emergence of a Western-educated elite, alternative models and discourses about
wealth, knowledge, and domestic life have developed with important implications for women's options in marriage.

Brides or Laborers: Education for Domesticity

Who, then, are the women who have had access to education in Maradi and in
Niger more generally, and what has been the character of that education? The
École de Filles sponsored by the Catholic Mission, for many years the best school
in Maradi, was founded originally as a state school in Zinder to educate the
métis children of French administrators and their African mistresses. Prior to
1921 the school served only boys and, like other schools in the country, suffered from a lack of trained teachers and rising numbers of students. With the
posting of Lieutenant Colonel Ruef to head the Military Territory of Niger in
1921, education became a higher priority in the colony; the numbers of students in school throughout the territory grew sporadically thereafter.

In 1921 Ruef ordered the creation of a special section for girls in the Zinder
school with the ostensible intention of sending the girls on to be trained at the
medical school in Dakar to become professional midwives (AOM/200 Mi 1693
2G20:12, AOM/200 Mi 1695 2G21). From 1921 to 1944 the school in Zinder
served both the boys and the girls of a special portion of the population: while
the school took in students who were of "indigenous" as well as mixed racial
parentage, the Ruef administration tended to regard it as an institution for "or-
phaned" *métis* children. The administration took a paternal interest in it, following the progress of the girls' class closely. These *métis* children were to serve
as exemplars of European culture. The girls in particular were to "civilize" the
colonies by embodying a dated European ideal of family life and domesticity.
As Karen Hansen remarks, "over the course of the nineteenth century in Eu-
rope and North America, the domestic domain took on changing meanings of
privacy, emotions, and moral authority that accorded domesticity a civilizing
function reaching far beyond the threshold of the home" (1992:3). It was in the
interest of this civilizing function that female schooling in the domestic arts
was promoted vigorously for this select population in the colony of Niger. Ruef

had high expectations of the influence of these "domesticated" women, remarking at the end of 1921 that "this first experiment has been a complete success and is a matter of great interest in terms of our civilizing influence" and later the following year, "feminine schooling is called upon to take a role of real importance in the Territory and has become a very favorable element of our influence." While more classes were created for *métisse* and elite girls in Niamey, the local village schools such as the school in Maradi "vegetated" for lack of qualified personnel (AOM/200 Mi 1695 2G21:14, AOM/200 Mi 1698 2G22:16).

Although the classes for girls had originally been created to prepare them for medical training, the notion of "civilization" embraced by the early administration required the girls to devote a large portion of their study to domestic training (*l'enseignement ménager*): the entire afternoon was taken up with sewing, mending, washing, and ironing. Like schoolgirls elsewhere in colonial Africa, they were encouraged to learn the skills of middle-class housebound domesticity at the very moment when growing numbers of European and American women were working outside the home. Nevertheless the more successful students (both *métisses* and *indigènes*) occasionally went on to the higher school in Niamey, from whence they might go on to medical school, or become secretaries and teachers' aids.

The emphasis on domestic training and marriage for these girls conflicted with the urgent needs of the colony for trained female medical personnel. Ruef seems to have imagined that part of the measure of France's success in "civilizing" this portion of Africa (thereby justifying the French colonial presence there) lay in France's ability to prepare these young women to become housewives after a dying European model. The ranking medical personnel of the colony, on the other hand, clamored increasingly for trained female personnel, since childbirth problems were (and still are) among the most pressing facing the health of the local population, and female staff were indispensable in handling pregnancy and childbirth. It was a matter of some frustration to the medical officers that the midwives trained and sent from the coastal regions were generally married to Dahomean functionaries; consequently, they could not move about freely, did not know the local languages, and inspired little confidence in the local women. The medical officers had little patience with the type of schooling and paternal protections offered to the young women schooled in Zinder, who were in their view a scarce and valuable resource. After criticizing the training in housework, the chief medical officer in 1935 remarked:

> As for these young girls, as soon as they reach puberty they are sought after for marriage by native functionaries, among whom they are in great demand. Only a few of the young *métisse* women go on to take the admission test to become midwives at the School of Medicine: two will be eligible in 1937 (AOM/200Mi 1768 2G35 30).

Six years later in 1943 the medical officer once again remarked that the problem of female staff was still severe and that meeting the needs for female personnel was critical to the success of the medical service in reaching the popula-

Photo 5: "The school in Doutchi–a class" ("Ecole de Doutchi–Une classe"). Dogondoutchi, April 6, 1955, donated by RRPP Chantoux, Collerie et Simon, 1957. A classroom in the Catholic school in Dogondoutchi (a Hausa-speaking region to the west of Maradi) provides a glimpse at an era in which a few Hausa girls gained Western education through mission schools. The non-Hausa names on the blackboard are perhaps a mark of the importance of Dahomean and other educated populations from outside Niger in the Nigérien schools of the period. French National Archives, Centre des Archives d'Outre-mer. All rights reserved. 30F1.20.AOF.6551.

tion, "the native female element being in general the most resistant" (AOM/ 200 Mi 1845 2G43 14).

After 1944 the Zinder school was used for boys, and the girls were sent to Fadan Gourma (which at that time fell within the administrative unit of Niger), where a Catholic mission took them on. It is probably during this period that the school became more rigorous academically, training more women to go on into higher education (AOM/200 Mi 2744 2G53 210).[9] The girls' school continued there until 1953, when Fadan Gourma was no longer part of Niger, and it was at that time that the school was finally moved to Maradi to keep it within the colony. The number of students in the girl's school, known by this time as the *Foyer des métisses*, never exceeded fifty and was usually limited to about thirty-five. Because the number of educated personnel available to fill medical and clerical positions prior to independence was still quite limited, these women had a good chance of being sent on for secondary education or of gaining a low-level position in the French administration or trade stores provided either that they did not marry or that their husbands and families approved.[10] During the colonial period this school was consistently better staffed and equipped than the schools built for "indigenous" students.[11]

After independence the school became a private girls' school available to anyone who could pay, and for many years continued to provide the best French education available in Maradi.[12] Recently, in an effort to eliminate single-sex schools (which are perceived to disadvantage girls) the Nigérien government has required all schools to become co-ed, and thus a longstanding institution that prepared a very few privileged women both for a particularly conservative brand of European marriage and for prominent roles in Nigérien society has lost its original character. A few other Catholic schools in Zinder, Dogondoutchi, and Niamey have provided women with a good education, but the expansion of religious schools (which in Africa have tended to be more interested than public schools in female education [Rescoussie 1973:19]) has been limited due to the administration's policy of avoiding possible confrontation with Muslim resistance among the local population.

For similar reasons the attempts of the Protestant Sudan Interior Mission to set up a school in Tibiri were consistently thwarted. Unlike the priests and sisters of the Catholic schools, however, the teachers of the SIM schools were rarely French and taught their classes in Hausa, generating even greater mis-

---

[9]   The education officer that year notes that the girls received "suitable training" and did well on the competitive exam to go into secondary school.

[10]   AOM/200 Mi 1695 2G21, AOM/200 Mi 1698 2G22:16, AOM/200 Mi 2744 2G53:210, AOM/200 Mi 2732 2G51:160; AOM/200 Mi 2067 2G58:16, APM/ "Rapport Annuel, 1954." APM/ "Rapport Annuel, 1964."

[11]   AOM/200 Mi 2067 2G58:16; in 1958 the École des Métisses had sanitary outdoor toilets when none of the other schools in the region had any facilities at all.

[12]   Up to 1977 the Catholic girls' school had the greatest success in preparing its students to pass the entry exams into secondary school of all the schools in Maradi. Since then it has continued to do better than most of the schools in the city, public or private. IP/ "Rapport Annuel," for the years 1970–1989.

trust on the part of the French administration. The government closed the SIM boy's school in Tibiri in 1933, in principle because the personnel were not licensed to teach in the French system. The missionaries were also forbidden to proselytize and were to focus on medical care rather than schooling. Tensions with the British in Nigeria periodically gave rise to suspicions that the missionaries were engaging in political activities, particularly during and after World War II.[13]

The missionaries nevertheless continued teaching quietly since they considered an ability to read the Bible in Hausa an important step towards becoming a Christian. By 1945, as a result of the mission's eighteen years of medical and social work, the local SIM community had grown to about 200 members and faced a demographic dilemma: many of the younger members of the community were men who were now preparing to marry, and, because it was harder to reach women than men, there were very few Christian women for them to wed.[14] Just as the French were arranging to transfer the *Foyer des métisses* from Fadan Gourma to Maradi, SIM began pushing hard for permission to set up a school for girls as a way of drawing young women into the community. The colonial government stalled, hoping that the Catholic mission could set up its school quickly and the issue of the girls' school could thus be defused (APM/ "Bulletin de renseignements, Cercle de Maradi, 1951"). In the meantime, in 1951, the SIM quietly began to set up a school for girls in Soura, a village between Maradi and Tibiri.

In its brief existence (1951–1966) the school in Soura never had more than forty students at a time. Parents in the region, seeing the success of the mission's medical efforts, brought in sickly infants and children who otherwise would not survive to be raised by the missionaries. Despite an SIM policy to the contrary, the Tibiri station found itself taking in orphans and foster children. The two female missionaries heading the Soura school were charged with raising them. Because the missionaries knew that they would probably only have the children for a short period of time before the girls' kin reclaimed them to marry them off at fourteen or fifteen, they focused on practical domestic skills and Bible study, calling the school (like the early *Foyer des métisses*) an *école ménagère*. The curriculum emphasized reading and writing in Hausa (with a view to being able to read the Bible) as well as hygiene, nutrition, sewing, and knitting. The older children were taught child care by helping to care for the infants and smaller children. As the school system grew in the postindependence era the older girls were sent to the public school in Maradi for part of the day.

Many of the girls went on to marry into Christian families, but others married Muslim men and were lost to the community. Although the school explic-

---

[13] APM/ "Rapport Politique, Cercle de Maradi, 1933;" AOM/FOM 386:77 Bis/8:6; APM/ "Rapport semestriel, Cercle de Maradi, le 30 juin, 1945." The reality was more complex: the mission was a potential vehicle for African converts to build power bases in competition for traditional offices, a tendency the missionaries themselves resisted (Robinson 1983:117).

[14] This discussion of the Soura school is based primarily upon a discussion with Rita Salls (Sebring, Florida, 11-16-90), the missionary who (together with Alberta Simms), presided over it for almost the entirety of its existence.

itly trained young women to become Christian wives and mothers, a number of the school's students went on to work at the SIM medical center at Galmi or to teach, and one (a *métisse*) went on to gain a position in the finance department of the national government in Niamey. Others went on to support their husbands in their teaching and pastoral duties. After 1965 the school was joined with the SIM boy's school in Tibiri and the school in Soura was closed. In all perhaps 100 girls went through the girl's school in Soura.

Thus two of the most striking efforts to educate girls in Maradi and in Niger as a whole prior to independence tangled with the delicate question of what role in society these women were expected to take on once they had completed their schooling. In both the *Foyer des métisses* and the Soura school the girls taken in were marginal members of society: children who either had no father present to look out for them or children whose health was so unstable that an unusual and perhaps dangerous upbringing could be justified by their kin. These were girls who, because they were atypical, were able to take advantage of educational opportunities from which other women were shielded. In both cases potentially conflicting goals emerged. On the one hand the schools groomed partners for marriage after an outdated European domestic pattern. On the other hand, the schools created a pool of women capable of meeting the country's urgent labor needs, particularly in the area of maternal and infant health. For the SIM women the mission's medical mission made it possible to combine their roles as church wives with their work as trained medical personnel. The earliest graduates of the *Foyer des métisses*, because they tended to marry educated functionaries before they completed secondary schooling, were less able to make this kind of compromise. Later, as secondary school for girls was promoted more vigorously after 1945, student marriages might be postponed until the young women had finished their schooling, making it more likely that they would have sufficient training to work as civil servants.

Neither the French colonial government nor the SIM missionaries were willing to emphasize female participation in the labor force at the expense of women's training to become wives and mothers. In reality a number of the SIM graduates did go on to enter the salaried work force and to do health and education work: like Africans elsewhere these women could put their training to uses not originally envisioned by their teachers.[15] But this was a secondary and unintended consequence of their schooling. As for the French girls' school, only after the *foyer* was headed by the sisters of the Catholic mission in Fadan Gourma and Maradi does the education provided seem to have been geared to prepare the girls directly to compete for secondary schooling and employment.[16] This early emphasis on domestic roles

---

[15]   Conflicts over the content and uses of female education for domesticity in Africa were common, and African women frequently turned their training to uses more in keeping with their prominence in the productive and income-earning realm (Hansen 1992).

[16]   There is some irony in the fact that two religious institutions that in theory advocated the subordination of women to men in practice relied upon strong, independent, and unmarried women for many of their efforts. These women succeeded far better than the French administration in training African women to go on to participate in the salaried work force.

for women has had a sustained effect upon local perceptions of the kinds of roles appropriate for educated women. In 1964 Henri Raulin interviewed boys and girls in their final year of primary school in the Maradi region and found that almost all hoped to earn a position working for the government. While the boys were interested in fields ranging from administration to veterinary services to medicine, all of the girls expected to become either teachers or nurses (1964:52, 54 Table I). Neither the government nor private educators have tended to train women for work in technical fields such as agronomy or veterinary science, despite their significant role in the agropastoral sector. Women in higher studies in Niger today continue to be concentrated overwhelmingly in the humanities (Adams and Kruppenback 1987:449). Women have only recently been trained in administration, finance, and planning, and in the national government their appointments have generally been limited to fields regarded as specifically touching upon women, such as health.

Ultimately, then, access to Western education has been linked for women in Niger to a particular image of femininity and domestic life. Women, in this image, are to create and maintain a European style middle-class household in which the husband is the master and provider while the wife teaches and promotes the values of cleanliness, health, and propriety. Of course the demand for educated female labor pulls against this middle class image of the homemaker. Bourgeois domesticity is possible only if women have leisure for knitting and embroidery, a luxury that resonates with the ideal of *zarafi*, or leisure, for secluded women of the merchant and aristocratic classes. The demand for educated female labor has meant that the ideal of the domesticated housewife has not generally been realized: educated women may remain single and work outside the home, or marry men of similar background. Married women often manage two-career households in which female chores are met through the labor of servants and junior female kin.[17] While the emblems of modernity and domesticity promoted through such education have become prominent elements of elite culture (from cutlery to crocheted tablecloths), elite households also prefer time-saving luxuries such as macaroni and washing machines. A "home" after the European model, ironically, frequently calls for the labor of illiterate servants, who may be male, and sufficient income to pay for them. Working women's use of these "boys" to perform traditionally female household tasks such as cooking occasionally provokes the ire of educated men, who argue that women's salaries aren't adequate to justify such an expense, that the children will be neglected, and that a "boy" can't cook good traditional sauces (Djermakoye 1975a). The educated wife remains a concept in flux, full of contradictions and possibilities.

---

[17] On the resulting demand for child labor see Coquery-Vidrovitch (1994:187–88); Oppong (1981:106–108); Moran (1992). On child fostering in the service of seclusion see Maher (1974:139).

From "Farm Donkey" to Mallama

Because rising rates of literacy occurred primarily in the postwar years and since independence, almost the entire Nigérien population of women born before 1952 have no Western education whatsoever (République du Niger 1985b:106). A woman such as Hajjiya Ta Abu is a remarkable exception. More typical of the Maradi women over thirty-five or forty years old who did obtain an education is Madame Rose, the *métisse* daughter of a Frenchman and a Dahomean functionary, who was educated "by the sisters" and was a primary school teacher for many years before her recent retirement. Madame Rose had lived in Maradi for about fifteen years with her husband, who owned a garage, before his death. Since then she has remained in Maradi and at the time of my research was a prominent member of the national women's association (AFN). Where Hajjiya Ta Abu, who has lived in Maradi since she was a girl and participated in the women's association from its inception under Diori, earned no national recognition for her activities, Madame Rose was "nominated" and then "elected" as one of the national representatives for Maradi Department in the National Assembly which was briefly reinstituted in 1989, despite the fact that she is a relative latecomer to the AFN, joining only after moving to Maradi in the late 1970s. Little wonder there was tension within the AFN over the differential treatment of educated and unschooled women by the government, treatment that inevitably coincided with racial and ethnic differences as well, since the earliest schools benefited *métisse* "orphans" and the Zerma region surrounding the capital of Niamey disproportionately.

While older women in the city of Maradi have rarely had access to Western education, from the mid-1930s on more and more women received a Koranic education, which had previously been reserved for boys. Prior to that time women were taught how to pray and how to wash, "enough so we wouldn't be *haram* [unlawful]," but not enough to read or write or recite special prayers ('Yar Fatake, 8-30-89).[18] As one older woman remarked, a woman who was too erudite might have trouble finding a husband (Mai Muni, 4-25-89). Women over sixty sometimes observed that in their day a woman who wanted a good understanding of Islam had to marry a mallam, and that the growth of Koranic schooling was a phenomenon associated with the "coming of the Europeans."[19] It is likely that the local population responded to Western education by supporting the learning it regarded as more relevant and appropriate for its children, and in particular its girls, who needed to be well trained in Islam to resist "heathen" customs. As early as 1921 Paul Marty observed 100 or so

---

[18]   This is, of course, in rather striking contrast with northern Nigeria where one of the legacies of the jihad has been a respect for female education. See Boyd (1989) and Sule and Starratt (1991).

[19]   Hajjiya Salamatou, 8-23-89; Hajjiya Zabaya, 9-13-89; Hajjiya Adama, 3-1-89; 'Yar Fatake, 8-30-89. The oldest women with a strong Muslim education were either married to a Mallam, or had fathers who were mallams: Maskomi, 8-20-89; Hajjiya Mai Saka, 8-23-89. Fulani women seem to have had a greater likelihood of getting a strong education that Hausa women; Fatchima, 2-1-89; Hajjiya Halima, 2-24-89.

Koranic schools, or *makaranta*, in the Maradi region, and noted that "sometimes the clear voices of one or two little girls make themselves heard above the sharp concert" of children reciting the Koran (1930:426).

The earliest Koranic schooling available to girls seems to have been provided in the evening by lantern light. Since girls were still expected to work in the day peddling goods for their mothers, they were often too tired to continue their studies for long before giving them up (Magajiya, 11-15-88; Hajjiya Ta Dogo, 2-2-89; 'Yar Fatake, 8-30-89; Hajjiya Gobarci, 11-16-88). Women born since 1945 were sent to daytime *makaranta* but the competition with their peddling duties was acute and continued to be tiring. Sometimes girls were sent to *makaranta* until they were old enough to peddle (at about age seven) and were then taken out; others were permitted to study only so long as their peddling was not affected (Hajjiya Gobarci, 11-16-88; 'Yar Fatake, 8-30-89; Amina Ta 'Yar Fatake, 11-6-89). Because girls were in any case always taken out of *makaranta* at puberty to be married, women only very rarely "arrived" at the culmination of their studies, namely the ability to recite the entire Koran by heart.

Today *makaranta* continues to be both an alternative to Western schooling and a source of competition for girls' time and energy. Because Islamic learning is a significant source of social capital in a milieu where "everybody knows it" and respected behaviors are associated with it, most parents in the city of Maradi today send their children to some form of Koranic school. Little girls seem to make up roughly one-third of the students and the potential for girls to achieve a relatively high level of learning is greater today than at any time in the past.[20] Although I knew of no women who had set themselves up as Koranic teachers in Maradi in the late 1980s, the possibility of women achieving enough Islamic education to earn the respectful title *mallama* or "scholar" is real today in a way it was not for the majority of their mothers and grandmothers.

Like Western schooling, *makaranta* has been largely an urban phenomenon. Women over fifty raised in rural areas only gained access to such an education in larger villages and cities (Dela Ta Tanin, 8-24-89; Hajjiya Gobarci, 11-16-88; Mariama, 8-29-89). While some villages in the Maradi region have a long tradition of Islamic scholarship, others do not, and only recently have Muslim schools been established in them.[21] Rural children who want an extensive Islamic education must come to Maradi to receive it, causing an enormous influx of poor *almajirai* Koranic students from villages throughout the Department during the dry season. While these children—who are always boys—do receive some Islamic education, their lives are extremely difficult: they sleep in the doorways of schol-

[20] In 1989 I watched an adolescent girl in Sabon Gari recite extremely long passages of the Koran publicly during one of the Great Festivals and she was roundly applauded by the gathered crowd and much admired by women and children in the neighborhood. She was a student in one of the newest and most expensive schools.

[21] In his late 1960s study of Muslim scholars in four villages in the region, Guy Nicolas found that the less Islamicized the village, the younger the scholar, suggesting that as Muslim schooling has grown young graduates have returned to their villages to set up schools for the first time (1975:604–605).

ars' houses, beg for food and money, and are treated (sometimes with good reason) with mistrust by the Maradi population, who are nevertheless obliged by Muslim norms to provide alms and food to them on daily basis.[22] Sending children to urban centers to "eat the dry season" is one way a rural family can eke out limited food reserves, so that the acquisition of Muslim education is in reality only of secondary importance for many of these boys. The children leave the city with the onset of the rainy season to return to their villages and help with farming.

With the rise of Islamic schooling generational differences between women have emerged. Older women's educational experience differs from that of their daughters not only in their access to Western education, but in their grasp of Islam, their sense of integration into the Muslim community, and their confidence in themselves as good and law-abiding Muslims. Younger women may have a grasp of Islam that provides them with spiritual and rhetorical resources unavailable to their mothers. As one middle-aged women who had been trying to learn to read the Koran by watching her children remarked:

When we were little we didn't learn to read the Koran, our peddling wouldn't allow for that. Back then people weren't enlightened like they are today. Today, when morning comes you tell your children to go off to *makaranta*. And there they are, they study, all the way until they can recite the whole thing. But in the past . . . there are a lot of adult women who don't have proper knowledge of Islam. We just go about our way and do our best to pray right. Yup. I'm trying to read now so that I won't do anything that is unlawful. But now we put our sons and daughters in *makaranta* ('Yar Fatake, 8-30-89).

Older women rely upon their children as links to a rapidly changing world that they have little means of understanding. Even if their children do not go on to become successful public sector employees, their Islamic and Western education makes them valuable intermediaries, conduits of information and analysis. But the opposition between senior women, whose judgement and experience ought to make them authorities, and juniors whose schooling makes them experts in a changing world, can occasionally generate tension.

Mariama is a middle-aged woman I visited on a number of different occasions. One day, when I asked her about her various children's progress in school, she had trouble remembering because she did not really understand the school system. She became very annoyed and ended our talk when her young daughter-in-law entered the conversation to help get the details right. So by the next time I visited she had gone to the trouble of finding out for herself exactly what levels her children were in. When in the course of our discussion I wished her daughters success in school she responded in this way, probably aware that she had been abrupt the last time we had spoken:

[22] Children from Maradi who want a higher Islamic education often go as *almajirai* to cities such as Daura in northern Nigeria, where they experience the same hardships. One of my informant's sons went to Daura to learn, and returned after only a week saying that it was too hard for him, unaccustomed as he was to this kind of severe existence. Hajjiya Ta Dogo, 2-2-89.

Amen! Well, we're just here trying to take it all in, Safiya. You know today, everything depends on intelligence. So, things in the world to-day, they're too much for me. Even though we hope the children will do well in school, maybe tomorrow [that will mean] they won't be here, they'll be off somewhere else. One day they're here, the next day they're off somewhere else studying. Off taking up learning by them-selves. Because, you know, today, if you don't have learning, then you are just like us farm donkeys who can't figure out worldly talk our-selves, right? (Mariama, 10-11-89).

This brief episode underscores the large gap in experience, opportunities, and self-image between women of different generations. Older women sometimes feel that their knowledge and experience is little valued, or that they are stupid be-cause they are not literate. The social hierarchy placing older women above younger women is threatened and the stature these women have earned with great diffi-culty over the course of their lives is in a sense diminished by the rapid achieve-ments of "children" who have been schooled. While women want their children to do well, they may lose touch with them because of Western schooling, especially if the children go off to Niamey or Zinder for higher studies or employment.

Female Education and the Negotiation of Marriage

Claire Robertson has argued on the subject of female education in Af-rica generally that the more active women are in the informal economy of a country, the more dysfunctional European education is. Such schooling de-prives girls of the "apprenticeships" in the activities most available to them (in this case farming and food transformation enterprises), denies their mothers valuable labor, and reinforces female dependence upon males in the future: unemployed primary and middle school graduates generally es-chew the kinds of economic activities their mothers had engaged in in the past, turning instead to marriage to successful men for their income and security.[23] The cases of women in Maradi support some of her conclusions but also indicate that the consequences of Western education are more mixed and ambiguous than she suggests.

Certainly, with tightening of the state budget and decreasing public sector appointments for school graduates, the disadvantages of Western education

---

[23] Robertson (1986:108–110). Robertson is not alone in this assessment; in an effort to make educa-tion in local languages available to children who probably will not enter the public sector, in 1979 the Nigérien government opened thirty-three "experimental" schools, one of which is in the city of Maradi. The courses are taught in local languages and the curriculum includes polytechnical in-struction, farming, and animal raising projects. Despite the schools' apparent success over more than a decade, they are still regarded as "experimental" and there is to my knowledge no discus-sion of expanding the program beyond its current alternative status (Oumarou 1984:69–70). Obvi-ously one of the problems with such schools in the eyes of Nigériens is that they do not confer the social and cultural capital of traditional Western education. Niger's current economic crisis and the decreasing likelihood that school-leavers will gain employment with the state may improve the status of the "experimental" schools.

may begin to outweigh the advantages in the perception of parents. Women who, like Madame Rose, found employment during the replacement of Dahomean functionaries with local labor or who later rode the tide of rising employment during the uranium boom, have been exceptional. However from the point of view of parents unemployment is not the only undesirable outcome of Western schooling: schooling presents the possibility that juniors will resist the controls of seniors, that girls will become pregnant before marriage, and that the cultural and social values of parents will not be respected by educated children.

The women of Hajjiya Indo's household provide examples of an array of experiences of and outcomes to female education. Hajjiya Indo's husband is a trader who has had contact with French merchants and therefore speaks some French, but has not been to school. She herself had only limited exposure to *makaranta* as a girl in Madarumfa. Later, as an adult in Maradi, she went to adult education classes offered as part of a literacy program targeted at members of the AFN.[24] She has since forgotten most of what she learned except for some mathematical skills she uses daily in her milk trade. The primary purpose of her participation in the "war on ignorance" program seems to have been to demonstrate good will and interest in the "progress" promoted by the Ali Saibou regime (Hajjiya Indo, 1-11-89).

Hajjiya's various trades have called for substantial labor, supplied by her children, hired labor, and her daughter-in-law, Hawa. While Hajjiya's own daughters were growing up Hajjiya relied upon Hawa's labor in her trade, so that in a sense her children's schooling was purchased at the expense of another child (who was married before the age of twelve). Hawa is very much a subordinate in the household–she works hard, is ill frequently, and rarely speaks or smiles. She attended *makaranta* in her nearby village as a child, but did not go to school, moving to Maradi when she married Hajjiya's son Hassan. Hajjiya has also relied upon the help of two hired workers from rural areas. Dije is a Fulani pastoralist who came to Maradi seeking work during the drought of 1984 after she was divorced by her husband. Dije is the subject of much teasing because of her poor Hausa and her general ignorance and confusion. Habi, a sturdy farm woman, also came to Maradi relatively recently after a divorce. She did some *makaranta* as a girl, but gave up when she decided she was not good at it.

Thus all three of Hajjiya's helpers are illiterate women of rural background who have come to Maradi for marriage and to earn money. By contrast, although Hajjiya's daughter Zuera, who is their approximate contemporary (all are between twenty and thirty years old), did help her mother

---

[24]   In the early postindependence years UNESCO funded a literacy project which created 349 literacy centers throughout the country; the numbers of centers increased through the 1970s to about 986 by 1980. Under Diori Hamani the centers promoted literacy in French, and like the early programs in many other independent African nations, the program was a failure because it was poorly adapted to the needs of rural adults (Oumarou 1984:70, Ouane and Amou-Taneh 1990).

with her various trades, she was able to attend primary school. At fifteen Zuera finished primary school and attempted once to gain entry into secondary school, but failed. Although school regulations would permit her to take the exam a second time the following year, she was instead married to a twenty-one-year-old school-leaver whose wealthy father had set him up as a trader between Niger, Burkina Faso, and Mali. Despite her parents' preference that she finish school before marrying, her suitor insisted that he could not wait; such a promising suitor could not be turned down. Although Zuera lived very comfortably in seclusion in her husband's compound in Ouagadugu, the marriage ended in divorce because of conflict with her younger co-wife and physical abuse by her husband. During my research she was living in her mother's house waiting for the divorce to be finalized and evaluating various suitors. She had no desire to set up an independent trade such as her mother's and wanted only a stable marriage to a wealthy man who would treat her well. Against her mother's wishes she eventually married a Nigerian functionary from a wealthy family with ties in Maradi and left her mother's house to live with him in Abuja, Nigeria. Zuera's education has not provided her with skills she can use to earn a living, but has rather made her, as Robertson would argue, more dependent than her illiterate mother upon men for her own support and status.

Zuera's younger sister Zainabu is a feisty young woman who not only went to primary school, but succeeded in entering secondary school. Many girls are married off before they can continue into secondary studies for fear they will become pregnant if they spend too much time with boys. Zainabu is proof that these fears are not altogether unfounded, since she was not able to finish her secondary schooling because she became pregnant.[25] She dropped out of school at about fifteen. She lives with her mother, who has borne the expense of raising the child. The father of the child, a soldier, is now in Niamey, and although he claims to want to marry her, in three years he had not arranged to return to Maradi for a formal ceremony. Zainabu is now taking secretarial courses in a private school at the expense of a different male admirer, a source of chagrin to her mother.

Where Zuera is interested only in marriage in the household of a respectable wealthy man and was extremely careful of her reputation while unmarried, Zainabu is single-mindedly pursuing her secretarial course and is flamboyantly unashamed of her sexuality. Despite her colorful reputation in the neighborhood, Zainabu has the kind of drive and determination that made her mother successful and is far more likely than Zuera to put her education to some kind of appropriate use, even if it means risking being considered a courtesan or prostitute to get where she wants. She is likely to

---

[25]   On the other hand close analysis of recent statistics on the age of first sexual encounters suggests that the popular stereotype of promiscuous schoolgirls is in fact off the mark. Girls with no schooling at all tend to have their first sexual relations earlier (at almost fifteen) than girls who have had some schooling (at sixteen and a half) precisely because unschooled girls are married off sooner (République du Niger 1992:68).

use successive relationships with men to provide herself eventually with the means to support herself independently. Zainabu has developed a kind of independence of mind, sexual freedom, and determination that is not easily measured by Robertson's economic assessment of women's education. Even if Zainabu does not find literate employment, she moves among men with an ease illiterate women find puzzling; she may, thus, use her education as cultural capital to gain herself other practical advantages.

Their youngest sister, Aisha, was married off at about fourteen to her cousin, Hajjiya's brother's son, during my stay. Aisha did not finish primary school. Hajjiya's inability to control Zuera or Zainabu, and the doubtful usefulness of Zuera's education other than to make her a rather elegant bride for a trader or functionary (in this case, one who doesn't even speak French), dampened Hajjiya's enthusiasm for her youngest daughter's schooling. Hajjiya was happy to have her youngest daughter safely married off into a suitable household nearby without finishing primary school. While Hajjiya has been happy to pay for her children's *makaranta*, she is less enthusiastic about supporting Western schooling, since even without schooling her children can help her with her trade, go into farming in her village, take up the transport business with their father, or help their uncle with his restaurant. Hajjiya seems to agree with Robertson that the disadvantages of Western education may outweigh the advantages.[26] However, if her daughters had been successful in becoming functionaries she might have felt differently.

One of Zuera's friends, Madame Hadiza, illustrates some of the advantages women who successfully complete a Western education enjoy and can bring to their parents. She has an independent income through her teaching, her own housing, freedom to move about on her own, and a degree of sexual independence unheard of for women who are not categorized as *karuwai*. For her mother the benefits of Madame Hadiza's education are significant, as Hadiza can afford to provide occasional gifts of cash and cloth. She also supplied the capital for starting her mother's cold drink trade. For Hadiza education has meant that she can choose to remain unmarried without suffering the stigma associated with non-marriage for most women; her income and housing make it possible for her to resist marriage arrangements proposed by her kin. For educated women such as Hadiza, their education brings not only independent income, but also a whole array of lifestyle options unavailable to illiterate women. However, the utility not only of Western education but of civil service employment itself has been severely called into question by the recent economic crisis, during which many functionaries received no salaries for extended periods of time. What this crisis will mean for female education in the longer term remains to be seen.

---

[26]   Disillusionment with the cost and lack of pay-off from schooling may affect parents' willingness to send boys to school as well as girls, given the high rate of unemployment for school leavers. (Roberta Ann Dunbar, personal communication June 14, 1993). The disaffection is heightened in the case of girls by the added risk that they will become pregnant before marriage.

Alhazai Ideology: Prosperity, Polygyny, and Seclusion

The postwar economic growth of the Maradi region drew "strangers" and "soldiers" to Maradi, created new income-generating options for women, and
opened up the market in urban land. It also gave rise to a class of male Hausa
merchants, known locally as the *alhazai* (the plural of Al Hajj) because they
have almost invariably performed the pilgrimage to Mecca. This class of men
has enormous influence in Maradi today, in some ways superceding the
Katsinawa *sarauta* aristocracy in importance. The most successful traders benefited from the postcolonial government's efforts to shift trade out of European
trade companies and into the hands of local merchants through new marketing
structures, the provision of credit, and investment in roads and communica-
tions (Grégoire 1986:180). The *alhazai* are consulted in all major political and
social decisions and are frequently called upon to fund various public works,
public displays of support of the regime in power (such as annual Samariya
popular theater competitions), and charity projects (such as the building of
mosques and schools). They were "invited" by the national government to buy
out a number of failing parastatals in the late 1980s. Their wealth creates public responsibilities in a setting where generosity and public-spiritedness are seen
as religious virtues. At the same time the demands made upon them, combined with the state's handling of the economy (particularly "illicit" trade with
Nigeria), have often placed them in subdued confrontation with the national
government, despite the origins of their success in national policies (Kotoudi
et al. 1988). It is not surprising, given these demands, that an element within
the *alhazai* class has begun to elaborate an ideology condemning ostentatious
redistribution in the form of building mosques, sending others to Mecca, and
providing wedding gifts. Instead, as these young members of the Islamic reformist movement, Izala, see it, capital should be invested in *madrasas* (schools
that provide a modern education combined with Islamic religious training) or
accumulated for "rational" investment (Grégoire 1993).[27]

The intense commercial ties between Maradi and northern Nigeria–particularly with Kano (Kotoudi 1988:30, Grégoire 1986:132–36)–have caused many
of these Hausa merchants to reinforce their ties with Nigerian merchants by
adopting Muslim norms common in Nigeria. One of Grégoire's informants explicitly links the growth of trade with the adoption of Nigerian Islamic practices:

> When merchants from Maradi went to Nigeria on business, they saw
> how their contacts there practised religion (prayer etc.) and then par-
> ticipated with them. When they came back to Niger they changed their
> customs and religious beliefs. They led the men who worked with them

---

[27] The Jama'atu Izalat al-bid'a wa Iqamat al-Sunna (Movement for Suppressing Innovations and
Restoring the Sunna) or Izala movement was founded in Jos, Nigeria, in 1978, defining itself in
opposition to the major Sufi brotherhoods of the region (the Qadiriyya and Tijaniyya). Members
are known in Hausa as 'yan Izala. For the rise of anti-Sufism in Nigeria see Umar (1993). For its
presence and meaning in Maradi, see Grégoire (1993).

to pray to God. That's how Islam replaced traditional religions (Grégoire 1993:108).

Note that the speaker, a Muslim scholar, implies that prior to the rise of the merchant class the only religious practice in the region was "traditional" animism, denying the long history of Islam in the Katsina court and dismissing the gradual adoption of Muslim practices by local farmers. Clearly the *alhazai* class has its own myths to tell about who is responsible for introducing "true belief" into the region.

The implication that those who do not practice religion as these merchants do are not Muslim is a powerful inducement for others to adopt *alhazai* and even Izala (reformist) practices. Polygyny is common among this class, and the wives of these large *commerçants* are kept more strictly in seclusion than had been usual in the past for women who were not married to notables or Muslim scholars.[28] Men in both urban and rural areas aspire to the prestige and moral capital of the merchant class, so that even households that can ill afford polygyny and seclusion may adopt them. While polygyny rates are high throughout Niger (overall 36.2 percent of women are in polygynous unions) the incidence is markedly higher (at 50.2 percent) in the Maradi region than in other regions of the country (République du Niger 1992:63). This practice is not limited to "backwards" rural areas. To the contrary, the polygyny rate appears to be highest in urban areas and among the educated. In other words it is closely associated with a higher standard of living (République du Niger 1992:63–64), and can, indeed, become a marker of urban prestige and prosperity. The ability of wealthy merchants to take more than one wife and to absorb the high cost of marriage creates competition between successful older men and less established "youth" for wives. Young men must delay marriage and full adulthood because as competition increases the cost of marriage rises. A kind of vicious cycle ensues: only successful married men can afford to take wives. Thus polygyny has become an important sign of status among men, not only because it represents a kind of wealth and adherence to Islam, but also because it reinforces the authority of senior men over junior men who have not yet achieved fully adult status through marriage (Raynaut 1971:136).

As practices from Nigeria become generalized, wealthy merchants have sought new means to distinguish themselves. Recently younger merchants have begun following the Izala movement emanating from Jos, Nigeria, setting them apart from other men in the city (who are primarily members of the Qadiriyya brotherhood, although a minority follow the Niassiyya branch of the Tijaniyya). The merchant class has always used Islamic identity to distinguish itself from the general population in a variety of ways. Formerly, Grégoire argues, simply being Muslim was sufficient to establish a distinctive merchant class identity:

[28] The linkage between these practices and the influence of Nigeria prompted Guy Nicolas to use the incidence of polygyny and seclusion as measures of the degree to which Islamic influences from Nigeria had affected various villages in the region (1975:605–606).

Then, for a long period, the performance of the pilgrimage and the acquisition of the *alhaji* title served a similar purpose, although nowadays this title is borne by so many people that it no longer functions as a sign of distinction. It would seem that now membership in the reformist religious movement called *Izala* has become a means for young, wealthy *alhazai* to develop their own unique sense of identity (Grégoire 1993:109).

The *Izala alhazai* further distinguish themselves from other merchants by requiring their wives to wear a black veil when they go out (Grégoire 1993:112), which sets these women apart visually from the majority of women in Maradi. Thus the wives of the *alhazai* serve consistently to establish their husbands' status, not only marking merchant class men off from farmers, functionaries, and petty traders, but also distinguishing among competing members of a single class.

However, we should not assume that because women serve as markers for male status that women themselves espouse the same understanding of status or that they rank one another according to the criteria debated by their husbands. The distinctions established through secluding women or through performing prayer in a particular way in a particular mosque seem primarily to be of interest to merchant class men. Maradi women at the time of my research seemed to take little interest in the doctrinal and ritual debates among and between different brotherhoods and movements, noting only with some curiosity differences in how the various competing parties pray.[29] Since all merchant class men aspire to secluding their wives, from the point of view of the women there is not a great deal of difference between them. No doubt my informants' distance from these debates is due in part to women's relative exclusion from Islamic learning until recently. But it also suggests that competition between merchant class men is enacted in debates and practices that have little salience to women themselves, who do not pray publicly and therefore do not have to take an open position one way or the other. Women's understandings of propriety and religious practice circulate in a much more diffuse realm. So far as I can determine, women evaluate one another according to a general sense of the respectable behavior appropriate to a given rank (*daraja*) rather than against a universalized standard of religious purity derived from a particular interpretation of key Islamic texts. Because women move in and out of different marriages over the course of their lifetimes, and because the living arrangements and economic requirements of those marriages may vary tremen-

---

[29]   Many West African Muslims pray with their arms straight, while Muslims elsewhere often cross their arms. Reformist movements often take up the crossed arm style of prayer and heated disputes may center on how one performs prayer rather than on doctrine. For a useful exploration of why ritual, rather than doctrine, can become so important see Launay (1992:104–31). In Maradi most people pray with their arms straight, and when they identify themselves with a Sufi order they regard themselves as members of the Qadiriyya. Members of the Niassiya branch of the Tijaniyya (a relatively recent strand of Islam in Maradi, developing from the mid-1950s) pray with their arms crossed. Both Sufi orders have set aside their differences to present a united front against the attacks of the 'Yan Izala movement (Grégoire 1993:110).

dously (in one a woman farms, in another she is strictly secluded, in the next she sells in the street), a woman who aspires to secluded marriage may nevertheless be quite realistic about the degree to which seclusion is practical at a given moment in her own or another woman's life. As we shall see in the final chapter, women debate among themselves what kinds of behavior are reasonable given the particular configuration of constraints any given woman works under. Only a woman firmly ensconced within the merchant class from childhood could expect all women to adhere to merchant class norms at all times.

This raises the question of whether a longer term pattern of intermarriage among subsections of the merchant class may not, in time, give rise to a class-based ideology that applies to both men and women, so that merchant class women's views of female worth come to differ from those of women who circulate in marriages with men of a variety of backgrounds. A woman such as Hajjiya Sa'a (whose home construction I discussed in Chapter 4) might be an indicator of the vision of such women, for her views about appropriate female behavior were markedly narrow compared to most of my informants (even the daughters of Muslim scholars or aristocrats), despite her brief marriage to a soldier. Since, in the present economy, it is likely that daughters of mallams and aristocratic families will aspire to marry men of the merchant class, whose standard of living is relatively high, it may be that these three social groups will converge somewhat to produce a class consciousness that is not disrupted by the slightly different perspective of women who move in and out of marriages with farmers, petty traders, strangers, and soldiers. However for the moment such clear-cut class differentiation does not appear to exist, and women's circulation into and out of quite different social milieus over the course of their lifetimes tends to militate against the emergence of class ideologies across gender lines. In any case the divisions within the merchant class, acted out in the realm of ritual, would seem to undercut any single vision of Islam. What all *alhazai* do seem to share, however, is a willingness to mark their status through the seclusion of the women in their families and households.

As Launay argues of the Dyula of Ivory Coast (a population with numerous affinities to the Hausa of Maradi), contrary to much of the literature on Sufism in Africa, historically Islamic practice in West Africa has evolved in quite local situations with communalist rather than universal contours. Piety in such settings is not an absolute, but is rather measured against what is possible for a given individual in a given locale: "Age and gender do not . . . determine how pious an individual really is, but rather constitute a grid for evaluating his or her actual behavior, a way of determining which individuals actually go beyond what is expected of them or instead fall short" (1992:191). Where proper religious behavior is measured against one's family background, age, and gender, practice itself is not the measure of an individual's piety. Ritual and practice only become important in themselves when behavior rather than social position determines one's proper relationship to Islam. The Wahhabi attacks on the "Suwarian tradition" in Koko described by Launay run parallel to the 'Yan Izala assault on the relatively tolerant form of Islam practiced in Maradi (in which only the wives of scholars and aristocrats were expected to veil and enter seclusion). Both purist Islamist movements reject the Sufi orders, ostentatious redistribution of wealth, and the authority of local scholarly traditions, and both create a fixed "universal" standard of piety while promoting distinctive (one might say "particular") behaviors and rituals that set its members apart from the older Islamic community. As in Koko, the younger educated elite, beseiged by demands for support from their kin, may find aspects of Izala asceticism appealing; in Maradi, however, they would have trouble reconciling its constraints on women with the employment of educated wives.

If, for men, women figure in such contests primarily as indicators of the behavioral standards of their husbands, for women in Maradi the older, more fluid, and situational understanding of piety and propriety continues to be important. Women I worked with seemed to admire and respect other women whose achievements made the most of the possibilities open to someone of that rank without compromising the respectable behaviors associated with a given social position. A woman in seclusion might be admired for sending her mother to Mecca on money earned through tailoring. Another woman of similar rank, such as Hajjiya Sa'a, who built an impressive house with money provided by her sons, might be envied but not admired. Industriousness and generosity rather than material wealth or displays of piety seemed to be valued. Since a woman could exhibit these qualities whether secluded or not, seclusion in itself did not make a woman admirable, neither did a display of independence and public mobility. Mature women who took up public trade might be admired—in spite of their visibility—if they used their wealth to advance the well-being of their daughters. Secluded women who simply watched television would be derided as "small" women. Often older woman engaged in public trade retired into seclusion not because of the criticisms of other women, but because their sons found such behavior objectionable. The women I knew who seemed to be universally admired by other women as "big women" came from a variety of backgrounds, but all worked extremely hard, supported numerous children and clients, and observed a certain decorum associated with "married women," which I shall discuss more fully in the final chapter.

The question of the relationship between such decorum and seclusion proper was the subject of considerable debate among women, for with the growth of the merchant class women in general have come to associate seclusion with prosperity. Many women therefore viewed seclusion positively, even if they were not secluded themselves. Because until quite recently neither polygyny nor seclusion have been systematically investigated or recorded in this region, it is not possible to provide statistical figures on the growth of these institutions.[30] Oral evidence of their growth gives some indication of how they have been understood locally, however. In the course of a discussion of various kinds of cloth, Hajjiya Jeka suggested that prior to World War II veiling and seclusion were very limited:

---

[30] To my knowledge the only systematic study of polygyny in the region has been the 1990 demographic survey (République du Niger, 1992), so we have no baseline information from which to measure change.

BMC: When you were a girl did women "wrap themselves up" in veils? Jeka: Oh, no, there weren't any veils back then. Oh no! You'd just wear a head scarf, if you had had some cloth woven and there was a little bit left over you'd have it made into a scarf, using the little scraps, you'd have them sewn together to make a head scarf. Back then there were no veils, not at all.
BMC: So you didn't have that kind of veil? [indicating a sheer imported veil.]
Jeka: No! No! Only the wives of elderly Muslim scholars, they'd keep them in their houses, their husbands would buy them a wawa [a large black cloth big enough to cover the body]. It was woven. It would be woven and sewn up, and brought to the house if it was a Mallam who kept his wife guarded in seclusion. Not all women were secluded [ba duk suke tsare], just the wives of the Imam and Al'kali. In the town. Like Al'kali Musa, the Al'kali of Limantci—he's dead now. But today it's very common, albarka has set in. Back then, not at all! Women would farm, you'd go out back and kill yourself with work, women did pounding and they'd do farm work . . . and you'd grind things with stones by hand . . . you'd get water, and seasonings from the bush (Hajjiya Jeka, 4-13-89).

Jeka associates the practice of veiling with seclusion and reports that when she was a girl both were limited to the wives of certain men. The increase in seclusion today is materially associated with imported cloth, while the limited seclusion of commoner women in her childhood prior to World War II is associated with a particular kind of locally woven cloth. Ordinary women were satisfied with simply covering their hair with makeshift head scarves.

Today most women in Maradi wrap themselves loosely in the kind of imported veil Jeka associates with modern seclusion, and even a woman who moved about publicly a great deal and would not characterize herself as "guarded" in seclusion would feel uncomfortable if she did not complete her dress with a veil to cover her head and shoulders. Thus veiling has entered into local understandings of female respectability. The preference for veiling among women is in part a question of fashion, status, and self-presentation, for women posing for photographs indoors invariably wanted to cover themselves with their veils. Most women in Maradi veil themselves with sheer colorful veils bearing patterns that reflect something of the taste, humor, and aspirations of the wearer. For example during my research a veil printed with a pattern of intertwined telephone receivers was very popular. The telephone, in this impoverished setting, is a symbol of relative wealth. It is also an emblem of communication breaching the confines of seclusion, for telephones enable women to converse and conduct business without leaving the home.[31]

---

[31]   Fatima Mernissi, reflecting on the telephone, remarks: "The first deadly blow to Harem architecture was the telephone. Many Gulf emirs still oppose it. In my childhood marble-floored palace, the telephone was kept with a double lock: 'men think if the lock disappears, we'll all be plotting erotic rendezvous in the Medina's dark alleys.' Aunt Habiba's best farce was the 'telephone dance.' She swirled around in her caftans with the locked telephone elegantly woven in her headgear." Text for an exhibit with Ruth Ward and Mansoora Hassan, "The Harem Within: Fear of the Difference" at the Alif Gallery in Washington D.C., Nov. 20-Dec. 15, 1993.

Young girls who leave the house without a head scarf will be roundly scolded, but they will not be obligated to wear a veil until they are married. Veiling accompanies marriage, and so it is that unmarried women who wear a veil can borrow some of the respectability of married women. Only *karuwai* would go out in public without such a veil; the wearing of a veil can be used to signify respectability and propriety even for women who are not married, while failure to wear a veil can be a signal a *karuwa* can use to announce her availability. Paradoxically, the veil offers both married and unmarried women greater mobility since it sets them off clearly from women whose motives for appearing publicly may be less socially acceptable, thus creating a kind of limited public seclusion.[32]

While women can to a certain degree use veiling to their advantage, the increase in "guarded" seclusion as the merchant class emulates Nigeria can hamper women, as we saw in the marital dispute brought before the iya, in which the wife declared that she wanted a field of her own and greater freedom to talk with women outside the compound. That she took the case to the iya at all is evidence both of how limited seclusion still is in the rural areas, and of the general understanding in Niger (unlike Nigeria) that married women have a right to a field of their own. But her failure to gain redress for her grievances exhibits the erosion of that right by women's invoking dependent status in order to control the *gamana* product, by seclusion as it spreads, and by urban mores that regard a husband's provision for his wives as more important than a woman's access to independent income.

Most women in Maradi who are not married to either a Muslim scholar or a merchant nevertheless submit voluntarily to restrictions to their movement (such as avoiding public spaces like the marketplace), and would not characterize themselves as being *tsare*, or "guarded" in seclusion. Women in such marriages who do regard themselves as secluded often use the term *kulle*, which literally means "locked up," a meaning rather at odds with the actual practice of *kulle* seclusion in this region. In Maradi the word *kulle* suggests a self-imposed seclusion allowing a woman to visit female kin or female neighbors, and such seclusion is understood as the norm for younger married women who are neither members of the aristocracy nor of the educated elite. By engaging in the kinds of behavior appropriate to respectable women, women police themselves and as a rule do not really regard themselves as being "locked up" by their husbands, despite the perceptions of outsiders. Even a woman who leaves the house rarely, going out only to visit her kin or to go to *biki* celebrations, may nevertheless retort when asked whether she is in *kulle*, "I'm a grown woman with kin to visit, children to marry off, and naming ceremonies to go to! How could I stay put!?" (Ta Durbawa, 10-27-89). Severe restrictions on a woman's movements are seen by many women in Maradi as appropriate only for young brides: a certain degree of mobility is regarded as a sign of adulthood and status.

Women in *tsare* seclusion, particularly the wives of merchants and Mallams, would not leave the house without permission from a husband who is rarely

---

[32]   Rugh (1986:122, 144, 146) notes the same kind of use of "modesty" clothing in Egypt to make it possible for women to work outside the home and to participate in male discussions when they are older.

home to grant it; it is this form of seclusion that is on the rise in Maradi.[33] The young woman who came before the iya was evidently not even permitted to visit her friends and kin, but could only talk to her co-wife. The isolation generated by such seclusion has, it must be confessed, important implications for sampling if one hopes to do extended interviews with women: the only women I had trouble re-interviewing after a successful initial encounter were women in such marriages (whose husbands occasionally forbade any further discussions), and my own networks tended not to lead me into the neighborhoods where such seclusion was practiced (such as Zaria for merchant class women and Limantci for the wives of mallams) precisely because such women are apt to be cut off from the most active female social networks, despite the importance of visiting (*ziyara*) among women who practice *kulle* seclusion. It is possible that my sense for women's measures of female worth would be quite different if I had had greater intercourse with such women. There is much more work that could be done around the related questions of the nature of the merchant class and of how women in Maradi experience and understand seclusion. I would suggest, however, that one measure of the growing isolation of women in *tsare* seclusion is precisely the inaccessibility to other women that made it less likely that I would meet them through female networks.

As Hajjiya Jeka's remarks reveal, this more rigorous seclusion is associated with *albarka*–the state of being blessed and prosperous. The growth of the *alhazai* class and the adoption of its norms is seen as a positive sign of Allah's approval of Maradi's moral state. It is evidence of a kind of abundance and fertility as the economy and population grows. Thus in a popular song praising the prosperity of Maradi under Sarki Buzu since World War II, the female praise singer Hajjiya Zabaya celebrates the growth of polygyny:

> While you have been in power, 'dan Bawa, older brother of Barmo,
> While he has been on the throne, everyone in Maradi has become an Al Hajj,
> In your time, father of 'dan Dodo, look, there are water pumps lined up everywhere,
> The one with one wife has married two,
> The one with two wives has married three,
> The one with three has married four,
> The one with four wives has filled out his four and stopped.[34]

The local understanding of Islam not only authorizes a man to take four wives, but promotes "filling out" the four as a positive virtue (Raynaut 1971:136). In this song wives are duplicated in abundance, like the water pumps lined up in the city. Where Jeka explicitly links increased seclusion and veiling with the

---

[33] This usage may be quite local. In other Hausa areas *kulle* seems to be more restrictive than *tsare*; see Callaway 1987:57; Latour 1992:51. The word *"tsare"* can mean both "arranged" and "guarded/protected"; regional differences in usage in the context of seclusion seem to hinge on which way the word is construed locally.

[34] Wa'kar Sarkin Maradi, Hajjiya Zabaya, recorded in Maradi, 9-13-89. Hajjiya Zabaya performs almost exclusively for women, and this particular song is much appreciated.

reduction of women's workload and with better living conditions more generally, Zabaya makes a similar linkage by juxtaposing improved access to water
in the city with the ability of *alhazai* men to take more wives, an association
that makes sense when one realizes that the secluded polygynous marriage
adopted by this class is only possible when women do not have to go out to
gather water and firewood and to do farming.[35] In rural areas it has only been
with fairly recent development efforts to build latrines and to provide general
access to wells and pumped water that seclusion has even been imaginable.[36]
Women in the city of Maradi are very grateful for the modern conveniences
that make their workloads lighter. Middle-aged women frequently remarked
to me that what made their marriages different from their mothers' was that
now there were milling machines and water pumps. With these amenities and
the monetization of the economy services have emerged in relatively prosperous rural areas to meet women's labor obligations. As one of William Miles's
rural informants comments, "Previously, there was no way to pay for water,
for firewood, for clothing. Now because of money, women need not leave their
homes to provide these things" (1994:260). Obviously in the many rural areas
where women's workloads are increasing rather than decreasing (the result of
increased cash demand, deforestation, and settlement in areas with low water
tables), such seclusion becomes impractical, deepening the gulf between village and city life, and between agriculturalists and traders.

   Since women's marital duties are tied to the activities of cooking and gathering water, these innovations make it possible for women to meet their marital obligations easily, leaving more *zarafi*–leisure, wealth, and opportunity–with
which to conduct a trade or visit with other women. As Guy Nicolas reported
in the region as early as the late 1960s, seclusion and polygyny have grown in
larger agglomerations, particularly those in which trade and Islamic scholarship flourish. Nicolas remarked that seclusion is often well received by women,
as it frees them from farm labor, and provides them (at least in theory) with
leisure to set up a trade or *sana'a*. These secluded women are set apart from
other women as extraordinary:

> If many men see in this new institution a means of keeping women
> from the fields, women themselves take advantage of it to gain access
> to an enhanced situation which tends to transform them as a group
> into a kind of privileged "class" . . . (1975:181).

Nicolas exaggerates the benefits of seclusion, neglecting to note that not all
women manage to set up a trade and that for urban women seclusion, particularly *tsare* seclusion, limits the kinds of trade they can enter. There can nevertheless be no doubt that, as Margaret Saunders has observed, "despite their air

---

[35] As Mernissi observes in Morocco, seclusion requires substantial investment for services in the
home (1987:142).

[36] Observers of northern Nigeria have generally followed Polly Hill in suggesting that seclusion
has only been possible there because the high water table made well digging easy and because the
use of donkeys replaced women as carriers (Hill 1972:24, 1977:84; Callaway 1987:59).

of male dominance, both polygyny and seclusion clearly reduce a wife's workload" and are seen as desirable by many women (1980:70). Women with little income and without entrée into public employment have a strong interest in the continuation of polygyny to alleviate the demands of domestic labor and to facilitate remarriage, a reality of life in Niger that makes it difficult for women as a group to work together to reform marital practice legally. Thus new conveniences, polygyny, seclusion, women's leisure trades, and regional prosperity are all conceptually bound together in *albarka*, and this linkage makes it difficult for women to embrace one portion of that notion without accepting the limitations it places on women at the same time.

Negotiated Mobility and Self-Imposed Seclusion

In Nigeria Barbara Callaway found that women of different classes had articulated a range of kinds of seclusion: *kullen dinga* ("continual" seclusion) practiced by the wives of the emir and Muslim scholars wherein the wife never leaves the home, *kullen tsari* ("arranged" seclusion) practiced by most women and entailing the husband's permission to go out, and *kullen zuciya* (seclusion "of the heart") adopted by the elite and involving the woman's judgement as to what is appropriate behavior, and leaving her a great deal of mobility in public. According to her the form of seclusion practiced correlated to the educational level of the husband (1987:55–57, 66).

In Maradi, in the absence of widespread Islamic education until recently, and in the absence of strict seclusion for anyone but the aristocratic class prior to World War II, seclusion has been understood more loosely, and generally has had less to do with male imposition than with female expressions of differences through the adoption of behavior appropriate to a woman of a particular status and background. If Barbara Callaway is correct, as I think she is, in stating that "where men live apart from women they cannot control them" (1984:433), then one might ask, who is imposing purdah? Husbands are rarely at home, women are left very much to their own devices, and yet women in *kulle* or in *tsare* maintain a kind of behavior that restricts their movements and options considerably.

Women in Maradi themselves play a very important role in the control of their own and other women's movements; to a very large degree these constraints are self-imposed. Elite women in Nigeria seem, by virtue of their greater familiarity with Islam, to have attempted to define seclusion in new ways in order to respect it while enjoying some freedom of movement. Women in Maradi have adopted a notion of *kulle* that is little informed by Islam and has more to do with conceptions of propriety and status. Thus a woman raised in a merchant class family who has had the privilege of living in merchant class homes most of her life will explain that she does not go out publicly and has never been inside the market because of *daraja*–worth, respectableness, and rank. In this context the negotiation of new interpretations of seclusion is difficult, since any behavior that does not conform to these notions of respectability is deemed inappropriate, regardless of the religious beliefs, intentions or circumstances of the woman involved. Hajjiya Sa'a, for example, would disparage all women who go to public events, married or unmarried, successful or disreputable, as *femmes passe-partout*–"loose, easy women," whose mere public presence and mobility is evidence of their immorality, of their "opening all doors." Condemnation of these women serves to uphold and validate her own voluntary seclusion and immobility. In Maradi there seems to be no elaboration of "seclusion of the heart." Women who do go out publicly veil themselves, but this practice does not entirely save them from the opprobrium brought upon them by the gossip of women such as Hajjiya Sa'a.

The participation of women in the "dominant model"–not to subvert it but to promote it for the advantages it provides to individual women in particular moments–makes change in marriage and female status a complex and difficult issue. If women were truly united in the solidarity created by the "female sphere," then it would be imaginable to promote legal reforms in the interests of women as a whole.[37] The reality of the "female sphere" is more complex: Indo, who at the age of fourteen ran away from her marriage to a wealthy polygynous trader, nevertheless married off her own schoolgirl daughter to just such an al Hajj; Iya, who lasted only nine months in her first marriage reinforces in her office as iya the marriage of the unhappy rural woman who has been secluded; Sa'a, who has quite consciously gained a great deal of independence due to her home ownership nevertheless rarely leaves the house even though she is past menopause and no longer married; Monique, who resented her ex-husband's philandering nevertheless participates in affairs with married men. Not only do women as a group have divergent interests, individual women are pulled in contradictory directions by their own experiences and choices. The notion of "appropriate behavior" makes it possible in some limited way for women to reconcile these contradictions: a young girl subject to "the foolishness of youth" does not behave according to the same standards as a grown woman; an aristocratic woman may act differently depending upon whether she is acting as a titled arbiter or as a private individual; a mistress may act differently from a wife. Ultimately, however, these differences tend to undermine any conscious effort on the part of women to alter the nature of marriage and relations between men and women.

If Islamic education has the potential to provide women with ways to justify new practices by reinterpreting Islam, then the expansion of *makaranta*, *madrasa*, and *Islamiyya* schooling may help women in Maradi to find new solutions to issues surrounding marriage.[38] John Esposito contends that the Koran

---

[37] Pittin (1979) has argued that women's co-residency in female-headed groupings cuts across class lines to create female solidarity in the face of the dominant male ideology. Callaway (1984) suggests that Hausa women's separate sphere means they may be in a better position than Western women to initiate change for women and to support politicians who promote women's interests.

[38] Certainly the growth of Islamic schooling in Katsina (Nigeria), promoted by some of the most conservative segments of Nigerian society, has had contradictory implications for Hausa women there, for such education provides women with tools to critique exploitation justified as "Islamic" by offering alternative interpretations of the Koran (Pittin 1990:22–23).

can be used to argue that women should have equal rights in divorce (II; 228) and that monogamy is in the spirit of Islam (IV: 3, 129). He is convinced that with a proper balance of *itjihad* (interpretation) and *ijima* (consensus) effective reforms can be made from within Islam (1982:109–111, 120–23, 132–33). He is not alone in arguing that consensus and interpretation can be at the heart of Islamic reform; Muhammad Ahmad Khalaf Allah has made similar arguments (see Stowasser 1993:12–13). Syria, Tunisia, and Iraq instituted Islamic legal reforms to polygamy and divorce by reference to competing legal traditions (Ahmed 1992: 146, 175, 242). However such reforms have not always been met with enthusiasm, and have had to be protected against Islamist reactions and the subordination of women's needs to the higher claims of nationalist discourses (Tessler et al. 1978, Hatem 1993:35). In order to be sustained meaningfully they must be supported by a broad base of women; in other words they must have their grounding in a genuine female consensus about how to interpret key religious texts. This observation begins to make sense of Elizabeth White's discovery of a correlation between educational achievement and Islamic legal reform (1978). She concludes from this correlation that educational advances are a function of legal reform, when the reverse might be argued with equal plausibility. The key issues then, are whether such consensus can be reached, whether women as a group are likely to come together to promote it, and whether the force of an alternative scholarly interpretation can offset the counterclaims of conservative readings of "traditional" Islam on the one hand and fundamentalist assumptions of access to scriptural purity on the other.

The ideological complexities set forth in the above discussion of women's actual behavior, however, would seem to indicate that mere legal reform alone would do little in and of itself to alter women's lives. As I argued in Chapters 1 and 2, neither the state nor the courts have exclusively or even directly affected marital practice. Instead, important changes resulted from women's being exposed to and embracing new kinds of opportunities while working to protect themselves from a variety of constraints. They have seized upon marriage to soldiers and strangers, education and public employment, immigration to urban areas, and acquisition of real estate. By acting out change rather than legislating it women have inadvertently and profoundly reshaped marital practices. More than any other factor contributing to the transformation of marital practices, women's visible movement into new domains will serve to reshape "consensus" and redefine "tradition." Instead of reworking appropriate behavior through reference to particular interpretations of Islamic texts, women rework it through spatial praxis. But as Hajjiya Sa'a's condemnation of other women shows, this reform will not come easily; prominent women's opponents will be other women as well as men. And such female opponents are unlikely to be arguing from interpretations of texts that can be debated, but rather base their position on a diffuse claim to propriety that is far more difficult to counter effectively.

The remaining two chapters of this book take up in different ways the question of how women's perceptions of marriage differ from men's, and of how women as a group are fragmented both by their experiences and by the tactics they deploy to make most of the options available to them. If it is increasingly the case that the wedding rituals in which women take part emphasize an organic understanding of marriage while men's wedding rituals take on the allure of a contractual arrangement, then men and women may enter marriage with quite different understandings of the nature of the union. In Chapter 7 I suggest that women's strategies in the face of the erosion of the moral force of the organic model have quite contradictory consequences. They may opt to sustain the ambiguity of the status of a union in order to retain the option to leave; they may lower or raise the significance of the *sadaki* payment with a view towards easing the dissolution of the union or towards establishing their own worth and substance; they may choose not to formalize a union at all and opt for outside marriage. These tactics undercut one another and place women in conflict with each other, particularly where women find themselves competing as wives and as mistresses. The final chapter, on a more positive note, raises the possibility that women's deliberate tactics to differentiate among one another have had some positive ramifications, unexpectedly subverting received notions about respectability, femininity, and what it means to be a "married woman."

7

Coping with Conflicting Models: Nurturing Ties, Maintaining Ambiguity, and Opting Out

Women in Maradi as a group have exhibited little propensity or ability to control marital practice through legislation or the courts. Nevertheless, given the competing understandings of prosperity, propriety, and domesticity circulating in the present moment, they must, as individuals, find means to protect themselves from interpretations of marriage conflicting with their own. Female wedding rituals suggest that women's understanding of marriage may differ profoundly from men's: the primary female celebrations marking the stages of marriage are permeated with organic images of growth, while the central ceremonies in which men currently take part suggest a more contractual understanding of marriage. For women weddings create and sustain social ties indispensable to their well-being, but those social ties go beyond the union between the husband and his new wife. The series of rituals making up marriage give rise to and crystallize *zummunci*, or the affection associated with kinship. Thus, as I argued in Chapter 5, weddings are not moments in which contracts are finalized, but rather processes through which a body of social relations is nurtured. Given that fundamentally different understandings of the character and obligations of marriage exist simultaneously in Maradi, as we have seen in the preceding chapter, how do women cope with the danger of entering into a union in which the husband's emerging expectations and preferences differ from those of his wife?

Retaining an element of conditionality or ambiguity is one means both women and men can employ to protect themselves in untested unions; an unsuccessful union is thus eluded by the argument that it never constituted a full marriage. Caroline Bledsoe's work in Sierra Leone and Liberia shows that men

143

and women can have quite different interests and expectations of marriage, and that women in particular may prefer to retain a certain degree of ambiguity about their marital status (Bledsoe 1980:7–8, Gage and Bledsoe 1994). Limiting the cost of key marriage expenses can protect women against the difficulties of extricating themselves from unsuccessful marriages. Certainly much of the literature on marriage in Africa has noted the seemingly direct relationship between high bridewealth and marital stability, while linking brittle marriage to relatively low bridewealth. Conversely (in keeping with the evidence offered in the Chapter 5), women might use the social capital arising from gift exchange to gain the stature to negotiate conditions which are more favorable to them. As Christine Oppong found, the better able a woman is to maintain herself financially, the more likely it is that the union will be "syncratic" (1981:122). Accepting a high bridewealth can signal a woman's financial autonomy, since she thereby suggests that she is confident that she can repay it. Finally, as seems to be quite common elsewhere in Africa, women might prefer informal unions in order to minimize the disappointments and pitfalls of marriages they can't control. Recent studies by Kristin Mann (1994), Wambui Wa Karanja (1987), Thérèse Locoh (1994), and Christine Obbo (1987) suggest that "outside marriage" appeals to women who hope to retain some independence while tapping into the resources men can provide. In this chapter I shall show that Hausa women in Maradi as individuals pursue all of these strategies in the face of the possibility that a marriage will prove disappointing.

Women's organic model of marriage persists partly because it provides them with a means of defining the character of a union in a setting where they lack the male right to repudiation. Because access to divorce is unequal, women's organic model offers them images and language for defining a union as partial, ambiguous, or incomplete, despite the completion of the masculine "tying of the marriage" and the transfer of *sadaki*. An emphasis on natural processes also provides women with potent symbolic capital to counterbalance male political power.[1] Further, it captures the broader social and affective ties that participation in wedding ceremonies creates, resources that women rely upon for emotional, economic, and political support beyond the marital union itself.

In the material realm, an examination of marriage registrations in Maradi suggests that when elite Hausa women control marriage negotiations they often attempt to keep *sadaki* payments low, despite the inflation of bridewealth evident from the registers in the first marriages of younger educated women. By keeping the bridewealth low, these women can ensure that they will have little difficulty ending any union that eventually proves undesirable. Women cannot control how men will construe marriage, but they can occasionally limit the potential damage of an interpretation that is not to their liking.

While some mature elite women work to keep marriage payments low, others (particularly Zerma functionaries) seem to use the marriage transactions

---

[1]   The force of such organic imagery emerges in traditional folktales, see Stephens (1991).

to establish and reinforce their own worth vis-à-vis their husbands. As we saw in Chapter 5, women can use marriage payments as a means of staging publicly their own social worth and standing. Women's strategies in the realm of bridewealth payment are therefore ambiguous and contradictory: while on the one hand it can be advantageous in material terms to keep the *sadaki* bridewealth payment low, it can also be a powerful social statement to demand a high *sadaki* payment. Which strategy a woman will pursue seems to depend upon her own position within the local socioeconomic milieu and her assessment of how the payments will be understood.

If women's strategies in the realm of bridewealth are contradictory, some women's preference for informal unions over marriage is even more so. By participating in extramarital liaisons with married men, such women contribute to the very marital conflict and instability they themselves hope to evade through "outside" unions.

Organic and Contractual Models

While the image of "tying the knot" would seem to suggest that the status of a marriage is understood as clear-cut–either the knot has been "done" or "undone"–in fact Hausa marriage allows for a certain amount of ambiguity. If "three threads" must be undone to finalize a divorce, what is the status of a marriage in which "two" have been "cut?" And who does the cutting? In what does it consist? Women in particular seem to experience marriage as something that grows, flourishes, and dies, a process poorly captured in the image of tying. For men, who are better able to control divorce and who can dictate the terms of their own and their young daughters' marriages, marriage probably seems quite unambiguous–it is women who are changeable and difficult to control.[2]

Women use language suggesting that, for them, marriage is something that "takes" [*arme ya kama*], rather like a dye, a seedling, a fire, or a pregnancy. It is essentially organic and must be nurtured and watched, but it can unaccountably expire for reasons beyond the control of the couple involved. When a marriage "refuses to take" [*arme ya 'kiya*] there is nothing anyone can do to save it–it will eventually "die," although that death may take time. A marriage that was perfectly healthy can be "killed" by others who want to sabotage it with gossip, ill-will, and cruelty. Women see the wedding ceremony as a process as well, something to be watched over, and the various ceremonies are rituals to promote growth, stages of that growth, and evidence that the marriage has "taken."[3]

---

[2] Organic processes and women combine in a Hausa proverb expressing the unpredictableness of life: "Duniya mace da ciki ce" ("The world/life is like a pregnant woman").

[3] The sense that rituals themselves cause growth, sociability, and maturity rather than simply marking or representing them is also shown in studies of other ceremonial processes of interest to women. See Audrey Richards' *Chisungu* (1956, reissued 1982) and Davison and the Women of Mutira (1989).

Thus while the "tying of the marriage" ceremony between the male kin of the bride and groom establishes the transfer of bridewealth and a legitimate marriage, this in and of itself is not regarded by women as the definitive moment in the wedding. The timing of the transfer of the "things for the room" and the *gara* gift for the groom a good week after the bride has gone to live with him suggests that women see that first week as a kind of test period. Hajjiya Indo, in the course of explaining the marriage expenses in her daughter Zuera's wedding, seems to have been unwilling to finalize the marriage by completing the *kan kaya* before she had been able to visit and see that her headstrong daughter was doing well in marriage to a Nigerian in a strange land. Zuera had been married twice before, and already had a room full of "things" stored at her mother's house, so there was no real need to purchase any new ones. As Hajjiya was describing the expenses to me, Zuera's close friend Fati listened in:

> Hajjiya: They brought me 150,000 naira, they said that was a "greeting." Then they came back, and they returned the gifts that had been given to her by other suitors, that was about 30,000 CFA.[4] Then the *sadaki* was 5,000 CFA. The gift for the mother [Hajjiya herself] was 1,500, and for the father [Zuera's paternal kin] 1,500. That's what we agreed upon, so as not to be disrespectful [since she is not a virgin]. That was that, we had finished with that, so they brought the colanut and tied the marriage. Then they said to me, "Shall we take her things?" And I said, "No, leave the things for a little while." They will come back in a few months. They don't know that [yet]...
> Fati: [Challenging, and a bit shocked] Well, now, Hajjiya, so only if they come back . . . they're going to take her [to her new home] without any things?!
> Hajjiya: Now I'm *going* to buy her things, but I'm going to do it down there. I *am* going to buy her things! I'll buy them. When I go down there I'll buy them, in her own room. She told me that when I had time I could sell the things she left here, so I can buy her more things down there. And if I don't sell them, then Zainabu [her younger sister] can have them. . . . When I go down there I can buy her a bed, a bed with a cupboard and everything.
> Fati: Well, it is less expensive down there.
> Hajjiya: Right, if Allah so wills it. I gave some friends some money and told them to buy me a "super" mattress, the big kind, for 300,000 naira, that's only about 10,000 francs here. So when they come back to get me I'll go there I'll take it and gather up every little thing, and I'll go there and buy things for her. Everything. And whatever God sends me, well, I'll give that to the bridegroom. But I don't want to waste a lot of money, that's why (Hajjiya Indo, 10-25-89).

Hajjiya Indo was not happy with her daughter's decision to marry a Nigerian man so far from Maradi. Nevertheless, rather than take advantage of the wealth

---

[4] One of the greatest expenses a successful suitor incurs is the *rama*, the repayment of the courtship gifts failed suitors gave to the woman. She is not expected to return them herself.

of the Nigerians, who had offered to carry Zuera's dowry "things" to her new home and had rented a station wagon for the trip, she chose instead to wait a little while before arranging the "carrying of the things." Zuera's friend was shocked, as this seemed to suggest that Hajjiya Indo was sending her daughter off without any "things" at all. As I have argued, the "things" help the bride to establish her space and standing in her new home. But Hajjiya fully expected that they would return to get the "things," at which time she would be able to return with them to visit her daughter herself.

Hajjiya's motive was more complex than mere parsimony, and Zuera probably had a hand in coming up with this arrangement. By holding off on giving the "things" Hajjiya had a pretext to go visit her daughter later, and could see for herself whether this marriage was likely to work out. Zuera would have the support of her mother's presence should her new situation prove less desireable than expected. The trip would also serve the double purpose of setting Hajjiya's mind at ease about her daughter's welfare while making something of a commercial enterprise of building Zuera's dowry. The difference in value between the CFA and the naira at the time of this research was such that Zuera and her mother counted on selling the "things" Zuera had stored in her mother's house since her previous marriage, and then using the cash generated to buy even more goods in Nigeria, where their money would go much further. Fati mistook Indo's hesitancy for a lack of interest in her daughter's well-being, when in fact Indo and Zuera had probably mutually agreed upon an arrangement to protect the new bride in a foreign setting. Although the formal Islamic ceremony had already taken place, as Hajjiya put it, she herself would not be settled with the marriage until she had seen "with her own eyes."

Women also seem to regard the "washing of the bride" as a significant moment in the marriage ceremony, and when this washing has not taken place, women don't regard the marriage as complete, regardless of whether the Islamic ceremony, "the tying of the marriage," has taken place. This was the case with Hajjiya Indo's other daughter, Zainabu. A woman who has a child before her first marriage creates an ambiguous situation: it is her first marriage, but since she is not a virgin the "washing" seems incongruous. In this case the groom had refused to return to Maradi to take part in the celebrations surrounding the ceremony in which the bride is washed, and therefore Hajjiya had refused to do the washing. As a consequence the marriage was in a peculiar kind of limbo. The groom's arrogance was clear evidence that he did not take his non-virgin bride particularly seriously. However this battle concerned not only Zainabu's status as a married woman, but also the paternity of Zainabu's little boy, the groom's son. If the groom could not come to Maradi and take up his responsibilities towards his bride, there was no reason why the bride should simply yield to him on the issue of the son's paternity. If the marriage were to be annulled, it was probable that Zainabu would be able to keep her son due to local readings of the status of this marriage. The boy would be considered illegitimate, but she and her mother would not lose custody of him.

Prior to the major changes in the economy simultaneous with the rise of the peanut economy and increasing Islamization in the region, both the bride and the groom were "washed" in their first marriage. Women complain that men are no longer "washed" and dyed with henna the way a *budurwa* bride is washed, which further separates women's experience of marriage from that of men, who would seem to be undergoing less of a ritual change in status than is the bride. In the mid-1960s a young man in Niamey describing his intolerable first marriage complained to ethnographer Suzanne Bernus that his family had induced him to come home to Maradi to marry a girl he had never met and to be "put in henna, that is put in prison for an entire week!" (1969:132). His characterization of the ceremony of washing as being like prison goes some way to explain why the custom has gone out of use, for young men are less and less inclined to submit to the decisions of their elders, and their greater economic independence today makes them resist being "tied." The disappearance of the *wanken ango* may also be linked to the rise of polygyny with the growth of cash cropping–men who marry three and four wives may take less interest in their own first marriage to a virgin than in the past (Raulin 1964:48). Certainly women greet the tokens of a bride's virginity (the bloodied bed sheets) with enormous skepticism today.

Nevertheless, the "washing" remains a key moment for Hausa women. The following unusual interchange underscores the peculiar significance women place upon the "washing." A'i had been raised as a Muslim in a rural village north of Maradi and was only converted to Christianity when she came to the city of Maradi as a middle-aged woman during the Sahel drought. She had just described to me the rough outline of her first wedding ceremony in her rural village. A friend of both of ours, Hawa (a Christian Hausa woman whose mother was also Christian), was listening.

> BMC: Did they wash the groom too?
> A'i: Yes! Oh, they would wash everybody. If you weren't washed, there was no pleasure in it–the woman would refuse to stay!
> Hawa: Is the "washing" when they put henna on you?
> A'i: Yes, it's the "putting on the henna."
> Hawa: Oh, so that's what "washing" is. When I was married I wouldn't let them do it to me, I refused.
> BMC: In the past the men put on henna, and they washed too, but now they refuse.
> Hawa: The reason I refused is that, since it's according to custom, I figured if I did it would be as if I had reverted to Islam, so I refused.
> A'i: Yes, that's right. I think that's right. At that time, if you didn't wash the bride, or the groom, it was something to cause a fight, people wouldn't agree about it. They would say, "Goodness, they didn't wash you, they didn't put henna on you, so if you die, you won't go to Paradise!" [She laughs.] (A'i Mai Muni, 4-25-89).

Regardless of the Muslim orthodoxy involved, older women seem to regard the "washing" as an integral part of the Islamic religious ritual, and without it the bride may feel that her salvation is threatened, her fertility in jeopardy, and the marriage incomplete. In fact, there is little in the Koran to support such a notion, and men who refuse to be "washed" probably do so partly because they regard the washing not as Muslim but as a relic of pagan custom. In rural Arna custom both the groom and the bride were washed at the household altar. As the household altars gradually disappear, they seem to have been replaced by "places to wash the bride," disassociated from animist practices. Men's washing has been eliminated from the ritual (Raynaut 1971:134). Whatever women's religious beliefs on the subject today, for Hajjiya Indo the problem of whether and how to complete the "washing" of her daughter Zainabu creates both a quandary and an opportunity. While the refusal of the groom to participate makes it difficult to complete the ceremony, it also creates a means for denying marriage to a son-in-law who has shown that he is not even willing to help her daughter save face.

The washing of the bride resonates with a number of other ritual ablutions: the washing of a woman after her menstrual period, the washing she does after sexual relations, and the washing following childbirth—all of which are related to fertility. Blood is released with the loss of virginity and the breaking of the hymen, and that blood is both dangerous and potent. In Arewa it was believed that menstrual blood could cure poisoning and hemorrhaging resulting from battle wounds (Latour 1992:66). Some believe that a virgin bride will bring *arziki* to a man through numerous offspring and prosperity (Asabe Hassan, 3-9-89). Many elderly women believe that if both the bride and groom aren't washed the union will be infertile.

Today prior to the actual "washing" the bride is decorated with henna, which is given several days to "take." It seems likely to me that the emphasis on the henna over the actual "washing" is a recent elaboration, associated with urban wealth and leisure. Here is how Hajjiya Fati, whose parents were villagers and who grew up in the city in a modest household, describes the changes:

> Today isn't like it used to be, since now people put a lot of money into it. Like today, they have the bride spend seven days in henna. They come and they put on the henna, people spend the day [and therefore eat a number of meals with her]—people spend a lot of money! In the past they didn't do that. If you put the bride [in henna], if it was a young girl like that one [her co-wife's daughter, a schoolgirl], then you'd go to the bush and get wood, one would make food, they'd get wood, little girls like her, they'd do the pounding [of the millet or sorghum grain] themselves, and the cooking, to bring to the bride. Now though, there's not all that, no pounding, just rice and macaroni. So the young girls don't do any work, or anything, they're all wrapped up with henna, Praise God. She [the bride] is all wrapped up with henna, and everything is taken care of. Back then, there wasn't this wrapping. You would just cook with your own hands and make *tuwo* [porridge made with local staple grains]. (Hajjiya Fati 11-17-88)

The imagery of working hands in the past and idle hands in the present in Hajjiya's vision is striking. The work of feeding social ties through the work of cooking food is contrasted with the display of wealth and leisure embodied in

Photo 6: "Hausa women–Gouchy (near Magaria) ("Gouchy–[environs de Magaria]
Femmes Haoussa"). January 21, 1956, donated by M. Jacques Alluson–Admin.
FOM. To my untrained eye this seemed an unremarkable photograph of Hausa
girls in a rural setting. When I showed it to women in Maradi they remarked with
delight, "It's a new bride (*amarya*) with her girlfriends!" While the bride is closely
veiled in costly imported cloth (*bazin*), her companions wear kerchiefs and ward
off the cold with blankets of locally woven indigo and of imported wool. Courtesy of the French National Archives, Centre des Archives d'Outre-mer. All rights
reserved. 30F1.23.AOF.6067.

imported foods and tied hands. She herself seems to be ambivalent about these
changes, interjecting the Islamic formula "Alhamdu lillahi" (Praise God) as her
narrative begins to sound as if she is ungrateful for the wealth that makes these
innovations possible. However to my ear, some nostalgia for the loving labor
exhibited in feeding kin and friends oneself rather than through money seeps
through nevertheless. Rural and poorer urban women were probably too busy
cooking and entertaining the numerous guests at the wedding to be able to
forgo the aid of the bride for very long.

   After the "putting on of the henna" the women and girls gather together
to watch as the bride is washed in water dyed blood red with henna and other
roots; the bride cries during the ritual, while her young friends sing songs. The
relevance of this ritual for a man, particularly a man who is likely to already be
sexually active (since he may be between twenty-five and thirty at the time of
his own first marriage), is a bit obscure, and it is perhaps not surprising that
men have lost interest, whether the ritual is originally non-Muslim or not.

However women's perception that this ritual is a key moment in the marriage, steeped as it is with the image of blood, and brought about through the "taking" of the henna dye, the literal feeding of social networks, and the gathering together of women seems to underscore women's more organic understanding of marriage. This ceremony calls for the presence and support of the all of the bride's female kin, and she is alternately comforted and teased by her girl-friends, who sing songs about marriage: it is a moment in which women's ties surface, not only ties to her new husband, but to the kin who will support her and attempt to help her make the marriage work. It is the only moment in which the bride herself, rather than her mother or paternal kin, is at the center of attention.

Even after the wedding ceremonies proper are finished, women still re-gard a marriage as incomplete until it has yielded children–the surest measure of the success of a marriage, its *arziki*: "It was only in my second marriage that *arziki* entered in, from that time I started to give birth and *arziki* set in, you see?" (Asabe Hassan, 10-11-89). If a marriage does not produce children within two years it is likely to be ended, regardless of how well the husband and wife get along, for both his kin and her own will begin to undermine it, and the woman's co-wives may ridicule her lack of fertility.[5] When asked why a mar-riage ended women often give the seemingly unresponsive answer that "Allah caused it to die." The answer says more than it seems to: if Allah does not bless a union with children and the support of one's kin, then it will end. It is a response women tend to give when they themselves did not want the mar-riage to end, but they could find no means of "holding" it.[6] And in such cases, the less said the better, for the women are generally depressed and demoral-ized by the failure of a marriage that seems to have been beyond their control.

Weddings as Creative Social Acts: Building *Zummunci*

In Chapter 5 we saw how important wedding transactions are to women's self-definition. The exchange of gifts is a creative act that brings social ties into being and makes them visible. Most of the time these ties are invisible, as are the benefits to be derived from them. However in tracing out a woman's "kin-ship" ties and placing them alongside those relationships that seem to protect her in times of stress, one can begin to see how the *zummunci* (or kinship and friendship) that a woman fosters through participation in the wedding celebra-tions of her friends and kin can have material and emotional benefits. Kande is a single woman with numerous children whom I visited many times over the course of my research. I was able to see that she had consciously built ties with her mother's kin near Dodo both by buying a farm there and by contributing to celebrations there. She had gone to Dodo to visit her kin after the harvest in

---

[5]   Such was the case in Hajjiya Ta Dogo's second marriage, 2-18-89.
[6]   As in Ta Kurya's childless fourth marriage to the man she had always loved, 2-1-89.

1989, and when she returned I dropped by to see how she was doing, and noted that her room was stuffed full of sacks of grain.

"Goodness," I remarked, "you've made quite an effort!" She responded with pleasure, "As a result of all the *zummunci* I have created, right?" (Kande, 11-16-89). She had been responsible for feeding many of these kin during the drought of 1984, so the ties had been serviceable in both directions. These ties have proven to be more useful to her than her ties with paternal kin in the city of Maradi proper, conservative Muslim scholars who have thwarted her efforts to earn income and to develop a support network through the Women's Association. While she had introduced me to her maternal kin and we had visited them together in Dodo, she does not visit her paternal kin in the neighborhood of Limanci very often, and never introduced me to them. As she commented to me bitterly:

> Muslim scholars today don't take responsibility for anyone but their own children. In the past there was *zummunci* among them. You see, *zummunci* has been spoiled now. In the past, if you had something, you would give to your nieces and nephews too, because of *zummunci*. It's not in this world that *zummunci* is valuable, it's in the afterlife, and from his grave a person would still look after his own children and his brother's children.... Today if you go to their house, then they will say you are just trying to get something from them, and so that makes you stay at home, and you try to look out for yourself. You don't go to your paternal kin. Because they will say you are just after money, they won't think you just came out of *zummunci*. So that spoils the *zummunci*, doesn't it? (Kande, 1-18-89).

Thus *zummunci*, or "kinship and friendship," is not simply blood relations; it is a feeling of closeness and mutual support created and nurtured through numerous visits, gift exchanges, and through occasional emergency support.[7] Kande has little to offer her urban paternal kin, so they see her as simply parasitic, whereas her rural maternal kin have much to gain from their ties to her. When they are ill they stay with her to visit the hospital; when they need to send children to urban schools she can take them in; and when they suffer a disastrous harvest she is proud and happy to provide for them as best she can. As the grain she stocked in her room shows, she also gains from this relationship. It is not simply grain that she has gotten from them, but also emotional support after the death of her second husband, and useful advice and contacts for her trade in food, wood, and pottery. These are among the benefits women seek when they invest in the considerable expense of participating in gift exchanges such as those described above. However creating such ties involves walking an economic tightrope: the benefits must offset the costs over time or the maintenance of the ties becomes a liability. Kande's abandonment of her paternal kin suggests that she has not found it useful to invest her money and energies there.

---

[7] Vaughan (1992) illustrates the importance of such ties to women's welfare elsewhere in Africa in times of famine.

As Enid Schildkrout argues, however, in some ways in building ties of this kind Kande has invested in the very marriage system that makes it so difficult for her to earn cash herself in the first place (1982). She has married off her own young daughter to a successful trader who keeps her daughter in seclusion. Kande is very fond of the young man because he drops by and gives her gifts of cash frequently, but the marriage is precisely the kind from which she herself had fled as a young girl, when she was too "young and foolish" to know that polygyny and seclusion in a wealthy household can be preferable to independence and mobility in poverty.

Where Schildkrout points out that through their investment in dowry women in a sense uphold a marriage system that sets limits on their own behavior, Guy Nicolas argues that the opportunity cost of investment in these social ties is far too high, and that the commitment to cash gifts and purchases made through the cash economy undermines the productive economy (1968:51, 56). In Kande's case this issue is rather more complex than it might at first appear. It has been partly to maintain her social ties that Kande has invested in a farm near her mother, which the latter manages for her. She has invested in production to feed her social relations as much as the reverse. It would be very difficult to disentangle the various threads that make up the fabric of the *zummunci* Kande has woven, some of which seem to be productive enterprises, others of which are more clearly ceremonial ties, and still others are simply emotional. And that is precisely the nature of *zummunci*, for if it appears to be baldly materialistic and acquisitive then it cannot survive, it is "spoiled." Only genuinely warm feeling can keep *zummunci* alive, for the maintenance of these social ties calls for the expenditures of enormous amounts of time and energy visiting kin. As one proverb expresses it, "zummunci a 'kafa take" ("kinship goes on foot").

If feeding one's *biki* or "celebration" ties calls for energy, time, and money, then they must be productive to be worth maintaining, and the awareness that these networks can be as much an expense as a source of support is also reflected in proverbs.[8] A *biki* partner who fails to return equivalent sums is a liability, and a junior who is not suitably grateful for the "help" he or she has been given is a loss. By the same token, the *biki* is a primary metaphor for one's "business," things one has a right to take part in and in which one has a legitimate interest.[9] By taking part in her kin and friends' celebrations, a woman establishes herself as an equal member in that community, with rights to protection and aid. Similarly by providing "help" to her younger kin a woman creates a social debt that she may call upon in the future. Men and women in Maradi are perfectly aware that

---

8   "Ban ci biki ba, biki ya ci ni?" ("Where there's no profit, why risk loss?") "Biki dai ba sarauta ba ne" ("Celebrations aren't titled offices," the equivalent of "All that glitters is not gold"). "Gaya mai zuciya biki, ba mai dukiya ba" ("Court the resolute, not the rich," more literally, "Invite those with a willing heart to your celebration, not those with wealth").

9   "Ina bikina da shi?" ("What business is it of mine?") For expressions surrounding *biki*, see Abraham (1962:99–100).

their efforts to secure social networks are costly and risky, but they do not have a great number of alternatives to this security network. Men have far more access than women to loans, government grants, and patronage ties with more wealthy individuals, and these may mitigate somewhat men's need to invest in expensive social networks. Women, on the other hand, cannot count on such institutions, and must therefore complement their investment in productive activities with social investments, which in turn may help them to continue their productive enterprises.

Claude Raynaut, analyzing men's gift transactions, argues that these do not so much create ties as express already existing relations (1972:286–87). For women *biki* participation is indeed a means of expressing alliances and social background; however, the expense of *biki* celebrations necessitates some selectivity as to which ties will be maintained and which neglected: ties that are neglected will "die" and the *zummunci* will be "spoiled." Thus in many ways the gift transactions have an organic quality themselves because they have the power to create and sustain ties, and to create and renew status rather than to simply "express" it.

This may be more true for women than for men, which would account for Raynaut's interpretation of these gift transactions: women must constantly reaffirm and recreate social ties because of their geographic mobility in marriage, which makes them "outsiders" to both their own kin group and their husbands'. Men's relative geographic stability may mean they have less need to invest consciously in these kinds of ties. Because men have access to a broader range of institutional support and broader trade, informational, and religious communities than women, they frequently invest their energies in these rather than simply in *zummunci*. Hajjiya Asma'u, whose successful enterprise I discussed at the close of Chapter 3, is in a sense the exception that proves this rule. Unlike other women, her success has made it possible for her to invest in forms of social capital that go beyond the family celebrations other women invest in: she gives out large quantities of food at the annual festivals as alms, very much as a wealthy male Al Hajj might do, and she has sent numerous kin (including her husband) to Mecca. Where less successful women must content themselves with building *zummunci*, Hajjiya Asma'u can build *jama'a* or membership in a broader Muslim community.

The creative aspect of weddings, so important to women because it generates *zummunci*, is poorly captured by the most prominent approaches to understanding the nature of marriage payments.[10] If marriage is an organic process that builds ties between two individuals and between those individuals and a network of other individuals, then existing analyses of marriage payments–which account for the payments in terms of a kind of cost/benefit balance, or as a means of distributing property based on pre-existing systems of descent and property relations, or as a means of reproducing the structures of

---

[10] For a summary of the range of approaches taken to the analysis of marriage payments see John Comaroff (1980).

dependency–all assume *a priori* the very things the wedding in fact creates: the establishment of the worth of the bride, a reaffirmation and consolidation of the kinship relations of the bride and her mother with other individuals, and debt relations created through "help" given by senior kin to junior kin, creating dependency.

The bride's family can only be recompensed for the loss of her labor and reproductive force if that force has been evidenced and her value measured: but it is through a bride's display of wealth and social ties in the *kan kwarya* or *gara* and later in her success in reproduction that her worth is established, and therefore it is the wedding and marriage itself that generates her value. Similarly, if dowry is seen as a kind of pre-mortem inheritance for the bride, to be associated with bilateral kinship systems emphasizing the conjugal unit, and if bridewealth marks her exclusion from inheritance in lineal descent groups, what are we to make of the Hausa system, which includes both? The transfer of *sadaki* to the bride's paternal kin in fact establishes her as a member of that kin group and a legitimate inheritor; by the same token, the bride's mother's gift to her and the groom creates bilateral ties that have little to do with inheritance, but rather provide for the bride's future security by showing that she is as powerful as her husband, and by providing insurance in the event of divorce. The transfer of the gifts seems to crystallize those social relations that define the bride's support group for the future rather than express already existing corporate alliances. Finally, if the control of bridewealth by senior males is seen as the means by which those men reproduce their control over juniors, that control can only be evidenced in the actual giving of the gift of bridewealth support, not through withholding it. Senior men and women retain their influence over juniors through the debt created by the transfer of gifts and support at the moment of marriage, and therefore it is by promoting and advancing marital ties that seniors–both male and female in this case–consolidate their control over juniors.

And this is perhaps why the images of "tying" and of organic growth are both prominent in Hausa marriage, for it is in the process of "tying" that various social ties become actualized. For women the organic processual aspect of marriage and social life is vividly experienced, where for men the contractual creation of ties through public social acts may appear to be more relevant; nevertheless it is through both that the marriage is created and sustained. With the increasing importance of participation in a commoditized economy, much of the symbolism in marriage ritual relating to the organic process of marriage has been submerged: the *sadaki* is to my knowledge never offered in the form of livestock today, and therefore the image of wealth through biological reproduction has been lost to the image of wealth through exchange; the cowries that symbolized the female and pregnancy have given way to currencies that have little symbolic content; gifts that in the past were provided through participation in production, such as locally produced cloth, calabashes, and grain, have largely been replaced with gifts purchased with cash. In order for the counterprestations women offer the groom to continue to serve as evidence of the bride's worth and her mother's *arziki*, they have had to originate in the cash economy.

With the sublimation of the organic/reproductive and processual imagery in weddings, the jural notion of marriage embedded in the image of "tying" and in the Islamic ceremony transferring the *sadaki* to the bride's male kin has gained in prominence. Rather than seeing the wedding as an organic process through which the couple become linked, a process that must be nurtured and tested to see whether it is "taking," marriage becomes a simple transaction, one that can be done or undone with ease by the husband, regardless of whether the union has been shown to have *arziki* through the production of children.[11]

Despite tremendous variations among them, women nevertheless share a quite different perspective on marriage, and occasionally ignore legalistic notions that do not suit them. Thus Zule simply left her rural husband when she had determined that the marriage was "dead," with little concern for whether the divorce had been legally effected and recorded, while Magajiya insists that a woman who has children with a husband is always in a sense married to him even if they divorce because they share an interest in the children (Zule, 3-9-89; Magajiya, 11-15-88). Magajiya's remark is evocative of the "polyandrous motherhood" Jane Guyer suggests emerges out of women's use of children to make long-term demands upon a wide range of men in successive unions: "Children mediate relationships which can hardly be set up or maintained in any other way, including marriage itself" (1994:237). Marriage, by Magajiya's reckoning, is equated with parenthood.

Women may, of course, deploy the "male" contractual model when it suits them, however. Legal rules, as Caroline Bledsoe remarks, can be "resources as well as sanctions"; in the Kpelle case, older Kpelle women espouse marriage as the norm for everyone but themselves (1980:177). In Maradi the restructuring of rights and obligations in rural marriages that placed the product of the *gamana* field at the wife's disposal was only possible because women found it convenient to adhere to a model of marriage in which men contract to care for their wives as dependents. Such a model provided the pretext for women to use their own income and production as they wished. Women speak of marriage, in this instance, as a kind of "promise" that the husband makes to provide for the bride, and any intrusion into her *gamana* production is then seen as a breaking of that promise. In using the contractual model to broker some space for independent production and income, however, women diluted the potency of the organic model, for it could no longer be said that "our women feed us" quite so directly, and women's role in marriage becomes thus more tenuously related to the reproduction and nurturing of life. When women are no longer "providers of food," the logic ensuring their access to land is undermined.

Part of the reason some women prefer to engage in informal liaisons rather than enter into the kind of contractual marriage men control and define may be that the processual understanding of marriage–in which women's needs and

---

[11] For a discussion of the negative consequences of the monetization of bridewealth for Zulu and Swazi women see Ngubane (1987).

demands must be responded to and their reproductive and productive powers respected–has declining currency today. Women's use of the contractual model has contributed to that decline, as has the resistance of youth to some of the symbolic subordination enacted in ritual, as evidenced in men's refusal to take part in the "washing." The effacement of the organic model makes it difficult for a woman to shape a marriage once it has already been "contracted." It becomes more appealing for women, therefore, to opt for various informal unions, which have yet to be fully defined within Maradi culture, as we shall see in a moment.

Elite Women and the Negotiation of Bridewealth

Given the tenuousness of the organic model, particularly in the urban setting where food is bought rather than produced directly through women's labor, women must sometimes protect their interests by working within the contractual paradigm. For an elite functionary woman this might mean protecting herself against the possibility that her husband will not respect her preference, for example, for a monogamous marriage, or that he will attempt to limit her mobility as seclusion in the region grows. The currency of the *alhazai* model of Islamic marriage makes it extremely difficult for elite functionary women to resist their husbands should they decide to emulate that form of polygynous marriage. As one functionary woman responded when I asked whether women do not sometimes stipulate prior to marriage that it is to be monogamous:

> Even if we agreed to such a thing beforehand, it would be meaningless. You know, there's no family code here, it just can't be done. It's only if you are married in a Christian church that you can impose a monogamous marriage. But if it's a Muslim marriage, men are authorized to have up to four wives. If there were a family code you could set stipulations (Hamsatu and Rahama, 8-20-89).[12]

Some elite women, given the choice between choosing a marriage over which they have little control and informal unions which they can end at will, seem to prefer to defer formal marriage for lengthy periods, particularly if they have been married and divorced once. This can lead to confusion and frustration between male admirers and unmarried women; women accept favors and gifts which under other circumstances would be understood as preludes to marriage.[13] Elite women who marry for the first time relatively late, usually between 15 and 20, do generally have more choice in their partners than other

---

[12]   Actually Christian marriage is no guarantee of monogamy. The two wives of a male member of the Protestant congregation were ostracized by other Protestant women for taking part in a polygynous household during my research. The family code has been much debated in Niger, as will be seen in the following chapter.

[13]   The male admirer of one of my unmarried functionary friends abruptly stopped seeing her when one of her older female kin told him that she didn't think her "daughter" had any intention of getting married.

young women.[14] But it is not clear that that choice has translated into particularly stable marriages, or that women who find themselves unmarried either through widowhood or divorce necessarily choose to remarry immediately. A number of factors militate against remarriage for elite women: first, certain government policies may actually promote non-marriage, such as the policy of preventing unmarried women from teaching in the urban centers where they would be more likely to meet men of their own background, and the frequent posting of civil servants to new locations where it may be difficult for both a husband and his wife to find employment. Second, these women have access to their own housing through the government and may invest in property with part of their income as well. They are therefore better able than most women to resist family pressure to remarry and may conduct alternative kinds of liaisons without the close scrutiny of their kin. Third, their independence has been won at great cost (in time devoted to education and in the expense of that education), and they are not particularly eager to remarry if it means that they must give up their income, mobility, or public persona.[15] Finally elite women have earned the title of "madame" and with it a certain latitude in their behavior. They are not expected to behave like other women, and respect for their success and learning (*arziki* and *ilimi*) may counterbalance the stigma of non-marriage somewhat.

When these women do remarry they seem to do all they can to ensure, on the one hand, that their husbands are impressed with their personal stature and, on the other, that they will not be trapped in the marriage by financial issues surrounding the return of the *sadaki* bridewealth payment given by the groom to the bride's family. Evidence in records of marriage registrations shows how contradictory the education of women can be in their attempts to negotiate and control their marriages. Because it is primarily men and women who have had some schooling or are employed by the state who register their marriages, these registrations provide some limited evidence on how these marriages have been affected by education, and how educated women have participated in marital negotiations. The earliest *Actes de mariage* record the marriages of lower-level administrative clerks, purchasers, and traders for the French trade houses, soldiers, and medical staff. Since independence, however, more and more of these registrations concern higher state functionaries, and more and more of the women involved (as brides, witnesses, and representatives) have also been employed by the state, particularly as teachers.

Evidence provided here was collected at the Mairie of Maradi from registries of the *Actes de mariage* for the years 1956 (the first year for which such records were available), 1965, 1970, 1985, and 1988. I studied all of the *Actes de*

---

[14]   This choice is so closely associated with education that when asked whether she had chosen her first spouse, one older woman responded, "No, I wasn't a schoolgirl."

[15]   This holding out for a husband who would suit a woman's choice of lifestyles is nicely captured in the words of one elite woman, "I still haven't found a suitor who suits my lifestyle" ("Jusqu'ici je n'ai pas trouvé un soupirant qui cadrerait avec ma vie").

mariage for 1956 (21), 1965 (70), and 1970 (66). Only 51 cases were studied from the registry for 1988, which was incomplete. Because the information provided in the registries varies over time, I have only discussed those issues which could be addressed over several sets of data, which eliminated records for 1956 and 1985 from much of the subsequent discussion.

The figures that follow chart the number of registered marriages at each level of *sadaki* payment listed in that year. In the 1956 registry there were three cases that do not show up on the chart: one in which the bridewealth offered was two cows, and two in which no bridewealth is listed. All were non-Hausa weddings. The peak in cases at the 10,000 CFA level probably represents the norm for this class at that time, but since the number of cases is so limited little can be deduced from this material. The information recorded did not enable me to determine such questions as the age differential between the spouses or the education of the bride.

By 1965 the information listed was more detailed, and the number of marriages recorded had more than tripled, from only 21 in 1956 to 70 in 1965. Because the registers began recording the recipient of the bridewealth as well as the names of the witnesses more can be determined about the character of the unions recorded. The bridewealth distributions suggest that 5,000 CFA was the "standard" dowry at that time for a Hausa marriage, and smaller peaks at 2,000 and 10–15,000 suggest that these represent the low and high ends of the dowry range.

In the 1970 registers the employment of both the bride and groom may be listed, but only rarely is anything recorded for the bride. Three peaks emerge on this chart as well, one at the 1–2,000 CFA range, another at the 5,000–10,000 range, and a third at the 15–20,000 range. Clear patterns begin to emerge when the age of the brides is correlated with the size of the dowry, and the more detailed information about the witnesses and couple make it possible to suggest that the lowest range tends to include older women who have their own female witnesses and who sometimes receive the "dowry" themselves; the middle range tends to include younger brides whose marriages do not include the unusual presence of women as witnesses; and the highest range once again includes older women, many of whom have listed some form of salaried employment. The bridewealth seems to correlate well with the age and education of the bride, but not with the age or education of the groom.

Unfortunately the most recent registers are in some ways less revealing than the 1970 register, for state pressure to keep ceremonial expenses down has meant that when marriages are registered both the clerks and the couple indicate a "standard" bridewealth payment automatically. This does not, of course, mean that all weddings are in fact contracted with the "standard" payment, but rather that the 15,000 CFA peak probably masks variations in the payments. Still, in the 1988 register some patterns emerge, and the more detailed information listed about the bride's employment is a new and interesting feature. A number of cases fall below the standard, in the 5,000–10,000 range, and a few fall well above at 50,000 CFA, the state-mandated cap on bridewealth payment.

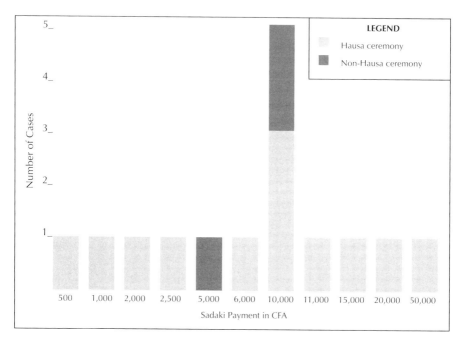

Figure 1: Actes de mariage, 1956

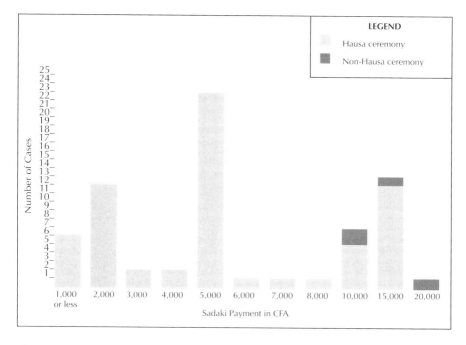

Figure 2: Actes de mariage, 1965

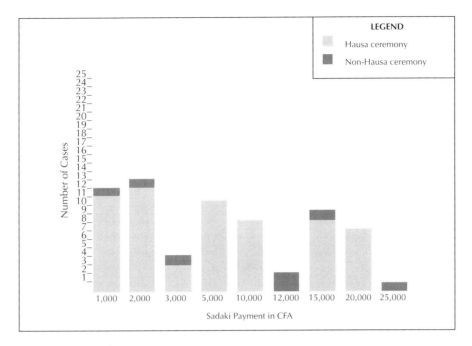

Figure 3: Actes de mariage, 1970

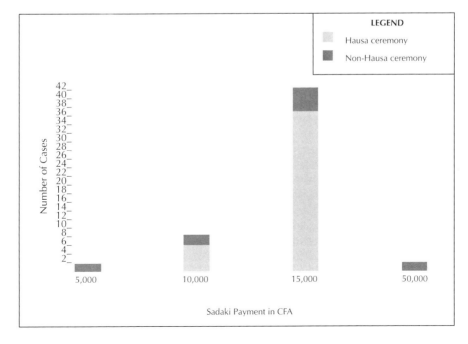

Figure 4: Actes de mariage, 1988

162   Marriage in Maradi

The lowest cases include anomalous marriages: a non-Hausa woman trader, a Christian couple, and four of the twelve cases in which the bride's employment is listed. The high cases are also exceptional: one includes a Tuareg woman, the other involves two students who are very close in age. Out of the 10 non-standard cases, five involve couples who are less than ten years apart in age. Half of the non-standard cases (both low and high) involve women whose salaried employment is listed.

In general, then, when the *Actes de mariage* recorded in any given year are charted according to the level of the *sadaki* bridewealth payment, a conspicuous peak emerges at a range which is the social norm for a woman's first marriage at that moment, and the majority of marriages for young women fall within this range. *Actes* recording a *sadaki* either above that level or below it are exceptional, but may be numerous enough to cause smaller peaks at either end of the scale. These cases often involve brides who are either older than the age of first marriage for elite women at that moment, or involve female representatives in the marriage arrangements. Perhaps because elite women often marry slightly later than most girls (who marry at about fourteen)[16] and may have more choice in their spouse, the age differential between spouses seems to be declining over time.[17] At the same time elite brides may find that because their kin have invested money in their education and absorbed the opportunity cost the loss of their labor represents, the bridewealth demanded is relatively high. Such high bridewealth can be a burden upon the couple's finances if they are young, and may be difficult for the bride to return if the marriage fails.[18] Educated women who are well over the normal age of first marriage (for whom the marriage registered may represent a second or third marriage) seem to negotiate bridewealth payments that fall into the lower end of a range.[19]

---

[16]   The 1990 demographic survey suggests a median first age of marriage for women in Maradi at 14.8, while overall nationally among women with some schooling the median age of first marriage is 17.1. Maradi women (together with women of Zinder) tend to marry slightly earlier than women in other regions of the country (15.1), although early marriage for women is a general pattern (République du Niger 1992:66).

[17]   In 1965, out of 64 marriages in which the age differential between the spouses could be determined, 29 involved couples within ten years of one another in age (45.3 percent). By 1970, the number had increased: out of 46 couples where the age differential between the spouses could be determined, 22 couples were within ten years of age of one another (47.8 percent). In 1988 30 couples out of 51 (58.8 percent) were within ten years of one another. In three-fourths of those cases the woman listed some form of employment.

[18]   In 1965 15 out of the 19 cases falling at the high end of the *sadaki* range involved women between 17 and 21, only one was the normative age of first marriage for girls, 13. Out of 17 cases at the high end of the *sadaki* range in 1970, 10 involved women between 17 and 21, none were younger. By 1988 *sadaki* had been standardized at 15,000 CFA and little can be determined from the registers, since applicants fill in 15,000 automatically. Many people believed this to be the maximum permitted by law, which was in fact 50,000 CFA.

[19]   In 1965 only one of the 19 cases which fell at the low end of the *sadaki* range involved a girl who was clearly entering her first marriage, 11 were ambiguous, the girl was between 14 and 19. But 9 cases involved women 20 or older. Similarly in 1970, out of 17 marriages at the low end of the scale, only three involved young girls, in this case 14 year olds. Seven were over 20, and the remaining seven were between 18 and 20. In 1988 all of the cases below the "standard" of 15,000 CFA involved women who were at least 16.

Because it is impossible to know from most of these records who negotiated the *sadaki* payment, I examined a number of exceptional cases particularly carefully: cases in which female witnesses represented the bride and received the bridewealth, suggesting that the bride was working on her own without male kin; cases where the bride herself or the bride's mother received the dowry; and cases where the bride was over thirty.[20] I then contrasted these cases with cases in which the bride was fourteen or younger–close to the normative age of first marriage for non-elite women–and in which the father or another male acted as representative and received the bridewealth.[21] Of the twenty-nine cases in which women seem to have controlled the negotiations, in eight cases the payment was high, in eleven cases it was low, and in ten it was within the norm at the time: translated into simpler terms, the dowry was unusual in two-thirds of the cases. In the fifteen cases where men almost certainly controlled the negotiations, the dowry was normal in ten, and exceptional only in one-third of the cases.

While this sample is very small, it does suggest that it makes a difference whether or not it is the bride and her female supporters who negotiate the *sadaki* and marriage arrangements as opposed to senior men. One might speculate that exceptional dowries can signify something about the bride that is not in the interests of her male kin: high dowry makes her unusually valuable, but the payment may be difficult to return and may place her own kin in the awkward position of presenting equally lavish return gifts. On the other hand low dowry might suggest that she is not well supported, that her male kin don't have wealth or prestige, and that she might therefore be mistreated. To insist upon the standard *sadaki* is to ensure that she will not be abused, to demonstrate an ability to provide an equivalent sum, and to suggest that although she may divorce, it will not be particularly easy. As Rabe's account of her marriage to the Chadian soldier recounted in Chapter 2 suggests, male kin do not necessarily have an interest in demanding or accepting an unusually high dowry.

Demanding a high dowry may be one way for an older woman who is negotiating for herself to assert her worth to her husband. In agreeing to such a brideprice she announces her ability to meet the sum in return gifts and her

---

[20] In 1965, out of fourteen cases where the mother or aunt of the bride acted as representative and received the dowry, in six the amount was the standard sum, at that time 5,000 CFA, but in eight cases (over half of the cases involving female representatives) the bridewealth was either unusually high or unusually low. In the one case where the bride was over thirty the bridewealth was high, and she proved to be six years older than her husband, the only such case in all the years studied. Two other unusually high cases involved non-Hausa women. In 1970 in all of the seven cases in which the dowry went to a female witness, the mother, or the bride, the sum was either unusually low (five cases) or unusually high (two cases). In the two cases involving women who were over 30 one was exceptionally high, the other exceptionally low. In 1988 in the four cases where a female witness or the bride received the payment, one was exceptionally low, the others "standard." There were no women over thirty.

[21] In 1965 there were eleven such cases, eight of which were average in bridewealth levels, one was high and two were low. In 1977 in three such cases the dowry was low and one was average. By 1988 the marriage age among women likely to register marriages had risen enough that out of a total of fifty-one brides, not one was the normative age of first marriage.

ability to repay the *sadaki* should she be called upon to do so.[22] Older women as a rule occasion relatively low dowries, however, both because they are no longer virgins, and because they themselves have an interest in keeping the *sadaki* low. Insisting upon a low bridewealth, the most common pattern for older independent women, is a way a woman (whether elite or commoner) can protect herself against difficulties returning the payment should she decide to initiate a divorce herself and thereby become responsible for returning it. Hajjiya explains this preference in the course of a discussion of the *sadaki* in her four marriages, all of which ended in divorce, and particularly in her final marriage to a soldier (exactly the kind of marriage that might have been registered):

> I don't know what the *sadaki* was in my first marriage, I was little [and so she neither received it nor was she present for the negotiations] but the marriages I did when I was older, when I was aware, it was 100 francs. A hundred francs, for the *sadaki* [in her second and third marriages]. They [her representatives] would argue and argue, saying he should give 1,000, and I would say, make it 100. *Sadaki* is trouble! Just a little bit is plenty, a little is enough. You know, even 100 francs. . . . Me myself [in her fourth marriage] I had said make it 100 francs, and my brothers fought and fought, and they finally received 1,000. But that 1,000 francs, I swear I had such a hard time paying that back! You know, 100 francs, that wouldn't have been hard, would it? That 1,000 francs, it was hard, there I was in seclusion, I couldn't sell anything, there was no source of pocket money, that was hard, where was I going to get that 1,000 francs? Who was going to give it to me? I didn't have money to buy seasonings for sauce, much less 1,000 francs![23]

Although the *Actes de mariage* can tell us nothing about elite women's attitudes or behavior when faced with polygyny or seclusion, they do seem to suggest that when women have a role in negotiating a marriage they may pursue either of two strategies. The first is to bolster their husband's estimation of them by seeking out a relatively high bridewealth. This is a strategy more plausible for educated women than for illiterate women like Hajjiya. Since Zerma women have benefitted from education more than Hausa women, it is perhaps not surprising that it is often Zerma women who pursued such a strategy in the *Actes de mariage* examined. The second strategy available to women is to protect themselves from financial difficulties should they decide to divorce their husbands by keeping the bridewealth low.[24]

---

[22] Five of the exceptionally high cases involved non-Hausa women, and only one of the low cases involved a non-Hausa woman; Hausa women would seem to prefer lower bridewealth payments, where many non-Hausa women prefer higher ones, perhaps because more of them are state employees and strangers to Maradi.

[23] Hajjiya Gobarci, 11-16-88. Unlike educated women Hajjiya did not command a high dowry in any of her marriages. It was only in her third marriage to a man who had more status, in which her brothers would have lost face if the sum were too low, that she had trouble over the bridewealth, even though the sum in question was very small for a marriage contracted in the 1960s, and certainly compared to the marriages of elite women at that time.

[24] Women's role in negotiating marriage payments is unexpected, but finds parallel elsewhere; see Oboler (1985:107) and Maher (1974:88).

Opting for Informal Unions

The *Actes de mariage* seem to support the theory that lacking control over interpretations of what constitutes an ideal marriage, women instead negotiate the size of the *sadaki* bridewealth paid in order to establish both their self-worth and their right to the option of divorce. This does not seem to be a particularly new phenomenon: Hajjiya Gobarci had a hand in defining the size of the *sadaki* in her second marriage c. 1950. But control of the conditions of entry and exit from marriage may be taking on more importance as expectations surrounding marriage change. With the understanding of marriage as a union in which the two parties have chosen one another, share a certain image of what constitutes success, and hope to work together to prepare their children for a similar life, the potential for disappointment in one's marriage is great. In response to my query as to whether marriage for them was better than it had been for their mothers, several young women felt that in some ways marriage may have become more difficult.

Today young women hope to marry someone they love—someone close to their own age and background in whom they have an emotional investment. They want to be respected and yet at the same time they want all the same guarantees that they and their children will be provided for that their mothers had enjoyed. The potential for disappointment is great, and the emotional cost of marital failure is, in these young women's minds, higher than in the past. As Madame Hadiza, speaking of her mother Hajjiya Larewa, remarked, "my mother didn't expect anything, and so she couldn't be disappointed."[25] Certainly Larewa went through several marriages, and experienced her share of divorces. But Larewa's ability to move in and out of marriage was in a sense enhanced by her lack of emotional commitment to her husbands. Her daughter Hadiza divorced her second husband because she and her co-wives fought incessantly, but she still loves him and would remarry him if she could. Increased emotional attachment generates greater friction between co-wives should the union become polygynous: it is no longer simply an issue of control of labor and resources, but also a question of one's self-worth and desirability.

In this context it is not surprising that some elite women prefer to enjoy less serious and less emotionally fraught alliances. A lengthy liaison with a man who is married and has wives in another city may be less painful and less humiliating should it fail than a formal marriage in which a woman is expected to live in the same house as her co-wives. The story of Monique, a well-educated schoolteacher in Maradi, illustrates the contradictions women encounter not simply in the world, but in their own behavior.

> Monique is the thirty-five-year-old daughter of a Hausa woman and a Togolese man who worked in Maradi prior to independence. She married a Hausa schoolteacher from Maradi in her first marriage. They

---

[25] Delu, an elderly woman, concurs, remarking, "as long as he was good and respectful it was a good marriage," 8-24-89.

were very happy together and had three children. She had a relationship to him that would have been considered altogether inappropriate
by many women. She even had him stay with her during childbirth,
which would shock most Hausa women.

Unfortunately her husband died ten years ago, and she has since
been disinclined to remarry. She is self-supporting, has her own
house from her father, and her children have been successful in
school. She maintained an informal relationship with a trader from
Ngigmi–a town very distant from Maradi–for about five years. She
had no desire to formalize it until two years ago, when she became
pregnant with her youngest son, and decided to marry the man for
the sake of the child.

She moved to Ngigmi to live with her new husband, leaving the
older children in the care of her illiterate mother in her house in Maradi.
Her husband had three wives already, and she became the fourth. The
wives differed enormously in educational level and did not get along
well. She found that her husband had numerous liaisons outside of
the home, and remarked, "With four wives, why did he need other
women? His sexual needs were amply satisfied!" She found that his
behavior was not challenged by the other wives, however, who as she
saw it, welcomed him with open arms when it was "their turn." She
found herself alone in confrontation with him and eventually obtained
a divorce and returned to Maradi.

She found that in her absence her children had done poorly in school,
and her daughter–who is extremely bright–failed in her second year
of CEG. She has devoted herself to attending to their education very
closely, and states that she has no intention of remarrying. She does,
however, see a number of men on a fairly regular basis.

Monique's contradictory reaction to her husband's philandering would
be amusing, given that she herself had been his mistress for several years,
were it not accompanied by real emotional pain. A relationship from which
she could maintain some emotional distance so long as they were not married changed abruptly as soon as she had the expectations of a wife and not
of a lover, and as soon as the spatial configuration of their union confronted
her with her position as only one of many sexual partners. Like the young
women in Nigeria described by Wambui Wa Karanja, a few educated women
in Maradi find it advantageous to maintain an informal liaison with a married man rather than marrying formally, because it can be preferable to be
the pampered mistress rather than the disappointed wife. However, unlike
the young women Karanja describes, who seem to choose Mr. Available (the
typical lover, who is married and wealthy) over Mr. Right (the ideal husband, who is young, well educated, and single) primarily upon financial
considerations (1987:256–57),[26] in Maradi the choice of Mr. Available has
advantages that are not only material but relate to a woman's maintenance

---

[26] These are terms used by female undergraduates in characterizing the men with whom they
might have relationships.

of her sense of self-worth and her emotional health.[27] Women are thus acutely aware of the potential disappointments of marriage caused largely by com- petition–emotional, sexual, and material–with other women, yet they them- selves sometimes promote that competition through the very stratagems they employ to avoid a disappointing marriage.

There are dangers in opting for outside unions, however. Some research suggests that in Africa unmarried women and women in informal unions have a higher risk of exposure to STDs (including AIDS) than married women (Caraël 1994). Evidence elsewhere also suggests that such women and their children are more vulnerable than formal wives who reside with their husbands during times of stress (Bledsoe 1980:172, Meekers 1994). Not only do such women miss out on some of the protections guaranteed to them as dependents in the local interpretation of marriage, unmarried women are also often scapegoated dur- ing droughts, famines, and moments of political instability; such harassment of single women has a long and troubling history in Hausaland (Pittin 1991, Folly 1993). Monique's status as educated "madame" provides her with some immunity from criticism, but most women enjoy neither her income nor her imposing physical presence, making it difficult for them to remain unmarried without some stigma and some physical risk.

One way a woman with fewer symbolic and material resources could pro- tect herself while remaining unmarried in the late 1980s was to join either the Association de Femmes du Niger, the national women's association, or the Samariya, the National Youth Movement. The Samariya provided young women with an acceptable venue for public display under the approved mantle of na- tional development propaganda. The AFN, on the other hand, ostensibly pro- vided mature women with a locus for participation in politics. I will argue that in Maradi the most striking implications of the women's association in the late 1980s lay less in its achievements in the realm of national politics under the single-party regime than in the uses to which it was put by women seeking sanction for their mobility, visibility, or choice not to remarry. Like most of the strategies available to women, the tactic of employing the women's association as a means to earn respectability and approval while moving into external public spaces was highly contradictory. In the following chapter, then, I shall address how women's associations have figured in the recalibration of respectability and of what it means to be a "married woman."

---

[27] In Maradi the financial advantages of a non-marital liaison among the elite are not all that considerable: in Monique's case she has her own home, so she does not gain access to housing through it, and with her own income, a small bar, and cloth trade on the side, she does not really need extra cash. The financial disadvantages of marriage to the same man were, however, consid- erable–she had to leave her job and her trade, as well as her children, to go to a city where she had no contacts.

8

Of "Prostitutes," the Public, and Politics

This chapter derives in many ways from my reflections upon the stresses and torn loyalties I myself experienced while conducting the fieldwork for this book. As I indicated in the introduction, part of my initial impulse to study the region involved a desire to capture and celebrate the female agency so neglected in most historical studies of the Hausa. I had, it must be confessed, a certain unspoken hope that some of the female solidarity found in other moments in African history might be evidenced here (Okonjo 1976, Van Allen 1976, Mba 1982). I knew, of course, that age, class, ethnicity, and religion would be likely to be important sources of differentiation among women (Strobel 1979), but I was not prepared emotionally (rather than theoretically) for what it would be like to face the reality of the tremendously fractured and fractious female populace I encountered in the field. I found myself unaccountably disappointed and distressed that, in the face of the substantial material constraints emerging from gender norms affecting all the women I worked with, women didn't seem inclined to come together as a unified group in order to effect change. Much of the preceding discussion will, I hope, have illuminated why, in negative terms, that might be. In this chapter I will propose a potentially positive reason why Hausa women in Maradi could, in particular moments, be quite theatrical in differentiating amongst themselves. I have come to think of this performance of distinctions in public arenas as a tactical politics of difference, one which, however contradictory, has earned women the single most important right they could have fought for collectively—namely, the right to participate openly and visibly in public politics.

In order to explain what I mean by this it will be necessary for trace out two related phenomena—the development of women's associations in Niger and the categorization and characterization of "married" and "unmarried" women in the Maradi region from the late 1950s to the late 1980s. The dual development of women's associations and the reconceptualization of women's status within or outside of marriage occurred at the intersection of national influences and interests with local circumstances and cultural categories. Beginning with the creation of the Union des Femmes du Niger in 1958 and progressing through the emergence of the Association des Femmes du Niger and the Samariya youth association in the mid-1970s, I argue that women's associations in Maradi have not served to crystallize a Hausa female subculture. Instead, Maradi women have used the different women's associations to emphasize age, marital, and status distinctions among themselves as part of a larger move to create a legitimate public persona for both married and unmarried women. Women thus participated in social transformation not by appeal to female solidarity or to a shared female culture but by drawing upon existing social forms to generate new possibilities for women in a changing political economy.

I refer to this extremely contradictory tactic as a politics of difference, for it is only by underscoring differences among women that it has been possible for women to redefine marriage, respectable behavior, and access to external political spaces. The danger of such a maneuver is, of course, that in emphasizing difference and in drawing upon existing categories and social forms to generate new social and political possibilities, there is a risk of heightening tensions among women and reinforcing accepted gender ideologies. Let me hasten to add that I am not arguing that women as a whole have consciously and deliberately engineered this tactic. To the contrary, I am suggesting that women's associations in Maradi in the late 1980s reflected fissures within the female body politic; in the pragmatics of bringing themselves into visibility and out of silence at a time when Islamic fundamentalism has been on the rise in the region, women drew upon and emphasized those fissures. I characterize this politics of difference as tactical not so much because it reflects the ongoing working-out of a conscious strategy but because it is important to see the alliances and identities entertained by women struggling to improve their personal and collective circumstances as frequently provisional and preliminary. These approaches may succeed in moving them, in uneven and contradictory fashion, toward ends that may not be fully articulated and that cannot always be achieved through direct and confrontational means. Research on women in the Muslim world is beginning to reveal the complexity of women's activism in such settings: women may choose to adopt a purely secular feminism, or they may attempt to work from within Islam to promote interpretations of the Koran that are more favorable to women, or they may call upon aspects of local understandings of Islam that they find liberating (such as veiling, education, and female companionship).[1] Strands within Islam can be empowering for women, and frequently serve as spiritual, rhetorical, and organizational resources for reform. Renée Pittin, in the course of setting out the tremendous contradictions inherent in a series of efforts to promote female education in Northern Nigeria, has argued that debates launched from within Islam can "have inherent limitations, inasmuch as they are carried out in an arena with

---

[1] For a survey of recent work see Moghadam (1991).

pre-set parameters, with an agenda established within the ideology, rather than being a critique of the ideology itself, placing it in a specific historical and social context" (Pittin 1990:22). However debates rarely occur in such a pristine ideological environment, and much of this book has been devoted to illustrating the rich array of discourses circulating in the rather different circumstances of Maradi which could also serve to modify, amplify, re-cast, or redefine the terms of debate. This chapter will show how discourses about women and associations for women launched at the national level in Niger found their way into local debates and maneuvers, simultaneously transforming local cultural categories and recasting the potential implications of the national associations themselves.

Because of the particular manner in which I was integrated into the social scene of Maradi, I found myself pondering the nature of women's associations there at length. When I first arrived in the city of Maradi, local authorities at the Mairie determined that I should make my contacts with women through the Association des Femmes du Niger (AFN), the women's wing of the military-dominated political party in power at the time. These male bureaucrats reasoned that men would be less likely to object to my interactions with their wives if it were clear that my research had been vetted through the appropriate state-controlled channels. I was therefore introduced to the women who headed the various neighborhood sub-units of the AFN, and these women then arranged for me to meet other women in their circle of friends, kin, and neighbors. The majority of the women I eventually managed to work with were not members of the AFN, and many indeed knew little or nothing about it. Nevertheless because I had made my earliest contacts through the women's association, AFN members took me under their collective wing, and I became something of a mascot for them whenever the AFN took part in highly visible public events. In a sense, if they were "my" informants, I was "their" researcher, and my public association with the AFN must have served them in some important way, given their insistence on my presence at these events. What was at stake here, I wondered? Why was it so important that I stand together with these women at parades and spectacles?

My puzzlement deepened the better I got to know some of the most active members of the women's association and as I became more alert to their ambivalence about the time-consuming activities of the AFN and to their hostility toward other groupings of women in the city, particularly toward the young unmarried women who were members of the Samariya youth organization. While the female members of the AFN and the Samariya were both active at political rallies, they kept quite distant from one another both socially and physically. This antagonism became most pronounced when I had to choose my loyalties in a highly public and visible arena: would I use my car to transport key members of the AFN to and from a political rally, or would I carry some of the young women I worked with who were prominent members of the Samariya? In one such moment a "big woman" in the AFN remarked to me with contempt that I would get no good "history" from the women in the Samariya.

Having discovered fairly early on in my research that if I wanted to gain the trust of women, I would have to forgo my original plan to work with both men and women, I was somewhat taken aback to discover that I might then have to choose to ally myself with only one group of women. In the end it was possible to remain publicly associated with the AFN while working quietly with some Samariya women. Nevertheless, such moments made it quite clear to me that any cultural feminist vision of a unified female sphere along the lines of Renée Pittin's early work in Katsina (1979) would not come close to describing the complex relations among women of differing age, marital status, and occupation in Maradi, and would in fact obscure some of the most important ways in which these women constitute themselves in formal political arenas.

In this chapter, then, I explore a performative and linguistic moment in which women in Maradi have played upon the dominant ideology of female respectability in marriage in order to redefine both "respectability" and what it means to be a "married woman." This performance takes place in the spatialized realm of the external public gatherings that constitute the most clearly recognized arena for formal politics. My observations on Hausa women's shifting roles in the regional economy have impressed upon me the urgency of women's increased access to the external public spaces of larger-scale trade, formal politics, and Western education. Most women throughout the Hausa-speaking region earn income through petty trade in prepared foods or small quantities of cloth and other trade goods. Women, increasingly restricted to their homes, must rely upon their young daughters to purchase inputs and to peddle the goods from door to door. Tempering scholars' enthusiastic depictions of the autonomy and vitality of the Hausa female sub-culture and its "hidden economy," Barbara Callaway remarks of women in Kano: "It should be emphasized . . . that there is little comparison between the wage sector and the hidden economy of women. The incomes of most women would not even support them at a subsistence level" (Callaway 1987:77). Scholars studying women in northern Nigeria suggest that despite Hausa ideology proclaiming the importance of men as providers for women, and despite the marginality of female enterprises, it is women themselves who increasingly take on the burden of feeding themselves and their children (Coles 1991, Frishman 1991, Pittin 1991). Hausa women's contributions to the household and national economies are rarely recognized, and national and regional policies can actively thwart women's income-earning efforts (Pittin 1990, 1991). To secure their rights to trade in the home and to gain greater access to public sector employment, larger-scale trade, and significant education, women in this region must first fight for their right and their daughters' rights to conduct their lives openly beyond the confines of their homes. Given the danger to which independent women in Hausaland are exposed, where such women have been systematically scapegoated and harassed at times of economic, ecological, and political stress (Pittin 1991), this is both a battle well worth winning and one that potentially subjects highly visible single women to heightened risks. It is therefore a fight best fought obliquely, through modifications and recalibrations of existing social forms, and through co-optation of sanctioned social and political discourses rather than through direct confrontation. This is all the more true as *'yan Izala* norms of respectability gain currency as this new generation of the *alhazai* elite grows in importance.

Unmarried Women and the Politics of Naming

In order to make clear what I mean when I suggest that women in Maradi have used existing social forms to create new political and economic possibilities for themselves, it will be useful to first set out some of the verbal categories available in Hausa for identifying and characterizing women of different marital status. The word used for an adult woman, *mata*, is also used to designate a wife, much as in French (*femme*) or in German (*Frau*) adulthood and marriage are linked in the words for "woman" and "wife." Prior to her first marriage (generally at puberty in the Maradi region) a marriageable girl is known as a *budurwa*, a term that implies virginity. A married woman who loses her husband either through divorce or widowhood may be known as a *bajawara*, which implies that she and the male kin who serve as her guardians (with whom she may live and who support her) are interested in finding her a new husband. Finally, a previously married woman who earns her keep through sexual favors is known as a *karuwa*. Such a woman is likely to live in a house together with other *karuwai*, and her means of income is known as *karuwanci*. Renée Pittin's (1979) research in Katsina (Nigeria) on the female-centered "houses of women" in which *karuwai* live reveals that women may enter into *karuwanci* temporarily, that they may marry a "client," and that in general women treat movement into and out of marriages as career moves, with *karuwanci* serving simply as one "career" option among several.

The long-standing institution of *karuwanci* presents translation difficulties for the English speaker, for although it bears some resemblance to prostitution, the relative permanence of the sexual relationships involved, the courtship those relationships entail, and the lack of enduring stigma practitioners encounter have prompted most English-speaking researchers to employ the word "courtesanship" instead. Hausa speakers in Niger, when speaking in French, often use the term *une femme-libre* to describe a woman who takes part in *karuwanci* rather than, for example, *une putin* or *une prostituée*, suggesting that indeed Hausa speakers do not regard this practice as being entirely congruent with Western prostitution. In Maradi, streetwalkers who come from other ethnic groups and who do not practice the domestic courtesanship women assimilated to Hausa culture prefer are openly derided and would not be called *karuwai*; Hausa speakers sometimes use the French loanword *passe-partout* to denote such women. The variations in forms of sex work in Maradi show some clear parallels with Luise White's work in Nairobi (1990); *karuwanci* corresponds most closely with what White refers to as the *Malaya* form and streetwalkers from other ethnic groups follow something more like the *Watembezi* form. For comparative purposes, then, one might choose to follow White's lead and analyze *karuwanci* as one form of prostitution among several. In this chapter I shall use the word "courtesanship" to refer to *karuwanci*. I retain the quotation marks, however, to remind the reader that we, too, are contributing to a debate about the moral character of *karuwanci*, sex work, "prostitution," and female sexuality, even in this act of translation.

This overview of linguistic categories, of course, obscures the extremely contested nature of naming. A great deal is at stake in which term is attributed to which women and by whom. There is little ambiguity about how to name a young girl who has never been married–she is a *budurwa* (virgin). Increasingly when a girl manages to continue her schooling beyond primary school, she might not marry until she is in her late teens or early twenties. In this case her status is ambiguous: the possibility that such a young woman has been sexually active prior to her first marriage complicates the question of whether she could reasonably be considered a *budurwa*. In general, however, a girl would be unlikely to enter into "courtesanship" without first having been married at least once. It is the large number of women who have been married at least once but are so no longer who are most difficult to categorize. Hausa language does not distinguish a divorcée from a widow or provide a broad term such as "single woman." For convenience I shall refer to all such ambiguous women as "nonmarried" in order to distinguish them clearly from "unmarried" pubescent girls, who have never been married. In 1979 Pittin asserted from her work in Katsina that while men may refer to any nonmarried woman who is not kin as a *karuwa*, women are more likely to use the more neutral term *bajawara*, a word that does not imply "courtesanship." She argued that men's preoccupation with "courtesanship" is a denial of the female sub-culture's recognition of non-marriage as an acceptable and respectable career option. Women, she asserts, are less concerned than men are with defining other women in relation to men: "The women have little emotional, moral, or political investment in the concept of women outside their husband's houses occupying a negative or stigmatized position" (1979:98). Women are more likely to use the word *bajawara* to describe another adult woman who is living outside marriage; men can imagine no option for women outside marriage other than "courtesanship."

In Maradi in the late 1980s the situation was more complex. Certainly, men in Maradi characterized some nonmarried women as "courtesans," while women were more likely than men to characterize some nonmarried women as *bajawara*. In Maradi today, however, when women refer to another woman as a *bajawara* they mean two things: first, that she is living with relatives and is under the authority of a senior male, and, second, that she and her guardian are pursuing or anticipating her remarriage. The word *bajawara* is no more appropriate than the word *karuwa* to describe an unmarried woman who lives on her own, earns own keep without recourse to sexual favors, and has no immediate interest in remarrying. *Bajawara* is a more positive term, but it is not more accurate. Consequently, single women in Maradi often maintain the pretense that they are interested in remarrying simply in order to be called *bajawara* rather that *karuwai*. The problem with conflating the categories of nonmarried women by promoting the notion that all nonmarried women ought to be considered *bajawara* is that it categorizes women who are pursuing remarriage with women who have no immediate interest in doing so. In Maradi women emphatically consider certain women to be *karuwai*, with something close to the moral opprobrium attached to the English word "prostitute," although the stigma is of a less lasting character. They also recognize that there are some women who are not married, have no intention of remarrying in the near future, and whose primary source of income is not connected to sexual favors. These women are the subject of considerable debate among Maradi women themselves, for if they are not *karuwai* and they are not *bajawara*, what are they?

I will now elucidate how the naming of nonmarried women has evolved in Maradi by tracing out the development of the political associations in which women have taken part during the postindependence era. It will become clear that the two issues are related, for as women begin to carve out a political place and persona for themselves, they must also create an appropriate public image, an image that neither *karuwa* nor *bajawara* adequately captures. This exercise in naming is a political exercise.

Party Politics in Niger

In order to make sense of the character and positioning of the primary women's associations in Niger's postindependence history, let me first sketch out the rise, decline, and recent resurgence of multiparty politics in Niger since 1945. With liberal reforms in politics in the French colonies following World War II, political parties were formed in the French colonial territories to send representatives to the new National Constituent Assembly in Paris. The Parti Progressiste Nigérien (PPN, the Progressive Nigérien Party), formed in 1946 by a group of elite intellectuals from the western Zerma speaking region of the country, emerged from a series of complex and shifting alliances and parties to gain control of the government of the newly autonomous Republic of Niger in 1958. The PPN leader Diori Hamani was named prime minister. In the following months the PPN proceeded to eliminate all opposition parties, reserving all positions for its own members. Upon Niger's full independence in 1960 Diori absorbed all the remaining non-PPN politicians into his own party, and henceforth Niger was a one-party state. In consolidating his control over the country, Diori gradually alienated the Hausa traditional rulers, who had continued to serve as the administrative apparatus under French rule and whose networks and power bases Diori attempted to co-opt through the creation of Party committees in each village. Diori formed a national "animation" agency, which was to create a pyramid of rural organizations that would replace local governments, bypassing the power networks built up by entrenched local powers. The rural party base would be founded on the state-directed cooperatives and a state-initiated youth movement.

The Diori regime's complacency and lack of interest in domestic problems eventually provoked a successful military coup in 1974. Many factors contributed to the coup, among them resentment of Diori's ties to the French government, his poor handling of negotiations for partial profits from the newly developing uranium mines, his alienation of traditional rulers, and, most important, his administration's cynical and inhumane manner of distributing relief grain from international donors during the Sahel drought of 1968–1974. The military government that took power under Seyni Kountché was very popular at first. Kountché used the brief surge in revenues from uranium to raise the minimum wage, improve national education, and make rural development and agriculture the nation's priority (Decalo 1990:268–69). His regime also developed a series of local-level institutions to replace Diori's village party committees with a "Development Society" based on the support of cooperatives, a renewed and expanded youth movement called the Samariya Youth Association, and a series of socioprofessional groups. Like Diori, Kountché hoped to mobilize popular support and channel political activity while bypassing any autonomous power bases at the local level (Charlick 1991:64–67).

As uranium revenues declined, the Kountché regime suffered numerous coup attempts and perennial student unrest, all of which Kountché survived. When he died in late 1987 of a brain tumor, he was succeeded by his chief of staff, Ali Saibou. Saibou seemed at first to have a strong hold upon his position, dealing moderately with student strikes. Saibou moved ahead with Kountché's plans to build a national charter and set up a committee to draft a constitution and to set dates for the elections of an assembly and president. In 1988 he launched a new party, the Mouvement National de la Société de Développement (MNSD, the National Movement for Society and Development) to facilitate the upcoming "civilian" presidential election. In spite of the relaxation of military rule under the Saibou regime, however, intellectuals and farmers alike were quietly skeptical of the apparent democratization under way; the MNSD was firmly in the hands of Saibou and the military government and the new constitution would be directed, controlled, and finally overseen by the military regime, even if a civilian were elected president of the party.

Popular discontent over the 1990 military attacks upon the Tuaregs, over the shooting of students in Niamey, and over austerity measures crystallized in a coalition between students and labor unions, who joined together to use strikes to pressure the Saibou regime to initiate a national conference for constitutional reform and to arrange multiparty elections. By March 1991 the Union Syndicale des Travailleurs du Niger (USTN) labor union had won an agreement from the MNSD government guaranteeing, among other things, access to the state media for opposition parties (*West Africa* 1991a). In an effort to limit the military control over the elections, the USTN forced Saibou to exclude the associations created or co-opted to form the base for the MNSD–the Samariya Youth Association, the Association of Traditional Leaders, the Islamic Association, and the Cooperatives–from the planning commission charged with arranging the national conference (*West Africa* 1991b). The MNSD candidate was defeated in multiparty elections held early in 1993, bringing a coalition government to power under Mahamane Ousmane, a civilian Hausa statistician from Zinder. The fate of the multiparty democracy movement is unclear at the moment of this writing. The military coup effected in January 1996 was ostensibly intended to move the nation beyond a constitutional impasse. The current head of government, Lieutenant-Colonel Ibrahim Bare Mainassara, immediately voiced an interest in working towards a new constitution and elections before the end of the 1996, and expressed the sentiment that what was needed was a stronger presidential regime and fewer political parties (three rather than seventeen) (*West Africa* 1996b). In July 1996 Mainassara declared himself to be the winner of a presidential election hotly contested by opposition party members, whose activities were immediately declared illegal (*New York Times*, July 11, 1996).

The Evolution of Women's Associations

Women's and youth associations have served as a means of mobilizing and making visible the power bases of the various political parties in Niger's postwar history. Youth associations in Niger (in contrast with the student unions) have not been formed spontaneously but were, rather, created to serve as wings of an existing political party. Youth group festivities have often served to distract from the vocal complaints of more politicized student groups and to entertain the large numbers of educated but unemployed youth. Similarly, until the civilian coup leading to the 1993 elections, there had not been an autonomous or spontaneously created women's political association in Niger. Prior associations were created as part of a political party or regime already dominated by men or were informal self-help and entertainment groupings absorbed into a political party. Women's groups could symbolize both a party's commitment to modernization and its roots in tradition. The problem parties have faced in mobilizing women as a party base has been that the women who have the greatest mobility and visibility within the external public sphere are precisely those nonmarried women whose character and status are most ambiguous.

Thus when the Parti Progressiste Nigérien (PPN) attempted to adopt the "courtesans" of Maradi in the 1960s to form the nucleus of its women's wing, it encouraged a change in naming. These *femmes-libres* represented qualities that the party regarded as signs of a modern, worldly woman. As Jacqueline Nicolas observed at the time, the "courtesan" "embodies the woman who has succeeded in freeing herself of the family yoke and has overcome certain taboos, a woman who lives on her own and who therefore is more likely to choose for herself the husband who suits her. The 'independent woman' is used by the PPN as their Egeria–companion and advisor to the kings! It is the party which had the word 'karuwa' changed to 'zawara.'"[2] The PPN attempted to

---

[2]   J. Nicolas (1967:59). A similar use of the *karuwai* by the PPN occurred in Arewa (Latour 1992:127–28). For parallel processes in Nigeria see Callaway and Creevey (1994:145).

replace the stigmatized term for "courtesan" with the neutral term for a woman between marriages (*zawara, bazawara,* and *bajawara* are variants of the same term) in order to legitimize the single women who served as the party's visible female base. However short-lived this renaming–certainly it no longer holds true today–it underscores the importance of nonmarried women to politics in a Muslim society where very few married women are in a position to join a political base publicly. Whether they were in strict seclusion or not, few respectable married women could have been called upon to parade on national holidays or to promote party propaganda. By choosing the word *bajawara* to replace *karuwa* the PPN was automatically implying that these single women were temporarily between marriages. These women were to be held up as progressive women and potential wives, not as women who had chosen a lifestyle that rejected or threatened the traditional ideal of marriage. It would have been difficult then, as it is today, for a young woman to state in any public manner that she had no interest in remarriage. Like many of my single female contacts in Maradi today, they would be far more inclined to profess an interest in marriage, "if only the right man would come along," while at the same time rejecting successive suitors. In part this is a strategy for finding a compatible or at least compliant husband. But it is also a strategy for avoiding criticism while maintaining an independent lifestyle.

The PPN's necessarily ambivalent relationship to "courtesanship" and independent women is made clearer in a rather Orwellian proposal made by the Union des Femmes du Niger (UFN, the Union of Nigérien Women), the party's women's association founded in 1958 under Diori and promoted by his wife, Aissa Diori: "The women of Niger demand that the party and the government give serious attention to the advancement of women at the national level. In particular the UFN calls for the creation of a female police force empowered to oversee urban morals and to prevent prostitution in cities and urban centers. . . " (cited in Clair 1965:139–40). This improbable proposal is followed by a series of demands that highlight the importance of women in the family:

> [They further demand] the schooling of Nigérien women so that they can soon bring their invaluable assistance to the education of children in the family, to the improvement of hygiene and nutrition, and to better child-raising practices and home economics. They also demand the creation of jobs specifically for women, particularly as stewardesses, waitresses, saleswomen, typists, stenographers, switchboard operators, police agents, and chauffeurs (cited in Clair 1965:140).

Women's education is proposed and justified here as a means to promote the well-being of children and to raise the standard of living for families. The dominance of the existing image of women as primarily wives and mothers meant that the UFN could only imagine laying political claim to education and jobs by publicly distancing itself from any interest in an immoral independent life outside the family. Through this juxtaposition the UFN implied that immoral sexual activities are the outcome of women's exclusion from education and employment in the formal economy: by promoting female jobs and education, the government would then encourage women to attend to their proper duties as wives and mothers.

Having established its interest in morality and the family, the UFN then went on to make a series of social and judicial demands which have yet to be fully implemented, modest though they may seem:

> The UFN demands that the government facilitate women's entry into judicial, social, and political careers; the liberation and upholding of women as wives and mothers; and the recognition by the state and by their husbands of their right to individual property. The UFN also demands that new legislation on marriage and the marriage contract be instituted guaranteeing a woman protection from divorce [repudiation] once she has had four children (cited in Clair 1965:140).

The UFN's defense of motherhood was not feigned: it was indeed interested in promoting women and in protecting the interests of women as mothers and wives.

In this juxtaposition of "courtesans" carrying the PPN banner and the cry for upholding women as wives and mothers we see the difficulties in mobilizing women politically in Niger: the women who are most available and visible as images of the modern woman at the same time threaten the accepted family organization. The renaming of *karuwai* as *bajawara* was in part an attempt to minimize the threat of these independent women.

It was the UFN that founded the original women's association in Maradi under the direction of Umma Aguiyar, a well-educated midwife from the Zerma-speaking region near the capital. Soon after the Maradi branch was formed, the internal divisions that have characterized the women's associations there began to emerge. While Madame Aguiyar acted as the president, the woman who was chosen as her vice president was Aisha Wandara, the sister of the traditional Hausa ruler of Maradi. Wandara had briefly held the title of iya, giving her authority over the members of the *bori* spirit possession cult when her brother was first enthroned. Her relative youth and independence, however, got her into trouble, and she was replaced by another woman of the aristocratic class after four years in office. Nevertheless, her spiritual and social ties to the spirit possession cult as well as her genealogical ties with members of the aristocracy made her an important asset to the UFN. Members of the cult, with which she remained closely associated, were often "courtesans," who as we have seen made up the nucleus of the women available to join the UFN. Wandara was the Union's link to Hausa women, who for the most part were not as well-educated as Zerma women in western Niger, and to the "courtesans" who could most visibly represent the PPN's women's wing in Maradi. Having lost her politically significant position as head of the *bori* cult, Aisha Wandara could nevertheless wield some power by acting as the state's link between a modern structure for women and the network of women most available to participate in that structure. By integrating a figure from the local female aristocratic hierarchy into the UFN, the PPN could make a political analogy between traditional forms of representation for women, and modern forms.

The existence of important titled positions for women in Maradi contrasts with the situation in northern Nigeria, where Pittin worked and where most research on Hausa women has been conducted. Local Maradi practices included women in the political process through titled positions for a few women in the aristocratic class, while commoner women could become prominent through the *bori* spirit possession cult, still practiced openly here and overseen by the iya. Independent women could find some protection from the dangers of marginality through *bori* cult membership, so that many "courtesans" were also part of the broad *bori* network. Thus the UFN could attempt to temper the possible negative associations attached to members engaged in "courtesanship" by drawing on the traditional sanction for *bori* that Wandara represented, as former head of the *bori* cult. The iya is chosen from among senior women in the family of the ruler, and both the traditional ruler, the sarki, and the iya can lay claim to their right to office in part because their family is seen as being closely allied with the *bori* spirits through inheritance: "su duk suna da bori" ("they all have spirits"). Such traditional sanction does not exist in northern Nigeria, where the cult is practiced very much in opposition to the desires of the Muslim rulers. The public acceptance of the *bori* cult, then, and the female title of iya altered the nature of women's participation in politics in Maradi, making it possible for at least one variegated segment of the female population (including some aristocratic women, bori members, and "courtesans") to participate in political events.

The early women's association entertained major political figures and participated in dry-season gardening. However, it is not entirely clear that "courtesans" had much choice in the matter of their participation. While the women who acted as leaders of the UFN in Maradi deny that "courtesans" were coerced into participating, older women often associate the UFN with "courtesanship," and in an interview I conducted in 1989 one former *karuwa* gave the following account of the experience of such women at the time:

> Hajjiya Gobarci: Back then they took all the women who weren't married, all the way from here and then all the way down the hillside, and they had to work a big field down in the valley, a government field.
> Me: Did you enjoy that?
> Hajjiya: How could you enjoy that?! They'd do dances late at night then, at that time, I had just come out of my marriage. Heavens! You'd do dances for Diori when he came (Hajjiya Gobarci, 11-13-1989).

With Diori's fall in 1974, the UFN slipped quietly into the background. When Kountché first took power, his government had a reputation for integrity and concern for the rural population devastated by the Sahel drought. As his regime began building the structures of the Development Society, local cooperatives and branches of the youth and women's associations were initiated in areas outside of the capital.

The traditional Samariya youth organizations were revived by the government in 1976 in part to implement major development infrastructure and in particular to construct wells and classrooms (Decalo 1990:190). Samariya comes from the word *samari* which means "youth" and, in particular, "young man." It generally refers to a man who has not yet gained enough experience and income to marry; it is also sometimes used by older men to refer to any junior male, married or not. In rural areas, when an invitation was sent out for men to work collectively on one another's farms, the *sarkin samari*, the head of the junior men, called them to work. Unmarried girls would be called by the corresponding leader of the young women, and while the young men labored the girls would sing and dance to make the farmwork more pleasurable. Such collective gatherings or *gaya* have become rare in rural areas today; hired labor has replaced the collective workforce.[3] Nevertheless the Nigérien government invoked this kind of collective work and festivity when it revived the Samariya in 1976.

The Samariya eventually became an important organ to encourage patriotism through the annual National Youth Festival (the Festival National de Jeunesse), where youth groups from throughout the country competed for prizes for the best ballets and plays presented on national themes. The festival plays became an important part of the Office de Radiodiffusion–Télévision du Niger broadcasts and consequently had a broad national audience beyond their local regions. Samariya members were also conspicuous in parades and generally danced and sang in local celebrations to entertain important visitors. The function of the Samariya was, on the surface, to retain "local" dance and culture. In reality, however, as Éliane de Latour observed, "All these festivities end up resembling one another. Oriented to the least common cultural denominator, the order and style of the rites is henceforth founded on national and Islamic values" (1992:148, see also 152).

The Women's Association of Niger (Association des Femmes du Niger) had a rather different genesis. In 1975, Kountché used the occasion of the International Year of the Woman to create a commission to study women's problems and to hold a series of public debates at the Institute for Research in the Humanities. These debates surveyed important issues ranging from women's status in the labor force to laws touching on women's rights in the family to female education. While the efforts of the UFN to promote women's issues, particularly those of educated urban women in Niamey, were recognized in passing, the Kountché regime quickly succeeded in redefining the terms of the debate: the interests of rural women were emphasized, and, therefore, women's issues were seen as part of a broader national development agenda. The women's association that emerged, the Association des Femmes du Niger (AFN), was consequently firmly in the hands of the Kountché regime. While the AFN had some success in advancing issues relevant to women, notably legal and available contraception (Dunbar and Djibo 1992),[4] other important efforts met

---

[3]   The *gaya* were disappearing in the Maradi region when Guy Nicolas conducted his research there in the late 1960s. See G. Nicolas (1975:188). For the same institution in northern Nigeria, see M.G. Smith (1981:59–60).

[4]   A law facilitating women's access to contraceptives was passed only in 1988. Prior to that time a woman was required to present her husband's written authorization (République du Niger 1992:43).

little success, most significantly the AFN's persistent attempts to promote a family code more favorable to women.[5] Despite Kountché's redirection of the women's association toward rural women's issues, the leadership and membership of the AFN remained concentrated in the major urban centers of Niamey and Zinder.[6] For women in Maradi, far from the capital, the significance of the AFN lay not in its specific social or economic programs, which in the end touched most of their lives only very marginally,[7] but, rather, in the possibilities the AFN presented for redefining women's roles and their access to public activity.

Struggling for Legitimate Independence: AFN and Samariya

Women in Maradi often see the UFN and the AFN as one seamless whole and use the same Hausa term to refer to both, '*kunjiyar mata* (women's association). Nevertheless, when the AFN was set up in Maradi, Madame Aguiyar kept quietly in the background; any clear association of the AFN with the UFN in the wake of the military coup would have been dangerous for the survival of the women's association and possibly for Madame Aguiyar as well. In 1975 Aisha Wandara regained the titled position of iya, making her the highest-ranking woman in the aristocratic class. Wandara's acquisition of full authority over the *bori* cult and its members, many of them "courtesans," made her the most logical choice to head the new women's association. Nevertheless, given the linkage between the earlier women's association and the recently deposed Diori regime, no one was eager to step forward publicly to head the successor association. Aisha Wandara described in tones of mingled irony and amusement how she came to be president of the new AFN in the same year that she regained the title of iya:

> In the end Madame Aguiyar said that she was tired, she said, "I can't do this anymore." So. She said I should become president, but I said I didn't want to. But then the préfet sent to the sarki [the traditional chief of Maradi and the iya's brother], asking why not, saying I should make myself a candidate. So they made me a candidate. . . . Madame Aguiyar had put away her presidency, she said she was tired, and that we should choose a new president from among us. That was in the time of Kountché. So that was that, there we were: no one was saying

---

[5] For a discussion of the pitfalls of promoting a family code in another Muslim context (Senegal), see Callaway and Creevey (1994:176–83). For a discussion of policies and practices surrounding contraception in Nigeria see Pittin (1986).

[6] Miles offers an anecdote illustrative of the chasm between rural units of the AFN and their superiors in larger cities: women in Yekuwa were asked to contribute money for a building in Zinder the purpose of which the local AFN head didn't know. The regional branch in Magaria relayed instructions, she explained, and "what they tell us to do, we do" (1994:282–83).

[7] For example women in Maradi have very limited knowledge, use, and access to modern methods of contraception, despite a broad interest in better birth spacing (République du Niger 1992:48, 55).

anything. So then the mayor asked the women: "Don't you women have anything to say? If there is no one else who wants to be a candidate, there is candidate Iya." He was reading from a piece of paper. And then everyone clapped and clapped [to cast their vote for her]. And that was that (Iya 'Yar Wandara, 11-16-89).

It is clear from this account that both the local public administration and the traditional authorities, all of whom were male, were actively involved in creating the new AFN. When the iya tells this story she tells it with humorous self-deprecation: when leadership calls, one is not given an opportunity to turn it down.

Iya Wandara was chosen to lead the new association for a number of reasons, one being her previous experience in the UFN. But the more significant reason was that she represented the intersection of several differing female interests in Maradi. As the leader of the *bori* spirit possession cult she represented female power, both political and spiritual: the AFN, like the UFN before it, needed that local form of power. However, the iya also traditionally represents the women of the major aristocratic families of the Maradi court who spend a great deal of time in her compound. Finally, she also represents women more generally, for women come to her for advice and help, whether they are members of the *bori* cult or not. With the iya at the head of the association, the government was assured of the sanction of an important cross-section of Maradi women.

Despite the apparently seamless transition from UFN to AFN, the character of the new women's association was radically altered by the establishment of the Samariya youth movement. The Samariya evoked not gender but age and seniority as primary elements of social order. By calling upon the image of the collective work group under the authority of seniors, the Samariya heightened the differences between young women and senior women. In rural areas around Maradi the Samariya of the late 1980s in some ways resembled the traditional model in which unmarried boys and girls worked cooperatively for the community. The members were often boys and girls too young to marry who were called upon to perform collective labor to the dancing and singing of the girls, accompanied by festive drumming. The groups also prepared plays and ballets for the national festival and helped with development projects such as well digging. In the town of Maradi proper, however, the Samariya groups had a rather different character. The membership was notably older; many of the young men were certainly old enough to marry (twenty-five to thirty-five years old) but perhaps could not afford to, and in some neighborhoods the girls were, in fact, young women, most of whom had been married at least once but were not any longer. Although the Samariya groups occasionally made an effort at dry-season gardening, their agricultural duties were relatively insignificant compared with their plays and ballets presented at the Maison des Jeunes and at the numerous political events which mark the year.

The character of the Samariya groups also varied immensely from neighborhood to neighborhood in the city of Maradi. In the most conservative neighborhoods, only prepubescent girls were permitted to be members. In newer neighborhoods, where the availability of rental housing increased the population of women who were neither living with kin nor married, the women in the Samariya were frequently "courtesans." In the newer neighborhood of Sabon Gari, for example, all of the young women in the Samariya lived in "houses of women" (*gidan mata*).[8] I asked a Samariya woman whether many of the members were *karuwai*, and she responded, "Not all of the women in the Samariya are *karuwai*, but lots of them are. Some of them are *budurwa* [unmarried virgins]" (Binta, 11-13-89). It is striking that she and the other women in Maradi I spoke to never contended that these nonmarried women were *bajawara*. Either Samariya members were "virgins" who had never been married (girls of ten to thirteen or so), or they were "courtesans." There was no room for anything in between.

The original UFN was frequently associated with *karuwai* and with *bori* members (G. Nicolas 1975:214). However the existence of the Samariya after 1976 altered the composition and range of associations in which women took part. The women who became members of the AFN were all, at least in theory, fully adult married women. It was now the Samariya that was very closely associated with "courtesanship," and the public and sexually mixed nature of their dancing and plays made the youth groups an appealing forum for women interested in public display.

One consequence of this division was that by the late 1970s and early 1980s women in the public realm no longer had a single arena in which to act together in the interests of women. Nonmarried women who were "courtesans" tended to join the Samariya, while married women and more "respectable" nonmarried women took part in the AFN. Whereas in the original women's association many "courtesans" and *bori* cult members were participants, the AFN eventually had a less diverse membership. It is possible that the existence of the Samariya also altered the composition of *bori* cult membership. The number of "courtesans" who participate in the *bori* cult may have dropped; the newer medium for public display and the closer association with more modern structures made possible in the Samariya were more appealing, particularly to young women with some education. The Samariya of the late 1980s was far more closely associated with "courtesanship" than was the *bori* cult, which in the past was considered the preserve of *karuwai*. As the "courtesans" shifted to the Samariya, the political utility of the *bori* cult for female support dropped significantly. Furthermore, as Maradi has adopted stricter Islamist practices as trade ties with conservative northern Nigeria increase, the cult has become a political liability to politicians attempting to unite around a common Islamic cultural heritage. Once the iya resigned from the presidency of the AFN in 1987, the few remaining *bori* members stepped into the background, leaving the AFN mostly to educated women, successful traders, and their clients.

One negative consequence of the division of women into the Samariya, the AFN, and the *bori* cult was that it undermined any solidarity the women might have been developing as a unified political group within the UFN. This

---

8 For a discussion of such houses in Katsina, see Pittin (1983).

fragmentation of women could serve the interests of the ruling regime, for it would work against opposition voiced by women at a time when the government was preoccupied with the demands of unruly students. Nevertheless, this division had the unexpected consequence of creating a more expansive political space for married and unmarried women who were not in fact engaged in "courtesanship." It is not entirely clear to me whether this space was consciously generated by Kountché and Saibou or whether it was an unintended outcome of the division of women between AFN and Samariya.[9] Certainly, by generating two potential fora in which women could participate, the government enabled a broader cross-section of the female population to become visible in the political context. It seems probable to me that, while the separation of women was promoted to make it more possible for married women to support the military regime visibly, no one anticipated that this separation could have counter-hegemonic and politicizing possibilities for nonmarried women. How did the creation of two groups give rise to such possibilities? I will argue that Maradi women themselves seized upon the occasion provided by these associations to debate, define, and renegotiate what it means to be "respectable," "married," and an adult "woman."

Debating Women

At the time of my research women who were not members of either the AFN or the Samariya often confused the two and saw no real difference between them, characterizing their membership as *matan zamani*, a euphemism for prostitute that means literally "modern woman." Members of the AFN, however, insisted on a difference between themselves and members of the Samariya. AFN members were "married women" who engaged in respectable behavior. By separating the AFN from the Samariya, the government made it possible for married women to take part in public political manifestations without being grouped with unmarried "courtesans."

What is the political significance of this linguistic differentiation? It enabled the Kountché and later the Ali Saibou regimes to promote a nationalism founded on the image of women as mothers and wives, even as it drew upon young women as a powerful form of entertainment and propaganda, harnessing the image of the "free woman" as an icon of modernization. For women this also meant that those who were not "courtesans" could participate in political events, at least in principle, without damaging their reputations. Married women found a forum suitable for women of their status. However, the

---

[9]   While Hausa-speaking women who are not of the elite educated class frequently described this phenomenon in passive constructions that imply that some outside force consciously intervened to separate women into specific groups ("Aka raba mata da karuwai" / "They separated out the women/wives from the courtesans"), women in a position to know more about actual strategies and directives from the party in power declined to discuss the subject, which they evidently regarded as politically sensitive. Nothing I have found in the published accounts from the period clarifies this question.

designation of AFN women as "married women" also made it possible for women who were not immediately interested in marriage to claim a terrain of public action without having to pretend to be potential wives (*bajawara*) under the tutelage of a senior male. This was new ground that the government made available, perhaps inadvertently. Women themselves laid claim to and reinforced that territory through dialogue among themselves and through public performative statements about what it meant to be a "married woman."

To return to the issues raised by Pittin in her work, while women had a sphere of their own and at times a language reflecting their values as opposed to those of men, the opposition that Pittin found in Katsina did not emerge in Maradi: one does not find that women refer to nonmarried women as *bajawara* while men call them *karuwai*. Rather, some women distinguish between different kinds of nonmarried women, clearly separating nonmarried women who exchange sexual favors for gifts and cash from nonmarried women who earn other kinds of income. Certainly women in Maradi are attempting to create a public arena in which nonmarried women can participate without being stigmatized as *karuwai*. Rather than subsume all nonmarried women into the category *bajawara*, however, they have accentuated distinctions among women and between the kinds of activities nonmarried and married women engage in to give moral legitimacy to the independence of some nonmarried women.

This act of legitimizing certain kinds of independence is extremely important for married women as well for as nonmarried women, for if women who are married are to participate in the public political and economic domain, they must be able to do so without any suggestion that they are behaving improperly and, in particular, without their being associated with women who are publicly known to engage in "courtesanship" or "prostitution." Where women in the Samariya danced and sang, AFN women at public gatherings made an attempt to behave in a dignified manner, clapping and chanting slogans. AFN women chose behavior suitable to their purported age and marital status. AFN gatherings could be very jolly affairs, but the form of the festivity needed to be distinguishable from that of the Samariya. Where Samariya women were openly flirtatious, AFN women deferred to men without being subservient. This image of AFN women had become current nationally, as Janet Beik's observation of the stereotyping of AFN members for a play in Zinder illustrates: the director instructed the actresses "to shake hands with the préfet but not to bow over in respect (as traditionally women would do when meeting an important man)" (1987:109).

Samariya women had equally clear notions of suitable behavior for themselves. I asked one *karuwa* if the "courtesans" could join the AFN if they wanted to; she responded that they could but that it would be hard to get along with married women whose husbands might be clients and that, in any case, "there's no dancing in the women's association, so it wouldn't be appropriate" (Hajjiya Gobarci, 11-13-89). The young Samariya members clearly enjoyed their dances and plays immensely, and no one seemed to feel that their behavior was inappropriate for their age or status as young girls and *karuwai*. One way a "courtesan" could demonstrate that she was a responsible citizen promoting the interests of society was to participate in the Samariya. Whereas in the past such women might have sought safety and refuge in the *bori* spirit possession cult, now they could turn to the government-sanctioned Samariya for legitimation, community, and protection.

While there were many AFN members who were not in fact married, their approach to legitimating their independence was to behave in a manner that resembled the married women as much as possible. They always wore headcloths and veils; they appeared restrained in public; they sat or stood with the married women in a crowd; they deferred to the older leaders of the Association. They behaved as if they were married women. Nonmarried AFN members were generally very hard-working women, who made do with meager incomes and relied in part upon the generosity of their AFN patrons to help them stay out of "courtesanship." Some originally came from rural areas and had few connections in Maradi. A few were very successful traders or producers, but the more successful nonmarried women were invariably older–often old enough to claim that they were too old to bear children and thus not planning to remarry. A few were government functionaries whose careers made remarriage difficult.

Some nonmarried women in the AFN may have been *bajawara*, but not all were necessarily looking for a marriage partner. Their approach, rather, seemed to be to associate themselves with women who were responsible, respectable, and married in order to maintain such a reputation for themselves. Since a Maradi woman's status as an adult is so closely associated with her status as a married woman, by mimicking the behavior of married women nonmarried women could establish themselves as fully adult women. Ironically, the most subversive implication of this performance was perhaps that these women were beginning to disassociate female adulthood from marriage (the equation of "woman" and "wife"); in appearing publicly as *mata* (adult women) and not *samari* (youth) they forced the public recognition that some fully adult women were not, in fact, married.

It is perhaps worth noting that I, too, was engaged, something less than fully consciously, in a performance of "marriedness" and "respectability." I covered my head with scarves and wore relatively modest clothing: opaque skirts that fell below the knee and blouses that covered my shoulders. I was not feigning marriage, for I was truly married; rather, I was making visible my marital status in a setting where it might not have been readily legible otherwise, given my husband's absence for much of my research. My respectable dress, my independence, and the fact that I had appeared before my contacts in the AFN fully approved through government channels made me, in effect, an excellent prop in their staging of respectability, marriage, and adulthood. I was close to the same age as many of the nonmarried women in the AFN, and I publicly engaged in my own work without participating in "courtesanship," which meant that my appearance alongside AFN women could be seen as an asset. This, I think, explains in part why AFN women insisted that I join them in the most public of events and why

187

they were dismayed by any prospect of my squandering this capital by being seen with the women of the Samariya. Conversely, by encouraging me to be seen publicly with them, they helped me to reinforce my own image as a "married woman."

Participation in the AFN was thus one way a woman could establish a reputation as an upright adult who behaved respectably, even if she was not married. This pushing at the edges of an accepted social category—*matan aure* (married woman)—is analogous to the stretching of other kinship and social categories. Just as older divorced and widowed women, despite their greater freedom of movement, were nevertheless treated as if they were married women, so these younger women mimicked married behavior and, in so doing, helped to redefine it. This manipulation of verbal categories is similar to the strategy Catherine Coles observed among Hausa women in Kaduna: younger women manipulated the category of "old women" (*tsofuwa*) in order to enjoy the greater mobility of women beyond child-bearing age (Coles 1990). However, such strategies are not guaranteed success. Popular perception of AFN women in Maradi was not always generous; some women in search of a marriage partner might temporarily bow out of AFN activities to avoid any possible association with "free women" and to make their availability for remarriage clear.[10]

Women argued among themselves about what constituted appropriate behavior, and their appearance in external public spaces following various behavioral norms was a way to create new public norms and perceptions of women. This interchange in 1989 between Iya Wandara and her niece, Rabi, illustrates the kinds of debates current in Maradi at that time. It is typical of many conversations I heard in which the respectability and status of various women was negotiated and established through gossip. The debate is unusual in that I happened to tape it while conducting a formal interview with the iya into which Rabi intruded. I asked the iya whether there had been many *karuwai* in the women's association when it was started. I used the general Hausa expression '*kunjiyar mata* for "women's association" rather than either of the French acronyms AFN or UFN.

> BMC: When they first started the women's association, didn't they call upon lots of *karuwai* to join?
> Iya: *Karuwai*? Yes, at that time the *karuwai* were put into the association.
> Rabi: No, that's not right. They did not put *karuwai* in!
> Iya: Well, they were the ones who weren't in seclusion; there were lots of them. All the married women were in seclusion.
> Rabi: No, it's only recently that they've put the *karuwai* in!
> Iya: No, today the married women are the majority.
> Rabi [challenging]: Where are they?

---

[10] One of my nonmarried acquaintances who had participated in street sweeping with married women in the AFN was severely chastised by her family for "going out with the Samariya." She stopped going to AFN events altogether in order to maintain a respectable image for potential suitors.

Iya [amazed at the question]: The married women in the women's as-
sociation? There are lots of them! The *karuwai* were all left to the
Samariya.
Rabi: They separated them?
Iya: Yes. Each of the women you see is a married woman who has a
husband. She is powerful in her home (*ta fi 'karfin 'dakinta*). She may
be an old women whose husband has died; now she isn't a *karuwa*.
You see, she has her own home, her daughters, and children. She's not
a *karuwa*. There aren't *karuwai* in the women's association (Iya 'Yar
Wandara, 11-16-89).

Two things strike me about this interchange. First, Rabi, who was not a
member of either the Samariya or the AFN, did not initially see any difference between the two; because the Samariya was so highly visible, she
thought of the Samariya when she heard me ask about *karuwai* and the
women's association. Her remark that the *karuwai* had only entered the association recently may reflect her memory that when she was much younger
the traditional rural Samariya work groups did not include "courtesans,"
more common in urban settings. Second, although the iya knew very well
that many of the women in the AFN were not married, when she generalized about AFN membership she described the typical AFN member as a
married woman, a woman with *karfin 'dakinta* - (the strength of her own
room or home). The expression is evocative, for it suggests both married
women who have enough influence with their husbands to be able to go
out to AFN gatherings, as well as any woman, married or not, who has the
ability to maintain herself and her children or dependants in a home or
room of her own. A woman who has the "the strength of her own room"
does not rely upon a man to pay her rent, although she may rely upon her
children for help. A woman who has been successful in trade might even
own or rent a house herself. The phrase thus calls to mind a woman with
either some economic self-sufficiency or enough intrahousehold stature to
be able to negotiate with her husband for a degree of independence and
mobility.

In the same exchange, Rabi, unconvinced, went on to enumerate women
whom she considered to be *karuwai* in order to prove that the women's association included them as members; the iya explained to her that each of them
was actually in the Samariya. Shifting tactics, Rabi then got Iya to name women
in their neighborhood who were members of the AFN. Rabi pointed out that
several of the women mentioned were not married. Iya then argued that they
were older women who are beyond marriage age. Finally, Iya mentioned one
woman who she conceded engaged in "courtesanship":

Iya: There's only one woman who has done *karuwanci*. [They establish
the woman in question.] But she isn't a *karuwa*.
Rabi: Good heavens, Hajjiya, she is too a *karuwa*, I swear to God!
Iya: Well, just because you are struggling with poverty doesn't make
you a *karuwa*. So she's having trouble. She just got into it.
Rabi: That's not true. She's been at it a long time. She didn't just start.

Iya was willing to make exceptions for a woman who is temporarily having trouble making a living, but in her own mind she made very clear distinctions between women who engage in *karuwanci* and women who for the most part avoid it.[11] Iya could distinguish among degrees of reliance upon gifts related to sexual favors and among different ways of associating with men. Rabi was less willing to see these distinctions, and as a married woman who rarely went out and saw little of how the two associations functioned, she had little understanding of why Iya would argue that some independent women are not *karuwai*. Note that neither woman made use of the word *bajawara*, which did not seem to be relevant to the discussion they were having.

This is not just verbal sparring, for much hangs on the issue of whether a woman, married or not, can take part in public activities–from politics to trading to education–without the perception of sexual impropriety. One of the factors limiting girls' education in Maradi, for instance, is the perception that it is inappropriate for a young married woman to go out to school. In a region where girls marry shortly after the onset of puberty, this perception is a powerful constraint to female education. The use of young girls as hawkers for married women who cannot leave the home to carry out their trade also serves to discourage women from sending girls to school. Of the many battles that the women's associations could be waging, one of the most important is to earn for women the right to be seen publicly without being stigmatized. As in the above conversation, this is a battle waged not simply with men but in debates among women themselves.

Conclusion

Since 1990, Niger has been drawn into the current of *multipartism* and democratization sweeping across West Africa; the Ali Saibou regime was forced in 1991 to cede power to a National Conference, which was to prepare the ground for the democratic national elections held early in 1993. It is, I think, an impressive measure of the success women have had in contesting external political space that on May 13, 1991, women in Niamey staged a well-publicized and highly visible protest against the virtual exclusion of female representation from the National Conference Planning Committee. While the powerful national trade union had managed to eliminate all other "democratic" institutions created or co-opted by the Saibou regime from the planning committee (including the Samariya and the Islamic Association), women staged a massive demonstration in the capital when the AFN was denied any representation. While the protest was organized and initiated from the Niamey offices of the

---

[11] One reason it can be difficult to distinguish a *karuwa* from a nonmarried woman who lives on her own is that sexual access, even for married women, is closely associated among the Hausa with gifts, and any courtship, whether sexual relations are involved or not, would also necessitate many gifts from the man.

AFN, the size of the demonstration and its success in forcing the inclusion of six women on the planning committee, despite the AFN's affiliation with the discredited Ali Saibou regime, suggests that women's rights to assemble in external public spaces and to have a voice in national politics are now broadly recognized. While the AFN itself has come under attack, the principle that women have the right to public political engagement and to representation has not.

If the Saibou regime attempted to co-opt women for its purposes, one might argue that women themselves managed to co-opt the AFN to gain representation for women even once the party with which it was originally allied had lost credibility. Whether, given Niger's current economic and political crises, women's voices and concerns will continue to receive attention is an important question. While urban women's groups succeeded in resuscitating the moribund debate concerning the Family Code (Dunbar and Djibo 1992), such issues are unlikely to be given priority in the near future. Nevertheless, women have demonstrated a willingness and ability to work together and appear publicly to promote representation of their interests in the national forum. The subtle manipulation of verbal categories setting out distinctions among women and establishing appropriate behavior for women of different status has been important in earning women the right to appear in such public demonstrations. The solidarity of women in May 1991 may have been possible only through a prior fracturing of women as a group: by emphasizing difference and establishing boundaries for behavior, women could open avenues for a broader segment of the female populace to appear openly in a political context than has recently been possible. That women in this instance carried banners of their own choosing rather than slogans for a male-dominated party shows how powerful this tactic has been. I do not wish here to reduce the politicization of women in Niamey to a consequence of debates among women in Maradi. Women's participation in politics in Niamey is a story deserving its own full treatment. I am suggesting instead that part of what made the women's march of May 1991 possible was the negotiation of a space for "respectable" women in public political fora by the AFN and that this accomplishment must be counted as quite a considerable success despite other setbacks for the women's association. Ironically the very performative aspect of the AFN that has so frequently been criticized (see a male supporter's scorn for the AFN's "folkloric side," Dunbar 1991:82-3) may prove to have had the most lasting implications for women's political empowerment.

This performative/linguistic tactic is fraught with contradiction, however. By setting themselves apart from the *karuwai* and the Samariya, women have played into the cultural stereotype that presents female sexuality as immoral and that defines proper behavior for women only in terms of marriage as the norm. The nonmarried woman can retain respectability only as long as she looks and acts as if she were married. By emphasizing divisions within the female body politic, women also run the risk of emphasizing tensions and conflicts with one another rather than with men. One thinks of the *karuwa* who remarked that it would be hard to get along with the married women of the AFN when some of their husbands are clients: the division between the two women's groups makes it possible for such women to avoid the immediate friction of meeting one another directly, but it also heightens the sense that the enemy is "those other women" rather than the men whose affections, attentions, and (perhaps most important) incomes are thus divided. If the cohesion of Pittin's female sub-culture is largely illusory, nevertheless, the fragmentation of women's groups itself distracts attention from some of the key sources of friction in gender relations in Maradi–sexual double standards, polygyny, the male prerogative of repudiation, and early marriage of women. These practices are given powerful sanction by their purported origins in Islam in a context in which Islamist solidarity is becoming an important factor in generating nationalist sentiment. The force of Islamist ideology in a general climate of resentment toward Western economic and political intrusion is considerable and has set the parameters within which women in Niger can realistically militate for change. Distanced from alternative readings of Islam and spirituality as the *bori* cult and the women's associations have become separated, women in the national associations find themselves subject to a potent Islamist cultural nationalism with little in the way of spiritual or religious alternatives to provide different models for women's roles in religion and society. As women in Maradi become better educated in Islam it is possible that they may find means to counter existing norms from within Islam, as has occurred in other parts of the Muslim world.

The dangers as well as the promise of the politics of difference were evident throughout the transition to civilian rule. The visibility and audibility of women in this process generated a backlash against young women of precisely the ambiguous status discussed above–secondary school students of marriageable age. In the market at Zinder several such women were beaten and stripped because of their "immodest" dress, and one was hospitalized (*West Africa,* 1993). A powerful measure of the positive potential in the ongoing process of negotiating women's entry into public space is that in such a moment large numbers of women rallied behind the young women rather than criticizing them for not dressing and behaving as if they were married women: once again women in the capital marched to protest these attacks and succeeded in forcing the government to intervene with police force (McCarus 1993a). While the attacks show how vulnerable single women are in times of national stress and suggest that Islamist sentiments are growing throughout the country, these incidents show how important the work of establishing women's access to external public space is and how tenaciously women in Niger are fighting for that access. This negotiation is still in process, and the alliances, divisions, and redefinitions women call upon in struggling for visibility and recognition are likely to shift many times.

The politics of differentiation women are engaging in underscores rather than erases the very real divergences within the female populace, emphasizing in subtle ways age differences and seniority, marital status, education, class, and rural versus urban origins. The interests of all women in Maradi or in Niger are not the same and in some cases run directly counter to one another. Although this strategy seems to have won recognition for women in Niger, it is not clear whether or how women in Maradi will move beyond the divide depicted here. Nevertheless, despite the considerable constraints women in Maradi encounter–within the household, the local economy, the national political arena, and the global economy–in terms of their access to critical resources, mobility, and education, they have been actively engaged in renegotiating gender relations and have found means, albeit contradictory, to counter some of the obstacles they face.

To borrow Judith Butler's formulation, this study can be seen as

> an effort to think through the possibility of subverting and displacing those naturalized and reified notions of gender that support masculine hegemony and heterosexist power, to make gender trouble, not through the strategies that figure a utopian beyond, but through the mobilization, subversive confusion, and proliferation of precisely those constitutive categories that seek to keep gender in its place by posturing as the foundational illusions of identity (1990, 34).

In reworking what it means to be a "married woman," Maradi women are subverting the most taken-for-granted of gender categories and enabling alliances between married women and nonmarried women. This is not, of course, the conclusion of a struggle but, rather, the emergence of a movement. To have begun staking a claim to the right to enter into the external public spaces of formal politics and large-scale trade is an extremely important first step toward achieving economic independence and political autonomy. In the wake of the Women's March of 1991 women's groups have mushroomed, with at least thirty-four formally recognized by 1995 (République du Niger 1995:7–8). After a long period of co-optation women themselves appear to have seized the initiative, and while their strategies and interests may be as numerous as the groups representing them, this increased female representation in public debate, however fragmented, will inevitably alter the political field significantly. It may be, in the end, that the most important thing I gave back to the women I worked with in Maradi was to stand in the hot sun with the "married women," wondering just what all the fuss was about.

CONCLUSION

What was the use of the enamel bowls and calabashes [given as wedding gifts]?

Well, that's history, the traditional kind. [Wato tarihi ne, irin na gargajiya].

Hajjiya Indo, 11-14-88

It would be a mistake to suppose that this book represents history as the women who were generous enough to share their homes, thoughts, and time with me would have presented it. My own attention to the ways in which shared idioms, institutions and rituals have been modified, adapted, and transformed by individuals attempting to navigate a changing political and economic landscape is quite distant from my informants' own emphasis upon continuities. For Hajjiya Indo history, "the traditional kind," resides neither in her own life story nor in the Arabic manuscripts from which her word *tarihi* is derived; history rests instead in the resonances of contemporary practices with past and future practices. If history is a story, then for her the important story is about tradition–*gargajiya*, or to translate somewhat literally, that which has been repeatedly inherited. Even in the act of recounting how gift exchange (for example) has changed, Maradi women insisted upon the important continuities with the past those exchanges represented. This book has explored this important paradox: the embodiment of continuity for such women is also the most significant locus of history and change. In attending to the domestic realm–the purported locus of stasis and reproduction–I have tried to recast what constitutes history and to relocate where agency is to be found. My thinking was powerfully shaped by the kind of "history" women in Maradi felt comfortable discussing with the young woman conducting the research: an educated "madame" who was married but had no children, an *anasara* [Christian foreigner] whose Hausa was far from flawless, an outsider whose sense of history was the product of years of training in the Western tradition.

That Western training emphasized a historical chronology quite different from the popular temporal markers more relevant to the women with whom I worked. Both men and women in the region tended to register the significant temporal divide in twentieth-century history not as a shift from the precolonial to the colonial era, or from the colonial to the postcolonial period, but rather as the loss of the "time of cowries" *(zamanin biringizau)* with the onset of the "time of searching for money" *(zamanin neman ku'di)*. One woman wryly captured the common local experience in a characteristic Hausa formulation balancing contrasting pairs: "In the past there was no money, but everything was cheap. Today there is money, but everything is expensive. Heavens!" (Hajjiya Fati, 11-17-88). With the growth of taxation, cash-cropping, and large-scale trade, particularly after the Second World War, a desperate search for cash has come to dominate the lives of farmers and traders, men and women in the region.

One reason why the temporal markers of the Western academic are not those of women in Maradi may be that, in fact, women's options over the course of the century have been altered less through the conscious engineering of the state than through the unexpected outcomes of a number of processes locally experienced as reiterations of "tradition." Work on gender in Africa has turned, of late, to the important question of how colonial constructions of femininity shaped marriage and domesticity (Hansen 1992, Walker 1990), occasionally accounting for contemporary gender tensions as the outcome of the colonial promotion of Victorian sensibilities through legislation and education (Okonjo 1976, Amadiume 1987). Certainly reactionary European gender constructs already under attack in the metropole found their way to Africa, and their impact has been particularly profound in regions where Christian missions have had a long history and in settler economies in which understandings of power and race have been inflected through gender. Nevertheless even in such regions local social forms and indigenous agency had important roles to play in determining the outcome of the encounter between European gender impositions and African "traditions" (Obbo 1988, Schmidt 1992).

Maradi experienced neither sustained exposure to Christian missions nor significant European settlement. Furthermore missionary and state interests could run quite counter to one another, while the colonial administration was itself torn over how to shape women's education and whether to legislate local marriage practices. Maradi's uneven and inconsistent exposure to European gender constructs had contradictory implications: alternative European models of marriage and womanhood were simultaneously resisted and absorbed by local populations situating them in the context of richly textured discourses of Islamic, Katsinawa, and Arna "tradition."

The difficulty and ambivalence the colonial state encountered in envisioning any serious legislative assault on local marriage practices (including bridewealth, early marriage for women, non-consensual unions, and polygyny) were heightened by the transfer of slave/free hierarchies onto hierarchies of wives as slavery declined. Particularly in aristocratic and merchant urban marriages, the domestic tasks performed largely by female slaves at the close of the nineteenth century fell increasingly to junior wives and concubines. Such women were brought into households through the idiom of marriage, but their social ties were weak enough that they could be treated as "captives" and implicitly recognized as such by the French administration well into the 1930s. Once the slave/free hierarchy had been recast as an intrahousehold matter of the ranking of wives, any meddling with marriage would have been profoundly disruptive in economic and political terms, and would be seen both by the colonial administration and by local populations as unduly intrusive. In general, then, matters to do with women were treated by the French colonial administration as domestic concerns to be governed by local habits and customs, *moeurs et coutumes*. "Tradition" served to mask a radical transformation of social and gender relations.

Vulnerable women were not passive in the face of such changes. The late nineteenth century and early twentieth century saw tremendous elaboration in the ritual gift exchanges traditionally associated with weddings, as women used this performative arena to stage publicly their own free status, to illustrate the strength of their social ties, and to imply that the *sadaki* bridewealth payment distinguishing a legitimate wife from a concubine had been transferred. As the economy was gradually transformed with the rise of taxation, cash cropping, and regional trade, these material exchanges made visible not only the character and status of the bride and her marriage, but also the skills of the bride and her mother in trade. Urban women in particular turned from the production and sale of local cotton thread and cloth to peddling imported cloth, metal and plastic goods, and processed foods. Thus the goods exchanged at marriage shifted over time, marking women's dependence upon a commodified economy in which they were increasingly marginalized.

With the growth of a military and bureaucratic apparatus under colonial and postcolonial rule, women in the region began to experience marriages of a new kind. Together with women of other regions they forged a new culture: that of *armen soji* or soldier marriage. Women in such marriages were exposed to other languages, cultures, and living arrangements. Their familiarity with the workings of the state and the benefits of owning urban property made them ground-breakers in the city of Maradi. Such women often invested in urban real estate and built rental housing suitable for single women and men, transforming the urban landscape by supporting the possibility of female-headed households and of single women managing outside of the "houses of women" occupied by "courtesans."

The growth of women's access to real property was also facilitated by the contradictions of the colonial state's interventions in the judicial realm. By privileging Maliki Islamic law over Katsinawa or Arna practices because it was codified and because it embodied an understanding of property familiar to Europeans, colonial officers inadvertently paved the way for women's access to landed property and for the expansion of Islamic practices in the region. Contrary to the assumptions in much of the literature on women and property in former French colonies, it does not appear to be the case in Maradi that the Napoleonic Code has come to dictate how property is actually transferred. Indeed, much of local judicial practice was never fully captured by the colonial or postcolonial state or the formal court system at all. Rather, such matters continue to be handled in a variety of dispute-mediation arenas well beyond the control of the state. While the discourses favored by the formal courts created under colonial rule have influenced the judicial field, shifting it towards Maliki law, they have not succeeded in dominating it.

If the state's intrusions in the realm of law have been partial and contradictory, so also have been its interventions in the realm of education. Education in Maradi has long focused on preparing aristocratic boys for their roles in the administration of the state, neglecting female education almost entirely. Two efforts at female education that have briefly affected Maradi's girls serve to illustrate the contradictions of colonial mission training for women. Both the *Foyer des métisses* staffed by Catholic sisters and the Sudan Interior Mission girls' school at Soura aimed at educating young women in domesticity to shape them to become exemplars of "civilized" behavior and suitable housewives for educated men. However the scarcity of trained female labor in the colony provided educated women with the possibility of entering into wage labor as teachers, nurses, and clerical personnel, an option that flew in the face of the domestic model. Debates within the colonial administration about the suitability of this domestic model for Niger's schoolgirls persisted throughout the colonial period because French medical officers recognized their own urgent need for female medical personnel familiar with local languages and cultures.

Maradi's families countered the growth of Western education by instilling in their children a proper understanding of Islam, and consequently Koranic schools proliferated under colonial rule. Such schooling interfered with young girls' increasingly urgent hawking activities, so that until recently few Muslim women in Maradi had prolonged exposure to Islamic education. However with the rise of the *'yan Izala* movement Islamic schooling after the Nigerian Islamiyya school model is gaining currency, and young girls today have the possibility of achieving a level of scholarship far higher than their mothers (and quite possibly their fathers as well) could attain. Thus the growth of education in the region has promoted not only the competing discourses of Western bourgeois domesticity and of female independence through salaried labor, it has also encouraged an intensification of Islamic learning and a counter-discourse of femininity emphasizing secluded domesticity. The colonial period, then, in many ways prompted the expansion of Islamic discourses, and gave rise to increasing economic, cultural, and religious linkages between the former belligerents of the Sokoto Caliphate and the kingdoms of Maradi and Tibiri.

Women in the region have drawn upon the rich array of discourses and cultural forms emerging from this complex historical overlay: pre-jihad Katsinawa traditions offer the possibility of laying claim to religious and judicial authority in the person of the iya, Islamist rhetoric can be deployed by wives to claim access to male income as dependents in marriage, bourgeois ideology can underwrite demands for luxury imported goods as wedding gifts, and the discourse of "modernization" promoted by the state can serve to protect women as they move into external public spaces. Women have made use of all of these discourses, and in their efforts to protect themselves from household arrangements detrimental to their well-being have sometimes employed inconsistent and contradictory strategies. These contradictions have contributed to the fragmentation of the female populace in Maradi, for women find themselves pitted more often against other women (co-wives, in-laws, mistresses, rural women versus urban, juniors against seniors) than against men. My purpose here has been neither to celebrate women's agency as innately praiseworthy nor to denigrate women's lack of solidarity as evidence of false consciousness. Rather it has been to show that major processes in the region cannot be understood without taking into account how women's micro-level maneuvers to channel and mediate change have fed back into broader processes to transform them.

Thus shifting patterns in the rural economy with the rise of cash cropping only make sense if one notes how both women and men have used the rhetoric of female dependency in marriage (a notion alien to local Arna understandings of marriage) to recalibrate both access to labor and the uses of the *gamana* and *gandu* product. Changes in the urban landscape enabling young men and women to live independently must be understood to have grown out of women's investment strategies. The conspicuous and otherwise mysterious emphasis in the local economy upon gift exchange becomes more transparent when seen as emerging at least in part out of women's increasingly desperate efforts to make visible their social status and to secure invaluable social capital. In other words major economic and social processes in the region are bound up in local contests over institutions and practices fundamental to defining gender relations. The history of the region is, in a sense, a history of struggles to define culture and gender.

These contests, I have argued in my final chapter, are not solely "about" the micro-politics and the micro-economics of gender in one region of Niger. They have important implications for Niger as a whole. Because of the early neglect of Western education in the Maradi region, Hausa speakers have been relatively marginalized in national political processes. The recent shift to multiparty politics seemed, briefly, to have altered the terms of power. However even as educated Hausa bureaucrats, traders, and white-collar workers have gained gradual recognition in politics in the capital, the important question has remained as to whether the largely illiterate rural Hausa population will begin to have a significant voice. One avenue Hausa-speaking regions may pursue to gain stature nationally is to ride on the coat-tails of politically prominent northern Nigeria. Such a strategy, which would be likely to enhance the appeal of Islamist ideologies current in Nigeria, would not, I think, be favorable for rural Hausa women in Niger, whose access to farmland, mobility, and independent income would almost certainly suffer. Neither would the rise of Islamic fundamentalism in Niger be welcomed by most women in Niamey, who had, until recently, taken their relative mobility and visibility somewhat for granted. In this context the struggles of Maradi's largely illiterate AFN women to stage publicly their right to access to external public spaces without censure have been, however contradictory, extremely important. Thus although the politics of difference AFN women pursued in the late 1980s set "married" respectable women apart from the "courtesans" of the Samariya, it contributed to providing women in general with a sanctioned claim to political participation at a time when other processes favored the expansion of seclusion.

My attention to the reformulation of tradition and the deployment of competing discourses resonates with Ayesha Imam's caution that real democracy would require autonomy for individual actors, not just the proliferation of parties. She observes that individual autonomy is often shaped by debates about "tradition" and "authenticity" in which women's rights, in particular, are seen as "foreign." The state's reluctance to act to protect women's rights is then "predicated on its estimation of the response its actions would provoke." She urges, therefore, "a focus on how to strengthen democratic processes at the level of daily life" (1992:105). The perplexing and contradictory struggles of AFN women in Maradi were, in a sense, struggles for autonomy at the level of daily life which ultimately contributed to shaping the national conference process in Niger. By 1990 Nigérien women's visible participation in events marking national political life had become a cultural commonplace–it had become a tradition, as it were. Thus when women protested their exclusion from the national conference, the transitional government was compelled to intervene to protect the now "traditional" representation of women in public affairs.

I insist upon the importance of women's admittedly contradictory uses of the AFN in part to counterbalance the received image of Africa's rural and provincial women as ignorant, passive, and conservative. Such imagery mars Anne-Laure Folly's otherwise useful film "Femmes du Niger: Entre intégrism et démocratie" ("Women of Niger: Between Fundamentalism and Democracy," 1993), in which the historic women's marches of 1991 and 1992 are depicted as having emerged *ex nihilo* in the capital out of the crucible of economic crisis. In reality the mobilization of women for those protests was made possible, at least in part, by years of unglamorous and unrecognized performative labor on the part of AFN and Samariya women throughout the country. Their sustained and carefully staged engagement bespeaks a political acumen out of keeping with the film's predictable portrayal of mute and uncomprehending rural women in need of consciousness raising by their educated urban sisters.

While it has been urban women, by and large, who have been the beneficiaries of what I see as a kind of popular female co-optation of the state's women's association, the possibility exists for rural Hausa women to carry through on what they helped to begin by supporting women's groups that protect the interests of women farmers. An attention to the concerns of such groups would have policy implications strikingly different from those emerging from the recognition of the needs of, for example, female bureaucrats. The focus upon women's interests in debates surrounding the Code Rurale (Rural Code) during the National Conference is perhaps a sign of a new and interesting elaboration in Nigérien women's activism in the capital (Dunbar and Djibo 1992:27–30). For this reason I see some positive elements in the recent fragmentation and proliferation of women's groups in Niger. However divided along party and other lines these groups may be, they have thus far been united in their efforts to retain for women as a whole the right to public protest, representation, and visibility. Where the assertion of the right to public visibility is also, more concretely, a claim to women's moral right to go to the polling stations themselves to vote, democracy itself is in the balance. On this score Folly's film (1993), showing footage of male voters at the polls and debates about whether Islam prohibits women's access to such spaces, is quite compelling. It remains to be seen how these ongoing struggles will play themselves out. To my Nigérien friends embarked upon this journey: "Allah ya kiyaye ku."

BIBLIOGRAPHY

Note: Authors are either listed alphabetically by "last" name or by the name they themselves use in citing their own works.

Abba, Souleymane. 1990. "La chefferie traditionelle en question." *Politique Africaine*, 38:51–60.

Abraham, R.C. 1962. *Dictionary of the Hausa Language.* London: University of London Press.

Abu-Lughod, Lila. 1986. *Veiled Sentiments: Honor and Poetry in a Bedouin Society.* Berkeley: University of California Press.

———. 1990."The Romance of Resistance: Tracing Transformations of Power Through Bedouin Women." In *Beyond the Second Sex: New Directions in the Anthropology of Gender*, ed P. Sanday and R. Goodenough, 311–37. Philadelphia: University of Pennsylvania.

———. 1993. *Writing Women's Worlds: Bedouin Stories.* Berkeley: University of California Press.

Adams, Milton N. and Susan E. Kruppenbach. 1987. "Gender and Access in the African School." *International Review of Education*, XXXIII: 437–53.

Adamu, Mahdi. 1978. *The Hausa Factor in West African History.* London: Oxford University Press.

Afonja, Simi. 1981. "Changing Modes of Production and the Sexual Division of Labor among the Yoruba." *Signs*, 7, 2:299–313.

Ahmed, Leila. 1992. *Women and Gender in Islam: Historical Roots of a Modern Debate.* New Haven: Yale University Press.

Amadiume, Ifi. 1987. *Male Daughters, Female Husbands.* London: Zed Books.

Ardener, Shirley. 1981. *Women and Space: Ground Rules and Social Maps.* New York: St. Martin's Press.

Baier, Stephen. 1981. *An Economic History of Central Niger.* London: Oxford University Press.

Barnes, Sandra. 1990. "Women, Property, and Power." In *Beyond the Second Sex: New Directions in the Anthropology of Gender*, ed. Peggy Sanday and Ruth Goodenough, 255–80. Philadelphia: University of Pennsylvania.

Barth, Henry. 1857. *Travels and Discoveries in North and Central Africa.* 3 vols. New York: Harper & Brothers.

Bay, Edna. 1995. "Belief, Legitimacy and the *Kpojito*: An Institutional History of the 'Queen Mother' in Precolonial Dahomey." *Journal of African History*, 36, 1:1–27.

Beik, Janet. 1987. *Hausa Theatre in Niger: A Contemporary Oral Art.* New York: Garland.

———. 1991. "Women's Roles in the Contemporary Hausa Theater of Niger." In *Hausa Women in the Twentieth Century*, ed. Catherine Coles and Beverly Mack, 232–44. Madison: University of Wisconsin Press.

201

Belloncle, G. 1980. *Femmes et développement en Afrique Sahelienne, l'expérience Nigérienne d'animation féminine 1966–76*. Paris: Éditions Ouvrières.

———. 1984. *La Question éducative en Afrique Noire*. Paris: Karthala.

Bernus, Edmond. 1973. "Drought in Niger Republic." *Savanna*, 2, 2: 129–32.

Bernus, Suzanne. 1969. *Particularismes ethniques en milieu urbaine: l'example de Niamey*. Paris: Institut d'ethnologie, Musée de l'homme.

Berry, Sara. 1987. *Fathers Work For Their Sons*. Berkeley: University of California Press.

———. 1993. *No Condition is Permanent: The Social Dynamics of Agrarian Change in Sub-Saharan Africa*. Madison: University of Wisconsin Press.

Blackwood, Evelyn. 1995. "Senior Women, Model Mothers, and Dutiful Wives: Managing Gender Contradictions in a Minangkabau Village." In *Bewitching Women, Pious Men: Gender and Body Politics in Southeast Asia*, ed. Aihwa Ong and Michael Peletz, 124–58. Berkeley: University of California Press.

Bledsoe, Caroline. 1980. *Women and Marriage in Kpelle Society*. Stanford: Stanford University Press.

Bledsoe, Caroline and Gilles Pison. 1994. *Nuptiality in Sub-Saharan Africa: Contemporary Anthropological and Demographic Perspectives*. Oxford: Oxford University Press.

Bourdieu, Pierre. 1977. *Outline of a Theory of Practice*, trans. Richard Nice. Cambridge: Cambridge University Press.

Bourgeot, André. 1990. "Le désert quadrillé: des Touaregs au Niger." *Politique Africaine*, 38:68–75.

Boyd, Jean. 1989. *The Caliph's Sister: Nana Asma'u, 1793–1865*. London: Frank Cass.

Bozzoli, Belinda with Mmantho Nkotsoe. 1991. *Women of Phokeng: Consciousness, Life Strategy, and Migrancy in South Africa, 1900–1983*. Portsmouth: Heinemann.

Butler, Judith. 1990. *Gender Trouble: Feminism and the Subversion of Identity*. New York: Routledge.

Callaway, Barbara J. 1984. "Ambiguous Consequences of the Socialisation and Seclusion of Hausa Women." *Journal of Modern African Studies*, 22, 3: 429–50.

———. 1987. *Muslim Hausa Women in Nigeria: Tradition and Change*. Syracuse: Syracuse University Press.

Callaway, Barbara J. and Lucy Creevey. 1994. *The Heritage of Islam: Women, Religion, and Politics in West Africa*. Boulder: Lynne Rienner Publishers.

Campbell, David John. 1975. "Strategies for Coping with Drought in the Sahel: A Study of Recent Population Movements in the Department of Maradi, Niger." Ph.D. dissertation, Clark University.

Caraël, Michel. 1994. "The Impact of Marriage Change on the Risks of Exposure to Sexually Transmitted Diseases in Africa." In *Nuptiality in Sub-Saharan Africa: Contemporary Anthropological and Demographic Perspectives*, ed. Caroline Bledsoe and Gilles Pison, 255–72. Oxford: Oxford University Press.

Carney, Judith and Michael Watts. 1990. "Manufacturing Dissent: Work, Gender, and the Politics of Meaning in a Peasant Society." *Africa*, 60, 2: 207–41.

Cassanelli, Lee. 1982. *The Shaping of Somali Society: Reconstructing the History of a Pastoral People, 1600–1900*. Philadelphia: University of Pennsylvania Press.

Chanock, Martin. 1985. *Law, Custom, and Social Order: The Colonial Experience in Malawi and Zambia*. Cambridge: Cambridge University Press.

Charlick, Robert. B. 1991. *Niger: Personal Rule and Survival in the Sahel*. Boulder: Westview Press.

Christelow, Alan. 1991. "Women and the Law in Early Twentieth Century Kano." In *Hausa Women in the Twentieth Century*, ed. Catherine Coles and Beverly Mack, 130–44. Madison: University of Wisconsin Press.

Clair, Andrée. 1965. *Le Niger, pays à découvrir*. Paris: Hachette.

Clapperton, Hugh. 1966. *Mission to the Niger*. Edited by E.W. Bovill. Cambridge: Cambridge University Press.

Cloud, Kathleen. 1986. "Sex Roles in Food Production Systems in the Sahel." In *Women Farmers in Africa*, ed. Lucy Creevey, 19–50. Syracuse: Syracuse University Press.

Coles, Catherine. 1990. "The Older Woman in Hausa Society: Power and Authority in Urban Nigeria." In *The Cultural Context of Aging: World-Wide Perspectives*, ed. Jay Sokolovsky, 57–81. New York: Bergin and Garvey.

———. 1991. "Hausa Women's Work in a Declining Urban Economy: Kaduna, Nigeria, 1980–1985." In *Hausa Women in the Twentieth Century*, ed. Catherine Coles and Beverly Mack, 163–91. Madison: University of Wisconsin Press.

Collion, Marie-Hélène J. 1982. "Colonial Rule and Changing Peasant Economy in Damagherim, Niger Republic." Ph. D. dissertation, Cornell University.

Comaroff, Jean. 1985. *Body of Power, Spirit of Resistance: The Culture and history of a South African People*. Chicago: University of Chicago Press.

Comaroff, John. 1980. "Introduction." In *The Meaning of Marriage Payments*, ed. J.L. Comaroff, 1–47. New York: Academic Press.

———. 1987. "*Sui generis*: Feminism, Kinship Theory, and Structural Domains." In *Gender and Kinship: Essays Toward a Unified Analysis*, ed. Jane Collier and Sylvia J. Yanagisako, 53–85. Stanford: Stanford University Press.

Cooper, Barbara M. 1992. "From the `Time of Cowries' to the `Time of Searching for Money': A History of Women in the Maradi Region of Niger, 1900–1989." Ph.D. Dissertation, Boston University.

———. 1993. "Cloth, Commodity Production, and Social Capital." *African Economic History*, 21:51–71.

———. 1994. "Reflections on Slavery, Seclusion, and Female Labor in the Maradi Region of Niger in the 19th and 20th Centuries." *Journal of African History* 35, 1:61–78.

———. 1995a. "The Politics of Difference and Women's Associations in Niger: Of 'Prostitutes,' the Public, and Policies." *Signs* 20, 4:851–82.

———. 1995b. "Women's Worth and Wedding Gift Exchange in 19th and 20th Century Maradi, Niger." *Journal of African History* 36, 1:121–40.

Coquery-Vidrovitch, Catherine. 1994. *Les Africaines: Histoire des femmes d'Afrique Noire du XIXe au XXe siècle*. Paris: Éditions Desjonquères.

"Coutumes Haoussa et Peul (Cercle de Maradi) 1933." 1939. *Coutumiers juridiques de l'Afrique Occidentale Française*. III, 265–301. Paris: Larose.

Creevey, Lucy. 1986. *Women Farmers in Africa, Rural Development in Mali and the Sahel*. Syracuse: Syracuse University Press.

David, Philippe. 1964. *Maradi: l'Ancien état et l'ancienne ville*. Niamey: République du Niger, Études Nigériennes no. 18.

Davison, Jean, with the women of Mutira. 1989. *Voices from Mutira: Lives of Rural Gikuyu Women*. Boulder: Lynne Rienner Publishers.

Decalo, Samuel. 1989. *Historical Dictionary of Niger*. Metuchen: Scarecrow Press.

———. 1990. *Coups and Army Rule in Africa*. New Haven: Yale University Press.

Denzer, LaRay. 1992. "Domestic Science Training in Colonial Yorubaland, Nigeria." In *African Encounters with Domesticity*, ed. Karen Tranberg Hansen, 116–42. New

Brunswick: Rutgers University Press.
Diarra, Fatoumata-Agnes. 1971. *Femmes Africaines en devenir: Les femmes zarma du Niger.* Paris: Anthropos.
Djermakoye, Djibo Moumouni. 1975. "La femme, la fonction et le foyer." *Sahel Hebdo,* February 17:9.
———. 1975. "Lettre." *Sahel Hebdo,* July 14:10.
———. 1975. "L'action libératrice des femmes doit toucher les femmes rurales." *Sahel Hebdo,* July 21:10.
Dunbar, Roberta. 1977. "Slavery and the Evolution of Nineteenth-Century Damagaram (Zinder, Niger)." In *Slavery in Africa, Historical and Anthropological Perspectives,* ed. S. Miers and I. Kopytoff, 155–77. Madison: University of Wisconsin Press.
———. 1991. "Islamic Values, the State, and 'the Development of Women': The Case of Niger." In *Hausa Women in the Twentieth Century,* ed. Catherine Coles and Beverly Mack, 69–89. Madison: University of Wisconsin Press.
Dunbar, Roberta and Hadiza Djibo. 1992. "Islam, Public Policy and the Legal Status of Women in Niger." Prepared for USAID/Niamey, Office of Women in Development.
Échard, N. 1975. *L'Experience du passé: Histoire de la société paysanne hausa de l'Ader.* Niamey: IRSH, Études Nigériennes no. 36.
———. 1991. "Gender Relationships and Religion: Women in the Hausa *Bori* of Ader, Niger." In *Hausa Women in the Twentieth Century,* ed. Catherine Coles and Beverly Mack, 207–20. Madison: University of Wisconsin Press.
Echenberg, Myron. 1991. *Colonial Conscripts: The* Tirailleurs Sénégalais *in French West Africa, 1857–1960.* Portsmouth, NH: Heinemann.
Edgar, B.L. 1924. *Litafi na Tatsuniyoyi na Hausa.* Edinburgh: T. and A. Constable, Ltd.
Egg, J., F. Lerin, M. Venin. 1975. "Analyse descriptive de la famine des années 1931 au Niger et implications méthodologiques." Paris: INRA.
Eliou, Marie. 1970. "Scolarité primaire et accès au second degré au Niger et au Sénégal, 1967." *Tiers Monde,* 11, 44:733–58.
Esposito, John. 1982. *Women in Muslim Family Law.* New York: Syracuse University Press.
Fala Habi Aboubacar, Gisèle. 1988. "L'art traditionnel de décorer l'habitat chez la femme haoussa dans l'Ader à Tahoua au Niger." Memoire de fin d'etudes (C.A.E.M.T.P.), École Normale Superieure d'Enseignement Technique et Professionnel, Université Cheikh Anta Diop, Dakar, Sénégal.
Feierman, Steven. 1990. *Peasant Intellectuals: Anthropology and History in Tanzania.* Madison: University of Wisconsin Press.
Folly, Anne-Laure. 1993. *Femmes du Niger: entre intégrisme et démocratie.* [Video.] New York: Women Make Movies.
Fisher, Humphrey J. 1991. "Slavery and Seclusion in Northern Nigeria: A Further Note." *Journal of African History* XXXII, 1:123–35.
Frishman, Alan. 1991. "Hausa Women in the Urban Economy of Kano." In *Hausa Women in the Twentieth Century,* ed. Catherine Coles and Beverly Mack, 192–206. Madison: University of Wisconsin Press.
Fuglestad, Finn. 1983. *A History of Niger 1850–1960.* Cambridge: Cambridge University Press.
Fuglestad, Finn and R. Higgott. 1975. "The 1974 Coup d'État in Niger: Towards an Explanation." *Journal of Modern African Studies* XIII, 3:383–98.
Gage, Anastasia and Caroline Bledsoe. 1994. "The Effects of Education and Social Stratification on Marriage and the Transition to Parenthood in Freetown, Si-

erra Leone." In *Nuptiality in Sub-Saharan Africa*, ed. Caroline Bledsoe and Gilles Pison, 148–66. Oxford: Clarendon Press.

Gervais, Myriam. 1995. "Structural Adjustment in Niger: Implementations, Effects & Determining Political Factors." *Review of African Political Economy* 63:27–42.

Greenberg, J. 1966. *The Influence of Islam on a Sudanese Religion*. Seattle and London: University of Washington Press, Monographs of the American Ethnological Society, #10.

Grégoire, E. 1986. *Les Alhazai de Maradi (Niger), Histoire d'un groupe de riches marchands sahéliens*. Paris: ORSTOM. Available in an English translation: 1992. *The Alhazai of Maradi: Traditional Hausa Merchants in a Changing Sahelian City*, trans. Benjamin Hardy. Boulder: Lynne Rienner Publishers.

———. 1990. "Le fait économique haoussa." *Politique Africaine* 38:61–7.

———. 1993. "Islam and the Identity of Merchants in Maradi (Niger)." In *Muslim Identity and Social Change in Sub-Saharan Africa*, ed. Louis Brenner, 106–15. Bloomington: Indiana University Press.

Guyer, Jane. 1984. *Family and Farm in Southern Cameroon*. Boston: Boston University Press.

———. 1994. "Lineal Identities and Lateral Networks: The Logic of Polyandrous Motherhood." In *Nuptiality in Sub-Saharan Africa: Contemporary Anthropological and Demographic Perspectives*, ed. Caroline Bledsoe and Gilles Pison, 231–54. Oxford: Oxford University Press.

Hama, Boubou. 1967. *Histoire du Gobir et de Sokoto*. Niger: Présence Africaine.

Hamani, Djibo. 1975. *Contribution à l'Étude de l'Histoire des États Hausa, l'Adar Précolonial (République du Niger)*. Niamey: IRSH, Études Nigériennes no. 38.

Hansen, Karen Tranberg. 1992. *African Encounters With Domesticity*. New Brunswick: Rutgers University Press.

Harrison, Christopher. 1988. *France and Islam in West Africa, 1860–1960*. Cambridge: Cambridge University Press.

Hatem, Mervat. 1993. "Toward the Development of Post-Islamist and Post-Nationalist Feminist Discourses in the Middle East." In *Arab Women: Old Boundaries, New Frontiers*, ed. Judith Tucker, 29–48. Bloomington: Indiana University Press.

Hay, Margaret Jean and Marcia Wright. 1982. *African Women and the Law*. Boston: Boston University African Studies Center.

Hill, Polly. 1969. "Hidden Trade in Hausaland." *Man*, 4, 3:392–409.

———. 1972. *Rural Hausa: A Village and a Setting*. Cambridge: Cambridge University Press.

———. 1977. *Population, Prosperity and Poverty: Rural Kano, 1900 and 1970*. Cambridge: Cambridge University Press.

———. 1985. "Comparative West African Farm Slavery Systems." In *Slaves and Slavery in Muslim Africa*. Vol II: *The Servile Estate*, ed. J.R. Willis, 33–50. London: Frank Cass.

Hiskett, Mervyn. 1960. "Kitab al Farq." *Bulletin of the School of Oriental and African Studies*, 23, 3:553–79.

———. 1973. *The Sword of Truth: The Life and Times of Shehu Usman Dan Fodio*. New York: Oxford University Press.

———. 1984. *The Development of Islam in West Africa*. London: Longman.

———. 1985. "Enslavement, Slavery and Attitudes towards the Legally Enslaveable in Hausa Islamic Literature." In *Slaves and Slavery in Muslim Africa*. Vol I: *Islam and the Ideology of Slavery*, ed. J.R. Willis, 106–24. London: Frank Cass.

Hogendorn, Jan. 1977. "The Economics of Slave Use on Two Plantations in the Zaria Emirate of the Sokoto Caliphate." *The International Journal of African Historical Studies* X, 3:369–83.

Hogendorn, Jan, and Paul Lovejoy. 1988. "The Reform of Slavery in Early Colonial Northern Nigeria." In *The End of Slavery in Africa*, ed. S. Miers and R. Roberts, 391–414. Madison: University of Wisconsin Press.

Imam, Ayesha. 1992. "Democratization Processes in Africa: Problems and Prospects." *Review of African Political Economy*, 54:102–105.

Isiugo-Abanihe, Uche C. 1994. "Consequences of Bridewealth Changes on Nuptiality Patterns Among the Ibo of Nigeria." In *Nuptiality in Sub-Saharan Africa*, ed. Caroline Bledsoe and Gilles Pison, 74–91. Oxford: Oxford University Press.

Jumare, Ibrahim M. 1994. "The Late Treatment of Slavery in Sokoto: Background and Consequences of the 1936 Proclamation." *International Journal of African Historical Studies*, 27 2:303–23.

Karanja, Wambui Wa. 1987. "Outside Wives and Inside Wives in Nigeria." In *Transformations of African Marriage*, ed. D. Parkin and D. Nyamwaya, 247–362. Manchester: Manchester University Press.

Klute, Georg. 1995. "Hostilités et alliances. Archéologie de la dissidence des Touaregs au Mali." *Cahiers d'Études africaines* 137, XXXV–1:55–71.

Kopytoff, Igor. 1990. "Women's Roles and Existential Identities." In *Beyond the Second Sex: New Directions in the Anthropology of Gender*, ed. Peggy Sanday and Ruth Goodenough, 75–98. Philadelphia: University of Pennsylvania.

Kopytoff, Igor and Suzanne Miers. 1977. "African 'Slavery' as an Institution of Marginality." In *Slavery in Africa: Historical and Anthropological Perspectives*, ed. Suzanne Miers and Igor Kopytoff, 3–81. Madison: University of Wisconsin Press.

Kotoudi, Idimama. 1988. "Les Alhazai de Maradi: leurs dieux sont à Kano." *Nigerama*, 2: 30.

Kotoudi, Idimama et al. 1988. "Débat sur les commerçants." *Nigerama*, 2: 26–29.

Landeroin, Captain. 1911. "Du Tchad au Niger. Notice historique." *Documents scientifiques de la mission Tilho, 1906–1909.* Vol. I:309–552. Paris: Ministère des Colonies.

Last, Murray. 1967. *The Sokoto Caliphate.* London: Longman.

Last, Murray and M. A. Al Hajj. 1965. "Attempts at Defining a Muslim in 19th c. Hausaland and Borno." *Journal of the Historical Society of Nigeria* III:231–40.

Latour, Éliane de. 1982. "La Paix Destructrice." In *Guerres de Lignages et Guerres d'États en Afrique*, ed. Jean Bazin and Emmanuel Terray. Paris: Éditions des Archives Contemporaines.

———. 1992. *Les temps du pouvoir.* Paris: Éditions de l'École des Hautes Études en Sciences Sociales.

Launay, Robert. 1992. *Beyond the Stream: Islam and Society in a West African Town.* Berkeley: University of California Press.

LeRoy Ladurie, Emmanuel. 1979. *Montaillou: the Promised Land of Error*, trans. Barbara Bray. New York: Random House.

Leroux, Henri. 1948. "Animisme et Islam dans la subdivision de Maradi (Niger)." *Bulletin d'IFAN*, 10:595–697.

Lévy-Luxereau, Anne. 1983. "Les femmes Hausa du Sahel Nigérien n'accèdent pas aux nouvelles techniques agricoles." *Penelope* 9:39–42.

Locoh, Thérèse. 1994. "Social Change and Marriage Arrangements: New Types of Union in Lomé, Togo." In *Nuptiality in Sub-Saharan Africa: Contemporary An-

thropological and Demographic Perspectives, ed. Caroline Bledsoe and Gilles Pison, 215–30. Oxford: Oxford University Press.

Lovejoy, Paul. 1978. "Plantations in the Economy of the Sokoto Caliphate." *Journal of African History*, XIX 3:341–68.

———. 1980. *Caravans of Cola: The Hausa Kola Trade 1700–1900*. Zaria: Amadu Bello University Press.

———. 1986. "Problems of Slave Control in the Sokoto Caliphate." In *Africans in Bondage*, ed. P. Lovejoy, 235–72. Madison: University of Wisconsin Press.

———. 1988. "Concubinage and the Status of Women Slaves in Early Colonial Northern Nigeria." *Journal of African History* 29, 2:245–66.

Lovejoy, Paul and Jan Hogendorn. 1993. *Slow Death for Slavery: The Course of Abolition in Northern Nigeria, 1897–1936*. Cambridge: Cambridge University Press.

MacGaffey, Janet. 1988. "Evading Male Control: Women in the Second Economy in Zaire." *Patriarchy and Class: African Women in the Home and the Workforce*. Boulder: Westview Press.

Mack, Beverly. 1990. "Service and Status: Slaves and Concubines in Kano, Nigeria." In *At Work in Homes: Household Workers in World Perspective*, ed. Roger Sanjek and Shellee Colen, 14–34. Washington, D.C.: American Anthropological Association.

Maher, Vanessa. 1974. *Women and Property in Morocco: Their changing relation to the process of social stratification in the Middle Atlas*. Cambridge: Cambridge University Press.

Maigari, Mahamane Chamsou. 1989. "Le médecin Lt.-Col. Ousmane Gazere déplore le faible taux de jeunes filles scolarisées." *Le Sahel*, 13 mars:2.

Mann, Kristin. 1982. "Women's Rights in Law and Practice: Marriage and Dispute Settlement in Colonial Lagos." In *African Women and the Law: Historical Perspectives*, ed. Margaret Jean Hay and Marcia Wright, 151–71. Boston: Boston University.

———. 1991. "Women, Landed Property and the Accumulation of Wealth in Early Colonial Lagos." *Signs* 16, 4:682–706.

———. 1994. "The Historical Roots and Cultural Logic of Outside Marriage in Colonial Lagos." In *Nuptiality in Sub-Saharan Africa: Contemporary Anthropological and Demographic Perspectives*, ed. Caroline Bledsoe and Gilles Pison, 167–93. Oxford: Oxford University Press.

Manning, Patrick. 1988. *Francophone Sub-Saharan Africa 1880–1985*. New York: Cambridge University Press.

Marks, Shula and Richard Rathbone. 1983. "The History of the Family in Africa: Introduction." *Journal of African History* 24: 145–61.

Marty, Paul. 1930. *L'Islam et let tribus dans la Colonie du Niger*. Paris: Librairie Orientaliste Paul Gauthier.

Masquelier, Adeline. 1993. "Narratives of Power, Images of Wealth: The Ritual Economy of Bori in the Market." In *Modernity and its Malcontents: Ritual and Power in Postcolonial Africa*, ed. Jean Comaroff and John Comaroff, 3–33. Chicago: University of Chicago Press.

Mauss, Marcel. 1967. *The Gift: Forms and Functions of Exchange in Archaic Societies*, trans. Ian Cunnison. New York: Norton.

Mba, Nina. 1982. *Nigerian Women Mobilized: Women's Political Activity in Southern Nigeria, 1900–1965*. Berkeley: Institute of International Studies, University of California.

Mbilinyi, Marjorie. 1989. "'I'd Have Been a Man': Politics and the Labor Process in Producing Personal Narratives." In *Interpreting Women's Lives: Feminist Theory and Personal Narratives*, ed. the Personal Narratives Group, 204–27. Bloomington: Indiana University Press.

McCarus, Chris. 1993a. "Election Showdown." *West Africa*, Feb. 22–28:289–91.

———. 1993b. "Ousmane romps home." *West Africa*, April 12–18:594.

Meekers, Dominique. 1994. "The Implications of Premarital Childbearing for Infant Mortality: The Case of Côte d'Ivoire." In *Nuptiality in Sub-Saharan Africa: Contemporary Anthropological and Demographic Perspectives*, ed. Caroline Bledsoe and Gilles Pison, 296–312. Oxford: Oxford University Press.

Miers, Suzanne and Richard Roberts. 1988. *The End of Slavery in Africa*. Madison: University of Wisconsin Press.

Mernissi, Fatima. 1987. *Beyond the Veil: Male-Female Dynamics in Modern Muslim Society*. Bloomington: Indiana University Press.

———. 1993. "The Harem Within: Fear of the Difference." Text for an exhibit with Ruth Ward and Mansoora Hassan at the Alif Gallery in Washington D.C., Nov. 20–Dec. 15.

Mignon, Jean-Marie. 1989. "Les mouvements de jeunesse dans l'Afrique de l'Ouest Francophone de 1958 aux années 1970–75." *Le Mouvement associatif des jeunes en Afrique noire francophone au XXe siècle*, ed. Hélène d'Almeida-Topor and Odile Goerg, 53–68. Paris: Harmattan.

Miles, William F. S. 1994. *Hausaland Divided: Colonialism and Independence in Nigeria and Niger*. Ithaca: Cornell University Press.

Mirza, Sarah and Margaret Strobel. 1989. *Three Swahili Women: Life Histories from Mombasa, Kenya*. Bloomington: Indiana University Press.

Moghadam, Valentine M. 1991. "Islamist Movements and Women's Responses in the Middle East." *Gender and History* 3 (3):268–84.

Monimart, Marie. 1989. *Femmes du Sahel, La désertification au quotidien*. Paris: Karthala.

Moore, Henrietta L. 1986. *Space, Text, and Gender: An Anthropological Study of the Marakwet of Kenya*. Cambridge: Cambridge University Press.

Moore, Henrietta and Megan Vaughan. 1994. *Cutting Down Trees: Gender, Nutrition, and Agricultural Change in the Northern Province of Zambia, 1890–1990*. Portsmouth: Heinemann.

Moran, Mary H. 1992. "Civilized Servants: Child Fosterage and Training for Status among the Glebo of Liberia." In *African Encounters with Domesticity*, ed. Karen Tranberg Hansen, 98–115. New Brunswick: Rutgers University Press.

Murray, Colin. 1980. "Migrant Labour and Changing Family Structure in the Rural Periphery of Southern Africa." *Journal of Southern African Studies* 6, 2:139–56.

New York Times. 1996. "Backers of Niger General Say He Won Election." Thursday, July 11:A7.

Ngondo a Pitshandenge, I. 1994. "Marriage Law in Sub-Saharan Africa." In *Nuptiality in Sub-Saharan Africa*, ed. Caroline Bledsoe and Gilles Pison, 117–29. Oxford: Oxford University Press.

Ngubane, Harriet. 1987. "The Consequences for Women of Marriage Payments in a Society with Patrilineal Descent." In *Transformations of African Marriage*, ed. David Parkin and David Nyamwaya, 173–82. Manchester: Manchester University Press.

Nicolas, Guy. 1968. "Processus oblatifs à l'occasion de la `Courtisation' des jeunes filles au sein d'une société africaine (vallée de Maradi – Niger)." Paris: CNRS.

———. 1975. *Dynamique sociale et appréhension du monde au sein d'une société hausa.* Paris: Musée National d'Histoire Naturelle.

———. 1986. *Don rituel et échange marchand dans une société sahélienne.* Paris: Institut d'Ethnologie.

Nicolas, Guy and Guy Mainet. 1964. *La Vallée du Gulbi de Maradi.* Bordeaux: IFAN, Études Nigériennes no. 16.

Nicolas, Jacqueline. 1967. *Les 'Juments des Dieux': rites de possession et condition féminine en pays hausa (vallée de Maradi, Niger).* Paris: Études Nigériennes no. 21.

Norman, David et al. 1979. "Technical Change and the Small Farmer in Hausaland, Northern Nigeria." African Rural Economy Program Paper, #21, Michigan State University, Department of Agricultural Economy.

Obbo, Christine. 1987. "The Old and the New in East African Elite Marriages." In *Transformations of African Marriage,* ed. David Parkin and David Nyamwaya. Manchester: Manchester University Press.

———. 1988. "Bitu: Facilitator of Women's Educational Opportunities." In *Life Histories of African Women,* ed. Patricia Romero, 99–112. London: Ashfield Press.

Oboler, Regina Smith. 1985. *Women, Power, and Economic Change: The Nandi of Kenya.* Stanford: Stanford University Press.

Okonjo, Kamene. 1976. "The Dual-Sex Political System in Operation: Igbo Women and Community Politics in Midwestern Nigeria." In *Women in Africa: Studies in Social and Economic Change,* ed. Nancy J. Hafkin and Edna G. Bay, 45–58. Stanford: Stanford University Press.

Ola-Davies, George. 1996. "The Coup in Niger." *West Africa,* 5–11 February:177–9.

Ong, Aihwa. 1995. "State Versus Islam: Malay Families, Women's Bodies, and the Body Politic in Malaysia." In *Bewitching Women, Pious Men: Gender and Body Politics in Southeast Asia,* ed. Aihwa Ong and Michael Peletz, 159–94. Berkeley: University of California Press.

Oppong, Christine. 1981 [1974]. *Middle Class African Marriage: A Family Study of Ghanaian Senior Civil Servants.* London: George Allen & Unwin.

Ortner, Sherry. 1974. "Is Female to Male as Nature is to Culture?" In *Women, Culture and Society,* ed. Michelle Rosaldo and Louise Lamphere, 67–88. Stanford: Stanford University Press.

———. 1984. "Theory in Anthropology since the Sixties." *Comparative Studies in Society and History* 26:126–66.

Ouane, Adama and Yvette Amou-Tanoh. 1990. "Literacy in French-Speaking Africa: A Situational Analysis." *African Studies Review* 33, 3:21–38.

Oumarou, Kané. 1984. "The Lifelong Education Center (F.E.P.) and other Learning Strategies for Post-Literacy in Niger." In *Learning Strategies for Post-Literacy and Continuing Education in Mali, Niger, Senegal and Upper Volta,* ed. by R.H. Dave, D.A. Perera, A. Ouane, 63–104. Hamburg: UNESCO.

Oyewumi, Oyeronke. 1993. "Inventing Gender: Questioning Gender in Precolonial Yorubaland." In *Problems in African History: The Precolonial Centuries,* ed. by Robert O. Collins, 244–52. New York: Markus Wiener.

Palmer, H.R. 1928. *Sudanese Memoirs, Being Mainly Translations from a Number of Arabic Manuscripts Relating to the Central and Western Sudan.* 3 vols. Lagos: Government Printer.

Parkin, David. 1978. *The Cultural Definition of Political Response.* London: Academic Press.

Parkin, David and David Nyamwaya. 1987. *Transformations of African Marriage.* Manchester: Manchester University Press.

———, eds. 1987. "Transformations of African Marriage: Change and Choice." *Transformations of African Marriage*, ed. Parkin and Nyamwaya, 1–16. Manchester: Manchester University Press.

Parpart, Jane. 1986. "Class and Gender on the Copperbelt: Women in Northern Rhodesian Copper Mining Communities, 1926–1964." In *Women and Class in Africa*, ed. Claire Robertson and Iris Berger. New York: Holmes and Meier.

Péhaut, Yves. 1970. "L'Arachide au Niger." *Études d'Économie Africaine* 1:11–103.

Peters, F.E. 1994. *The Hajj: The Muslim Pilgrimage to Mecca and the Holy Places.* Princeton: Princeton University Press.

Pellow, Deborah. 1991. "From Accra to Kano: One Woman's Experience." In *Hausa Women in the Twentieth Century*, ed. Catherine Coles and Beverly Mack, 50–68. Madison: University of Wisconsin Press.

Périé, Jean. 1939. "Notes historiques sur la région de Maradi (Niger)." *Bulletin de l'Institut Français d'Afrique Noire* I:377–401.

Phillips, Arthur and Henry F. Morris. 1971. *Marriage Laws in Africa.* London: Oxford University Press.

Piault, Colette. 1965. *Contribution à l'étude de la vie quotidienne de la femme Maouri.* Paris: Études Nigériennes no. 10.

Pittin, Renée. 1979. "Marriage and Alternative Strategies: Career Patterns of Hausa Women in Katsina City." Ph.D. University of London.

———. 1984. "Migration of Women in Nigeria: The Hausa Case." *International Migration Review*, 18, 4:1293–314.

———. 1990. "Selective Education: Issues of Gender, Class and Ideology in Northern Nigeria." *Review of African Political Economy* 48:7–25.

———. 1991. "Women, Work and Ideology in Nigeria." *Review of African Political Economy* 52:38–52.

Pool, Janet. 1971. "A Cross-Comparative Study of Aspects of Conjugal Behavior among Women of 3 West African Countries." *Canadian Journal of African Studies* VI, ii:233–59.

Raulin, H. 1964. *Techniques et bases socio-économiques de sociétés rurales du Niger occidental et central.* Niamey: IFAN, Études Nigériennes no. 13.

———. 1984. "Techniques et instruments aratoires au sud du Sahara." *Cahiers ORSTOM, série Sciences Humaines*, XX, 3–4:339–58.

Raynaut, Claude. 1971. "Organisation spatiale et organisation sociale d'un village Hausa du Niger." *Cahiers d'Outre-Mer* 94, XXIV:123–57.

———. 1972. *Structures normatives et relations électives: étude d'une communauté villageoise haoussa.* Paris: Mouton.

———. 1975. Le cas de la région de Maradi (Niger)." *Secheresses et Famines du Sahel*, ed. J. Copans, Vol II, 5–43. Paris: Maspero, 1975.

———. 1976. "Transformation du système de production et inégalié économique: le cas d'un village haoussa (Niger)," *Canadian Journal of African Studies* X, 2:279–308.

———. 1977. "Aspects socio-économiques de la préparation et de la circulation de la nourriture dans un village hausa (Niger)." *Cahiers d'Études Africaines* 68, XVII, 4:569–97.

———. 1984. "Outils agricoles de la région de Maradi (Niger)." *Cahiers ORSTOM, série Sciences Humaines*, XX, 3–4:505–36.

Raynaut, Claude and Souleymane Abba. 1990. "Trente ans d'indépendence: repères et tendances." *Politique Africaine*, 38:3–29.

République du Niger. 1979. "Le role économique des femmes dans la zone du Projet Maradi (Arrondissements de Madarounfa, Aguié, Tessaoua, Guidan-Roumdji)." Niamey: Service de Plan.

———. 1980. *Annuaire statistique, 1978–79.* Niamey: Ministère du Plan.

———. 1980. *Recensement agricole, 1980.* Tome II. Niamey: Ministère du Développement Rural.

———. 1985a. "Données Brutes, Département de Maradi." *Recensement général de la population, 1977, Résultats definitifs.* Niamey: Ministère du Plan.

———. 1985b. "Rapport d'Analyse." *Recensement général de la population, 1977, Résultats definitifs.* Niamey: Ministère du Plan.

———. 1988. *Annuaire Statistique, 1986–87.* Niamey: Ministère du Plan.

———. 1989. *2ème recensement général de la population 1988, Résultats provisoires.* Niamey: Ministère du Plan.

———. 1989. *Recensement général de la population 1977.* Niamey: Ministère du Plan.

———. 1993. *Enquête Démographique et de Santé 1992.* Niamey: Ministère des Finances et du Plan.

———. 1995. "Niger Women: Myth and Reality." Niamey: Ministry of Social Development, Population and Women [sic] Advancement.

Rescoussie, Pierre. 1973. "L'enseignement secondaire dans 18 États francophones d'Afrique et Madagascar." *Afrique Contemporaine* 67:11–26.

Richards, Audrey. 1982 [1956]. *Chisungu: A Girl's Initiation Ceremony among the Bemba of Zambia.* New York: Routledge.

Robert, André. P. 1955. *L'Évolution des coutumes de l'ouest Africain et la législation Française.* Paris: Éditions de l'Encyclopédie d'Outre-Mer.

Roberts, Pepe. 1981. "'Rural Development' and the Rural Economy in Niger, 1900–75." In *Rural Development in Tropical Africa,* ed. J. Heyers, P. Roberts, and G. Williams, 193–221. New York: St. Martin's Press.

———. 1988. "Rural Women's Access to Labor in West Africa." In *Patriarchy and Class: African Women in the Home and the Workforce,* ed. Sharon Stichter and Jane Parpart, 97–114. Boulder: Westview Press.

Roberts, Richard. 1984. "Women's Work and Women's Property: Household Social Relations in the Maraka Textile Industry of the Nineteenth Century." *Comparative Studies in Society and History* 26, 2:229–50.

———. 1988. "The End of Slavery in the French Soudan, 1905–1914." In *The End of Slavery in Africa,* ed. Suzanne Miers and Richard Roberts, 282–307. Madison: University of Wisconsin Press.

Roberts, Richard and Suzanne Miers. "The End of Slavery in Africa." In *The End of Slavery in Africa,* ed. Suzanne Miers and Richard Roberts, 3–68. Madison: University of Wisconsin Press.

Robertson, Claire. 1984. *Sharing the Same Bowl: A Socioeconomic History of Women and Class in Accra, Ghana.* Ann Arbor: University of Michigan Press.

———. 1986. "Women's Education and Class Formation in Africa, 1950–1980." *Women and Class in Africa,* ed. Claire Robertson and Iris Berger, 92–114. New York: Africana Publishing Co.

Robertson, Claire C. and Martin Klein. 1983. "Women's Importance in African Slave Systems." In *Women and Slavery in Africa,* ed. Claire Robertson and Martin Klein, 3–25. Madison: University of Wisconsin Press.

Robinson, Pearl. 1983. "Traditional Clientage and Political Change in a Hausa Community." In *Transformation and Resiliency in Africa As Seen by Afro-American*

Scholars, ed. Pearl T. Robinson and Elliott P. Skinner, 105–28. Washington D.C.: Howard University Press.

———. 1994. "The National Conference Phenomenon in Francophone Africa." *Comparative Studies in Society and History* 36:575–610.

Rosaldo, Michelle Zimbalist. 1974. "Women, Culture, and Society: A Theoretical Overview." In *Women, Culture & Society,* ed. Michelle Rosaldo and Louise Lamphere, 17–42. Stanford: Stanford University Press.

Ross, Paul J. 1987. "Land as a Right to Membership: Land Tenure Dynamics in a Peripheral area of the Kano Close-Settled Zone." In *State, Oil and Agriculture in Nigeria,* ed. M. Watts, 223–47. Berkeley: University of California, Institute of International Studies.

Rugh, Andrea. 1986. *Reveal and Conceal: Dress in Contemporary Egypt.* Syracuse: Syracuse University Press.

Salifou, André. 1971. *Le Damagaram ou le Sultanat de Zinder au XIXè siècle.* Niamey: CNRS, Études Nigériennes no. 27.

Saunders, Margaret. 1978. "Marriage and Divorce in a Muslim Hausa Town (Mirria Niger)." Ph.D. dissertation, Indiana University (Bloomington).

———. 1980. "Women's Role in a Muslim Hausa Town." *A World of Women: Anthropological Studies of Women in Societies of the World,* ed. Erika Bourguignon, 57–86. New York: Praeger.

Scheub, Harold. 1988. "And So I Grew Up: the Autobiography of Nongenile Masithathu Zenani." In *Life Histories of African Women,* ed. Patricia Romero, 7–46. London: Ashfield Press.

Schildkrout, Enid. 1982. "Dependence and Autonomy: The Economic Activities of Secluded Hausa Women in Kano, Nigeria." *Women and Work in Africa,* ed. E. Bay, 55–83. Boulder: Westview Press.

Schmidt, Elizabeth. 1992. *Peasants, Traders and Wives: Shona Women in the History of Zimbabwe, 1870–1939.* London: James Currey.

Scott, James. 1990. *Domination and the Arts of Resistance: Hidden Transcripts.* New Haven: Yale University Press.

Shennan, Andrew. 1989. *Rethinking France: Plans for Renewal 1940–1946.* Oxford: Clarendon Press.

Shettima, Kole Ahmed. 1995. "Engendering Nigeria's Third Republic." *African Studies Review* 38, 3:61–98.

Smith, M.G. 1959. "The Hausa System of Social Status." *Africa* 29:239–52.

———. 1967. "A Hausa Kingdom: Maradi Under Dan Baskore 1854–1875." In *West African Kingdoms in the Nineteenth Century,* ed. D. Forde, 93–122. London: Oxford University Press.

———. 1965. "The Sociological Framework of Law." In *African Law: Adaptation and Development,* ed. H. Kuper and L. Kuper, 24–48. Berkeley: University of California Press.

———. 1981 [1954] "Introduction." In *Baba of Karo: A Woman of the Muslim Hausa,* ed. and trans. Mary F. Smith, 11–34. New Haven: Yale University Press.

Smith, Mary F. (ed. and trans.) 1981 [1954]. *Baba of Karo: A Woman of the Muslim Hausa.* New Haven: Yale University Press.

Spittler, G. 1977. "Urban Exodus: Urban-Rural and Rural-Rural Migration in Gobir (Niger)." *Sociologia Ruralis* 17, 3:223–35.

Stephens, Connie. 1991. "Marriage in the Hausa *Tatsuniya* Tradition: A Cultural and Cosmic Balance." In *Hausa Women in the Twentieth Century,* ed. Catherine Coles and Beverly Mack, 221–31. Madison: University of Wisconsin Press.

Steverlynck, Theresa. 1984. "Les femmes rurales dans le développement." FAO, Rapport de Mission.

Stowasser, Barbara. 1993. "Women's Issues in Modern Islamic Thought." In *Arab Women: Old Boundaries, New Frontiers*, ed. Judith Tucker, 3–28. Bloomington: Indiana University Press.

Strobel, Margaret. 1979. *Muslim Women in Mombasa, 1890–1975*. New Haven: Yale University Press.

Sudarkasa, Niara. 1986. "The Status of Women in Indigenous African Societies." *Feminist Studies* 12, 1:91–103.

Sule, Balaraba and Priscilla Starratt. 1991. "Islamic Leadership Positions for Women in Contemporary Kano Society." In *Hausa Women in the Twentieth Century*, ed. Catherine Coles and Beverly Mack, 29–49. Madison: University of Wisconsin Press.

Suret-Canal, Jean. 1971. *French Colonialism in Tropical Africa, 1900–1945*, trans. Till Gottheiner. New York: Pica Press.

Tessler, Mark A. with Janet Rogers and Daniel Schneider. 1978. "Women's Emancipation in Tunisia." In *Women in the Muslim World*, ed. Lois Beck and Nikki Keddie, 141–58. Cambridge: Harvard University Press.

Thom., D.J. 1975. "The Niger-Nigeria Boundary 1890–1906." Papers in International Studies, African Series, no. 23, Ohio University.

Tinguiri, Kiavi Limam. 1990. "Crise économique et ajustement structurel (1982–1988)." *Politique Africaine*, 38:76–86.

Umar, Muhammad Sani. 1993. "Changing Islamic Identity in Nigeria from the 1960s to the 1980s: From Sufism to Anti-Sufism." In *Muslim Identity and Social Change in Sub-Saharan Africa*, ed. Louis Brenner, 154–78. Bloomington: Indiana University Press.

Urvoy, Yves. 1938. *Histoire des Populations du Sudan Central*. Paris: Larose.

Usman, Yusufu Bala. 1981. *The Transformation of Katsina, 1400–1883*. Zaria: Ahmadu Bello University Press.

Van Allen, Judith. 1976. "'Aba Riots' or Igbo 'Women's War'? Ideology, Stratification, and the Invisibility of Women." In *Women in Africa: Studies in Social and Economic Change*, ed. Nancy Hafkin and Edna Bay, 59–86. Stanford: Stanford University Press.

Vaughan, Megan. 1992. "Famine Analysis and Family Relations: Nyasaland in 1949." In *The Social Basis of Health and Healing in Africa*, ed. Steven Feierman and John M. Janzen, 71–89. Berkeley: University of California Press.

Waldeman, Marilyn R. 1965. "The Fulani Jihad: A Reassessment." *Journal of African History* 6:333–55.

Walker, Cherryl, ed. 1990. *Women and Gender in Southern Africa to 1945*. London: James Currey.

Wallace, Christine. 1978. "The Concept of Gandu: How Useful is it in Understanding Labour Relations in Rural Hausa Society?" *Savanna*, 7, 2:137–50.

West Africa. 1990. "Massacre Allegations." *West Africa*, June 25–July 1:1090.

———. 1991a. "Unions Win Key Gains." *West Africa*, 15–21 April:574.

———. 1991b. "Work Resumes." *West Africa*, 20–26 May:818.

———. 1993. "Constitution adopted." *West Africa*, 18–24 January:72–3.

———. 1996a. "Coups and Democracy." *West Africa*, 5–11 January:168.

———. 1996b. "Niger: Civilian Rule Project." *West Africa*, 19–25 February:251.

White, Elizabeth. 1978. "Legal Reform as an Indicator of Women's Status in Muslim Nations." In *Women in the Muslim World*, ed. Lois Beck and Nikki Keddie, 52–68. Cambridge: Harvard University Press.

White, Luise. 1990. *The Comforts of Home: Prostitution in Colonial Nairobi.* Chicago: University of Chicago Press.

Wright, Marcia. 1993. *Strategies of Slaves and Women: Life Stories from East/Central Africa.* New York: Lilian Barber.

Yanagisako, Sylvia and Jane Collier. 1990. "The Mode of Reproduction in Anthropology." In *Theoretical Perspectives on Sexual Difference,* ed. Deborah Rhode, 131–41. New Haven: Yale University Press.

Yusuf, Ahmed B. 1974. "A Reconsideration of Urban Conceptions: Hausa Urbanization and the Hausa Rural-Urban Continuum," *Urban Anthropology* 3:200–21.

Primary Sources

Archives Nationales du Niger (ANN)

I have referred to these in the text using only the archive catalogue designations. The full description of the document appears below.

14.1.2   M. Périé, "Carnets monographiques du cercle de Maradi, 1945."
14.1.9   "Monographie du Cercle de Maradi, 1955."
14.1.12   A. Capitaine Brantonne, "Extrait de la monographie de la Residence de Tessaoua, Moeurs et Coutumes, Cercle de Maradi, 1901."
         B. "Monographie du Lieutenant Villomé, 1913."
14.2.3   "Rapport trimestriel d'ensemble, 1935."
14.2.8   "Bulletins mensuels, 1946."
14.3.2   M. Gosselin, "Rapport de tournée, 1934."
14.3.59   Monoucut, "Rapport de Tournée, 1941."

Archives de la Préfecture de Maradi (APM)

The "Archives" is in reality a small stack of uncatalogued papers I managed to peruse. For lack of a better system I have organized them chronologically. It is unclear who authored most of these reports.

Brantonne, "Histoire, Poste El Hassan, Risedence de Tessaoua [sic], 22 oct. 1901."
"Histoire politique et administrative de la Subdivision de Maradi" [c. 1923].
"Rapport politique, Cercle de Maradi, 1933."
Périé, "Histoire Complet, 1940."
"Rapport annuel d'ensemble, Cercle de Maradi, 1944."
"Rapport semestriel, Cercle de Maradi, 1er Semestre, 1945."
"Rapport Annuel, Situation Politique, Cercle de Maradi, 1947."
"Rapport Economique, Cercle de Maradi, 1948."
"Bulletin de renseignements, Cercle de Maradi, Jan. 1951."
M. Sellier, Commandant de Cercle, "Rapport Annuel, Cercle de Maradi, 1954."
Service de l'Agriculture, "Elements de Geographie du sous secteur Agricole de Maradi, 1958."
"Rapport annuel, Cercle de Maradi, Partie sociale, 1964."
"Rapport annuel, Arrondissement de Maradi, Partie sociale, 1967."

Archives - Projet Maradi (PM)

Where the author is not indicated I have noted "PDRM" as author to show that the source in question was produced for the Projet de Développement Rural de Maradi.

P. Brasset, J. Koechlin, and Cl. Raynaut. 1984. "Rapport de mission socio-géographique: proposition pour un zonage agro-écologique du Département de Maradi."

Grégoire, Emmanuel and Cl. Raynaut. 1980. "Présentation générale du Département du Maradi." Université de Bordeaux II, Programme de Recherches sur la Région de Maradi.

Issa, M. Harouna. 1981. "Analyse de la formation des femmes dans les CPR et son impact dans le milieu rural." Rapport de Stage: Projet Developpement Rural de Maradi. 16 juillet – 16 sept.

LeGal, P.Y. 1984. "Systèmes de production agricole et systèmes de culture." Programme Recherche Developpement.

———. 1985. "La gestion de la force de travail sur 14 exploitations haoussas."

de Miranda, E. 1979. "Étude des déséquilibres écologiques et agricoles d'une région tropicale semi-aride au Niger: le problème de l'utilisation des ressources naturelles dans 3 villages haoussas." Rapport de synthèse du sous-programme de recherches agro-écologique sur la région de Maradi, Université de Bordeaux II.

PDRM. 1983. "Réévaluation du Projet Maradi." Tome 1: "Bilan."

PDRM. 1984. "L'impact des ex-stagiaires des Centres de Promotion Rurale du Département de Maradi."

PDRM. 1986. "Les exploitations agricoles au sud du Département de Maradi."

PDRM/G.R.I.D.(Groupe de Recherches Interdisciplinaires de Développement). 1988. *Le développement rural de la région au village: analyser et comprendre la diversité.* Bordeaux: Université de Bordeaux II.

PDRM/U.S.E. (Unité Suivi-Évaluation). 1986. "Les systèmes de Culture au sud de Département de Maradi: Analyse des pratiques culturales et de leur influence sur les rendements (Synthese)."

Raynaut, Claude. 1977. "Rapport sur les études socio-économiques menées dans l'un des villages témoins: Serkin Haoussa." Université de Bordeaux II, Programme de Recherches sur la région de Maradi.

Archives d'Outre Mer (AOM)

FOM refers to items in the collection of the Agence de la France d'Outre Mer (the numbers following give the carton and dossier in which the document is to be found). AP refers to items in the collection Affaires Politiques of the AOF (likewise the numbers following refer to the carton and dossier). 200Mi designates the microfilm of AOF records; the microfilm can be consulted in the Archives Nationales in Paris, or in the Archives d'Outre Mer in Aix-en-Provence (the reel number follows, and after the slash are the document designations of the original collection in Dakar).

Photographs:
Agence des Colonies: 1ère série, 11
3.280   "Niger - Fileuse"
3.184   "Niger - Jeune fille tamisant du mil pilé"

5.933   "Cercle de Dosso - Subd. de Dogondoutchi
         Dogondoutchi - le marchand de tissus et de plats émaillés. Donateur: M.
         Jacques Alluson - Admin. FOM Mars 1955."

Agence des Colonies: 1ere série, 12
6.067   "Gouchy (environs de Magaria) Femmes Haoussa. Donateur: M. Jacques
         Alluson - Admin. FOM 21 Jan. 1956."
6.551   "Ecole de Doutchi - Une classe. Donateur: RRPP Chantoux, Collerie et
         Simon, 1957."
3.269   "Niger - de gauche à droit: jeunes filles Djerma - Haoussa - Bella."

Agence des Colonies: 2eme série, Carton 60 (Niger)
no. 3 "Jeune femme Haoussa allant porter son repas à son marie."

FOM/141/98 "Rapport agricole annuel," 1933, 1935.
FOM/386/77bis/8 "Rapport statistique annuel," 1946.
200Mi 1191/K15 Letter from Lt. Gov. Soudan Francais to Gov. Gen. AOF, Sept 15, 1899.
Circular from Délegué Ponty to Commandants de cercle, Feb. 1, 1901.
200Mi 1191/K16 "Rapport sur l'esclavage: Enquête." From the Gov. Gen. de l'AOF
         to the Ministre des Colonies, 1903.
200Mi 1192/K17 "Enquête sur l'esclavage en AOF," par l'admin. Poulet, le 18 mars,
         1905.
200Mi 1194/K24 Décrét Loubet, 12 dec., 1905.
200Mi 590/3F:12-16 Mission Tilho, "Rapport no. 3 à M. le Ministre des Colonies,
         nov. 1907."
200Mi 1671/2G13:16 Venel, "Rapport d'ensemble, Territoire Militaire du Niger, 1913."
200Mi 1693/2G20:12 Col. Ruef, "Rapport d'ensemble annuel, Territoire du Niger,
         1920."
200Mi 1695/2G21:14 Col. Ruef, "Rapports politiques, Territoire du Niger, 1921."
200Mi 1698/2G22:16 Col. Ruef, "Rapport politique mensuel, Territoire du Niger,
         premier trimestre, 1922."
Col. Ruef, "Rapport politique mensuel: Rapport agricole, 3ème trimestre, 1922."
200Mi 1768/2G35:30 Le Médecin, Lt. Col. Muraz, "Rapport médical, Colonie du
         Niger, 1935."
200Mi 1845/2G43:14 Foerster, "Rapport annuel, Service de Santé, Colonie du Niger,
         1943."
200Mi 1891/2G48:64 Roehrig, "Rapport statistique annuel, Inspection Academique,
         Colonie du Niger, 1948."
200Mi 1982/2G53:99 Toby, "Rapport d'ensemble, Colonie du Niger, 1953."
200Mi 2732/2G51:160 Roehrig, "Rapport annuel, Inspection Academique, Colonie
         du Niger, 1951."
200Mi 2744/2G53:210 "Rapport annuel sur l'enseignement au Niger, 1953."
200Mi 2067/2G58:16 Terramoisi, A.J. "Rapport annuel sur le fonctionnement du
         Service de l'Inspection des Ecoles, 1958."

Inspection Primaire - Commune de Maradi (IP)

"Rapports annuels," 1970 through 1989.
"Rapport de fin de l'année," 1974 through 1988.
"Rapport de rentrée, 1988-89."
"Taux de scolarisation, 1988-89."

Tribunal de Première Instance, Maradi

"Relevé du Registre des jugements supplétifs, du Registre des jugements de divorce, du Registre des actes de répudiation, Conseil de Famille, Reconnaissance d'enfants, et Autres," 1985 through 1989.

Mairie

"Registre des Actes de mariage," 1956, 1965, 1970, 1985, 1988.

Interviews Cited

Most informants have been assigned a pseudonym to protect their privacy. Taped interviews conducted in Niger are on deposit with the Archives of Traditional Music at Indiana University in Bloomington. Unless otherwise indicated, interviews were conducted in Maradi.

A'i Mai Muni, 4-25-89.
Abdou Mondanchirou (Justice of the Peace), 11-9-89 (not on tape).
Aisha Labo, 2-1-89, 2-21-89.
Al'kali and Magatakarda (Gidan Al'kali), 10-17-89 (not on tape).
Amina (Fura Girki), 10-15-89.
Amina Ta 'Yar Fatake, 11-6-89.
Asabe Hassan, 1-21-89, 3-9-89, 8-14-89, 10-11-89.
Atu, 8-29-89, 10-7-89.
Binta, 11-13-89.
Buga, 4-14-89.
Chisholm, Liz (S.I.M., Sebring, FL), 11-16-90.
Cimma (Fura Girki), 10-15-89.
Cimma and Zule Ta Zabaya, 10-13-89.
Delu Ta Tanin, 8-24-89.
Fatchima, 2-1-89, 2-5-89.
Hadiza Ta Durbawa, 9-4-89, 10-27-89.
Hajjiya Adama, 3-1-89.
Hajjiya Aisha, 2-28-89, 8-24-89.
Hajjiya Akbar, 2-19-89.
Hajjiya Asma'u, 10-24-89.
Hajjiya Aya, 4-24-89.
Hajjiya Fati and Mariama, 11-17-88.
Hajjiya Gaba, 3-10-89, 3-16-89, 4-25-89.
Hajjiya Gobarci, 11-16-88, 11-13-89.
Hajjiya Habi and Saude (Fura Girki), 10-15-89.
Hajjiya Halima, 2-24-89.
Hajjiya Hasiya, 9-4-89, 10-27-89.
Hajjiya Indo, 11-14-88, 10-25-89, 1-11-89.
Hajjiya Jeka, 2-12-89, 2-14-89, 4-13-89.
Hajjiya Larewa, 9-4-89.
Hajjiya Mai Sa'ka, 8-23-89.
Hajjiya Rabe (Ta Indo), 2-1-89.
Hajjiya Salamatu, 8-23-89.

Hajjiya Ta Abu, 8-31-89.
Hajjiya Ta Dogo, 2-2-89, 2-18-89, 2-29-89.
Hajjiya Zabaya, 9-13-89.
Hamsatu and Rahama, 8-20-89.
Inspecteur des Écoles Secondaires, Maradi 11-7-89 (not on tape).
Iya Wandara, 8-30-89, 11-16-89.
Kande, 11-15-88, 1-18-89, 11-16-89.
Laure, 8-29-89.
Magajiya, 11-15-88, 1-17-89.
Mai Buhu, 2-21-89.
Malaya, 9-4-89, 10-14-89.
Mariama, 8-29-89, 10-11-89.
Maskomi, 8-20-89, 10-8-89.
Rabe, 1-21-89, 11-17-89.
Rahama, 8-20-89.
Salla (Fura Girki), 10-15-89.
Salls, Rita (S.I.M., Sebring, FL), 11-16-90.
"Sarkin Gobir" (Fura Girki), 10-15-89.
Ta Kurya, 2-18-89, 2-1-89.
Tanin, 3-15-89.
Tanin and Almajira, 3-15-89.
'Yar Fatake, 8-30-89.
'Yar Jibiya, 11-10-89.
Zuera, 1-10-89.
Zuera Abdu, 8-29-89.
Zule, 3-9-89.

INDEX

A'i Mai Muni (Christian woman), 148
Abolition. *See* Slavery
Ader, 67
Agriculture, 40-61. *See also* Land, La-
 bor, Female investment, Inherit-
 ance, Commercial crops, Gandu,
 Gamana
Aguiyar, Umma, 178–79, 181–82
AIDS, 167
Aisha, 129
Al'ada (custom), xxxiii
Al'kali (Muslim judge, *qadi*), 74–78
Albarka (blessings, prosperity), 110,
 137, 139. *See also Arziki*
Alhazai (pl. *Al Hajj*, returned male pil-
 grim; the merchant class). *See* Mer-
 chant class
Almajirai (mendicant Koranic stu-
 dents). *See* Koranic schooling
Alms, 154
Amadou, Hama, xli
Amarya (new bride), 150
Anasara (Christian foreigner), 193
Animation feminine, 57–58
Anti-sufism. *See Izala*
Arme (=*aure*, marriage), xxxi
Armen soji (marriage to a soldier). *See*
 Soldier marriage
Arna (non-Muslim Hausa population
 of the Maradi valley), xxxiii, xlii, 3,
 6, 12, 48, 149, 194, 195, 197
 effacement from historical record,
 75–76
Aro (rent-free loan of land), 78, 79, 81

Arziki (fortune, wealth, luck), 95, 100,
 107, 110, 149, 151, 156
Arzikin mutane (wealth in people),
 95
Association des Femmes du Niger (national women's association initiated
 under Seyni Kountché, AFN), xix–
 xx, xxiii, xlviii, 87, 123, 168–92, 197–
 98
 and adult education 127
 as a support network 152, 167
Auren sadaka ("marriage of alms," in
 which no *sadaki* is offered), 36, 97–
 98
Autonomous female sphere, 140, 171,
 173
Bagalam (neighborhood), xx, xxii
Baiko (betrothal, the "giving of
 power"), 10
Baiwa (gift, female slave), 10
Bajawara/Bazawara (previously married
 woman who is not presently mar-
 ried), 172–74, 176, 185
Bambara groundnuts, 50
Baraka/barka. See Albarka
Barnes, Sandra, 86
Bay, Edna, xxxiii
Beik, Janet, 185
Bella, 71
Benin, 79
Bernus, Suzanne, 148
Berry, Sara, 21
Bi'kon soji (forcible return of runaway
 bride), 35–38

219

Biki (wedding or birth celebration), xx, 136, 153–54, 153 n8,9. *See also* Wedding gift exchange, Zummunci

Biringizau. See Cowries

Black market, 130

Bledsoe, Caroline, xxix, 1, 84, 143, 156

Blood, 149–51

Bori (spirit possession cult), xxii, xxxiii, xliii, 25, 27, 79, 178–79, 182–83, 191

Borno, 6, 65

Bourdieu, Pierre, xxvii

Bourgeois marriage. *See* Domesticity

Brazzaville Conference, 15

Brideprice. *See Sadaki*

Bridewealth. *See* Wedding gift exchange, *Sadaki*

Budurwa (previously unmarried virgin), 148–51, 172–73, 183

Buga, 22–23, 79

Bureaucracy, xxxviii

Butler, Judith, 192

Calabashes, 94–95, 103, 155, 193. *See also* Faifai, Wedding gift exchange

Callaway, Barbara, 139, 171

Captive. *See* Slavery

Carney, Judith, 19

Cash, 102, 194
    exchange of wedding gifts for, 105

Catholic Mission, 116–19, 196

Centres de Promotion Rurale (CPR). *See* Projet de Développement Rural du Département de Maradi (Projet Maradi)

CFA (currency of French West Africa), devaluation of, xlii

Chad, 38, 163

Chiefs, xxxvi, 12, 111–12, 174

Child labor, 64, 114–15, 124, 171, 189, 196

Childbearing
    and emancipation of slaves, 10
    and female hierarchies, 11
    as *arziki* in marriage, 151

Christian marriage, 157 n12, 162

Christian Missions, 112, 194. *See also* Sudan Interior Mission, Catholic Mission, Protestant community

Cloth, xxxvii–iii, 53, 92–94, 100–103, 135, 150, 155, 195. *See also* Trade goods, Female income, Dress

Clothing. *See* Cloth, Veiling

Coles, Catherine, 187

Comaroff, John, 106

Commercial crops, xxxv, 39, 50, 194. *See also* Peanut production, Millet production, Cotton production

Companionate marriage, xlvii, 165

Concubinage, 6
    and free wives, 9–13
    and titled offices, 67. *See also* Slavery

Contraception, 180

Contractual model of marriage, xlvii, 49, 142, 145–51

Cooperatives, xl, 54, 61, 174

Cotton spinning, 92–94, 98, 103

Cotton production, xxxv, 46

Coup d'état, of 1974, xxxix, 17, 179
    of 1996, xli, 176

Courts. *See* Judicial practice

Coutumier juridique, 11–12, 75

Cowry, 66, 100, 101, 194

Co-wives. *See* Polygyny, *'Kishiya*

Credit, 49
    and land, 85

Currency, 66, 100–101. *See also* CFA, Cash

Custom. *See* Al'ada, Gargajiyya, Judicial practice

Customs barriers, xxxvi

Dahomey, xxxiii, xxxviii, 111, 118–19, 127

Dakar, 15

Damagaram, 5, 67

Daraja (respectability, standing). *See* Respectability

'Darmen arme ("tying of the marriage"; ceremonial transfer of *sadaki*), 10, 92–94, 144, 146, 155

David, Philippe, 67
de Gaulle, Charles, 15
Décret Mandel, 15–16
Dije, 127
Diori, Aissa, 177
Diori Hamani, xxxviii, xliii, 17, 174–75
Divorce, 24, 32–33, 34–35
  defined as action brought by a woman, 32
  and remarriage, 66–67
  and return of *sadaki*, 20, 93, 158–67
  See also Judicial Practice, Repudiation
Dodo (village), 151–52
Dogondoutchi (region), 118
Domestic/Public binary, xliii–xliv
Domestic sphere, xxvii–xxx
Domesticity, discourses of, xlii, xlvii, 109, 110–42, 194, 196
Dowry. *See* Wedding gift exchange (*kayan 'daki*), *Sadaki* (Fr. *dot*)
Dress, 191. *See also* Cloth, Veiling
Drought
  and scapegoating of single women, 167
  drought of 1984, 127
  Sahel drought, 17, 47, 54, 99, 102, 175
Durbi, xxxiii, 74
Dyula, 133
Echenberg, Myron, 70–71
École de Filles, 116–19
Education, xxxviii, xlvii, 110–29, 141, 196
  adult education, 127, 177
  and appeal of Samariya youth group, 183
  and competition for girls' labor, 115, 124, 189
  and marriage age, 18–19, 159, 162
  and Projet Maradi, 55
  and Uranium revenues, 175
  as part of dowry, 105
  education and early marriage of women, 189

emphasis on health and hygiene for women, 58, 177
"experimental schools" (technical schooling), 126 n23
teachers and marriage, 158, 165
See also Ilimi, Koranic schooling, Infrastructure
Elite (educated functionary class), xxxviii, xlii, 32, 84, 110, 116, 129
Elite women and marriage, 157–67, *See also* Education, Bureaucracy
Esposito, John, 140–41
External public space, 87
Fadama (river valley land), 50–51, 79
Fadan Gourma, 120
Faifai (round mat used by women to cover calabash), xxiii–xxv, 65
Family code, 157, 181, 190
Famine
  and scapegoating of single women, 167
  of 1913–14, 46
  of 1930–31, xxxv, 46
Fatauci trade, 69
Fati, 146–47
Female income, 33
  and education, 129, 196
  and ownership of real property, 88
  and syncratic marriage, 144
  cold drink trade, 129
  food processing, xxxvii, 51–53, 60–61, 152
  processing peanut oil, 60–61
  sana'a or female trades, 138
  spinning cotton (*zare*), xxxvii, 2
  tailoring, 134
  trade in imported goods such as cloth and rubberware (*robbobi*), 83–84, 134
  trade in local pottery and firewood, 152
  wife's personal income in marriage, 49
  See also Child labor, *Zarafi*

Female farming. *See* Agriculture, Gamana, Land

Female investment, in real property, xliv, 70, 83–89, 153, 195, 197
 in agriculture, 60–61, 153
 in moveable property (*kayan 'daki*), 63–64, 88, 105, 197
 in rental properties, 87
 See also Zummunci

Female sub-culture, xxix

Fisher, Humphrey, 6

Flood, xxxvii

Folly, Anne–Laure, 198–99

Food processing enterprises. *See* Female income

Forced labor on "government fields," xxiii, xxiv, 46–48, 50

Foyer des métisses, 116–20

French colonial rule, xxxiv
 fear of Islamic resistance, 112, 119
 See also French West Africa

French West Africa, 38–39

Fulani
 in Maradi, 112–14, 127
 in Nigeria, xxxv, 6

Fura Girki (village), xx, 79, 80

Gamana (land used in usufruct by a dependent), xxi, xliv, 22, 41–61, 81, 136, 156, 197
 See also Agriculture, Land

Gandu (land managed by the household head), xxxi, 40–45, 79. *See also* Agriculture, Land

Gara. See Wedding gift exchange

Gargajiya (traditional, customary), 193

Gobirawa (19th c. immigrants from Gobir), xx, xxxii, xxxvii

Gramsci, Antonio, xxx

Greniers de réserve (reserve granaries), xxxv, 46

Gudummawa. See Wedding gift exchange

Guyer, Jane, 156

Habi, 127

Haiwa hoe, 5

Hajjiya Asma'u, 60–61, 154

Hajjiya Ta Abu, 112–14, 123

Hajjiya Indo, 127–29, 140, 146–47

Hajjiya Zabaya, 137

Hajjiya Gobarci, 164–65

Hajjiya Jeka, xxiii–xxvi, 65–69, 134, 137

Hajjiya Larewa, 165

Hajjiya Sa'a, 83–84, 133, 140

Hansen, Karen, 116

Hawa (Christian woman), 148

Hawa (daughter-in-law of Hajjiya Indo), 127

Hé!. See Wedding gift exchange

Hill, Polly, 40

Hogendorn, Jan, 3

Horses, 99, 100

Hospitality, xxv

House of the Al'kali. *See* Judicial Practice

House of the Judge. *See* Judicial Practice

Houses of Women, 63, 84, 183, 195

Housing 87, 129, 188. *See also* Female investment (in real property)

Idda, 30–31

Igiyar arme (marriage ties), 10
 marriage of the "thread of Allah," 66

Ijima, 141

Iler hoe, 5

Ilimi (learning, knowledge), 110

Imam, Ayesha, 198

Indigénat (code governing indigenous French subjects), xxxvi, xxxviii, 15–16, 38–39

Indirect rule, xxxiv, xxxvi

Infrastructure, xxxv, xl, 20, 39, 175
 and labor of Samariya youth association, 179–80
 and seclusion, 137–38
 See also Education, Medicine, Labor saving devices

Inheritance
 disputes concerning, 32

pre-mortem inheritance (*kyauta*), 81, 82
shifts in understandings of, 39, 73–83
See also Maliki law, Land
Inputs to agriculture
animal traction, 55–57
female exclusion from circuits of access to, 59 n28
fertilizer and manure, 56, 79–80
seeds and insecticides, 59–61
technology, 5
Insurance, wedding gifts as, 105–6
Intercropping, 55
Islam, xvii. *See* Merchant class, Katsinawa, Islamic Brotherhoods, Izala, *Albarka*, Maliki law
Islamic fundamentalism. *See* Merchant class, Izala
Islamic Brotherhoods, xxi, xlii
Qadiriyya and Niassiyya branch of Tijaniyya, 131–34
Wahhabi, 133
See also Izala
Itjihad, 141
Iya, xxxiii, 25–28, 34, 49, 136, 140, 178–79, 181–82, 187–89, 196
Izala (Anti-Sufi Islamic reform movement), 130–33, 172, 196
Jacquinot decree, 16
Jama'a (sense of membership in Muslim community), 154
Jama'atu al-bid'a wa Iqamat al-Sunna. *See* Izala
Jekadiya, 65–68
Jihad of Usman 'dan Fodio, xxxii–xxxiv, 3
Jingina (pawning), 79
Judicial practice, xlv
customary law, 21
"greeting money," 32, 26
Iya's home, 25–28, 136
Neighborhood forum, 22–25
overemphasis upon courts in work on marriage, 21, 34

preference for reconciliation, 23, 26, 28, 79
Sarki's Court, 28–30
the House of the Al'kali, 30–31
Tribunal (the House of the Judge), 28, 31–33, 74
See also Coutumier juridique
Justice indigène, 39
Kaduna, 187
Kan kwarya. *See* Wedding gift exchange
Kan kaya. *See* Wedding gift exchange
Kande, 151–54
Kano rail line, xxxv, xxxviii, 99
Kano, precolonial, 100
colonial, xxxiv
Karanja, Wambui wa, 144, 166
Karuwa ("courtesan," prostitute), xxxi, 27, 87, 128, 172–74, 195, 197
and political parties, 176, 185
matan zamani, 184
Katsina, pre-jihad, xxxiii
colonial, xxxiv
independence era, 171, 173, 179
Katsinawa (19th c. immigrants from Katsina), xx, xxxii, xxxvii, xlii, 6–7, 39, 48, 51, 77, 194, 195–96
Kayan 'daki. *See* Wedding gift exchange
Khalaf Allah, Muhammad Ahmad, 141
'Kishiya (Co-wife; jealous rivalry, especially between co-wives) 13, 20, 28–30
Koranic schooling, xlvii, 115, 123–26, 127, 196, 127, 129, 130
almajirai, 124–25
and Islamic supports for women, 169
and legal reform, 140–41
Kountché, Seyni, xxxix–xl, xliii, 17–18, 175, 179, 184
Kpelle, 156
Kulle (secluded marriage). *See* Seclusion
'Kunjiyar mata (women's association). *See* Association des Femmes du Niger, Union des Femmes du Niger

Labor-saving devices, xxiv, 58
  and seclusion, 137–38
Labor
  division of labor in agriculture, 12
  female, xlvi, 49–50, 149
  junior male labor in *gandu*, 40–41
  labor of bride in wedding, 149
  replacement of slave labor with la-
    bor of subordinate wives, 9–13
  servants to replace labor of em-
    ployed wives, 122
  wage labor of junior males, 16, 20
  women's access to labor, 56–57
  See also Child Labor
Land
  and claims to social ties, 80
  definitional battles, 81–82
  fragmentation of, 44, 46
  security of tenure, 82
  shift from communal to freehold
    tenure, 76–78
  women's access to, xvii, xlvi, 25–26,
    55
  See also Inheritance, Maliki law, Ag-
    riculture, *Gamana, Fadama,*
    Zummunci
Landeroin, Captain, 11
Latour, Éliane de, 18, 20, 76, 105, 180
Launay, Robert, 133
Law. *See* Judicial practice, Maliki law
Legal reform of marriage, xlv, 14–18,
  140–41, 143, 178, 194
Liberia, 143
Limanci (neighborhood), xxi, 152
Locoh, Thérèse, 144
Lovejoy, Paul, 3
Mada (village), xxiii, xxiv
Madame (as social status), 158, 167,
  193
Madame Monique, 140, 165
Madame Hadiza, 129, 165
Madame Rose, 123
Madarumfa (village), 127
Magajiya, 27, 156
Magistrate. *See* Judicial Practice

Maguzawa. See Arna
Mai gida ("owner of the house"), 41,
  85–86
Mainassara, Colonel Ibrahim Barre, xli,
  176
Mairi (Fura Girki), 80
Makaranta. *See* Koranic schooling
Maliki law, 17, 31, 38, 48, 74–78, 195.
  See also Judicial practice
Mallamai (Koranic scholars as class),
  110–11, 131, 152
Mann, Kristin, 144
Maradawa (people of Maradi valley),
  xx
  neighborhood in city, 22
Maradi
  growth of city, xxxviii, xlv, 85–86
  transfer of city to plateau, xxxvii, 85,
    113
  warfare with Sokoto, 196
Mariama (Fura Girki), 79
Mariama (Maradi), 125–26
Marks, Shula, xxx
Marriage
  age at first marriage, 16, 18–19, 189,
    191, 194
  consent in, 15, 36–38, 194
  expense of, 16, 93
  female dependency in, 39
Married woman. *See Matan arme*
Marty, Paul, 74–75, 123
Maskomi, 79–80
Matan arme (married woman), xxxi,
  167, 172, 184
Mauri, 50
Mauss, Marcel, 91
Medicine, need for female personnel
  in, 116–22, 196
Merchant class, xxi, xxxviii, xlii, xlvii,
  19, 39, 82, 86, 110–11, 130–39, 172
Métisses, 116–21
Migration
  as form of resistance, xxxv, 47
  of women from rural to urban ar-
    eas, 24

women as perennial migrants, 62–63, 78
Miles, William, 46, 69, 138
Military rule, colonial, xxxvi, 69–73
and education, 113–14
independence era, xxxix, xl, 18, 175–76
See also Soldier marriage, *Bi'kon soji*
Millet production, xxxvi, 47
and wedding gifts, 155
stigma on sales, 52
MNSD (National Movement of the Society for Development, party initiated by Ali Saibou), xl, 175
Mokoyo (neighborhood), xx
Monocropping, 56
Moore, Henrietta, xxvii
Mulkin zafi (hot rule), 69
Nairobi, 172
Napoleonic code, 38, 73, 178, 195
National debt, xlii
National Conference, xli, 189, 198
Ngigmi (town), 166
Niamey, xxxviii, 83, 119, 121, 126, 180, 181, 197
Nicolas, Guy, 43, 153
Nicolas, Jacqueline, 176
Nigeria, xvii, xxxii, xxxviii, xl, xlii, 38, 86, 111, 130, 166, 169, 179, 197
decline of slavery in, 3
seclusion and slavery in, 6
Nonmarried women, 158, 173
Normative Farming Arrangement, 43–46
Nyamwaya, David, xxx
Obbo, Christine, 144
Office de Radiodiffusion-Television du Niger (ORTN), 180
Operation Hirondelle, xxxviii
Oppong, Christine, 144
Organic model of marriage, xlvii, 26, 104, 107, 142, 145–51, 155
Ortner, Sherry, xxvii
Ousmane, Mahamane, xli
Outside marriage, 85, 144, 156

Paradise
and social ties, 152
and state of marriage, 68–69
and washing of bride, 148
Parkin, David, xxx
Parti Progressiste Nigérien (local branch of the Rassemblement Démocratique Africaine, PPN-RDA), 17, 174–75, 176–79
Pastoral economy, xxxvi
Peanut production, xxxv, xxxvii, 46–61, 99
Performance, 170, 171, 186, 190–92, 198
Périé, Jean, 22
Pilgrimage, xliv, 25, 61, 84, 105, 130, 134, 154
Pison, Gilles, 1
Pittin, Renée, 169, 171, 173, 179, 185, 191
Political parties, xxxviii, 174, 197
Politics of difference, 168, 197
Polyandrous motherhood, 156
Polygyny, xlvii, 20, 191, 194
and elite women, 157
and ranking of wives, 13
and remarriage, 139
and rise of Merchant class, 131–39
elite men and, 16
Muslim men's responsibility in polygynous marriage, 28–30
rates of, 14
serial polygyny, 13, 82–84
Presidency, xli
Projet de Développement Rural de Maradi (PDRM, Projet Maradi), xix, 54–57
Property, separate male and female, 33, 178. *See also* Female investment
Prostitution. *See Karuwa*
Protestant Community, 148, 157 n12. *See also* Sudan Interior Mission
Purdah. *See* Seclusion
Queen Mother, xxxiii. *See also* Iya
Rabe, 35–38, 163
Railroad. *See* Kano rail

Rathbone, Richard, xxx
Raynaut, Claude 41, 154
Registration
    Actes de mariage, 158–64
    Takarda: paper records of birth, mar-
        riage, and divorce, 30–31, 65–66
Republican discourse, xli, xlv, 14, 76
Repudiation, 32, 144, 178, 191
    and women's right to retain *sadaki*,
        35
Resistance, xxvii. *See also* Migration
Respectability (*daraja*), 132, 139, 171,
    184
Ribat (military outpost), 4
Rimji (slave village), 3–6, 8
Robert, André, 15
Robertson, Claire, 126, 129
Robinson, Pearl, xl
Ross, Paul, 80
Ruef, Lieutenant Colonel, 116–17
Rural code, 198
Sa lalle. See Washing of the bride
Sabon Gari (neighborhood), xx,
    xxxviii, 83
Sadaki ("brideprice"-bridewealth pay-
    ment from groom to bride's family,
    referred to in French as *dot* or
    "dowry"), xxxi, xlviii, 100, 155, 194
    and authority of seniors, 16
    and implication of free status, 37
    and marital stability, 144
    female negotiation of, 142–45, 157–
        65
    one of many gifts from groom, 91–
        94
Saibou, Ali, xl, xliii, 18, 175, 184, 189–
    90
Salla, 58–59
Salt, 93, 100
Samariya (cooperative work group,
    national youth association), xl, 167,
    169, 170, 174, 176, 179–80, 182–84,
    187, 197, 198
Sana'a. See Female income
Sara, 38

Sarauta (titled position, aristocratic and
    courtly class) 18, 82, 130 110
    and participation of Iya in women's
        associations, 178, 181–82
    and rural women seized in "mar-
        riage," 24, 25
    See also Katsinawa
Sarki Kure, 13, 112
Sarki Kollodo, 13, 79–80
Sarki Buzu 'dan Zambadi, 28–30, 181
Sarki (chief, leader), and taxation,
    xxxvi. *See also* Judicial practice
Sarki Labo, 13
Saunders, Margaret, 138–39
Schildkrout, Enid, 153
Scott, James, xxvii
Seclusion, xxxiv, xvii, xlvii, 3, 20, 109
    and external public spaces, 88
    and merchant class ideology, 111,
        130–142
    increasing seclusion of rural
        women, 25–28, 33
    Kulle, 136–40
    Tsare, xx, 136, 138, 139
Senegal, 111
Sharia. *See* Maliki law, Judicial prac-
    tice
Sierra Leone, 143
Single women. *See* Nonmarried
    women, *Budurwa*
Slavery, xvii, 1–14, 194
    and alternative forms of "mar-
        riage," 12–14, 92, 106
    and colonial state, xliv–xlv
    and education, 114–15
    and free female status, xlvii
    freedom through childbearing, 10
    legal emancipation, 8–14, 21
    redemption fee, 10
Smith, M.G., 3, 7, 40
Social debt, 91, 103, 108
Social networks, xx, xxii, xlvii, 137
Social differentiation, 110. *See also*
    Sarauta, Elite class, Merchant class,
    Tallakawa, Mallamai

Soil deterioration, 58–60
Sokoto Caliphate, xxxii, 3, 6, 24, 100, 196
Soldier marriage, 65, 69–73, 83, 128, 130, 133, 163, 195
Soura (village), 119–22, 196
Spatial praxis, xliii–xliv, xlvii
Stranger marriage, 86, 130
Structural Adjustment, xlii
Sudan Interior Mission (SIM), 54, 102, 119–22, 196
Sufism, 131–34
Supreme Military Council, xl
Suret-Canale, Jean, 38
Suwarian tradition, 133
Ta Kurya, xxiii–xxvi
Takarda. See Registration
Talla (peddling). *See* Child labor
Tallakawa (commoners), 7, 110
Tambara (female title), 97
Tarihi (written history, tradition), xxvi, 193
Taxation, xxxv, xxxvi, 194
   and duties of *mai gida*, 41, 46, 52
   and free status, 7–8
   and peanut production, 47
   and perception of education, 114
   and wives, 7
   burden on Hausa in Niger, 46
   in precolonial Maradi, 4, 44
Tchin-Tabaraden, xl
Thread of marriage. *See Igiyar arme, 'Darmen arme*
Tibiri (town), xx, 13, 119, 196
Tilho-O-Shee Mission, 11
Time of Searching for Money, 194
Tirailleurs Sénégalais, 70. *See also* Military rule, Soldier marriage
Titled positions, xxxiii, 116
   Maradi, xxxiv
   Sarkin Arna, xxxiv
   See Iya, Durbi, Sarki, Magajiya, Jekadiya, Maskomi, Tambara
Togo, 165
Trade goods, xxxvii, 101, 104, 193, 195

Trade companies, 46, 99, 100, 158
Tradition, 198. *See Tarihi, Gargajiyya,* Judicial practice
Trans-Saharan trade, xxxv, 100
Tsare. See Seclusion
Tsofuwa (old woman), 187
Tuareg
   marriage in Maradi, 162
   military attacks on, xl, 175
   rebellion, xli–xlii
Union des Femmes du Niger (UFN, national women's association initiated under Diori Hamani), 17, 169, 177–79
Union Syndicale des Travailleurs du Niger (USTN, the national labor union), 175
Unmarried women. *See Budurwa*
Uranium, 175
Vaughan, Megan, xxvii
Vegetable gardening, 50, 179
Veiling, 9, 135–36, 150, 169
Vichy government of AOF, xxxvii, 35
Victorian ideals, 1, 194
Villomé, Lieutenant, 11
Virilocal marriage, 62–63, 78, 154. *See also* Migration
Voulet-Chanoine Expedition, xxiv
Wa'kar Sarkin Maradi, 137
Wallace, Christine, 40
Wandara, Iya Aisha, 25–28, 178–79, 181–82, 187–89
Washing of the bride (*Wanken Amarya*), 147–51, 157
Washing of the groom (*Wanken Ango*), 148
Watts, Michael, 19
Wedding ritual, xvii, xlvi
Wedding gift exchange, xlvi, 90–107, 195, 197
   and trade goods 100–102
   counter-prestations as denial of servile status, 107
   Gudummawa (gifts to "reinforce" those offered by major partici-

pants in wedding or birthing ceremony), 94, 95, 96

Kan kaya (the bearing of gifts to the bride), 94–96, 146–47

Kan kwarya (bearing of "overflowing calabashes" to groom by bride's supporters *(Gara, Hé!)*, 17, 96, 146, 155

Kayan 'daki ("things for the room," decorative gifts to the bride for her to arrange in her room), xxiii, xxxi, xlvii, 23, 63–64, 94–96

Rama (repayment of gifts of failed suitors), 146 n 4

See also Sadaki ("brideprice," Fr. *dot*), Female investment (moveable property), *Zummunci, Auren sadaka*

White, Luise, 172

White, Elizabeth, 141

Widowhood and remarriage, 66–67, 158

Witchcraft accusation, 28–30

Women's associations, *see* Association des Femmes du Niger, Union des Femmes du Niger

Women's marches, of May 1991, 189–92
of 1992, 198

World War II, xxxvii, 35–38, 139, 194

'Ya 'Daya (village), 80

'Yan Daka, xx

Zainabu, 128–29

Zarafi (leisure), 122, 138

Zare. See Cotton spinning, Female income

Zaria, xxi

Zerma, xxxviii, 5, 69, 71, 78, 86, 112, 116, 123, 144, 164, 178

Zinder, 100, 116–17, 126, 181, 185

Ziyara (visiting), 137

Zuera, 127–29, 146–47

Zule, 156

Zummunci (friendship, kinship, social investment), 80–81, 143, 151–54